Lecture Notes in Computer Science 7312

Commenced Publication in 1973
Founding and Former Series Editors:
Gerhard Goos, Juris Hartmanis, and Jan van Leeuwen

Barbara M. Chapman   Federico Massaioli
Matthias S. Müller   Marco Rorro (Eds.)

OpenMP
in a Heterogeneous World

8th International Workshop on OpenMP, IWOMP 2012
Rome, Italy, June 11-13, 2012
Proceedings

 Springer

Volume Editors

Barbara M. Chapman
University of Houston
Department of Computer Science
4800 Calhoun Rd, Houston 77204-3010, TX, USA
E-mail: chapman@cs.uh.edu

Federico Massaioli
Marco Rorro
CASPUR
Via dei Tizii, 6, 00185 Rome, Italy
E-mail: {federico.massaioli, marco.rorro}@caspur.it

Matthias S. Müller
Dresden University of Technology
Center for Information Services and High Performance Computing (ZIH)
Zellescher Weg 12, 01062 Dresden, Germany
E-mail: matthias.mueller@tu-dresden.de

ISSN 0302-9743   e-ISSN 1611-3349
ISBN 978-3-642-30960-1   e-ISBN 978-3-642-30961-8
DOI 10.1007/978-3-642-30961-8
Springer Heidelberg Dordrecht London New York

Library of Congress Control Number: 2012939165

CR Subject Classification (1998): C.1, D.1, F.2, D.4, C.3, C.4

LNCS Sublibrary: SL 2 – Programming and Software Engineering

Typesetting: Camera-ready by author, data conversion by Scientific Publishing Services, Chennai, India

Printed on acid-free paper

Springer is part of Springer Science+Business Media (www.springer.com)

Preface

OpenMP is a widely accepted, standard application programming interface (API) for high-level shared-memory parallel programming in Fortran, C, and C++. Since its introduction in 1997, OpenMP has gained support from most high-performance compiler and hardware vendors. Under the direction of the OpenMP Architecture Review Board (ARB), the OpenMP specification has evolved, reaching the recent release of Specification 3.1. Heterogeneous systems, where conventional CPUs are combined with one or more many-core accelerators, are raising new interest in directive-based approaches to parallel programming, like OpenMP. The appealing computing power offered by heterogeneous hardware makes the old problem of software portability even more complicated. Code porting can no longer be restricted to making computing intensive routines suitable for a given architecture. Since architectural diversity is now built into heterogeneous systems themselves, to fully exploit their computing power, one single application may need to contain two or more versions of the same code section, suited for different subsystems. This year, the IWOMP conference took its title from the important role that OpenMP can play in helping programmers to generalize the design of their codes, so that it can be mapped onto accelerators or conventional CPUs, leaving the low-level parallelization work to the compiler.

The community of OpenMP researchers and developers in academia and industry is united under cOMPunity (www.compunity.org). This organization has held workshops on OpenMP around the world since 1999: the European Workshop on OpenMP (EWOMP), the North American Workshop on OpenMP Applications and Tools (WOMPAT), and the Asian Workshop on OpenMP Experiences and Implementation (WOMPEI) attracted annual audiences from academia and industry. The International Workshop on OpenMP (IWOMP) consolidated these three workshop series into a single annual international event that rotates across the previous workshop sites. The first IWOMP meeting was held in 2005, in Eugene, Oregon, USA. Since then, meetings have been held each year, in Reims, France, Beijing, China, West Lafayette, USA, Dresden, Germany, Tsukuba, Japan, and Chicago, USA. Each workshop has drawn participants from research and industry throughout the world. IWOMP 2012 continued the series with technical papers, tutorials, and OpenMP status reports. Furthermore, to stress the importance of the research activities in the field of compilers, runtime systems, and tools as a driving force for the OpenMP evolution, IWOMP traditionally hosts one of the meetings of the language committee. The first IWOMP workshop was organized under the auspices of cOMPunity, and thereafter, the IWOMP Steering Committee took care of organizing and expanding this series of events. The success of the IWOMP meetings is mostly due to the generous support from numerous sponsors.

The cOMPunity website (www.compunity.org) provides access to all presentations proposed during the meetings and to a photo gallery of the events. Information about the latest conference can be found on the IWOMP website at www.iwomp.org. This book contains the proceedings of the 8th International Workshop on OpenMP which was held in Rome in June 2012, where 18 technical papers and 7 posters were presented out of more than 30 works submitted to the call for papers. The workshop program also included a tutorial day and the keynote talk of Bjarne Stroustrup, the creator and developer of the C++ programming language.

The interest shown this year again in the IWOMP conference witnesses the strength, the maturity, and the diffusion of the portable, scalable model defined by OpenMP, and confirms the critical role played by this series of events in the development of the specification and its adoption.

June 2012

Barbara M. Chapman
Federico Massaioli
Matthias S. Müller
Marco Rorro

Organization

Program and Organizing Chair

Federico Massaioli   CASPUR, Italy

Sponsor Contact Chair

Barbara M. Chapman   University of Houston, USA

Tutorial Chair

Ruud van der Pas   Oracle America, USA

Poster Co-chairs

Alejandro Duran   BSC, Spain
Christian Terboven   RWTH Aachen University, Germany

Program Commitee

Dieter an Mey   RWTH Aachen University, Germany
Eduard Ayguadé   BSC/UPC, Spain
Massimo Bernaschi   IAC-CNR, Italy
James Beyer   Cray Inc., USA
Mark Bull   EPCC, UK
Bronis R. de Supinski   NNSA ASC, LLNL, USA
Alejandro Duran   BSC, Spain
Rudolf Eigenmann   Purdue University, USA
Massimiliamo Fatica   NVIDIA, USA
Guang R. Gao   University of Delaware, USA
William Gropp   University of Illinois, USA
Lei Huang   Prairie View A&M University, USA
Ricky Kendall   Oak Ridge National Laboratory, USA
Raymond Loy   Argonne National Laboratory, USA
Craig Lucas   NAG Ltd, UK
Larry Meadows   Intel, USA
Matthias S. Müller   ZIH, TU Dresden, Germany
Stephen Olivier   University of North Carolina, USA
Marco Rorro   CASPUR, Italy

Mitsuhisa Sato   University of Tsukuba, Japan
Eric Stahlberg   OpenFPGA and Wittenberg University, USA
Christian Terboven   RWTH Aachen University, Germany
Ruud van der Pas   Oracle America, USA
Michael Wong   IBM, Canada

Steering Committee Chair

Matthias S. Müller   ZIH, TU Dresden, Germany

Steering Committee

Dieter an Mey   RWTH Aachen University, Germany
Eduard Ayguadé   BSC/UPC, Spain
Mark Bull   EPCC, UK
Barbara M. Chapman   University of Houston, USA
Rudolf Eigenmann   Purdue University, USA
Guang R. Gao   University of Delaware, USA
William Gropp   University of Illinois, USA
Ricky Kendall   Oak Ridge National Laboratory, USA
Michael Krajecki   University of Reims, France
Rick Kufrin   NCSA/Univerity of Illinois, USA
Kalyan Kumaran   Argonne National Laboratory, USA
Federico Massaioli   CASPUR, Italy
Larry Meadows   Intel, USA
Arnaud Renard   University of Reims, France
Mitsuhisa Sato   University of Tsukuba, Japan
Sanjiv Shah   Intel
Bronis R. de Supinski   NNSA ASC, LLNL, USA
Ruud van der Pas   Oracle America, USA
Matthijs van Waveren   Fujitsu, France
Michael Wong   IBM, Canada
Weimin Zheng   Tsinghua University, China

Additional Reviewers

Gary Elsesser
Jeffrey Sandoval
Francesco Salvadore

Table of Contents

Optimization and Accelerators

Task Parallelism

Validation and Benchmarks

Poster Papers

Specification and Performance Evaluation of Parallel I/O Interfaces for OpenMP

Kshitij Mehta, Edgar Gabriel, and Barbara Chapman

Department of Computer Science, University of Houston
{kmehta,gabriel,chapman}@cs.uh.edu

Abstract. One of the most severe performance limitations of parallel applications today stems from the performance of I/O operations.
Numerous projects have shown, that parallel I/O in combination with
parallel file systems can significantly improve the performance of I/O
operations. However, as of today there is no support for parallel I/O operations for applications using shared-memory programming models such
as OpenMP. This paper introduces parallel I/O interfaces for OpenMP.
We discuss the rationale of our design decisions, present the interface
specification and a prototype implementation with the OpenUH compiler. We evaluate the performance of our implementation for various
benchmarks on different file systems and demonstrate the benefits of the
new interfaces.

1 Introduction

Amdahl's law stipulates that the scalability of a parallel application is limited by
its least scalable section. For many scientific applications, the scalability limitation comes from the performance of I/O operations, due to the fact that current
hard drives have an order of magnitude higher latency and lower bandwidth than
any other component in a computer system. Parallel I/O allows (efficient) simultaneous access by multiple processes or threads to the same file. Although the
adoption of parallel I/O in scientific applications is modest, it has been shown
that in combination with parallel file systems parallel I/O can lead to significant
performance improvements [1].

I/O options are limited as of today for applications using shared memory
programming models such as OpenMP [2]. Most OpenMP applications use the
routines provided by the base programming languages (e.g. Fortran, C, C++) for
accessing a data file. In order to maintain consistency of the resulting file, read
and write operations are performed outside of parallel regions. In case multiple
threads are accessing a file, access to the file handle should be protected e.g.
within a *omp critical* construct to avoid concurrent access by different threads.

Another approach has each thread utilizing a separate file to avoid race conditions or synchronizations when accessing a single, shared file. While this approach
often leads to a better performance than the previously discussed methods, it has
three fundamental drawbacks. First, it requires (potentially expensive) pre- and
post-processing steps in order to create the required number of input files and

B.M. Chapman et al. (Eds.): IWOMP 2012, LNCS 7312, pp. 1–14, 2012.
© Springer-Verlag Berlin Heidelberg 2012

merge the output files of different threads. Second, it is difficult to support application scenarios where the number of threads utilized is determined dynamically at runtime. Third, managing a large number of files often creates a bottleneck on the metadata server of the parallel file system. The latter could become relevant in the near future as the number of cores of modern micro-processors are expected to grow into the hundreds or even thousands.

This paper introduces the notion of parallel I/O for OpenMP applications. We discuss and evaluate design alternatives, present an initial set of interfaces and evaluate the performance using a prototype implementation in the OpenUH compiler. The main goal of the new interfaces is to improve the performance of I/O operations for OpenMP applications by providing threads the ability to perform I/O using a single file without having to explicitly lock the file handle or synchronize access to the file using ad hoc methods.

The parallel I/O interfaces suggested here introduce the ability of collaboration among threads on shared data items through collective I/O interfaces, to specify more work per operation through list I/O interfaces and allow to exploit OpenMP specific features for I/O, specifically to write private data items to file in an efficient manner.

The organization of the paper is as follows: Section 2 discusses existing parallel I/O interfaces. In Section 3 we present the new set of interfaces to support parallel I/O in OpenMP applications along with design alternatives. Section 4 presents a prototype implementation of the interfaces in the OpenUH compiler framework, while Section 5 evaluates the performance of this implementation for various micro-benchmarks. Finally, Section 6 summarizes the contributions of this paper, and gives an overview of outstanding items and currently ongoing work.

2   Related Work

The most widely used parallel I/O specification is based on the Message Passing Interface (MPI) [3], which has introduced the notion of parallel I/O in version two. The most notable features of MPI I/O compared to standard POSIX style I/O operations are i) the ability to express in advance, regions of interest in a file on a per process basis using the *file-view*; ii) the notion of collective I/O operations, which allows processes to collaborate and transform often suboptimal I/O requests of each process into a more file-system friendly sequence of I/O operations; iii) and support for relaxed consistency semantics which pushes the responsibility to create a consistent file from the file-system to the application.

Unified Parallel C (UPC) is an extension of the C language for parallel computing based on a partitioned global address space (PGAS). UPC provides an abstraction for parallel I/O [4] mostly following the MPI I/O specification. The main difference with MPI I/O comes from the fact that UPC I/O does not have the notion of derived data types and thus has to use List I/O interfaces.

Other popular I/O libraries include HDF5 [5] and pNetCDF [6]. Although both libraries support the notion of parallel I/O, they are layered on top of MPI I/O and do not introduce significant new features.

3   Interface Specification

In the following, we discuss various design alternatives for parallel I/O interfaces in OpenMP, followed by the actual specification.

Directive based interfaces vs. runtime based library calls. The primary design decision is whether to use compiler directives to indicate parallel execution of read/write operations, or whether to define an entirely new set of library functions. The first approach would have the advantage that the changes made to an application are minimal compared to using an entirely new set of functions. Furthermore, it would allow an application to execute in a sequential manner in case OpenMP is not enabled at compile time.

Additionally, the syntax of the directive based parallel I/O operations are implicitly assumed to behave similarly to their sequential counterparts. This poses the challenge of having to first identify which functions to support, e.g. C I/O style `fread/fwrite` operations vs. POSIX I/O style `read/write` operations vs. `fprintf/fscanf` style routines. Furthermore, due to fact that OpenMP also supports Fortran and C++ applications, one would have to worry about the different guarantees given by POSIX style I/O operations vs. the record-based Fortran I/O routines or how to deal with C++ streams. Because of the challenges associated with the latter aspects for a parallel I/O library, we decided to define an entirely new set of library functions integrated into the runtime library of an OpenMP compiler.

Individual vs. shared file pointers. The notion of parallel I/O implies that multiple processes or threads are performing I/O operations simultaneously. A preliminary question when designing the interfaces is whether to allow each thread to operate on a separate file pointer, or whether a file pointer is shared across all threads. Due to the single address space that the OpenMP programming model is based on, shared file pointers seem to be the intuitive solution to adapt. Note, that the overall goal is that all threads are able to execute I/O operations on the shared file handle without having to protect the access to this handle.

Collective vs. individual interfaces. A follow-up question to the discussion on individual vs. shared file pointers is whether threads are allowed to call I/O operations independent of each other or whether there is some form of restriction on how threads can utilize the new I/O functions. Specifically, the question is whether to use collective I/O operations, which request all threads in a parallel region to call the I/O operations in the same sequence and the same number of times, or whether to allow each thread to execute I/O operations independent of each other. Although collective I/O operations initially sound very restrictive, there are two very good reasons to use them. First, collaboration among the threads is a key design element to improve the performance of I/O operations. The availability of multiple (application level) threads to optimize I/O operations is however only guaranteed for collective interfaces. Second, individual file I/O operations could in theory also be implemented on a user level by opening the file multiple times and using explicit offsets into the file when accessing the data. Therefore, we decided to support collective I/O interfaces in the current specification.

However, using collective I/O interfaces also requires a specification of the order by which the different threads access the data. The current specification read/writes data in the order of the thread-id's. However, relying on a thread's id is not a robust method of coordinating file operations implicitly among threads, especially in case of using nested parallelism. The OpenMP specification makes it clear that relying on thread id order for things such as predetermining the work a thread gets from a worksharing construct is at best benignly non-conforming (as in the case of a *static* schedule used by a parallel loop).

Despite this fact, we opted for now to base implicit ordering among threads on the total thread id order due to the lack of useful alternatives. If the order of data items can be determined using a different mechanism in an application, interfaces that allow each thread to specify the exact location of the data item in the file are also provided. Our future work exploring parallel file I/O in OpenMP will consider it in the context of nested parallelism and explicit tasks, particularly as the latter continues to evolve and mature.

Synchronous vs. asynchronous interfaces. Synchronous I/O interfaces block the execution of the according function to the point that it is safe for the application to modify the input buffer of a write operation, or the data of a read operation is fully available. Asynchronous interfaces on the other hand only initiate the execution of the according operation, and the application has to use additional functions to verify whether the actual read/write operations have finished. Internally, asynchronous I/O operations are often implemented by spawning additional threads in order to execute the according read/write operations in the background. In a multi-threaded programming model, where the user often carefully hand-tunes the number of threads executing on a particular processor, creating additional threads in the background can have unintended side affects that could influence the performance negatively. For this reason, the initial version of the OpenMP I/O routines only supports synchronous I/O operations.

Algorithmic vs. list I/O interfaces. A general rule of I/O operations is, that the more data an I/O function has to deal with, the larger the number of optimizations that can be applied to it. Ideally, this would consist of a single, large, contiguous amount of data that has to be written to or read from disk. In reality however, the elements that an application has to access are often not contiguous neither in the main memory nor on the disk. Consider for example unstructured computational fluid dynamics (CFD) applications, where each element of the computational mesh is stored in a linked list. The linked list is in that context necessary, since neighborhood conditions among the elements are irregular (e.g. a cell might have more than one neighbor in a direction), and might change over the lifetime of an application. The question therefore is how to allow an application to pass more than one element to an I/O operation, each element pointing to potentially a different memory location and being of different size.

Two solutions are usually considered: an algorithmic interface, which allows to easily express repetitive and regular access patterns, or list I/O interfaces, which simply take a list of *<input buffer pointers, data length>* as arguments. Due to the fact that OpenMP does not have a mechanism on how to express/store repetitive patterns in memory (unlike e.g. MPI using its derived data types), supporting algorithmic interfaces would lead to an explosion in the size of the interfaces that would be cumbersome for the end-user. Therefore, we opted to support list I/O interfaces in the current specification, but not algorithmic interfaces. We might revisit this section however, since *Array shaping*[7] is being discussed under the context of OpenMP accelerator support.

Error Handling. As of today, OpenMP does not make any official statements to recognize hardware or software failures at runtime, though there is active investigation of this topic by the OpenMP Language Committee (LC). Dealing with some form of failures is however mandatory for I/O operations. Consider for example recognizing when a write operation fails, e.g. because of quota limitations. Therefore, the I/O routines introduced in this paper all return an error code. The value returned is either *0* (success), or *-1* (failure). In case of a failure, the amount written/read is undefined. This model follows the (user friendlier) error behavior of the MPI I/O operations which give stronger guarantees compared to the POSIX style function and the error codes returned in the *errno* variable.

3.1 Introduction to the Annotation Used

In the following, we present the C versions of the parallel I/O functions introduced. Since all functions presented here are collective operations, i.e. all threads of a parallel region have to call the according function, some input arguments can be either identical or different on each thread. Furthermore, the arguments can be either shared variables or private variables. Table 1 shows the interfaces, focusing on the read operations for the sake of brevity. For convenience, we introduce the following annotation to classify arguments of the functions:

- *[private]*: The argument is expected to be a private variable of a thread, values between the threads can differ.
- *[private']*: Argument is expected to be different on each thread. This can be either achieved by using private variables, or by pointing to different parts of a shared data structure/array.
- *[shared]*: The argument is expected to be a shared variable.
- *[shared']*: An argument marked as *shared'* is expected to have exactly the same value on all threads in the team. This can either be accomplished by using a shared variable, or by using private variables having exactly the same value/content.

3.2 Interface Specification

The *file management functions* consists of two routines to collectively open and close a file. All threads in a parallel region should input the same file name when

Table 1. OpenMP I/O general file manipulation routines

File Management Interfaces

int omp_file_open_all([shared] int *fd, [shared'] char *filename, [shared'] int flags)
int omp_file_close_all([shared] int fd)

Different Argument Interfaces

int omp_file_read_all ([private']void* buffer, long length, [shared]int fd, [shared']int hint)
int omp_file_read_at_all ([private']void* buffer, long length, [private']off_t offset
                          [shared]int fd, [shared']int hint)

                                                    [shared]int fd, [shared']int hint)
int omp_file_read_list_all ([private']void** buffer, int size, [shared]int fd, [shared']int hint)
int omp_file_read_list_at_all ([private']void** buffer, [private']off_t* offsets, int size,
                               [shared]int fd, [shared']int hint)

Common Argument Interfaces

int omp_file_read_com_all ([shared]void* buffer, [shared']long length,
                           [shared]int fd, [shared']int hint)
int omp_file_read_com_at_all ([shared]void* buffer, [shared']long length,
                              [shared']off_t offset, [shared]int fd, [shared']int hint)
int omp_file_read_com_list_all ([shared]void** buffer, [shared']int size,
                                [shared]int fd, [shared']int hint)
int omp_file_read_com_list_at_all ([shared]void** buffer, [shared']off_t* offsets,
                                   [shared']int size, [shared]int fd, [shared']int hint)

opening a file. The *flags* argument controls how the file is to be opened, e.g. for reading, writing, etc.. The returned file descriptor *fd* is a shared variable. Note, that it is recommended to use as many threads for opening the file as will be used later on for the according read-write operation. However, a mismatch in the number of threads used for opening vs. file access is allowed, specifically, it is allowed to open the file outside of a parallel region and use the resulting file handle inside of a parallel region. Having the same number of threads when opening the file as in the actual collective read-write operation could have performance benefits due to the ability of the library to correctly set-up and initialize internal data structures. Note also, that a file handle opened using *omp_file_open_all* can not be used for sequential POSIX read/write operations, and vice versa.

The *different argument interface* routines assume that each thread in a collective read/write operation passes different arguments, except for the file handle. Specifically, each thread is allowed to pass a different buffer pointer and different length of data to be written or read. This allows, for example, each thread to write data structures that are stored as private variables into a file.

In the explicit offset interfaces, i.e. interfaces that have the keyword *at* in their name, each thread should provide the offset into file where to read data from or write data to. If two or more threads point to the same location in the file through the according offsets, the outcome of a write operation is undefined, i.e. either the data of one or the other thread could be in the file, and potentially even a mixture of both. For read operations, overlapping offsets are not erroneous.

For implicit offset interfaces, data will be read or written starting from the position where the current file pointer is positioned. Data will be read from the file in the order of the threads' OpenMP assigned IDs.

All functions also take an argument referred to as *hint*. A hint is an integer value that indicates whether buffer pointers provided by different threads are contiguous in memory and file, or not. For the sake of brevity we omit details at this point. The specification also contains List I/O interfaces, which are not discussed here due to space limitations.

The *common argument interfaces* define functions where each thread has to pass exactly the same arguments to the function calls. The main benefits from the perspective of the parallel I/O library are that the library has access to multiple threads for executing the I/O operations. Thus, it does not have to spawn its own threads, which might under certain circumstances interfere with the application level threads.

In the following, we show a simple example using the interfaces described above.

```
int fd;     //global file handle
char* buf;  //global data buffer

#pragma omp parallel
{
    char* private_buf;  //private data buffer
    long len = 100000000;

    omp_file_open_all (&fd, "input.out", O_RDONLY);
    // Read data into private buffer
    omp_file_read_all(private_buf, len, fd, NULL);
    omp_file_close_all(fd);

    do_something (buf, private_buf);

    omp_file_open_all (&fd, "result.out", O_CREAT|O_RDWR);
    // Write data from global buffer
    omp_file_com_write_all(buf, len, fd, NULL);
}
...
#pragma omp parallel
{
    // write more data from global buffer
    omp_file_com_write_all(buf, len, fd, NULL);
    omp_file_close_all(fd);
}
```

4   Implementation in the OpenUH Compiler

We developed a parallel I/O library which provides collective I/O operations based on POSIX threads. The library is organized in multiple logical components, the most important of which we present in the following.

The *base function* collects the input arguments provided by all threads in a single array. All threads sychronize at this point through a barrier, after which the master thread begins analyzing the input arguments and redirects control to the contiguity analyzer or the work manager. The remaining threads are put to sleep and wait for an I/O assignment.

The *contiguity analyzer* performs the optimization of merging buffers by scanning the input array of memory addresses to look for contiguity between them. If the analyzer finds discontiguity between buffers, it passes the contiguous block found so far to the *work manager* and proceeds with the scan on the rest of the array. Large sized blocks are split amongst threads instead of assigning an entire block to a single thread.

The *work manager* performs the task of assigning blocks of data to be read/written to threads. Once it accepts a contiguous block of data from the contiguity analyzer (or from the base function), it assigns the block to the next available worker thread and sets the *ASSIGNED* flag for the thread. It also manages the internal file offset used for those interfaces that do not accept a file offset explicitly. The work manager can be programmed to wake up a thread immediately once an I/O request is assigned to it or wake up all threads once the contiguity analyzer completes its analysis and the *FINISH* flag is set.

The *low level interfaces* list the functions available to a thread for performing I/O. As an example, for a thread with multiple I/O assignments, it creates an array of *struct iovec* and calls the *readv / writev* routines.

The parallel I/O library has been integrated in the runtime of the OpenUH compiler. OpenUH [8], a branch of the Open64 4.x compiler suite, is a production quality, fully functional C/C++ and Fortran optimizing compiler under development at University of Houston that supports the bulk of the OpenMP 3.0 API, including explicit tasking. It is freely available[1] and used as a basis upon which language extensions (e.g., Co-array Fortran) and new ideas for better supporting OpenMP during both the compilation and runtime phases are explored.

Since the collective I/O interfaces were originally developed as part of a stand-alone library for POSIX threads, integration of the library with the compiler and providing the OpenMP syntax discussed previously required some modification. The bulk of the integration work was to take advantage of the functionality of the compiler's OpenMP runtime within the parallel I/O library. This includes using the runtime's functionality to determine the number of threads in a parallel region, thread ID's etc. Furthermore, the parallel I/O library has been modified to take advantage of the highly optimized synchronization routines among threads instead of the original implementation in the parallel I/O library.

---

[1] http://www.cs.uh.edu/~hpctools/OpenUH

5   Performance Evaluation

In the following, we evaluate the performance of the prototype implementation on two storage systems using a set of micro-benchmarks that implement commonly used I/O patterns in OpenMP applications and/or options to express I/O patterns in OpenMP applications. In this paper, we focus on write operations, although most micro-benchmarks can easily be extended to read operations as well. In the following, we provide a brief description of the microbenchmarks used.

1. Writing in parallel to one file using the ordered directive Threads write non-overlapping parts of a large shared buffer to a shared file using POSIX `write()` operations in this benchmark. Since the file descriptor is shared between all threads, access to it is protected by executing an *ordered for* loop. Note that access to the file descriptor could also be protected using OpenMP's *critical* section. This test exposes the performance drawback that can be seen when access to a shared file needs to be exclusive. As such, this is a worst case scenario when threads write to a common file.

2. Writing in parallel to separate files All threads perform writes to separate, individual files in this benchmark. Each thread has exclusive access to its own file and can perform I/O without requiring any interaction/synchronization with other threads. For many scenarios, this access pattern will lead to the maximum I/O bandwidth achievable by an OpenMP application.

3. Collective write using omp_file_write_all This benchmark aims to evaluate the collective interface *omp_file_write_all*. Threads write non-overlapping parts of a large, shared matrix to a common file. The file is opened using *omp_file_open_all*. The shared matrix is ultimately written multiple times using a *for* loop to achieve the desired file size. The access to the open file does not require synchronization between threads.

5.1   Resources

For our experiments, we use two PVFS2 (v2.8.2) [9] file system installations. One has been setup over nodes of a cluster that employ regular hard drives, whereas the second installation has been setup over an SSD based storage.

PVFS2 over the Crill Compute Cluster The crill compute cluster consists of 16 nodes, each node having four 2.2 GHz 12-core AMD Opteron processors (48 cores total) with 64 GB main memory. Each node has three 4x SDR InfiniBand links, one of them being reserved for I/O operations and two for message passing communication. A PVFS2 file system has been configured over the crill nodes such that all 16 crill nodes act as PVFS2 servers and clients, and a secondary hard drive on each node is used for data storage.

PVFS2 over SSD Apart from regular hard drives, the crill cluster has a RAMSAN-630 Solid State Disks (SSD) based storage from Texas Memory Systems. This SSD is made of NAND based enterprise grade Single Level Cell (SLC) flash. The SSD installation has four 500GB cards, thus making a total of 2TB. It has two dual port QDR Infiniband cards, and we use one of two ports on each card. The peak I/O bandwidth of the SSD storage is 2 GB/s. The PVFS2 parallel file system configured over the SSD employs two separate I/O servers, each I/O server serving exactly half of the SSD storage. Tests have been executed multiple times, and we present in each case the average of the bandwidth values observed across various runs. Also, we flush all data to disk using *fsync* before closing a file to ensure we do not see effects of data caching.

5.2   Results

First, we present the results of the first two micro-benchmarks described above. These benchmarks do not utilize the new interfaces presented in this paper, but allow to set upper and lower bounds for the expected performance of the collective OpenMP I/O interfaces.

The left part in figure 1 shows the bandwidth obtained on the crill-pvfs2 file system when threads perform I/O to a shared file. The I/O bandwidth observed reaches a maximum of 212 MBytes/sec, independent of the number of threads used. This can be explained by the fact that the benchmark serializes the access to the file handle and therefore the I/O operation itself. The right part of fig 1 shows the results obtained with the second micro-benchmark where threads write to individual files. The bandwidth obtained in this case is significantly higher than when threads write to a shared file, reaching a maximum of almost 500 MBytes/sec. This value is an indication of the upper bound on the I/O performance that can be achieved from a single node. Note however, that for many production codes this solution would require a separate merging step, which would degrade the overall bandwidth obtained. Results of the same two microbenchmarks executed on the SSD storage revealed a similar trend in the performance can be seen for both, the first benchmarks achieving a

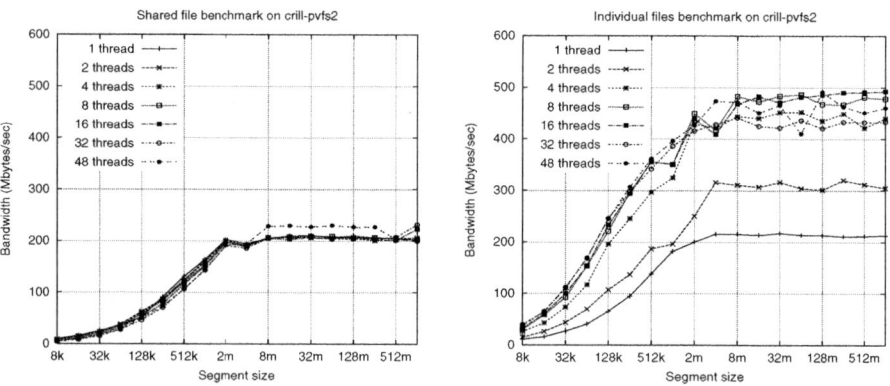

Fig. 1. Shared file microbenchmark(left) and individual files microbenchmark(right) on crill-pvfs2

maximum average write bandwidth of 160 Mbytes/sec, and the second benchmark 356 Mbytes/sec. We omit the graphs due to space restrictions.

Fig 2 shows the performance of *omp_file_write_all* on crill-pvfs2 platform.
Note that *omp_file_write_all* is a collective function where every thread provides a fixed amount of data and the data points shown on this graph (segment size) indicate the total amount of data written across the threads by each
omp_file_write_all call. The results indicate that our prototype implementation
of the new OpenMP I/O routine presented in this paper achieved a bandwidth
in excess of 500 Mbytes/sec. Performance for 1, 2 threads reaches a maximum
of 214 Mbytes/sec and 360 Mbytes/sec respectively, whereas it is much higher
for a larger number of threads. The benefits of multiple threads performing I/O
are clear in this case. It can also be seen that overall, increasing the segment
size, i.e. the amount of data written in a single function call, results in increasing performance. However, the bandwidth obtained does not necessarily increase
beyond a certain threshold. For the crill-pvfs2 file system, the main limitation
comes from how fast data can be transferred out of the node, while for the SSD
storage the limitation is sustained write bandwidth of the storage itself.

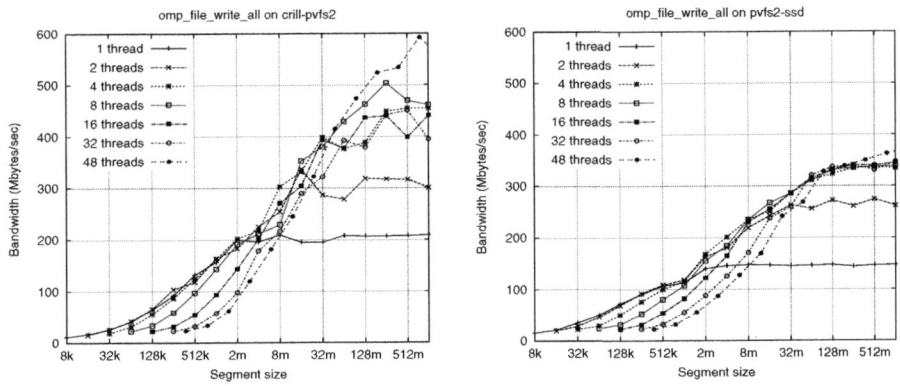

Fig. 2. omp_file_write_all on crill-pvfs2 (left) and pvfs2-ssd (right)

Fig. 3 shows a comparison of all three micro-benchmarks for 16 threads. Despite the fact that *omp_file_write_all* writes to a shared file, its performance is
consistently better than when writing to a shared file using explicit serialization.
The new collective I/O routines presented in this paper perform typically close
to the performance of the second micro-benchmark, which – as discussed – often represents a best-case scenario. Furthermore, taking into account that the
'separate files' scenario would require an explicit merging step after executing
the application, the new routines clearly represent the best of three solutions
evaluated in the corresponding micro-benchmarks.

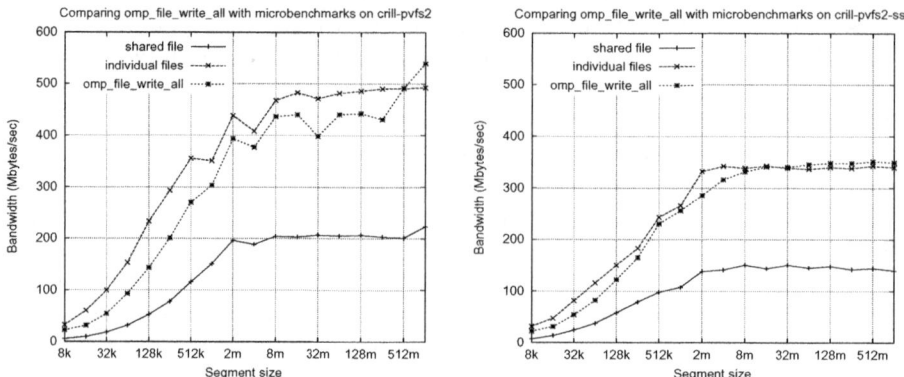

Fig. 3. Comparing microbenchmarks with omp_file_write_all for 16 threads on crill-pvfs2 (left) and pvfs2-ssd (right)

5.3 BT I/O

The new OpenMP I/O routines have also been evaluated with two OpenMP applications. We present here results obtained with the Block-Tridiagonal (BT) NPB benchmark [10], which has in its MPI version an I/O performance component. An OpenMP version of the BT benchmark is available since version 3 of NPB, however without the I/O part. We extended the NPB OpenMP BT benchmark to include I/O in a way similar to its MPI-IO implementation. Note, that subtle differences remain between the two implementations, most notably that the OpenMP version does not read the data back for verification after the write operation.

Experiments have been performed with the class D benchmark, where approximately 128 Gigabytes of data are written over the course of the program (approximately 2.5GB of data over 50 iterations). Table 2 shows the time spent in I/O operations over both file systems for various numbers of threads. I/O was performed such that data was split between threads and every thread was involved in writing data. The overall results indicate, that the I/O time can be improved by a factor of around 2.5 for this application. The time spent in I/O operations is constantly decreasing until 4 threads, and stays constant afterwards, since the limitations of the two file systems described in the previous subsection have been reached. While the results indicate that the I/O performance might not necessarily scale to arbitrary numbers of threads, it is important to note, that the prototype implementation of the new interfaces did lead to a significant performance improvement, which allowed to push the performance of the I/O operations. An advanced user might be able to achieve the same performance through regular POSIX style I/O routines. However, our interfaces have the advantage of a) providing good performance for non I/O expert, b) taking advantage of the multi-threaded execution environment in an OpenMP application, and c) offer support for a number of scenarios such as collectively writing private variables that would be very difficult to achieve without compiler support.

Table 2. BTIO results showing I/O times (seconds)

No. of threads	crill-pvfs2	pvfs2-ssd
1	410	691
2	305	580
4	168	386
8	164	368
16	176	368
32	172	368
48	168	367

6   Conclusions

This paper introduces a set of interfaces for performing parallel I/O in OpenMP applications. We discuss design alternatives and present the architecture of a prototype implementation. Using a set of micro-benchmarks we evaluate the performance of the implementation on two different platforms. The results obtained indicate the potential of the new interfaces in case a high-performance parallel file system is used.

An important question is arising about the interoperability of the MPI I/O specification with the interface routines suggested in this paper. A hybrid application using both OpenMP and MPI would have to choose at the moment between the two competing specifications. Depending on whether it uses one file per process or one file across multiple processes, it could use the OpenMP I/O or the MPI I/O routines, but not both simultaneously. However, an interesting approach in combining the two specifications could be given in that the MPI I/O library could use internally the OpenMP I/O routines to enhance the performance of the I/O operations on a per-node basis. This could become especially attractive with the upcoming MPI-3 standard, which allows a hybrid application to register *helper threads* with the MPI library to enhance the performance of communication and I/O operations.

In the future, we plan to extend this work into multiple directions. First, the interface specification itself will be updated to take advantage of recent developments in OpenMP into account, such as array shaping or explicit tasks. Second, a tremendous amount of optimizations are possible in the parallel I/O library itself, such as explicitly controlling the number of active threads reading/writing data, exploiting data locality in NUMA architectures for I/O operations and combining multiple resources (e.g. local disk + network storage) to enhance the performance of the I/O operations.

Acknowledgments. We would like to thank Brett Estrade, who had editorial contributions to the first version of the paper. Partial support for this work was provided by the National Science Foundation's Computer Systems Research program under Award No. CNS-0833201 and CRI-0958464. Any opinions, findings, and conclusions or recommendations expressed in this material are those of the authors and do not necessarily reflect the views of the National Science Foundation.

References

1. Gabriel, E., Venkatesan, V., Shah, S.: Towards high performance cell segmentation in multispectral fine needle aspiration cytology of thyroid lesions. Computational Methods and Programs in Biomedicine 98(3), 231–240 (2009)
2. OpenMP Application Review Board: OpenMP Application Program Interface, Draft 3.0 (October 2007)
3. Message Passing Interface Forum: MPI-2.2: Extensions to the Message Passing Interface (September 2009), http://www.mpi-forum.org
4. El-Ghazawi, T., Cantonnet, F., Saha, P., Thakur, R., Ross, R., Bonachea, D.: UPC-IO: A Parallel I/O API for UPC. V1.0 (2004)
5. Group, H.D.F.: HDF5 Reference Manual. Release 1.6.3, National Center for Supercomputing Application (NCSA), University of Illinois at Urbana-Champaign (September 2004)
6. Li, J., Liao, W.K., Choudhary, A., Ross, R., Thakur, R., Gropp, W., Latham, R., Siegel, A., Gallagher, B., Zingale, M.: Parallel netcdf: A high-performance scientific i/o interface. In: Proceedings of the 2003 ACM/IEEE Conference on Supercomputing, SC 2003, pp. 39–49. ACM, New York (2003)
7. Ayguadé, E., Badia, R.M., Bellens, P., Cabrera, D., Duran, A., Ferrer, R., González, M., Igual, F.D., Jiménez-González, D., Labarta, J.: Extending openmp to survive the heterogeneous multi-core era. International Journal of Parallel Programming 38(5-6), 440–459 (2010)
8. Liao, C., Hernandez, O., Chapman, B., Chen, W., Zheng, W.: OpenUH: An optimizing, portable OpenMP compiler. In: 12th Workshop on Compilers for Parallel Computers (January 2006)
9. PVFS2 webpage: Parallel Virtual File System, http://www.pvfs.org
10. Wong, P., der Wijngaart, R.F.V.: NAS Parallel Benchmarks I/O Version 3.0. Technical Report NAS-03-002, Computer Sciences Corporation, NASA Advanced Supercomputing (NAS) Division

The Design of OpenMP Thread Affinity

Alexandre E. Eichenberger[1], Christian Terboven[2], Michael Wong[3],
and Dieter an Mey[2]

[1] IBM T.J. Watson Research Center, Yorktown Heights, New York, USA
alexe@us.ibm.com
[2] Center for Computing and Communication,
JARA, RWTH Aachen University, Germany
{terboven,anmey}@rz.rwth-aachen.de
[3] IBM Software Group, Toronto, Ontario, Canada
michaelw@ca.ibm.com

Abstract. Exascale machines will employ significantly more threads than today, but even on current architectures controlling thread affinity is crucial to fuel all the cores and to maintain data affinity, but both MPI and OpenMP lack a solution to this problem. In this work, we present a thread affinity model for OpenMP, which will be shown to work well with hybrid use cases, too. It maintains a separation of platform-specific data and algorithm-specific properties, thus offering deterministic behavior and simplicity in use.

1 Introduction

On Exascale machines, higher performance will likely be achieved by significantly scaling the computing power combined with a smaller increase in total memory capacity. Systems will run significantly more threads than today and these threads will share deeply-hierarchical memory architectures, as it is the case today already. For applications, this implies the need to exploit parallelism at every possible level, e.g., using MPI [10] for process-level, coarse-grain parallelism and OpenMP [8] for outer-loop, medium-grain parallelism as well as for inner-loop, fine-grain parallelism. Since memory accesses to remote locations incur higher latency and lower bandwidth, control of thread placement to enforce affinity within parallel applications is crucial to fuel all the cores and to exploit the full performance of the memory subsystem on Non-Uniform Memory Architectures (NUMA).

However, both programming models lack a solution for this problem. The user is constrained to employ vendor-specific approaches which mostly are not portable between different systems and often set a unique affinity policy for the whole application, without the option to change behavior for a given parallel region. This underlines the need for a common affinity mechanism that is integrated in the OpenMP standard.

In this work, we present a solution to control thread affinity in OpenMP programs, which will be shown to be compatible with MPI in hybrid use cases. It maintains a separation of platform-specific data and algorithm-specific properties, thus offering deterministic behavior and simple employment by the application users in most scenarios.

B.M. Chapman et al. (Eds.): IWOMP 2012, LNCS 7312, pp. 15–28, 2012.
© Springer-Verlag Berlin Heidelberg 2012

This work explains in detail the proposal made by the Affinity Subcommittee of the OpenMP Language Committee to incorporate support for thread affinity in OpenMP 4.0.

This paper is structured as follows: Chap. 2 discusses related work and vendor-specific affinity proposals. Chapter 3 describes the underlying machine model used in Chap. 4 outlining the behavior of threads inside places and the affinity policies. Chapter 5 explains use scenarios and the reference implementation, followed by Chap. 6 on possible future enhancements. We close with Chap. 7 as our summary.

2   Related Work

OpenMP [8] provides a standard, easy to use programming model for multiprocessors, without any notion of the hardware an OpenMP programming is running on. This has been noted by OpenMP implementors, who use appropriate operating system calls to offer compiler vendor-specific environment variables to pin software threads to processors [3]. These approaches will be described in Chap. 2.1, however, they are not portable and we are convinced that the low-level control of thread pinning from within an OpenMP program does not provide the right level of abstraction necessary to program current and future system architectures. This is particularly true when two or more levels of parallelism are employed[4].

Several proposals to extend OpenMP with support for thread and also data affinity have been made in the past, including the extension by low-level APIs as well as higher-level concepts. This work most significantly differentiates from previous ones by the introduction of places as an abstraction of architecture details, with which the application user may control the program execution. A similar concept named location [12] as both an execution environment as well as data storage has been proposed before by Huang et al., again borrowing ideas from X10's place and Chapel's locale. All this previous work heavily influenced this proposal.

Libraries such as the *Portable Hardware Locality (hwloc)*[2] provide a low level of hardware abstraction and offer a solution for the portability problem by supporting many platforms and operating systems. This and similar approaches may provide detailed hardware information in a tree-like structure. However, even some current systems cannot be represented correctly by a tree, such as an 8-socket AMD Operton or Intel Xeon system, where the number of hops between two sockets vary between socket pairs. Still we believe that dealing with this information is too low-level for most application programmers.

2.1   Current Implementation-specific Approaches

All implementations have in common that they did not introduce a specific naming scheme to identify processor cores, but rather use the core numbering scheme provided by the operating system. They are configuration specific in that they have been designed by vendors to easily and quickly support contemporary systems.

The KMP_AFFINITY environment variable in the **Intel** compilers [7] allow to bind OpenMP threads to cores. If unspecified, threads remain unbound. The environment variable may contain enumerations of single core numbers in any order or ranges of core numbers with and without the definition of a stride, as well as sets of core numbers using the same scheme enclosed in curly brackets. Thus, threads may be bound to specific cores, but also to a set of cores representing a whole part of the machine. Furthermore, it knows about the specifiers *compact* and *scatter*: specifying compact assigns the OpenMP thread $n+1$ to a free thread context as close as possible to the thread context where the n-th OpenMP thread was placed, and specifying scatter distributes the threads as evenly as possible across the entire system. Adding the specifier *verbose* instructs the runtime to print information regarding the detected machine topology as well as the actual thread binding. In order to distribute four OpenMP threads over two sockets and four cores on the machine illustrated in Fig. 1, one could either set KMP_AFFINITY to "scatter" or "0,4,8,12".

While the facility provided by Intel is very flexible and addresses many use cases, it does not support nested OpenMP well. The way in which thread binding for compact and spread is computed does not allow any changes after the program has started. However, the features of the Intel implementation influenced this proposal heavily.

The GOMP_CPU_AFFINITY environment variable controls the binding of threads to specific cores in the OpenMP runtime of the **GNU** compilers, libgomp[5]. The variable may contain enumerations of core ids in any order or ranges of cores with and without the definition of a stride. If specified, the OpenMP threads are bound in the order in which they are started to the given cores, one thread per core. If more threads are started than cores specified in the list, the assignment continues from the beginning of the list. If the variable is unspecified, the assignment of threads is up to the host system.

The **Oracle** compilers[9] offer the SUNW_MP_PROCBIND environment variable to influence the binding of threads, which is disabled by default. If the environment variable is set to *true*, the threads are bound to the available cores in a round-robin fashion, although the starting core is determined by the OpenMP runtime, unless exactly one core number is given. If a list of core numbers is specified, the OpenMP threads will be bound in a round-robin fashion to these cores.

The **PGI** compilers[11] do not bind threads to cores unless the user sets the environment variable MP_BIND to *yes*. If binding is enable, the environment variable MP_BLIST may contain a list of core numbers the threads are being bound to, one thread per core in a round-robin manner.

The **IBM**™compilers[6] support binding via the environment variable XLSMPOPTS. This can be set to bind=SDL=n_1,n_2,n_3 or bindlist=SDL=$n_1,\ldots,n_i$. SDL is a system detail level and can be PROC, PROC_CORE, L2CACHE, or MCM, which is a node. Both allow to bind threads to multiple logical processors. The first option specifies an enumeration with the integers n_1 being the starting resource id, n_2 is the number of requested resources, and n_3 is the stride, which specifies the increment used to determine the next resource id to bind, ignoring extra resources if the number of resources specified is greater than the number of threads. In the latter option the list of integers enumerates the resources to be used during binding. When the number of threads t is greater than the number of resources x, t threads are divided among x resources according to the following formula: The $\lceil t/x \rceil$ threads are bound to the first $t \bmod x$ resources. The $\lfloor t/x \rfloor$ threads are bound to the remaining resources.

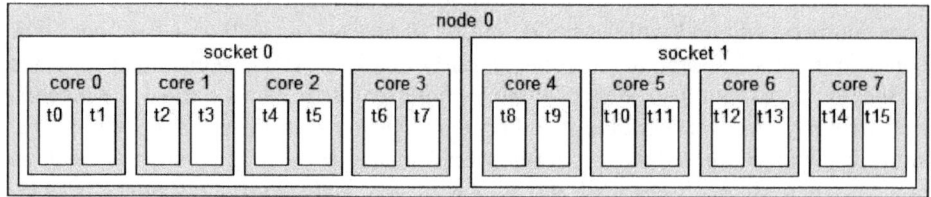

Fig. 1. Linear system with 2 sockets, 8 cores, and 16 hardware threads

The features provided by the GNU, Oracle, PGI and IBM implementations work well for many use cases, but again do not provide support for nested OpenMP. The binding of a thread to a single core is too restrictive for several scenarios. In order to distribute four OpenMP threads on two sockets and four cores on the machine illustrated in Fig. 1, using the GNU, Oracle or PGI implementations one has to set the respective environment variable to "0,4,8,12". For the IBM runtime one could either set the environment variable XLSMPTOPS to "bind=PROC_CORE=0,4,4" or otherwise to "bindlist=PROC_CORE=0,4,8,12".

3   Machine Model

HPC machines are typically built using a hierarchy of building blocks that are increasingly shared among the threads in the systems. For example, a few hardware threads share a common core including functional units and first level cache. Cores are then replicated to form a chip or socket, where they share a common cache hierarchy and ports to external caches or memory devices. At the next level, chips or sockets are assembled to form a node or a system. An example of a linear system is depicted in Fig. 1.

While we could conceivably build a machine model that precisely represents such hierarchies of machine resources, we decided against such detailed representation for the following reasons. First, it is difficult to find a precise, detailed representation that encompasses all of the current and up-coming HPC architectures. Second, we would have to provide a detailed interface for the user to interact with the representation. This interaction would be required by application writers who aim at generating portable code, as they might desire one kind of affinity on a machine with one set of features, and another type of affinity on a machine with a distinct set of features. Third, detailed representation and associated affinity policy are bound to introduce additional runtime overhead during parallel region creation.

3.1   Places

Because of the above reasons, here we propose to use a simple representation of resources rooted in the concept of a *place*: a place is defined as a set of hardware execution environments (e.g. hardware threads, processor cores, GPU lanes) that is treated by OpenMP as one unit of location when dealing with OpenMP thread affinity. A place is a clear delineation of OpenMP thread placement: on one hand, the user can fully specify the places to be used for each of the OpenMP threads in a given parallel region; and on the other hand, the OpenMP runtime has full flexibility to place and migrate OpenMP threads within any of the execution environments mapped to a given place. This definition is very flexible as it lets the user specify the affinity that matters for the user's application by determining the assignment of OpenMP threads to places while leaving sufficient amount of flexibility to the runtime to perform runtime-driven load balancing within the allocated resources.

We propose to give the user full control over the allocation of resources to each place in the system. For example, consider a user wanting to determine the placement of OpenMP threads to the hardware cores in the system and let the OpenMP runtime environment determine load balancing among the threads within each core. Using the system depicted in Fig. 1 as an example, this user would define a set of up to 8 places, one per physical core, and allocate two hardware threads per place, e.g., hardware threads t_0 and t_1 for the first place, an so on. Consider a second user that wants to maintain full control over affinity and disallow the OpenMP runtime to perform any runtime load balancing. Using the same machine, this user would define a set of up to 16 places, each containing exactly one hardware thread. A third user may want to give the runtime full control over thread placements, and thus would assign all hardware threads to a unique place, e.g., including hardware threads t_0 to t_{15}.

3.2 Place List

Now we consider how the places in the system relate with one another. The *place list* is defined as an ordered list of places. Consider the list (t_0), (t_1), (t_2), ... to (t_{15}) representing a list of 16 places, each including a single hardware thread. This list represent one possible walk through the hardware threads in Fig. 1 such that threads sharing cores be next to each others, and then threads associated with neighbor cores be next to each other, and so on. For example, place (t_0) is followed by place (t_1) as they share a common core, and then by places (t_2) and (t_3) as they all share a common chip. Note that the place list is not a reliable indicator of the degree of sharing since, for example, neighbor places (t_6) and (t_7) have a core in common but neighbor places (t_7) and (t_8) only share the same node, but neither core nor chip.

This concept of a place list also applies to two-dimensional torus-like structures. In this case, a suitable list of places including one hardware thread each is obtained by, for example, zigzagging among the threads of the first chip before listing the threads of the next chip.

3.3 Model Specification

The thread-affinity machine model consists of an ordered list of places along with a set of execution environment resources dedicated to each place in the list. While we expect most users to rely on a default vendor-specific, machine-specific machine model, we also provide a mechanism for a user-defined machine model. Like other parameters in the OpenMP model, this can be provided as an environment variable (OMP_PLACES) using the semantic provided in Fig. 2. The value of OMP_PLACES can be one of two

```
"OMP_PLACES" = <place-list> | <abstract-name>

      <place-list> = <place-interval> "," <place-list> | <place-interval>
   <place-interval> = <place> ":" <len> ":" <step> | <place> ":" <len> |
                      <place> | "!" <place>

         <place> = "(" <resource-list> ")"
   <resource-list> = <resource-interval> "," <resource-list> | <resource-interval>
<resource-interval> = <resource> ":" <len> ":" <step> |
                      <resource> ":" <len> | <resource> | "!" <resource>

   <abstract-name> = <word> | <word> | ... | <word>

      <resource> = non-negative integer
         <len> = positive integer (not null)
        <step> = integer
```

Fig. 2. Place list syntax

types of values: either an abstract name describing a set of places or an explicit list of places described by non-negative numbers.

When appropriate for the target machine, abstract names such as threads and cores should be understood by the execution and runtime environment. While the precise definitions of the abstract names are vendor-specific, these definitions should correspond to the intuition of informed users, i.e. cores defining each place corresponds to a single physical core (having one or more hardware threads). Vendors may also add abstract names as appropriate for their target platforms.

Alternatively, the OMP_PLACES environment variable can be defined using an explicit ordered list of places. A place is defined by an unordered set of nonnegative numbers enclosed by parenthesis and comma separated. The meaning of the numbers is implementation-dependent, but generally represent the smallest unit of execution exposed by the execution environment, typically a hardware thread. The exact syntax is defined in Fig. 2, the examples below define a model with 4 places containing 4 hardware threads each:

```
OMP_PLACES="(0,1,2,3),(4,5,6,7),(8,9,10,11),(12,13,14,15)"
OMP_PLACES="(0:4),(4:4),(8:4),(12:4)"
OMP_PLACES="(0:4):4:4"
```

3.4   Strengths and Limitations of the Machine Model

As formulated, the thread-affinity machine model is static for the duration of the execution of the OpenMP program and provides for a single, linear level of abstraction, namely a list of places. The model only permits thread migration within each given place; however, the user is free to define as coarse a place as required by load-balancing needs. While the model limitations may theoretically impact the performance of specific applications, we believe that the model strikes a good balance between efficiency and expressivity, because most machines' building blocks and applications' parallelism are hierarchical in nature. Similarly, the parallelism in most HPC applications is hierarchical, with coarse-grain, outer-loop parallelism, which, in turn, includes nested, fine-grain, inner-loop parallelism. As a result, the linear partition of places will often be perfectly partitioned at the outer-loop levels. Examples in section 5 fill further illustrate this point.

4   Affinity

4.1   Threads per Place

While places deal with hardware resources, we have not yet defined how the software threads under control of the OpenMP runtime are mapped to the places. The OpenMP standard already has a mechanism to cap the maximum number of concurrently working OpenMP threads in the system. This upper limit is stored in the runtime as the Internal Control Variable (ICV) *thread-limit-var* and is set by the OMP_THREAD_LIMIT environment variable.

It has to be defined how to cap the number of OpenMP threads in the presence of a place-list. One approach would be to simply let the runtime create as many OpenMP threads as needed for each place as long as the total number does not exceed the *thread-limit-var* ICV. While flexible, this approach suffers from a few issues. First, one place could temporarily consume all OpenMP threads, thus leaving no more threads for other places at a given instance of time, thus creating imbalance in the system. Second, not all architectures and operating systems efficiently support over-subscription of software threads to hardware threads. Third, performance may become more difficult to predict if some places have a large number of OpenMP threads while others have very few.

Thus one approach is to use a fix, static policy mapping an equal number of OpenMP threads to each place defined in the system (plus or minus one). Defining P as the number of places in the place list, the number of OpenMP threads per place is capped at $\lfloor thread\text{-}limit\text{-}var/P \rfloor$ OpenMP threads, with the first *thread-limit-var* mod P places having their cap increased by one.

Figure 3 illustrates the assignment of OpenMP threads to an 8-place target machine with a thread limit of, respectively, 8, 32, and 20 OpenMP threads. Note that this approach does not preclude supporting heterogeneous machines with strong and weaker cores. Consider, for example, the mapping of threads for a machine with 1 strong core and 6 weak cores. In this case, the user can create two places associated with the hardware threads of the strong core, and 6 places associated with hardware threads of the weak cores. As a result, even though each place is capped to an equal number of OpenMP threads, the strong core will effectively execute up to twice as many OpenMP threads as each of the weak cores.

The drawback of this approach is that it reuses OMP_THREAD_LIMIT in a slightly different context. Another approach would be to introduce an alternative environment variable, or use the number of hardware resources listed in OMP_PLACES.

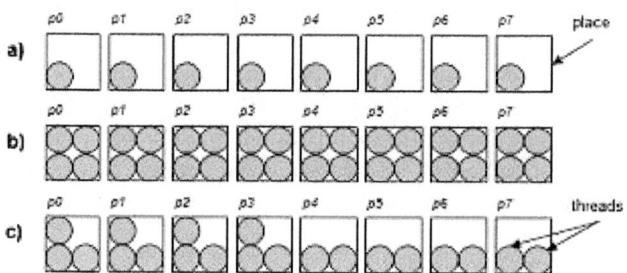

Fig. 3. Threads per places for varying thread limits (OMP_THREAD_LIMIT)

4.2 Affinity Policies

The new `affinity` clause on the parallel construct determines the selection of places, which remains fixed for the duration of the parallel region. When designing the affinity policies, our aim was to provide effective affinity for a large set of application patterns while remaining at a high level so as to provide an interface that is portable across threading levels and platforms. The main affinity policies are *spread* and *compact*, whose features are highlighted below.

- **Spread.** When using the spread affinity, the user requests the OpenMP runtime to spread the worker threads evenly within the places in the system, as much as possible. We expect users to select this affinity policy in order to increase the resources available to each worker thread. The spread policy also logically sub-divides the machine in equally sized sub-partitions so as to enable suitable affinity in presence of nested parallelism.
- **Compact.** When using the compact affinity, the user requests the OpenMP runtime to pack the worker threads on the same place as the master, as much as possible. We expect users to select this affinity policy in order to exploit fine-grain instruction-level parallelism among the created threads while aiming to preserve data locality among the different threads to the same subset of the memory hierarchy.

The detailed behavior of an OpenMP implementation is defined in terms of ICVs. First, we define the *place-list-var* ICV as an ordered list describing all OpenMP places available to the execution environment. Its value is constant during the duration of the program. The user can set its value with the OMP_PLACES environment variable, or a default, vendor-specific value is used. Second, we define the *place-partition-var* ICV as an ordered list that corresponds to one contiguous interval in the place list and describes the places currently available to the execution environment for a given `parallel` directive. Its initial value is set to include the entire place list as defined by the *place-list-var* ICV. Its value may change when creating a parallel region using the *spread* affinity policy. There is one copy of this ICV per data environment. Third, the policies impact how the OpenMP threads are numbered within a parallel region.

Figure 4 illustrates the affinity policies, where the middle column shows a visual depiction of parallel constructs with specific affinity policies, the rightmost three columns

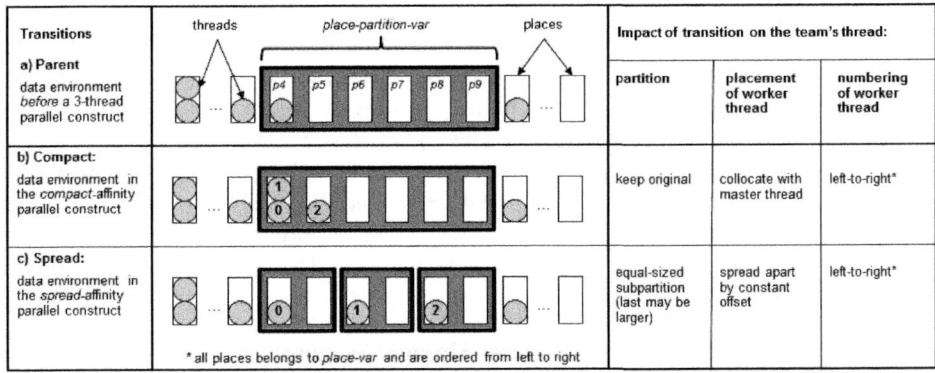

Fig. 4. Compact and Spread affinity policies

summarize the impact on the three parts of the execution environment, respectively, partition, thread placement, and thread numbering. In this figure, circles illustrate threads, white boxes depict places and grey boxes indicate the values of *place-partition-var* ICVs. Figure 4(a) depicts a (parent) thread owning a partition of the machine with six places, p_4 to p_9, before executing a `parallel` construct with three threads.

Let us focus first on the impact of affinity on partitions. We see in Fig. 4 that the spread policy subdivides the partition of the parent thread. The original *place-partition-var* ICV, including places p_4 to p_9, is partitioned in three equal-sized, contiguous sub-partitions, where the master thread gets p_4 and p_5, one worker thread gets p_6 and p_7, the other worker gets p_8 and p_9. In general, when the parent's partition cannot be divided evenly, only the last partition includes more places than the other partitions. When a `parallel` construct requests more threads than there are places in the parent's place partition, some threads will be mapped to the same places. For example, when requesting 8 threads on a partition with 4 places, the places are sub-partitioned in 4 sub-partitions of unit size, each with 2 OpenMP threads mapped to it. The *thread-limit-var* ICV is also adjusted to reflect the reduced thread limit within each partition. For the compact policy, each team thread inherits the full partition of the parent. Consider now the placements of the worker threads of the `parallel` construct. For the compact policy, shown in Fig. 4(b), the worker threads are co-located with the master thread, as much as possible. Assuming that there are at most two OpenMP threads per place, the execution environment assigns one worker thread on the same place as the parent/master thread (here: p_4) and one thread on the place following the parent/master thread (p_5). For the spread policy, depicted in Fig. 4(c), each worker thread is assigned to the first place in its sub-partition, namely p_6 and p_8 here.

For both affinity policies, worker threads that are assigned to places with lower place numbers have lower thread numbers than worker threads assigned to places with higher place numbers. The thread number of worker threads assigned to the same place is implementation-defined. Note that places are numbered by their respective positions in the *place-list-var* ICV. When there are not enough OpenMP threads available within a given place, the number of worker threads returned by the parallel region as well as the affinity of the threads becomes implementation-defined.

To formally define the policies, we assume a parallel construct requesting a team of size T with *place-partition-var* including P consecutive places. Places are ordered by indices; in particular, the place following a given place x (namely, the x'th place in *place-list-var*) corresponds to place $x + 1$. Using this numbering, we define the lowest numbered place in the current *place-partition-var* as P_{first}, and we define the place on which the master thread executes as P_{master}. When referring to a place that falls outside of the current place partition (namely P_{first} to $P_{first+P-1}$, inclusively), that place defaults back to the P_{first} place.

Affinity Policy and Its Impact on Team Threads Mapping to Places. *compact:* The execution environment first takes OpenMP threads that are both available and executing on the P_{master} place. If it needs additional OpenMP threads, it then takes available threads from the place following P_{master}, and so on, until it forms a team of T threads. *spread:* When requesting a team with fewer OpenMP threads than there are places in the place partition, the team threads are spaced $S = \lfloor P/T \rfloor$ places apart. The first thread executes on place P_{first}, the next team thread on place $P_{first+S}$, and so on until all worker threads have been assigned[1]. Otherwise, there is at least one thread per place. In this case, each place executes at least $\lfloor T/P \rfloor$ threads, with the first places (P_{first} to $P_{first+(P \bmod T)-1}$) executing one additional team thread.

Updated *place-partition-var* ICV in the Data Environment of the Team Threads. *compact:* Each team thread inherits the *place-partition-var* of the parent thread. *spread:* Consider first the case where team threads are spaced $S = \lfloor P/T \rfloor$ places apart. In this case, the *place-partition-var* of the parent thread is partitioned into P non-overlapping partitions of length S (with an exception for the last partition which is extended up to the last place, $P_{first+P-1}$). Each thread then gets the partition that includes the place where it executes. Otherwise, each thread gets a *place-partition-var* that solely includes the place where it executes.

Thread Number of Team Threads Depending on Affinity Policy. *compact:* The smallest thread numbers are assigned to the worker threads located on P_{master}; the next smallest numbers are assigned to the worker threads located on the place following P_{master}, and so on. *spread:* The smallest thread numbers are assigned to the worker threads located on P_{first}; the next smallest numbers are assigned to the worker threads located on the place following P_{first}, and so on.

4.3   Runtime Library Routines

In order to provide an interface to the affinity policies that is coherent with the handling of other clauses such as the num_threads clause for the parallel construct, we propose adding two library calls, omp_get_proc_bind() and omp_set_proc_bind() in order to, respectively, retrieve and set the affinity policy of the current data environment.

---

[1] A special case occurs when P_{master} is not located at a multiple of S places after P_{first} (namely, when $P_{first+x*S} < P_{master} < P_{first+(x+1)*S}$ holds true for some integer x). In this case, the execution environment skips creating a worker thread on $P_{first+x*S}$.

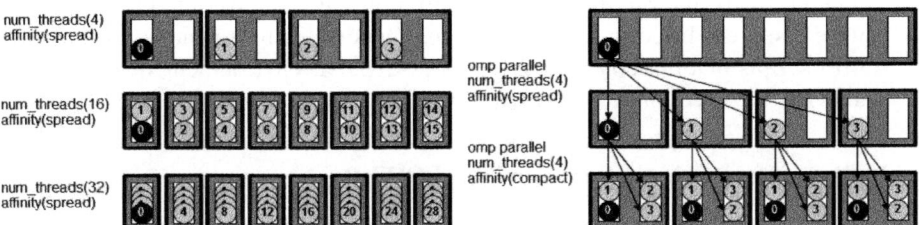

Fig. 5. Use Scenarios

5   Use Scenarios and Implementation

Before we discuss the reference implementation, we want to illustrate use scenarios:

1. **Varying level of concurrency.** Consider an application that has many phases and assume we are targeting an 8 cores machine with 2 hardware threads per core. For phases with little parallelism or data sharing, the thread distribution shown in Fig. 5 (left, top) may be used, with one OpenMP thread per core. In a phase where threads have some data locality in common, a thread distribution like in Fig. 5 (left, middle) may be beneficial, as each software thread is mapped on a dedicated hardware thread and two threads per core share the same cache hierarchy. In a third phase, with high level of parallelism, memory latency can be hidden by over-committing software threads per hardware thread, as shown in Fig. 5 (left, bottom). For load balancing within a core, one would use one place per core with a thread limit of at least 32. While a user could vary the level of concurrency by using the num_threads clause prior to this affinity proposal, the application writer had no way to determine where its worker threads would be mapped. Using the appropriate OMP_PLACES and OMP_THREAD_LIMITS environment variables as well as the appropriate num_threads and affinity clauses, a user can now reliably distribute the worker threads across cores and consistently across target machines and OpenMP runtime vendors.
2. **Distinct data sharing patterns.** The second use scenario illustrates a nested parallelism case, where outer loops are parallelized with little data reuse between threads, and where inner loops are parallelized with data reuse and false sharing between threads. Figure 5 (right) illustrates this scenario, where a spread affinity is used at the top level and a compact affinity is used at the inner level of parallelism.
3. **Restricting OpenMP threads.** In a third use scenario, a user may simply want to restrict the OpenMP threads to a subset of the machine. A typical example is when a single shared memory machine is used for several MPI processes. In such case, a typical user will aim to reduce the interferences of the MPI processes among themselves by logically partitioning the shared memory machine and assigning a distinct subset of cores to each MPI process. In this case, the user can simply define the OMP_PLACES environment of each MPI process to include the specific cores assigned to each process. Even in the absence of affinity policies (e.g. OMP_PROC_BIND set to false), where OpenMP threads are allowed to

migrate freely, the runtime is required to limit the OpenMP threads to only hardware resources listed in the list of places. We expect most vendors to provide for MPI scripts that directly set the OMP_PROC_BIND environment variable so as to alleviate the need for the user to perform such repetitive tasks.

5.1   Reference Implementation on IBM POWER

We have created a reference implementation in an experimental OpenMP runtime targeting POWER™platforms running on AIX and Linux. The changes to the runtime were fairly limited. We added one global, static *place-list* ICV, switched the global, static *bind-var* and *thread-limit-var* ICVs to become scoped within the data environment of the OpenMP threads, and added one new *place-partition-var* ICV, also within the data environment of the OpenMP threads. While adding ICVs to the data environment can potentially impact performance, as this data must be copied from the master thread into the context of the team members of a parallel region, we have found no noticeable slowdown as affinity policies can be trivially encoded in two bits of data and the *thread-limit-var* ICV value can be reconstructed on demand from other data available in the data environment of a given OpenMP thread.

The second change to the experimental runtime was to change our default OpenMP thread selection policy invoked when creating a team of threads for a parallel construct. Like many other OpenMP runtimes, we keep a pool of software threads ready to be awoken when needed. In our implementation, the master selects the threads for a given parallel task, taking some general measure of load balance between the cores in the system, and then signals the software threads to get them to exit an idling loop or sleep state. We have found that using spread or compact affinity policies were slightly faster than our default policy because these deterministic policies have less code checking out for load across each cores in the system. The one cost introduced by this proposal is that now the code has to query which affinity policy is to be used and switch to the appropriate code.

Overall, the impact on a parallel region overhead was less than 1 %. Also, this proposal does not impact performance critical parts of the runtime such as the handling of barriers. Changes are really limited to switching the thread selection algorithm in the parallel construct code from one (default) policy to two additional policies, and selecting the right policy depending on the value of the *proc-bind-var* ICV in the current data environment.

6   Future Enhancements

A number of issues remain open based on the discussion in the Affinity Subcommittee. We intend to comment on the outcome in the final paper:

– *Requesting more threads than available.* If a parallel region requests for more threads than currently available in the sub-partition, the number of threads returned by the parallel construct is currently implementation-defined. One possible option is to cap the maximum number of threads to the number of threads within the current partition. Another option is to provide for additional threads in the current partition (provided there are some) by breaking the current sub-partition and return to taking threads from the full place-list.

- *Threads per Place.* A finer control to allow the user to set the number of threads per place was asked for. One suggestion is to use a new environment variable or internal control variable, OMP_PARTITION_LIMIT.
- *Assignment of Thread Numbers.* A great deal of interest revolve around the default assignment of threads. Should it naturally be left to right in the same order as places in a list, or some form of round-robin fashion?
- *Explicit Setting of Partition.* One possible enhancement is to let the user explicitly query the machine model and possibly set the current *place-partition-var* ICV for the current data environment. This scenario can easily occur when user-thread programs call parallel libraries, or when legacy user-thread applications want to speedup inner-loops using the convenience of OpenMP. In such a scenario, the user would create its user threads (e.g. pthreads), map them to known locations in the machine, and then possibly produce an OMP_PLACES excluding these known locations.
- *Other Affinity Policies.* As it stands, the current proposal has two affinity policies, spread and compact. Potentially, we could add another policy that instructs the runtime to select places within the current partition in a way that evenly distributes the threads among the places in the sub-partition, particularly if less places are asked for than are available. Another policy of interest is one that 'breaks' free of the current sub-partition so as to allow a given parallel construct to escape the confines of its logical sub-partition and gets thread from the entire machine.

7 Summary

We have proposed a machine model abstraction that allows decoupling the OpenMP runtime from architectural details from the target platform while preserving most aspects relating to thread locality by using the abstraction of a place list. OpenMP directives allow the user to select, for each parallel construct, the thread affinity policy that best suits the parallel region. One affinity policy is the *spread* policy, which spread the OpenMP threads evenly among the places in the machine, and then logically sub-partitions the place list so that each team member gets an even subset of the machine for nested parallel regions. The other affinity policy is *compact*, which allocates the worker threads as much as possible on the same place as the master thread. We have demonstrated the use of these policies based on several use scenarios. A reference implementation demonstrated that the overhead due to this proposal is minimal.

Acknowledgments. We would like to acknowledge the input of Kelvin Li and Mary Chan, as well as the helpful comments from the anonymous reviewers. This work has also tremendously benefited from discussions at the OpenMP Affinity Subcommittee. This work has been supported and partially funded by Argonne National Laboratory and the Lawrence Livermore National Laboratory on behalf of the U.S. Department of Energy, under Lawrence Livermore National Laboratory subcontract no. B554331.

28   A.E. Eichenberger et al.

References

1. OpenMP Pragma and Region Instrumentor (OPARI)
2. Broquedis, F., Clet-Ortega, J., Moreaud, S., Furmento, N., Goglin, B., Mercier, G., Thibault, S., Namyst, R.: hwloc: A generic framework for managing hardware affinities in hpc applications. In: 2010 18th Euromicro International Conference on Parallel, Distributed and Network-Based Processing (PDP), pp. 180–186 (February 2010)
3. Terboven, C., an Mey, D., Schmidl, D., Jin, H., Wagner, M.: Data and Thread Affinity in OpenMP Programs. In: Proceedings of the 2008 Workshop on Memory Access on Future Processors: a Solved Problem?, MAW 2008, pp. 377–384. ACM International Conference on Computing Frontiers (2008)
4. Schmidl, D., Terboven, C., an Mey, D., Bücker, M.: Binding Nested OpenMP Programs on Hierarchical Memory Architectures. In: Sato, M., Hanawa, T., Müller, M.S., Chapman, B.M., de Supinski, B.R. (eds.) IWOMP 2010. LNCS, vol. 6132, pp. 29–42. Springer, Heidelberg (2010)
5. GNU. GNU libgomp (2012)
6. IBM. IBM C/C++ Version 11.1 and FORTRAN Version 13.1 (2009)
7. Intel. Intel C++ Compiler XE 12.0 User and Reference Guide (2010)
8. OpenMP ARB. OpenMP Application Program Interface, v. 3.1 (July 2011)
9. Oracle Solaris Studio 12.2: OpenMP API User's Guide. Oracle (2012)
10. Snir, M., Otto, S., Huss-Lederman, S., Walker, D., Dongarra, J.: MPI-The Complete Reference, 2nd (revised) edn. The MPI Core, vol. 1. MIT Press, Cambridge (1998)
11. The Portland Group. PGI Compiler User's Guide (2011)
12. Huang, L., Jin, H., Yi, L., Chapman, B.: Enabling locality-aware computations in OpenMP. Sci. Program. 18(3-4), 169–181 (2010)

Auto-scoping for OpenMP Tasks

Sara Royuela[1], Alejandro Duran[2], Chunhua Liao[1], and Daniel J. Quinlan[1]

[1] Lawrence Livermore National Laboratory
{royuelaalcaz1,liao6,dquinlan}@llnl.gov
[2] Barcelona Supercomputing Center
alex.duran@bsc.es

Abstract. Auto-scoping analysis for OpenMP must be revised owing to the introduction of asynchronous parallelism in the form of tasks. Auto-scoping is the process of automatically determine the data-sharing of variables. This process has been implemented for worksharing and parallel regions. Based on the previous work, we present an auto-scoping algorithm to work with OpenMP tasks. This is a much more complex challenge due to the uncertainty of when a task will be executed, which makes it harder to determine what parts of the program will run concurrently. We also introduce an implementation of the algorithm and results with several benchmarks showing that the algorithm is able to correctly scope a large percentage of the variables appearing in them.

1 Introduction

Parallel programming models play an important role in increasing the productivity of high-performance systems. In this regard, not only performance is necessary, but also convenient programmability is valuable to make these models appealing to programmers. OpenMP provides an API with a set of directives that define blocks of code to be executed by multiple threads. This simplicity has been a crucial aspect in the proliferation of OpenMP users.

Each application has its own specific requirements for the parallel programming model. Loop-centered parallel designs are useful for certain problems where the inherent parallelism relies in bounded iterative constructs. This model becomes of little use when dealing with unbounded iterations, recursive algorithms or producer/consumer schemes, adding excessive overhead, redundant synchronizations and therefore, achieving poor performance. These limitations have driven the evolution of OpenMP from loop-centered designs to adaptive parallelism. This new form of parallelism is defined by means of explicit asynchronous tasks. Tasks are units of work that may be either deferred or executed immediately. The use of synchronization constructs ensures the completion of all the associated tasks. This model offers better solutions for parallelizing irregular problems than loop-based approaches. Furthermore, tasks are highly composable since they can appear in parallel regions, worksharings and other tasks.

The use of OpenMP task directives requires programmers to determine the appropriate data-sharing attributes of the variables used inside the task. According to the

B.M. Chapman et al. (Eds.): IWOMP 2012, LNCS 7312, pp. 29–43, 2012.
© Springer-Verlag Berlin Heidelberg 2012

OpenMP specification, the data-sharing attributes of the variables referenced in an OpenMP task can be **shared**, `private` or `firstprivate`. Although OpenMP defines a default data-sharing attribute for each variable, this might not always be the one that ensures the correctness of the code. Thus, programmers still need to scope[1] them manually most of the time. This process is tedious and error-prone considering the large amount of variables that can potentially appear in each construct. Rules for the automatic scope of variables in OpenMP parallel regions have been presented and tested in the past. However, the process of analyzing OpenMP tasks is quite different because of the uncertainty introduced by tasks regarding when are those tasks going to be executed. Due to this uncertainty, the first challenge is to determine the regions of code that execute concurrently with a given task in order to be able to find out possible race conditions. The second challenge is to discover how variables are used inside and outside the task to assign the proper data-sharing attribute according to the information collected.

The contributions of this paper are the following:

- A new algorithm for the automatic discovery of the data-sharing attributes of variables in OpenMP tasks to enhance the programmability of OpenMP. The algorithm determines the code that is executed concurrently with a task and the possible race conditions of the variables within the task. Then, it scopes these variables with the data-sharing that ensures the correctness of the code.
- An implementation of the proposed algorithm in the Mercurium source-to-source compiler and proof of the auto-scoping benefits by testing its implementation on several OpenMP task benchmarks. We present the results of the variables that have been automatically scoped and those which the compiler has not been able to determine the scope. We also compare our results with the results obtained with the Sun Studio 12.3 compiler.

2 Motivation and Related Work

OpenMP data-sharing attributes for variables referenced in a construct can be predetermined, explicitly determined or implicitly determined. *Predetermined* variables are those that, regardless of their occurrences, have a data-sharing attribute determined by the OpenMP model. *Explicitly determined* variables are those that are referenced in a given construct and are listed in a data-sharing attribute clause on the construct. *Implicitly determined* variables are those that are referenced in a given construct, do not have predetermined data-sharing attributes and are not listed in a data-sharing attribute clause on the construct (See OpenMP Specifications 3.1 [6] for more details). All variables appearing within a construct have a default data-sharing defined by the OpenMP specifications (either are predetermined or implicitly determined); nonetheless, users are duty bound to explicitly scope most of these variables changing the default data-sharing values in order to fulfill the correctness of their codes (i.e., avoiding data race conditions) and enhance their performance (i.e., privatizing shared variables).

---

[1] In this paper we use the word scope referring to data-sharing attributes.

Listing 1.1. Code with OpenMP task from Floorplan BOTS benchmark

```
1  /* Method that computes all possible positions of a set of cells within a board.
2   * @param id identifier of the current cell.
3   * @param FOOTPRINT surface already used in the board.
4   * @param BOARD whole board that can be used.
5   * @param CELLS set of cells to be placed in the board.
6   * @return The number of possible combinations of the cells within the board */
7  static int add_cell(int id, coor FOOTPRINT, ibrd BOARD, struct cell *CELLS)
8  {
9    int   i, j, nn, area, nnc = 0, nnl = 0;
10   ibrd  board;
11   coor  footprint, NWS[DMAX];
12
13   /* For each possible shapes of the current cell */
14   for (i = 0; i < CELLS[id].n; i++)
15   {
16     /* Compute all possible locations of the north-west corner of the shape */
17     nn = starts(id, i, NWS, CELLS);
18     nnl += nn;
19     /* For each possible location */
20     for (j = 0; j < nn; j++)
21  #pragma omp task untied private(board, footprint, area) \
22  firstprivate(NWS, i, j, id) \
23  shared(FOOTPRINT, BOARD, CELLS, MIN_AREA, MIN_FOOTPRINT, N, BEST_BOARD, nnc)
24  {
25     /* Extent the shape from the computed north-west corner position */
26     struct cell cells[N+1];
27     memcpy(cells, CELLS, sizeof(struct cell)*(N+1));
28     cells[id].top = NWS[j][0];
29     cells[id].bot = cells[id].top + cells[id].alt[i][0] - 1;
30     cells[id].lhs = NWS[j][1];
31     cells[id].rhs = cells[id].lhs + cells[id].alt[i][1] - 1;
32     memcpy(board, BOARD, sizeof(ibrd));
33
34     /* If the cell cannot be layed down in the board, prune the search */
35     if (!lay_down(id, board, cells))
36       continue;
37
38     /* Calculate the current footprint with the new cell layed down */
39     footprint[0] = max(FOOTPRINT[0], cells[id].bot+1);
40     footprint[1] = max(FOOTPRINT[1], cells[id].rhs+1);
41     area         = footprint[0] * footprint[1];
42
43     /* If the current cell is the last one */
44     if (cells[id].next == 0)
45     {
46       /* If the area is minimum, update global values */
47       if (area < MIN_AREA)
48  #pragma omp critical
49  {
50             MIN_AREA        = area;
51             MIN_FOOTPRINT[0] = footprint[0];
52             MIN_FOOTPRINT[1] = footprint[1];
53             memcpy(BEST_BOARD, board, sizeof(ibrd));
54  }
55     }
56     /* If the area is still smaller than best area, try to fit more cells */
57     else if (area < MIN_AREA)
58     {
59  #pragma omp atomic
60       nnc += add_cell(cells[id].next, footprint, board, cells);
61     }
62  }
63   }
64
65  #pragma omp taskwait
66    return nnc + nnl;
67  }
```

In Listing 1.1 we show a section of code from the *Floorplan* benchmark contained in BOTS [2]. In this code we find a task within a *for-loop* construct. We have specified data-sharing attributes for all variables used in the task, although some of this variables do not need an explicit data-sharing attribute because OpenMP rules applying for implicitly determined variables already specify the appropriate attribute. We aim to improve the programmability of OpenMP by defining a new algorithm which analyzes the access to variables appearing in OpenMP tasks and automatically defines the proper scope of these variables. The compiler should be capable of accurately scoping the variables by analyzing a) the immediately previous and following synchronization points of the task, b) the accesses done to the variables appearing within the task in all the concurrent codes to the task and c) the liveness of these variables after the task. In those cases in which the compiler cannot automatically scope a variable, it should warn the user to manually do this work. Due to the effectiveness of the algorithm, we prove that the work of the manual scope of variables can be considerably reduced and, therefore, the programmability of OpenMP can be highly improved.

Lin et al. [10] proposed a set of rules which allow the compiler to automatically define the appropriate scope of variables referenced in an OpenMP parallel region. They use a data scope attribute called **AUTO**, which activates the automatic discovery of the scope of variables. These rules apply to variables that have not been implicitly scoped, like the index of worksharing *do-loops*. Their algorithm aims to help in the auto-parallelization process but it has several limitations such as:

- It is only applicable to **parallel**, **parallel do**, **parallel sections** and **parallel workshare** constructs.
- It recognizes OpenMP directives, but not API function calls such as **omp_set_lock** and **omp_unset_lock**, enabling the report of false positives in the data race condition process.
- Their interprocedural analysis and array subscripts analyses are limited. Conservatively, most of the times arrays are scoped as shared while they could be privatized.

They implemented the rules in the Sun Studio 9 Fortran 95 compiler and tested the enhancement in the programmability with the PANTA 3D Navier-Stokes solver. They found that OpenMP required the manual scoping of 1389 variables, rather than the 13 variables that need to be manually scoped using the process of automatic scoping. They proved that the performance obtained by the two versions is the same.

Voss et al. [5] evaluated the application of the auto-scoping in OpenMP to the automatic parallelization. They implemented the same **AUTO** data-sharing attribute as Lin et al. did, but in the Polaris parallelizing compiler. They used a subset of the SPEC benchmark suite for the evaluation and they revealed that many parts cannot be scoped by the compiler, thus disabling the auto-parallelization in those sections of the program. Their limitations are the same as in the work of Lin et al. [10] since the rules used in the automatic scoping process are the same.

Oracle Solaris Studio 12.3 [7] extends the rules already implemented for the automatic scope of variables in parallel regions to support tasks. It defines a set of five rules that helps in the automatic scope of variables. However, it does not define an algorithm to find the concurrent code of a task and the way to determine the occurrence of data race conditions. Furthermore, this implementation has several restrictions:

- The rules are restricted to scalar variables, and do not deal with arrays.
- The set of rules is not applicable to global variables.
- The implementation cannot handle nested tasks or untied tasks.
- It recognizes OpenMP directives, but not runtime routines such as *omp_set_lock* and *omp_unset_lock*, enabling the report of false positives in the data race condition process.

The analysis of data race conditions in OpenMP programs is needed for many analytic purposes, such as auto-scoping and auto-parallelization. Y. Lin [9] presented a methodology for the static race detection. His method distinguishes between *general races*[2] and *data races*[3]. We base our data race analysis in the method presented by Lin, taking into account only data race conditions. This is motivated by the fact that those are the only race situations that can affect the correctness of OpenMP programs.

We base our work on the increasing need of asynchronous parallelism methods and the good results obtained with algorithms that auto-scope variables in OpenMP parallel regions. Since, to the best of our knowledge, there is no previous work on the exhaustive definition of concurrent regions of code in the existence of tasks, we introduce a new algorithm that detects all regions of code that can be executed in parallel with a given task and, based on this information, determines the scope of variables in the task. The algorithm differs from the previous proposals in that it has a methodology based on a parallel control flow graph with synchronizations that discovers all regions executing concurrently with a task. Furthermore, our algorithm takes into account OpenMP directives and OpenMP API calls to determine data race situations and it can deal with arrays and global variables.

3   Proposal

Our proposal is to extend the clause **default** used with the OpenMP task directive in order to accept the keyword **AUTO**. The clause **default(AUTO)** attached to a **task** construct will launch the automatic discovery of the scope of variables in that task. In Algorithm 1 we present the high-level description of the proposed algorithm. For each variable referenced inside the task region, which is neither local to the task nor a variable with an explicitly predetermined data-sharing attribute, the algorithm returns one of the following results:

- UNDEFINED: The algorithm is not able to determine the behavior of the variable. This variable will be reported to the user to be manually scoped.
- PRIVATE: The variable is to be scoped as **private**.
- FIRSTPRIVATE: The variable is to be scoped as **firstprivate**.
- SHARED: The variable is to be scoped as **shared**.
- SHARED_OR_FIRSTPRIVATE: The variable can be scoped as either **shared** or **firstprivate** without altering the correctness of the results. It is an implementation decision to scope them as **shared** or **firstprivate**.

---

[2] A *general race* occurs when the order of two accesses to the same memory location, where at least one is a *write*, is not enforced by synchronizations.

[3] A *data race* is a *general race* where the access to the memory is not protected by a critical section.

Algorithm 1. High-level description of the auto-scoping algorithm for OpenMP tasks
***

1. Define the regions of code that execute concurrently with a given task. These regions are defined by the immediately previous and following synchronizations of the task and belong to:
   - Other tasks scheduled in the region described above.
   - Other instances of the task if it is scheduled within a loop or in a parallel region.
   - Code from the parent task between the task scheduling point and the synchronization of the task.
2. Scope the variables within the task depending on the use of these variables in all regions detected in the previous step and the liveness properties of the variables after the execution of the task.

***

The algorithm works under the hypothesis that the input code is correct and that the input code comes from an original sequential code that has been parallelized with OpenMP, otherwise, the results of the algorithm may be incorrect. Based on that, suppose the analysis of a task t; the algorithm computes the scope $sc(x)$ of every variable $x \in X$, where X is the set of variables appearing within t that have not explicitly determined scope and are not local variables of the task. In order to do that, the algorithm proceeds as it is shown in Algorithm 2.

Algorithm 2. Detailed algorithm for the auto-scoping in OpenMP tasks
***

1. Determine the regions of code executing concurrently with t, referred to as *concurrent regions* in this paper. These regions can be other tasks, other instances of the same task and code from the parent task. In order to do that, we first define the following points:
   Scheduling The task scheduling point of t as defined in the OpenMP specification. Any previous code in the parent task is already executed before the task starts its execution.
   Next_sync The point where t is either implicitly or explicitly synchronized with other tasks in execution. Any code after this point will be executed after the completion of t.
   Last_sync The immediately previous synchronization point to the *Scheduling* point of t. If this synchronization is a `taskwait`, then we take into account the previous nested tasks since they may not be finished.
   With these points, we can define the concurrent regions to be the following:
   - The region of code of the parent task that runs concurrently with t, bounded by *Scheduling* and *Next_sync*.
   - The regions defined by the tasks that run concurrently with t, bounded by *Last_sync* and *Next_sync*. Other instances t' of t are concurrent with t when t is scheduled within a `parallel` construct or within a loop body.
2. $\{\forall s : s \in X\}$, where s is a scalar, apply the following rules in order:
   (a) If s is a parameter passed by reference or by address in a call to a function that we do not have access to, or s is a global variable and t contains a call to a function that we do not have access to, then $sc(s) = $ UNDEFINED.

(b)If s is not used in the concurrent regions, then:

    i.If s is only read within t, then $sc(s) =$ SHARED_OR_FIRSTPRIVATE.

    ii.If s is written within t, then:

        A.If s is a global variable and/or s is alive after *Next_sync*, then $sc(s) =$ SHARED.

        B.If s is dead after the *exit* of the task, then:

          –If the first action performed in s is a write, then $sc(s) =$ PRIVATE.

          –If the first action performed in s is a read, then $sc(s) =$ SHARED_OR_FIRSTPRIVATE.

(c)If s is used in the concurrent regions, then:

    i.If s is only read in both the concurrent regions and within the task, then $sc(s) =$ SHARED_OR_FIRSTPRIVATE.

    ii.If s is written either in the concurrent regions or within the task, then we look for data race conditions (data race analysis specifics are explained at the end of this algorithm). Thus,

        A.If we can assure that no data race can occur, then $sc(s) =$ SHARED.

        B.If a data race can occur, then $sc(s) =$ RACE.

3. $\{\forall a \mid a \in X\}$, where a is an array or an aggregate, apply the following rules in order:

    (a)$\{\forall a_i \mid i \in [0..N]\}$, where a_i is a use of a or a region of a (if a is an array) or a member of a (if a is an aggregate), and N is the number of uses of a, compute $sc(a_i)$ applying the same methodology used for scalars.

    (b)Since OpenMP does not allow different scopes for the subparts of a variable, we compute $sc(a)$ by mixing the results obtained in the previous step following the rules below:

        i.If $\{\forall a_i : sc(a_i) = \text{SC} \mid i \in [0..N]\}$, then $sc(a) = \text{SC}$.

        ii.If $\{\exists a_i, a_j : sc(a_i) = \text{SC}_1 \wedge sc(a_j) = \text{SC}_2 \mid i, j \in [0..N] \wedge i <> j \wedge \text{SC}_1 <> \text{SC}_2\}$, then:

          A.If $\{\exists a_i : sc(a_i) = \text{UNDEFINED} \mid i \in [0..N]\}$, or $\{\exists a_i, a_j : sc(a_i) = \text{RACE} \wedge sc(a_j) = \text{SHARED} \mid i, j \in [0..N] \wedge i <> j\}$, then $sc(a) = \text{UNDEFINED}$.

          B.If $\{\forall a_i : sc(a_i) = \text{SHARED_OR_FIRSTPRIVATE} \vee sc(a_i) = \text{SHARED} \mid i \in [0..N]\}$, then $sc(a) = \text{SHARED}$.

          C.If $\{\forall a_i : sc(a_i) = \text{PRIVATE} \vee sc(a_i) = \text{RACE} \mid i \in [0..N]\}$, then $sc(a) = \text{RACE}$.

          D.If $\{\exists a_i, a_j : sc(a_i) = \text{SHARED_OR_FIRSTPRIVATE} \wedge (sc(a_j) = \text{RACE} \vee sc(a_j) = \text{PRIVATE}) \mid i, j \in [0..N] \wedge i <> j\}$, then $sc(a) = \text{FIRSTPRIVATE}$.

4. $\{\forall v : sc(v) = \text{RACE} \mid v \in X\}$, based on the hypothesis that the input code is correct, we privatize v (otherwise a synchronization would have existed to avoid the race condition). Therefore,

    –If the first action performed in v (or in any part of v if v is an array or an aggregate) within t is a read, then $sc(v) = \text{FIRSTPRIVATE}$.

    –If the first action performed in v (or in all parts of v if v is an array or an aggregate) within t is a write, then $sc(v) = \text{PRIVATE}$.

Data Race conditions. In the previous algorithm we need to analyze whether the variables within a task are in a data race situation or not. Data race conditions can appear when two threads can access to the same memory unit at the same time, and at least one of these accesses is a write. To determine data race conditions, we have to analyze the code appearing in all the concurrent regions and in the task. Variables that appear in more than one of these regions within blocks that are not protected by synchronization constructs (**atomic** or **critical**) or runtime library lock routines (*omp_set_lock* and *omp_unset_lock*) can trigger a data race situation.

Under the assumption we make that the code is correct and, since OpenMP defines an unexpected behavior for the algorithms containing race conditions, the variables scoped as RACE are privatized. Depending on the use made of the variable within the task it will be PRIVATE (if it is first written) or FIRSTPRIVATE (if it is first read).

Limitations. The only limitation of the algorithm is the incapability of dealing with tasks containing calls to functions which code is not accessible at compile time; in this case all variables that can be involved in this functions cannot be scoped. The variables affected are global variables and parameters to the unaccessible function that are addresses or passed by reference.

Regarding the implementation, the compiler might be unable to determine the previous synchronization point, *Last_sync*, and/or the next synchronization point, *Next_sync* (i.e., the point belongs to a function that calls the function where the analyzed task is scheduled); in these cases only the variables that are local to the function (including its parameters) where the task is scheduled can be automatically scoped. The rest of variables must be scoped as UNDEFINED and reported to the user to be manually scoped.

Strengths. The algorithm is perfectly accurate when the input code fulfill the hypotheses, so it never produces false positives and the reported results are always correct. Specific rules cover the cases when the algorithm cannot determine the data-sharing attribute of a variable. The undetermined variables are reported back to the user.

The methodology we use to determine the regions of code that run concurrently with a task, based on the definition of the synchronization points of the task, models an algorithm that is insensitive to the scheduling policy used in runtime.

Example. In the code presented in Listing 1.1 a task is defined within a loop construct. The algorithm proposed will compute the following result for the variables appearing within the task: variable *cells* does not need to be scoped because it is local to the task; global variables *N*, *MIN_AREA*, *MIN_FOOTPRINT* and *BEST_BOARD* are scoped as UNDEFINED due to the occurrence of the system call *memcpy* and because we do not have access to the code of this function; the same happens to the parameter *board*, passed by reference to *memcpy*; variable *nnc* is scoped as SHARED because it is written within the task, it cannot produce a data race because the access is protected in an atomic construct and its value is alive at the exit of the task; variables *area* and *footprint* are PRIVATE because the algorithm detects a race condition (different instances of the task can write to the variable at the same time) and their values are written without being read; variables *i*, *j*, *id*, *BOARD*, *CELLS*, *FOOTPRINT* and *NWS* are scoped as SHARED_OR_FIRSTPRIVATE because they are only read.

4 Implementation

Mercurium [3] is a source-to-source compiler for C/C++ and Fortran that has a common internal representation (IR) for the three languages. The compiler defines a pipeline of phases that transforms the input source into an output source which is afterwards passed to the back-end compiler (gcc, icc, etc). We have implemented the algorithm presented in Section 3 within a new phase along with other analyses that are required for the computation of the scope. These analyses are *control flow analysis, use-definition chains* and *liveness analysis*. All of them are both intra- and inter- thread, and intra- and inter- procedural.

We define a parallel control flow graph (PCFG) [8] with specific support for OpenMP:

- OpenMP pragmas and OpenMP API function calls are represented with special nodes attaching the specifics of each case, i.e.: additional clauses, creation of parallelism (**parallel**, **task**) or synchronization (**taskwait**, **barrier**).
- All implicit memory flush operations introduced by the OpenMP directives are made explicit. For example, a flush is implied during a barrier region and this is represented with the introduction of a **flush** before the **barrier** and a **flush** after the **barrier**.
- For each OpenMP worksharing without a **nowait** clause, we add a node representing the implicit **barrier** that occurs at the end of the worksharing.
- All task synchronization points are represented with special edges symbolizing the boundaries of the region where the task can be executed. These edges connect:
  1. The scheduling point of the task with the entry of the task.
  2. The exit of the task with the synchronization point that synchronizes the task with its parent (i.e., a **taskwait**) or with the threads of the team (i.e., a **barrier**).

Nodes in the PCFG can be *simple* (nodes containing *basic blocks* or *OpenMP stand-alone directives*) or *complex* (nodes containing a subgraph: *OpenMP non-stand-alone directives*, loop constructs, function calls or conditional expressions). In Fig. 1 we show a basic class diagram of the PCFG. The visitor pattern is used to traverse the Mercurium IR and generate the graph. The graph is composed by a unique *complex* node that contains the whole graph. Nodes are connected by means of edges.

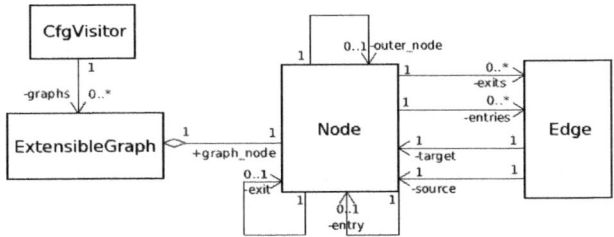

Fig. 1. Basic class diagram of the PCFG

Focusing on the representation of tasks in the PCFG, in Fig. 2 we show a code scheme with different tasks (**task** blocks) and synchronization points (**taskwait** and **barrier** blocks) embedded in a sequential code (*section X* blocks). In Fig. 3 we show a simplified version of the resultant PCFG. *Section* blocks represent code executed sequentially that can result in one or more *simple* or *complex* nodes in the detailed PCFG; these blocks are connected among them by flow (solid) edges whereas tasks are connected by synchronization (dotted) edges; this edges (dotted) do not imply control flow as the other edges (solid) do, so they must be analyzed distinctly.

We take into account nested tasks (including nesting due to recursive functions) and the semantics of the different synchronization points when we connect tasks in the PCFG:

- A **taskwait** synchronizes just the previous tasks that are scheduled by the encountered task of the **taskwait** (in Fig. 3, the **taskwait** only synchronizes **task** A, but not **task** B).
- A **barrier** synchronizes any previously scheduled task that has not yet been synchronized (in Fig. 3, the **barrier** not only synchronizes **task** C and **task** D, but also **task** B).

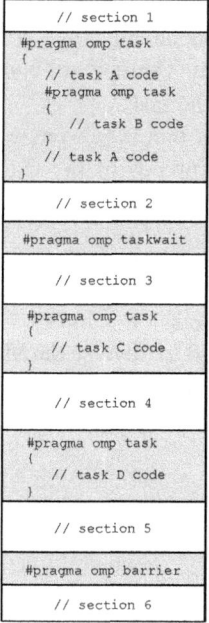
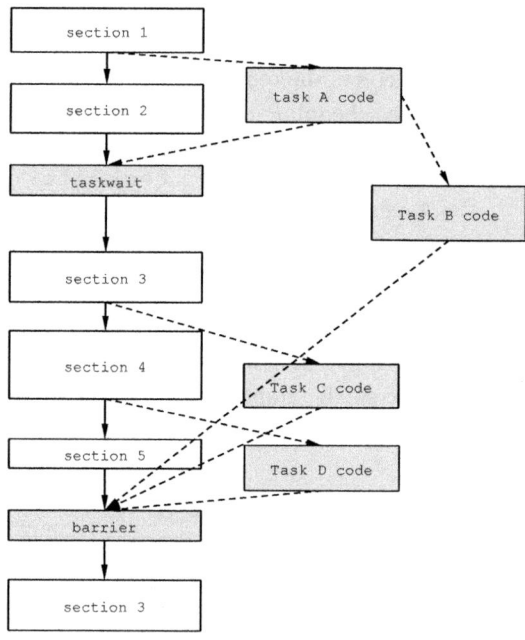

Fig. 2. Code scheme with tasks

Fig. 3. Abstraction of the PCFG used during the auto-scoping that shows the connections of the tasks in Fig. 2

In Fig. 4 we show the flow chart with the analyses performed in the compiler in order to have enough information to compute the scope of variables. The steps we follow are described below:

1. Create the PCFG, as it is defined previously, for each function involved in the analysis.
2. Compute the use-definition chains. This analysis computes for each node the set of variables that are read before than being defined (*UPPER_EXPOSED*) and the set of variables that are defined *(KILLED)*. Variables that have an undefined behavior are classified in a special set called *UNDEFINED* (Address parameters -pointers or parameters passed by value- of functions that are called in a different file from the file where they are defined have an undefined behavior. The occurrence of such calls cause an undefined behavior in all global variables).

   Information is propagated from *simple* nodes to *complex* nodes.
3. With the use-definition information, we then perform liveness analysis. This analysis computes the sets of variables that are alive at the entry of each node (*LIVE_IN*) and the variables that are alive at the exit of each node (*LIVE_OUT*).

   Information is propagated from *simple* nodes to *complex* nodes.
4. Apply the algorithm shown in Section 3 for the automatic discovery of the scope of variables in OpenMP tasks. The algorithm has been fully implemented except for the support for aggregates. In our implementation we have decided to further specify the variables scoped as SHARED_OR_FIRSTPRIVATE as follows:
   - All scalar variables are defined as FIRSTPRIVATE because the cost of the privatization should be comparable to the cost of one access to a shared variable. In the worst case (*s*, scalar variable, is only used once), performance is not affected and, in the best case (*s* is used more than once) performance is improved.
   - Due to the likely high cost of privatizing an array, all array variables are defined as SHARED. Only in those cases where the positions of the array are accessed many times it may be advantageous to privatize the array.

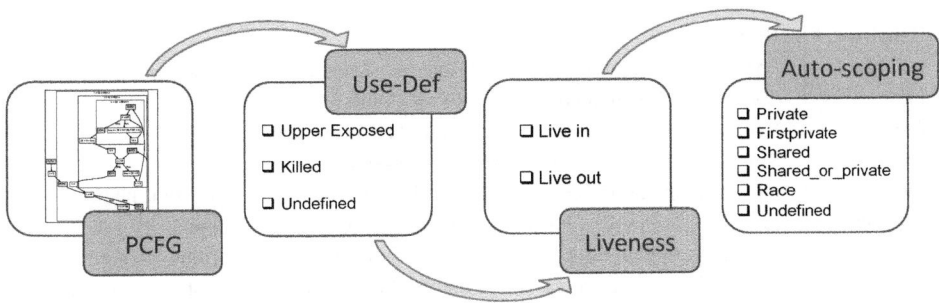

Fig. 4. Flow chart of the Mercurium analyses used in the Auto-Scoping process

Mercurium offers two different ways to use the analyses:

1. Some flags added in the command line trigger the analysis of all the input sources. These analyses are performed in the middle-end, next to all transformations applied in this stage. Moreover, some flags allow the synthesized information to be output in different formats: textually and graphically (as a PCFG).
2. The compiler provides an API with methods allowing the use of the analyses on demand. The analyses can be used in any stage of the compiler and they can be applied to any section of the IR. The main functions provided are:

   PCFG Generation: Creates one PCFG for each function included in a region of IR, or, if the IR does not contain a function, then creates one PCFG with the sample of code contained in the IR.
   Use-definition analysis: Computes use-definition analysis for every node contained in a PCFG.
   Liveness analysis: Computes liveness analysis for every node contained in a PCFG.
   Task analysis: Computes auto-scoping for every task node contained a PCFG.

5 Evaluation

For the evaluation of the proposed algorithm, we have used the Barcelona OpenMP Tasks Suite [2] and other benchmarks, all developed in the Barcelona Supercomputing Center. Table 1 presents the description of the benchmarks used in our evaluation. Table 2 describes the principal characteristics of each benchmark: the language of the source code, the number of lines and the number of tasks and the method used in the functions containing tasks (it can be iterative, recursive or both).

Table 1. Short description of the benchmarks used in the evaluation

Benchmark	Description
Alignment	Dynamic programming algorithm that aligns sequences of proteins.
FFT	Spectral method that computes the Fast Fourier Transformation.
Fib	Recursive version of the Fibonacci numbers computation.
Health	Simulation method for a country health system.
Floorplan	Optimization algorithm for the optimal placement of cells in a floor plan.
NQueens	Search algorithm that finds solutions for the N Queens problem.
Sort	Integer sorting algorithm that uses a mixture of sorting algorithms to sort a vector.
SparseLU	Linear algebra algorithm that computes the LU factorization of a sparse matrix.
UTS	Search algorithm that computes the number of nodes in an Unbalanced Tree.
Stencil	Stencil algorithm over a matrix structure.
Cholesky	Linear algebra algorithm that computes the Cholesky decomposition of a matrix.

Table 2. Principal characteristics of the benchmarks used in the evaluation

	Source language	Lines count	Number of tasks	Method
Alignment	C	694	1	iterative
FFT	C	4859	41	recursive
Fib	C	45	2	recursive
Health	C	551	2	iterative & recursive
Floorplan	C	344	1	iterative & recursive
NQueens	C	405	1	iterative & recursive
Sort	C	486	9	recursive
SparseLU	C	309	4	iterative
UTS	C	283	1	iterative & recursive
Stencil	C	218	1	iterative
Cholesky	C	70	6	iterative

Since we want to evaluate the enhancement of programmability, we have computed the number of variables that have been automatically scoped. A summary of the results comparing Mercurium implementation with Sun Studio 12.3 implementation is shown in Table 3. This table contains the amount of variables that have been automatically scoped organized according to their scope[4], the amount of variables that the algorithm has been unable to scope[5] and the percentage of successfulness for each benchmark in both compilers as well as the mean of successfulness for each compiler.

Table 3. Automatic scoping results of Mercurium and Sun Studio 12.3 compilers for different benchmarks

	Mercurium					Sun Studio 12				
	SHARED	PRIVATE	FIRSTPRIVATE	UNDEF	(%)success	SHARED	PRIVATE	FIRSTPRIVATE	UNDEF	(%)success
Alignment	0	5	5	11	47.61%	0	5	5	11	47.61%
FFT	5	0	241	1	99.58%	0	0	241	1	99.58%
Fib	2	0	4	0	100.00%	1	0	4	0	100.00%
Health	0	0	3	1	75.00%	1	0	2	1	75.00%
Floorplan	2	2	6	5	66.67%	1	1	6	7	53.33%
NQueens	0	0	6	0	100.00%	0	0	6	0	100.00%
Sort	0	0	34	3	91.89%	0	0	34	3	91.89%
SparseLU	1	3	7	6	64.70%	0	3	1	14	22.22%
UTS	2	0	4	0	100.00%	1	0	4	1	83.33%
Stencil	0	0	6	1	85.71%	0	0	6	1	85.71%
Cholesky	0	0	16	0	100.00%	0	0	16	0	100.00%
TOTAL					**84.65%**					**78.05%**

Regarding to the Mercurium compiler, the overall result shows that a significant amount of variables, almost the 85%, can be automatically scoped. Most of the variables that cannot be automatically scoped are global variables. The compiler is not able

---

[4] Sun Studio auto-scopes as PRIVATE all variables that are local to a task. We have purged this variables from the results to simplify the comparison between the two compilers and because these variables have a predetermined data-sharing attribute.

[5] The two compilers have different behavior regarding to the variables that cannot be automatically scoped: Mercurium does not make any decision about these variables and it shows a warning with the list of variables that have not been scoped. Sun Studio automatically scopes these variables as SHARED and it warns the user about this decision.

to determine a correct data-sharing attribute for these variables because either there is a call to a function which code is not located in the same file as the call, or the previous synchronization point of the tasks cannot be specified. In some cases, such as the *Alignment* or the *Cholesky* benchmarks, the algorithm is able to find data race conditions and privatize the variables. In some other cases, such as the *Floorplan* benchmark, the algorithm dismisses data races, and keeps variables as shared.

Regarding to the Sun Studio compiler, the 78% of variables can be automatically scoped. The results are the same for the two compilers in most cases. Specific weaknesses of the Sun Studio 12.3 implementation make the difference in the results. I.e., in the case of the *SparseLU* benchmark, Mercurium obtains better results because it implements support for nested tasks and Sun Studio does not. In other cases such as the *Floorplan* benchmark, array variables can not be auto-scoped by Sun whereas they are auto-scoped by Mercurium. An important difference between the two compilers is the treatment of variables that are free of data race conditions and can be shared or firstprivate: Mercurium classifies arrays as shared and scalars as firstprivate whereas Sun Studio classifies all variables that are only read as firstprivate. Sun Studio applies this rule for scalars and also in some arrays as we have proved in benchmarks such as *Floorplan* and this decision can affect the performance in the occurrence of large arrays.

Overall, our algorithm detects 6.65% more variables than Sun Studio compiler. The results in both compilers reveal that the main handicap for the automatic discovery of data-sharing attributes in tasks are global variables. In the case of Mercurium, the major difficulty is defining the previous and next synchronization points of a task. We have to improve the PCFG implementation in order to have enough context information to determine these two points. If we are able to define the regions of code that are concurrent, all variables that are undefined in the current results will be automatically scoped.

6   Conclusions and Future Work

We have developed an automatic mechanism to improve the programmability of OpenMP by relieving the programmer from the tedious work of manually scoping variables within tasks. The mechanism consists of a new algorithm based on compiler analyses such as use-definition chains and liveness analysis, and the OpenMP synchronization points. This algorithm scopes automatically the variables appearing in OpenMP tasks with the use of the clause **default(AUTO)**. We have proved the benefits of this new method implementing the algorithm in the Mercurium compiler and testing it with a set of benchmarks. Our results show that the majority of variables can be scoped by the compiler and that the main difficulty is the treatment of global variables. The variables that cannot be automatically scoped are reported to the user to proceed to manual scoping.

In the future we want to enhance the implementation in Mercurium by adding support to aggregates and improving the PCFG generation to have the necessary context information to define the concurrent regions of a task in any case. We also plan to implement the algorithm in the ROSE [4] source-to-source compiler and take advantage of its features for dealing with multiple files and library calls. We want to make the compiler capable of recognizing the most common C library calls, such as memory allocation methods, in order to avoid the incapacity of auto-scoping global variables and address parameters in the occurrence of such calls. The automatic scoping of variables is part of the solution to other problems of compiler analyses and optimizations. This analysis can, for example, lead us to enhance auto-parallelizing tools and provide support to OpenMP correctness tools. We plan to use the auto-scoping analysis to automatically define data-dependencies between tasks[1].

Acknowledgements. We would like to acknowledge the support of the European Commission through the ENCORE project (FP7-248647), and the support of the Spanish Ministry of Education (contracts TIN2007-60625, CSD2007-00050), and the Generalitat de Catalunya (contract 2009-SGR-980). This work performed under the auspices of the U.S. Department of Energy by Lawrence Livermore National Laboratory under Contract DE-AC52-07NA27344.

References

1. Duran, A., Ayguadé, E., Badia, R.M., Labarta, J., Martinell, L., Martorell, X., Planas, J.: OmpSs: a Proposal for Programming Heterogeneous Multi-Core Architectures. Parallel Processing Letters 21(2), 173–193 (2011)
2. Duran, A., Teruel, X., Ferrer, R., Martorell, X., Ayguadé, E.: Barcelona OpenMP Tasks Suite: A Set of Benchmarks Targeting the Exploitation of Task Parallelism in OpenMP. In: 38th International Conference on Parallel Processing, ICPP 2009, Vienna, Austria, pp. 124–131. IEEE Computer Society (September 2009)
3. Barcelona Supercomputing Center. The NANOS Group Site: The Mercurium Compiler, http://nanos.ac.upc.edu/mcxx
4. Quinlan, D., et al.: Rose compiler infrastructure (2012), http://rosecompiler.org
5. Voss, M., Chiu, E., Chow, P.M.Y., Wong, C., Yuen, K.: An Evaluation of Auto-Scoping in OpenMP. In: Chapman, B.M. (ed.) WOMPAT 2004. LNCS, vol. 3349, pp. 98–109. Springer, Heidelberg (2005)
6. OpenMP ARB. OpenMP Application Program Interface, v. 3.1 (September 2011)
7. Oracle. Oracle Solaris Studio 12.3: OpenMP API User's Guide (2010), http://docs.oracle.com/cd/E24457_01/html/E21996/index.html
8. Royuela, S.: Compiler Analysis and its Application to OmpSs. Master's thesis, Technical University of Catalonia, 1012
9. Lin, Y.: Static Nonconcurrency Analysis of OpenMP Programs. In: Mueller, M.S., Chapman, B.M., de Supinski, B.R., Malony, A.D., Voss, M. (eds.) IWOMP 2005 and IWOMP 2006. LNCS, vol. 4315, pp. 36–50. Springer, Heidelberg (2008)
10. Lin, Y., Terboven, C., an Mey, D., Copty, N.: Automatic Scoping of Variables in Parallel Regions of an OpenMP Program. In: Chapman, B.M. (ed.) WOMPAT 2004. LNCS, vol. 3349, pp. 83–97. Springer, Heidelberg (2005)

A Case for Including Transactions in OpenMP II: Hardware Transactional Memory

Barna L. Bihari[1], Michael Wong[2], Amy Wang[2],
Bronis R. de Supinski[1], and Wang Chen[2]

[1] Lawrence Livermore National Laboratory
[2] IBM Corporation
{bihari1,bronis}@llnl.gov
{michaelw,aktwang,wdchen}@ca.ibm.com

Abstract. We present recent results using Hardware Transactional Memory (HTM) on IBM's Blue Gene/Q system. By showing how this latest TM system can significantly reduce the complexity of shared memory programming while retaining efficiency, we continue to make our case that the OpenMP language specification should include transactional language constructs. Furthermore, we argue for its support as an advanced abstraction to support mutable shared state, thus expanding OpenMP synchronization capabilities. Our results demonstrate how TM can be used to simplify modular parallel programming in OpenMP while maintaining parallel performance. We show performance advantages in the BUSTM (**B**enchmark for **U**n**S**tructured-mesh **T**ransactional **M**emory) model using the transactional memory hardware implementation on Blue Gene/Q.

1 Introduction

While the concept of transactions has been around for nearly two decades [6], we still need efficient, production-quality implementations of transactional memory (TM). TM could greatly simplify shared memory programming while maintaining efficiency. However, software TM (STM) is often considered a research toy [3] while commercially available chips have only recently supported hardware TM (HTM) [5].

The two implementation strategies for TM exhibit significant differences. HTM modifies the memory system, typically through modifications to the L1 and/or L2 caches, to support atomic execution of groups of memory instructions. STM, which does not use special hardware, handles all memory conflicts in software. Thus, STM has substantial runtime overheads, while HTM has been limited to prototype architectures.

IBM® recently announced the first production-quality HTM system in the Blue Gene/Q® (BG/Q) platform. We anticipate that other vendors will provide similar support in the near future. Several ongoing efforts are evaluating its applicability, efficiency and ease of use (see [14], [15]). The preliminary results are encouraging and HTM support can greatly simplify efficient and correct synchronization of multiple threads. Prior work [11,17] has proposed TM support within OpenMP [12]. With the advent of commercially available HTM implementations, our results demonstrate that we should incorporate TM into the OpenMP specification in order to make these benefits easily accessible.

B.M. Chapman et al. (Eds.): IWOMP 2012, LNCS 7312, pp. 44–58, 2012.

This paper continues our case for including transactions in OpenMP. We build on our preliminary STM results that combined an STM system, which provided the TM primitives, with an OpenMP implementation, which provided all other shared memory functionality [16]. We again explore performance with the BUSTM benchmark code. However, we use a more complex, fully 3-D geometry in many of our experiments. Our initial studies treated performance as a secondary focus; this work shows that HTM can provide significant speed-ups and scalability. Since we have not highly optimized BUSTM for the system, our results are preliminary, but very encouraging.

The rest of this paper is organized as follows. Section 2 discusses existing OpenMP synchronization while Section 3 contrasts TM to other concurrency control techniques. Section 4 presents our proposed TM extensions for OpenMP and Section 5 describes the BG/Q TM implementation. Section 6 details our experimental results, including several runs in three different synchronization modes (TM, atomic, and critical) that contrast existing OpenMP constructs with our proposed solution.

2   Current OpenMP Synchronization Mechanisms

OpenMP currently includes four synchronization mechanisms: locks, barriers, atomics and critical sections. These mechanisms synchronize objects in shared memory but are either limited in their performance and applicability or are difficult to use correctly. TM provides greater flexibility and ease of use; our results show it can also be performant.

Using locks for synchronization on a per construct basis leads to fine-grained locking that can produce complex associations between data and synchronization as multiple locks are held and released through intersecting lifetimes. A failure to acquire and release these locks in the correct order can lead to deadlocks and data races. They are not composable and, thus, break modular programming. Alternatively, developers can use coarse-grained locking strategies. However, using few locks can lead to unnecessary convoying of execution and loss of performance. Developers can synthesize more directed synchronization mechanisms from OpenMP atomics. However, these techniques usually remain low level and suffer from problems similar to locks. Thus, we must use more advanced abstractions as OpenMP programs increase in size and complexity.

OpenMP barriers and critical sections provide higher level abstractions. However, barriers enforce synchronization across all threads in a team, which is frequently a much larger scope than the programmer requires. OpenMP critical sections provide a directed, high-level synchronization mechanism. However, the OpenMP specification precludes nesting of critical sections. Further named critical sections allow additional complexity that is often unnecessary and undesirable.

Parallel programming is complex, whether it is developing the program, reasoning about the program or looking for bugs. TM provides a higher level of abstraction than existing OpenMP synchronization mechanisms without unnecessary restrictions or complexities. TM results in simpler design, simpler reasoning, and maintenance, while allowing specialized synchronization support for different platforms. Above all, it enables simple lexical or dynamic nesting, even across library interfaces.

3 Prior Approaches to Concurrency Control

3.1 Mutual Exclusion

Perhaps the most common form of concurrency control for shared-memory parallel programming is mutual exclusion. In general, mutual exclusion ensures program correctness, that is, serializability, by limiting access to shared-memory variables to one thread at a time. Mutual exclusion achieves this restriction by using mutually exclusive locks, also known as just locks or mutexes. For a thread to access a shared-memory variable, it must first acquire the lock that protects the shared-memory variable. When a thread has completed its access to the shared-memory variable, it releases the lock.

The concept of mutual exclusion appears straightforward and easy to apply. However, mutual exclusion quickly becomes unwieldy in large-scale software. Further, it is extremely difficult nearly to write both correct and efficient large-scale multithreaded software using mutual exclusion [7].

3.2 Non-blocking Atomic Primitives and OpenMP Atomics

Another, less common mechanism to synchronize shared-memory accesses uses non-blocking atomic primitives, such as compare-and-swap (CAS) or load-linked store-conditional (LL/SC), or more recently, OpenMP atomics. These approaches support non-blocking algorithms that can offer substantial concurrency. However, only expert parallel programmers typically use them as they are error prone even for simple data structures, such as queues [10].

3.3 Lock Elision

TM essentially supports optimistic speculation. An alternative speculative technique simply elides the lock. In most cases, no synchronization conflict will occur and the accesses can be performed without acquiring the lock. Hardware techniques can track temporary results and then commit them if no conflict has occurred [13].

In essence, lock elision is an implementation technique of TM that allows optimistic execution of a critical section by eliding the write to a lock, so that the lock appears to be free to other threads. A failed transaction results in execution restarting at the beginning of the lock and actually acquiring the lock. The existing hardware cache coherency mechanism is used to track read and write sets, which is consistent with their intended use. although now they are usually tagged with a special transactional bit. However, this mechanism also effectively limits the size of transactions to a cache size while a general TM mechanism can allow bigger transaction sets. Lock elision benefits from being backwards compatible to existing code that does not have to be rewritten, and, if no hardware support for TM is present, the lock is just acquired.

3.4 Integrated TM Language Support

Several languages include TM support, including Programming Clojure, Scala, Haskell, Perl, Python, Caml, and Java. For C++, significant work has explored language-level and library implementations. Several vendors provide compilers that support STM [4,8,9]. Most vendors have used C++ as the model for TM because it has the more complex language constructs than C and Fortran. Issues that have been explored include:

- Memory model and atomics (C++11);
- Support for member initializers;
- Support for C++ expressions;
- Integration of non-transactional and TM constructs;
- Embedding non-transactional synchronization within TM constructs;
- Structured block nesting;
- Multiple function entry and exit points;
- Static (templates) and dynamic (virtual functions) polymorphism;
- Exceptions thrown from within TM constructs;

The expectation is that transferring TM to C or Fortran will be straightforward.

4 Proposed OpenMP Extension

We propose to integrate TM into OpenMP. TM is not new; Herlihy and Moss proposed it in 1993 for lock free data structures [6]. However, since that introduction, it has exploded in popularity due to a promise of easy parallel programming. TM solves the concurrency control problem. Case studies have shown that TM reduces the challenge of parallel programming compared to mutual exclusion [18]. TM raises the level of abstraction from basic support for mutable shared state to advanced support. TM can coexist with current OpenMP concurrency mechanisms.

TM simplifies development of deadlock-free programs since functions can be composed regardless of order. Thus, TM supports a modular programming model in which software is written by composing separate and interchangeable modules together. Modular programming is fundamental to all of OpenMP's base languages.

Our proposed syntax for the invocation of TM is simple by design and by definition. We use the following notation in C/C++:

```
1 #pragma tm_atomic [(safe_mode)]
2 {
3        < code >
4 }
```

The syntax in Fortran is essentially identical.

5 Blue Gene/Q TM Implementation

BG/Q support for TM involves three aspects. The BG/Q compute chip includes a versioning L2 cache that can associate version numbers with cache tags. Thus, the cache can contain multiple instances of the same address. This mechanism allows the BG/Q compiler and runtime to implement TM support. In this section, we describe these compiler and runtime techniques.

5.1 Compiler Support

The compiler is responsible for translating the `tm_atomic` enclosed region into two function calls to the TM runtime: `tm_begin` and `tm_end`. The compiler must also generate register save and restore code in case a transaction is aborted and must be retried. The `safe_mode` clause asserts to the compiler that the TM region does not contain irrevocable actions such as I/O or writing to device memory space. Without this assertion, the runtime assumes that the transaction is unsafe, which requires the system to use jail mode protection. A rollback caused by a jail mode violation restricts concurrency as the TM runtime immediately retries the transaction in the irrevocable mode. Entering and exiting jail mode requires two system calls. We can avoid the overhead of these calls by using the `safe_mode` clause.

5.2 TM Runtime

A key aspect of TM support is detection of memory access conflicts. Our TM runtime implements two conflict detection schemes: eager and lazy. Users can choose which detection scheme to use via the `TM_ENABLE_INTERRUPT_ON_CONFLICT` runtime environment variable. In the eager scheme, threads receive interrupts upon WAW, WAR, and RAW conflicts. We base conflict arbitration on the age of the transactions to favor survival of the older one. In the lazy scheme, all transactions, including doomed ones run to the commit point at which arbitration and invalidation occur. When we abort a transaction, the thread rolls back to the start of the transaction and retries immediately.

We support irrevocable actions inside a transaction as the runtime can revert to a single global lock when an irrevocable action occurs. The runtime also reverts back to a single global lock when a hardware transaction fails more than a configurable number of times. Users can adjust this threshold via the `TM_MAX_NUM_ROLLBACK` runtime environment variable. The runtime implements flat transaction nesting semantics in which commit and rollback are to the outermost enclosing transaction.

The BGQ L2 cache is 16 way set associative and 10 out of 16 ways can be used to store speculative states without an eviction. Since the L2 is 32MB in size and as such, it can buffer approximately 20MB of speculative state. Capacity overflow can also happen when the ways in a set are exhausted. When a transaction suffers capacity overflow, the TM runtime retries the transaction `TM_MAX_NUM_ROLLBACK` number of times; that is, in the same way as rollbacks due to access conflicts. The reason is that it is likely that capacity related rollbacks are transient, for example, due to too many concurrent transactions running at the same time.

Our runtime provides several counters that can facilitate TM optimization. Users can use the `TM_REPORT_LOG` to trigger printout of the counters. Four settings control the level of detail reported: `TM_REPORT_LOG=ALL/SUMMARY/FUNC/VERBOSE`. The `TM_REPORT_NAME` environment variable can specify the name of the report file. The runtime provides utility functions to print and to inspect counter values, which allows users (or tools) to collect the statistics and to generate reports in any format. The `TM_REPORT_STAT_ENABLE` environment variable enables the inspection routines.

The counters collect the following information per thread:

1. totalTransactions
2. totalRollbacks

3. totalSerializedJMV
4. totalSerializedMAXRB
5. totalSerializedOTHER

We capture the total number of transactions that a thread commits in totalTransactions and the total number of retries that it attempts in totalRollbacks. If execution of an irrevocable action serializes a thread, we increment its totalSerializedJMV counter (JMV stands for jail mode violation). totalSerializedMAXRB tracks the total number of times that a thread is serialized due to retrying TM_MAX_NUM_ROLLBACK times. We track other non-obvious serialization causes in the totalSerializedOTHER counter.

6 Experimental Results Using BUSTM

We now present computational experiments to show HTM behavior and performance on BG/Q. We use the BUSTM (Benchmark for UnStructured-mesh Transactional Memory) code. We show results in BUSTM's deterministic and probabilistic modes on two different types of meshes that represent two different unstructured mesh connectivities. For more details on the benchmark, we refer the reader to our previous work [1,2,16].

Unlike our previous work, we emphasize performance in terms of execution time and scalability. However, BUSTM has not been optimized to run on any particular system, including BG/Q. The TM runtime provides several options that we have not yet explored. The runtime software, while quite stable, is still in limited availability as it continues to evolve. Thus, our results represent a preliminary set of performance numbers on a new system with novel technology and are likely to improve in the future.

6.1 Geometries Used

Prism Mesh around a Cylinder. Our first example is the same grid of 119893 triangular prism cells arranged as a 2-D layer of 3-D cells that we used in earlier work [16]. The mesh has 420060 faces (some quadrilateral, others triangular) and 123132 nodes. This mesh has a fixed number of potential conflicts although the actual number of conflicts, which we observe with the totalRollbacks counter, varies between runs.

Tetrahedral Mesh around a Sphere. Our second example of a real unstructured mesh is a fully 3-D tetrahedral mesh composed of 362,429 cells, a total of 739,480 triangular faces, and 67,938 nodes. The actual geometry around which this mesh was constructed is a 10° wedge of a sphere. This mesh is fully 3-D: all interior cells are connected to the nearest neighbors through all of their faces. Thus, the connectivity graph, which significantly impacts the memory access pattern for the face- and particle-loops, is qualitatively and quantitatively different than that of the triangular prism mesh.

6.2 Experiments in Deterministic Mode

BUSTM's deterministic mode models conservative finite volume schemes, in which the outer loop is over the cell faces on which the heavy computation occurs [1,2]. This

```
1 #pragma tm_atomic
2 {
3   gradient[cell_no_1] += incr;
4   gradient[cell_no_2] -= incr;
5 }
```

```
1 #pragma omp parallel for
2   for (i=0; i < max_face; i++){
3     left_neighbor = left_cells[i];
4     right_neighbor = right_cells[i];
5     update_cells(incr,
6       left_neighbor, right_neighbor);
7   }
```

Fig. 1. Gradients accumulated within a transaction in update_cells

Fig. 2. Loop that calls update_cells

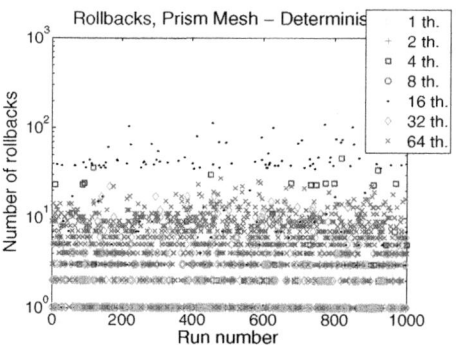

Fig. 3. Rollbacks across 1000 runs on prismatic mesh, in deterministic mode

Fig. 4. Total number of rollbacks and errors on prismatic mesh, in deterministic mode

mode takes the mesh data, the number of threads, and the iteration count as input. We replace the face-by-face flux computations with the simpler *numerical divergence* of a mesh-function that we define on an unstructured mesh in a cell-centered sense. This emulation computes the gradient of a function. If the function is constant, its gradient and, thus, its divergence is zero. Fig. 1 shows the gradient transaction, which may seem rather trivial, but it is purposely chosen in such a way so that we can later easily replace it with equivalent atomic statements for side-by-side performance comparisons.

Since BUSTM loops over the faces, as Fig. 2 shows, conflicts can occur if different faces concurrently update the same cell. These conflicts only actually occur, if update_cells does not use transactions or other synchronization such as a critical section, and two updates happen at the same physical time. Thus, the probability of conflicts is extremely low and, in fact, many of our experimental runs had no conflicts.

Prism Mesh. Fig. 3 shows that the number of rollbacks in each of 1000 runs is always less than 120, and often zero. Fig. 4 shows the sum of the number of rollbacks that TM incurs over the same 1000 runs versus the total number of errors committed (without TM) for thread counts between 1 and 64. Unlike in the STM case [16], the number of TM retries (i.e., "rollbacks") is comparable to the number of errors with the unsynchronized code. Both curves exhibit similar trends with increasing thread counts:

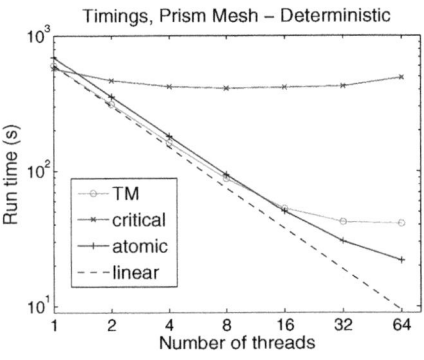

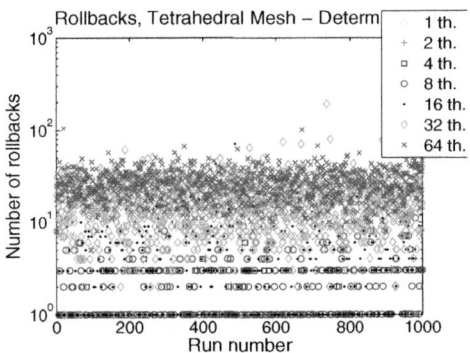

Fig. 5. Actual run time on prismatic mesh, in deterministic mode

Fig. 6. Rollbacks across 1000 runs on tetrahedral mesh, in deterministic mode

the number of conflicts increases significantly with the number of threads, except on 8 threads where we obtained no rollbacks at all. Fig. 3, which also clearly shows this local anomaly, also indicates a large variation in the number of rollbacks across runs with 16 threads where the spread from run to run is wider than on 64 threads, for example. Since the errors and rollbacks exhibit similar trends in Fig. 4, we believe that the details of the connectivity of this particular mesh and/or the cell ordering may be responsible for this conflict pattern. Overall, conflicts rarely occur relative to the number of potential conflicts. Despite the relatively small mesh, only 0.0017% of all cell updates incur conflicts even on 64 threads. No rollbacks or errors occur with just two threads (or one, which is expected).

In order to compare to other synchronization techniques, we ran the code, with trivial code modiifications, in two other modes as well. Fig. 5 shows timings for *TM*, *atomic*, which uses the `atomic` directive, and *critical*, which replaces the transaction with a `critical` region; *linear* corresponds to perfect speed up. BG/Q has an efficient implementation of the `atomic` construct so *atomic* exhibits almost linear scaling through 64 threads. However, the gradient computation of Fig. 1 involves three variable updates (one for each dimension). Indeed, when we replace the one transaction with three `atomic` constructs, the larger overhead of transactional memory ends up being amortized over a larger code section so *TM* becomes actually slightly more efficient with fewer than 16 threads, as Fig. 5 shows. As we expect, *critical* scales poorly, lagging the other methods even with just two threads.

Tetrahedral Mesh. Fig. 6 and Fig. 7 plot the pattern and number of rollbacks with the fully 3-D mesh. We again see few (less than 100 for most runs) conflicts during each run. Fig. 6 is qualitatively similar to Fig. 3 although we see fewer conflicts with 16 threads. Fig. 7 now shows a monotone increase in rollbacks with the number of threads and the absence of anomalies that we have seen in Fig. 4. The distribution of conflicts across the runs exhibits a pattern in which higher thread counts result in a proportional increase in rollbacks. The number of unsynchronized errors again follows, in a qualitative sense, the pattern of rollbacks, although it is not monotone. The number of potential

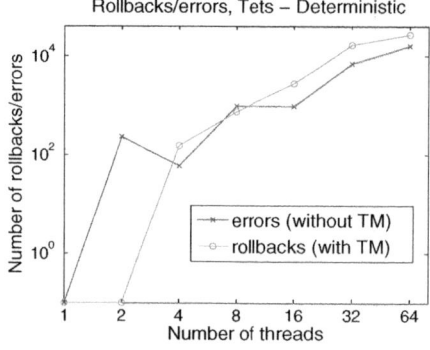

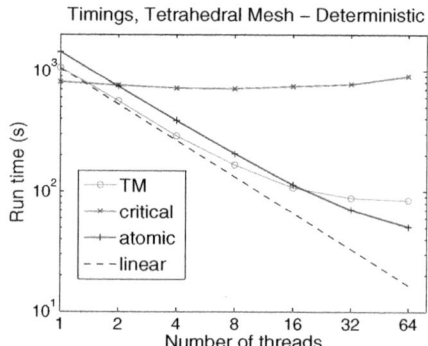

Fig. 7. Total number of rollbacks and errors on tetrahedral mesh, in deterministic mode

Fig. 8. Actual run time on tetrahedral mesh, in deterministic mode

```
1 #pragma tm_atomic
2 {
3    cell_counter[cell_no]++;
4 }
```

```
1 #pragma omp parallel for
2 for(i=0; i<max_particles; i++){
3    next_cell = rand();
4    while(inside){
5       mark_cell(next_cell); // cell touched
6       next_face = rand();
7       next_cell = neighbor(next_face);
8       if(next_cell < 0)inside = 0;
9    }
10 }
```

Fig. 9. Cell counter incremented within a transaction in function mark_cell

Fig. 10. Particle loop calls mark_cell

conflicts is again the number of cells (362,429) times the number of faces per cell (4), which yields a conflict probability of 0.00013% even for the run that exhibits the most conflicts (190). This extremely small conflict probability occurs with a small 3-D mesh by today's standards; larger meshes would be expected to incur even *fewer* conflicts.

For the timings, Fig. 8 shows that *atomic* again scales well up to 64 threads, and it is actually linear with up to 16 threads. *TM* is about 10% faster than *atomic* with fewer than eight threads and scales well up to 8 threads, after which it slowly degrades in scalability to about 70% of the ideal linear speed-up. The break even point between *TM* and *atomic* is again 16 threads. As before, *critical* is faster with just one thread. However, it actually slows down slightly as the thread count increases.

6.3 Experiments in Probabilistic Mode

We now present results for the probabilistic mode [1,2] to understand how well TM suits real Monte Carlo applications. We again use the unstructured bookkeeping in BUSTM in order to emulate the behavior of particles. Fig. 9 illustrates a simple transaction that safely increments a single cell-based integer and Fig. 10 shows the loop that distributes

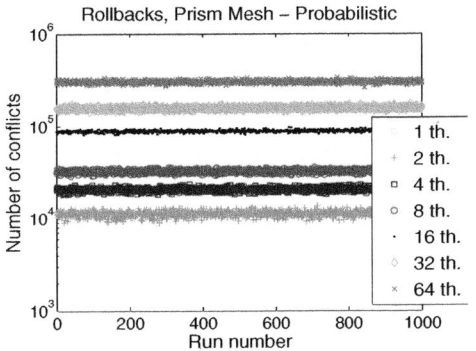

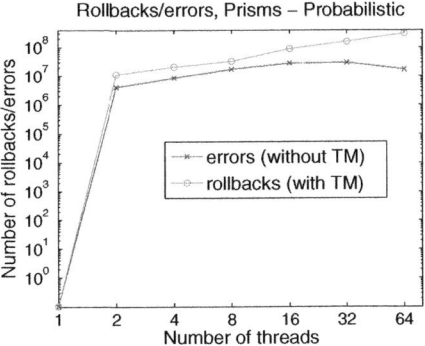

Fig. 11. Rollbacks across 1000 runs on prismatic mesh, in probabilistic mode

Fig. 12. Total number of rollbacks and errors on prismatic mesh, in probabilistic mode

the particles across the threads. Again, the transaction itself in Fig. 9 is trivial because of our anticipated timing comparisons to `atomic`. For error checking, we use a separate counter that we increment for each particle every time it touches a cell.

Prism Mesh. Our first probabilistic experiments use the triangular prism mesh. We report conflict statistics that the TM runtime reports. Each of our 1,000 runs uses 12,000 random particles (10% of the number of cells). Fig. 11 shows a much higher number of conflicts than in the deterministic case. The conflicts are fairly consistent for a given thread count with a relatively narrow spread from run to run, and appear almost linearly proportional to the number of threads. We observe the opposite trend from the deterministic case between the total number of TM rollbacks and the total number of unsynchronized errors in Fig. 12 in that that TM performs many more rollbacks than unsynchronized errors (without TM), sometimes by an order of magnitude. This phenomenon may arise from the much heavier computational load imposed by frequent invocations of the random number generator. Also, higher conflict-rate scenarios can lead to multiple rollbacks on the same memory location, thus considerably increasing the number of rollbacks. In fact, on some rare occasions, we exceed the default maximum number of rollbacks of 10, thus invoking jail mode and serializing the entire transactional loop.

The single statement transaction of Fig. 9 is easily replaced with an `atomic` or `critical` directive. Because of this, however, *TM* no longer gains an advantage due to multiple `atomic` constructs being included in a single transaction. Nevertheless, Fig. 13 shows that *TM* again scales well, as does *atomic*. Again, *critical* has constant execution time independent of thread count.

Tetrahedral Mesh. We now show probabilistic experiments on the tetrahedral mesh. Each of our 1,000 runs uses the same number of random particles as mesh cells. Fig. 14 shows an unexpected pattern in terms of the number of rollbacks. Surprisingly, we incur the most rollbacks with 16 threads, with a much lower conflict rate on 32 and 64 threads. This anomaly can only be explained by the unique connectivity of this 3-D mesh in this particular scenario. Fig. 15 shows that another anomaly occurs in the number of

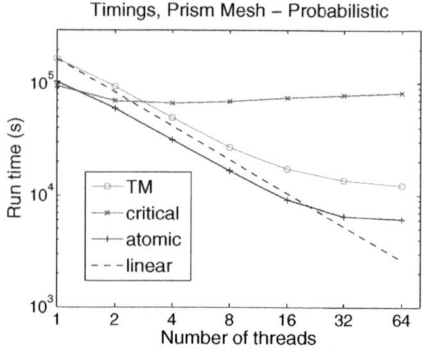

Fig. 13. Actual run time on prismatic mesh, in probabilistic mode

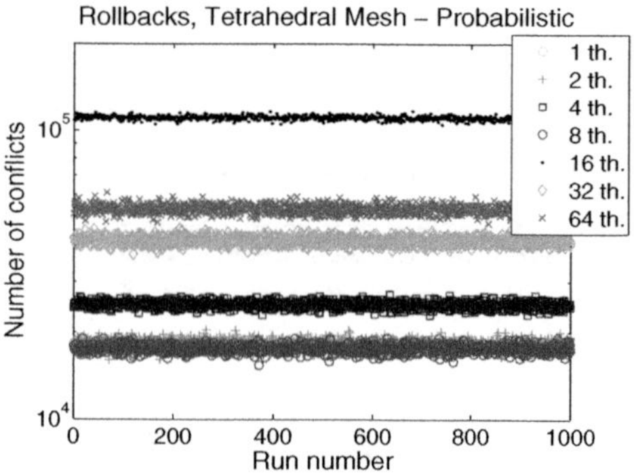

Fig. 14. Rollbacks across 1000 runs on tetrahedral mesh, in probabilistic mode

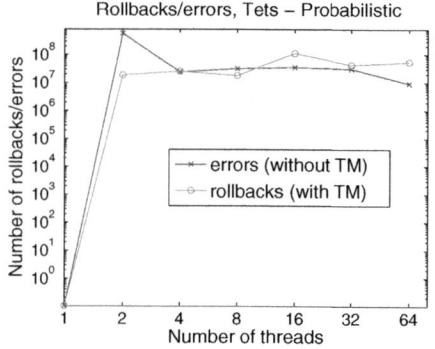

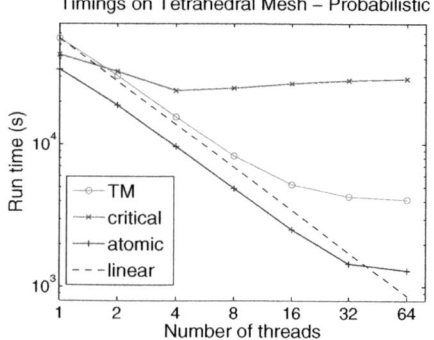

Fig. 15. Total number of rollbacks and errors on tetrahedral mesh, in probabilistic mode

Fig. 16. Actual run time on tetrahedral mesh, in probabilistic mode

incorrect results without TM with two threads, but on the rest of the thread counts the error trend follows, qualitatively speaking, that of the rollbacks. Overall, the total number of resolved conflicts and committed errors is again a small fraction of the number of updates. For example, even on 16 threads, the conflict probability is only 0.045% on this relatively small mesh.

In terms of timings, Fig. 16 shows that *TM* again scales well up to 16 threads, with marginal improvements on 32 and 64 threads. As expected, *critical* has constant execution time, while *atomic* scales better than in the prism case, probably because the mesh is larger. The difference between *atomic* and *TM* is again due to the larger overhead of TM for a single statement.

7 Conclusions, Current and Future Work

We explored the HTM support of IBM's newly introduced Blue Gene/Q platform through the BUSTM code. In order to understand the potential benefits of HTM in different scientific computing scenarios, we ran BUSTM in two different modes on two different unstructured meshes. In all cases TM scaled well up to at least 16 threads, with further, albeit smaller gains on 32 and 64 threads. Wherever TM had three memory locations to protect instead of just one, it outperformed the OpenMP `atomic` construct. Further, it outperformed the OpenMP `critical` construct in all cases and by an order of magnitude or more on 64 threads. Thus, our preliminary evaluation of this new HTM technology shows that TM offers substantial benefits in all cases.

Our explicit goal is the inclusion of TM into the OpenMP specification. Our performance comparisons only required substitution for OpenMP directives, thus retaining composability and the benefits of modular programming while retaining efficiency.

Finally, this reinforces our position that the deterministic and probabilistic algorithms shown here, while they represent different numerical algorithms, are well-suited to transactions since conflicts rarely occur. We continue to study the outlier cases presented here, to add new potential meshes, to include more complicated operations in the transactions, and to search for new algorithms to add to BUSTM's portfolio.

Acknowledgements. The authors wish to thank John Gyllenhaal and Scott Futral of LLNL for numerous fruitful discussions on this subject and for support of this work. The IBM authors gratefully acknowledge the help of Kelvin Li and Mary Chan. The first author also acknowledges past financial support from Rockwell International, Boeing, and Hypercomp, Inc. in developing the unstructured mesh bookkeeping used in the experiments, and from Icon Consulting and IBM in writing the BUSTM code.

This article (LLNL-PROC-528852) has been authored in part by Lawrence Livermore National Security, LLC under Contract DE-AC52-07NA27344 with the U.S. Department of Energy. Accordingly, the United States Government retains and the publisher, by accepting the article for publication, acknowledges that the United States Government retains a non-exclusive, paid-up, irrevocable, world-wide license to publish or reproduce the published form of this article or allow others to do so, for United States Government purposes.

license to these patents. You can send license inquiries, in writing, to: IBM Director of Licensing, IBM Corporation, North Castle Drive, Armonk, NY 10504-1785, U.S.A.

The following paragraph does not apply to the United Kingdom or any other country where such provisions are inconsistent with local law: INTERNATIONAL BUSINESS MACHINES CORPORATION PROVIDES THIS PAPER "AS IS" WITHOUT WARRANTY OF ANY KIND, EITHER EXPRESS OR IMPLIED, INCLUDING, BUT NOT LIMITED TO, THE IMPLIED WARRANTIES OF NON-INFRINGEMENT, MERCHANTABILITY OR FITNESS FOR A PARTICULAR PURPOSE. Some states do not allow disclaimer of express or implied warranties in certain transactions, therefore, this statement may not apply to you.

This information could include technical inaccuracies or typographical errors. Changes may be made periodically to the information herein; these changes may be incorporated in subsequent versions of the paper. IBM may make improvements and/or changes in the product(s) and/or the program(s) described in this paper at any time without notice.

Any references in this document to non-IBM Web sites are provided for convenience only and do not in any manner serve as an endorsement of those Web sites. The materials at those Web sites are not part of the materials for this IBM product and use of those Web sites is at your own risk.

IBM may have patents or pending patent applications covering subject matter described in this document. The furnishing of this document does not give you any license to these patents. You can send license inquiries, in writing, to: IBM Director of Licensing, IBM Corporation, 4205 South Miami Boulevard, Research Triangle Park, NC 27709, U.S.A.

All statements regarding IBM's future direction or intent are subject to change or withdrawal without notice, and represent goals and objectives only.

This information is for planning purposes only. The information herein is subject to change before the products described become available.

If you are viewing this information softcopy, the photographs and color illustrations may not appear.

Trademarks
IBM, the IBM logo, ibm.com, and Blue Gene/Q are trademarks or registered trademarks of International Business Machines Corporation in the United States, other countries, or both. If these and other IBM trademarked terms are marked on their first occurrence in this information with a trademark symbol, these symbols indicate U.S. registered or common law trademarks owned by IBM at the time this information was published. Such trademarks may also be registered or common law trademarks in other countries. A current list of IBM trademarks is available on the web at "Copyright and trademark information" at http://www.ibm.com/legal/copytrade.shtml.

Intel, Intel logo, Intel Inside, Intel Inside logo, Intel Centrino, Intel Centrino logo, Celeron, Intel Xeon, Intel SpeedStep, Itanium, and Pentium are trademarks or registered trademarks of Intel Corporation or its subsidiaries in the United States and other countries.

Linux is a registered trademark of Linus Torvalds in the United States, other countries, or both.

Java and all Java-based trademarks and logos are trademarks or registered trademarks of Oracle and/or its affiliates.

Other company, product, or service names may be trademarks or service marks of others.

References

1. Bihari, B.L.: Applicability of Transactional Memory to Modern Codes. In: International Conference on Numerical Analysis and Applied Mathematics 2010 (ICNAAM 2010) Conference Proceedings, pp. 1764–1767. APS, Rodos (2010)
2. Bihari, B.: Transactional Memory for Unstructured Mesh Simulations. Journal of Scientific Computing (to appear, 2012)
3. Cascaval, C., Blundell, M.C., Michael, H.W., Wu Cain, P., Chiras, S., Chatterjee, S.: Software Transactional Memory: Why is it Only a Research Toy? ACM Queue 6(5), 46–58 (2008)
4. Dice, D., Shalev, O., Shavit, N.: Transactional Locking II. In: Dolev, S. (ed.) DISC 2006. LNCS, vol. 4167, pp. 194–208. Springer, Heidelberg (2006)
5. Haring, R., The IBM BlueGene Team: The IBM Blue Gene/Q Compute Chip. In: Hot Chips 24: A Symposium on High Performance Chips, Palo Alto, CA (2011)
6. Herlihy, M., Moss, J.E.B.: Transactional memory: Architectural Support for Lock-Free Data Structures. SIGARCH Comput. Archit. News 51(2), 289–300 (1993)
7. Herlihy, M., Shavit, N.: The Art of Multiprocessor Programming. Morgan Kaufmann Publishers (February 2008)
8. IBM. IBM XL C/C++ for Transactional Memory for AIX, V0.9 Language Extensions and Users Guide (May 2008), http://dl.alphaworks.ibm.com/technologies/xlcstm/xlcstm-whitepaper.pdf
9. Intel. Intel C++ STM Compiler, Prototype Edition 2.0 (2008), http://softwarecommunity.intel.com/articles/eng/1460.htm/
10. Michael, M.M., Scott, M.L.: Simple, Fast, and Practical Non-Blocking and Blocking Concurrent Queue Algorithms. In: Proceedings of the Fifteenth Annual ACM Symposium on Principles of Distributed Computing, PODC 1996, pp. 267–275. ACM, New York (1996)
11. Milovanović, M., Ferrer, R., Unsal, O.S., Cristal, A., Martorell, X., Ayguadé, E., Labarta, J., Valero, M.: Transactional Memory and OpenMP. In: Chapman, B., Zheng, W., Gao, G.R., Sato, M., Ayguadé, E., Wang, D. (eds.) IWOMP 2007. LNCS, vol. 4935, pp. 37–53. Springer, Heidelberg (2008)
12. OpenMP ARB. OpenMP Application Program Interface, v. 3.1 (July 2011)
13. Rajwar, R., Goodman, J.R.: Speculative Lock Elision: Enabling Highly Concurrent Multithreaded Execution. In: Proceedings of the 34th Annual ACM/IEEE International Symposium on Microarchitecture, MICRO 34, pp. 294–305. IEEE Computer Society, Washington, DC (2001)
14. Schindewolf, M., Schulz, M., Gyllenhaal, J., Bihari, B., Wang, A., Karl, W.: What Scientific Applications Can Benefit from Hardware Transacional Memory? In: International Conference for High Performance Computing, Networking, Storage and Analysis (SC 2012), Salt Lake City, Utah (November 2012) (currently under review)
15. Wang, A., Gaudet, M., Wu, P., Ohmacht, M., Amaral, J.N., Barton, C., Silvera, R., MIchael, M.: Evaluation of Blue Gene/Q Hardware Support for Transactional Memories. In: PACT (submitted, 2012)

16. Wong, M., Bihari, B.L., de Supinski, B.R., Wu, P., Michael, M., Liu, Y., Chen, W.: A Case for Including Transactions in OpenMP. In: Sato, M., Hanawa, T., Müller, M.S., Chapman, B.M., de Supinski, B.R. (eds.) IWOMP 2010. LNCS, vol. 6132, pp. 149–160. Springer, Heidelberg (2010)
17. Woongki, B., Minh, C.C., Trautmann, M., Kozyrakis, C., Olukotun, K.: The OpenTM Transactional Application Programming Interface. In: PACT 2007: Proceedings of the 16th International Conference on Parallel Architecture and Compilation Techniques, pp. 376–587. IEEE Computer Society, Washington, DC (2007)
18. Zyulkyarov, F., Gajinov, V., Unsal, O.S., Cristal, A., Ayguadé, E., Harris, T., Valero, M.: Atomic Quake: Using Transactional Memory in an Interactive Multiplayer Game Server. In: Proceedings of the 14th ACM SIGPLAN Symposium on Principles and Practice of Parallel Programming, PPoPP 2009, pp. 25–34. ACM, New York (2009)

Extending OpenMP* with Vector Constructs for Modern Multicore SIMD Architectures

Michael Klemm[1], Alejandro Duran[2], Xinmin Tian[1], Hideki Saito[1], Diego Caballero[2], and Xavier Martorell[1,3]

[1] Intel Corporation
{michael.klemm,xinmin.tian,hideki.saito}@intel.com
[2] Barcelona Supercomputing Center
{alex.duran,diego.caballero}@bsc.es
[3] Universitat Politecnica de Catalunya
xavim@ac.upc.edu

Abstract. In order to obtain maximum performance, many applications require to extend parallelism from multi-threading to instruction-level (SIMD) parallelism that exists in many current (and future) multi-core architectures. While auto-vectorization technology has been used to exploit this SIMD level, it is not always enough due to OpenMP semantics and compiler technology limitations. In those cases, programmers need to resort to low-level intrinsics or vendor specific directives. We propose a new OpenMP directive: the simd directive. This directive will allow programmers to guide the vectorization process enabling a more productive and portable exploitation of the SIMD level. Our performance results show significant improvements over current auto-vectorizing technology of the Intel® Composer XE 2011.

1 Introduction

Moore's Law is still alive and well and bestows an exponential growth of the number of transistors on a chip [1]. Due to fundamental constraints on energy consumption and cooling [21], CPU vendors cannot push performance of single-core CPUs at the usual pace. The available transistor budget is instead spent to increase the number of cores per die and to widen the arithmetic Vector Processing Units (VPU) by doubling the length of SIMD vectors. The evolution from Intel® Streaming SIMD Extensions (SSE, 128 bit) to Intel® Advanced Vector Extensions [9] (AVX, 256 bit) to the instructions of the Intel® Knights Ferry prototype [7] (512 bit) are a good example.

Applications must make effective use of the available VPUs together with parallelization to leverage the full potential of today's multi-core architectures. While OpenMP* [20] is a widely accepted industry standard for thread parallelism, it does not offer any means to express SIMD parallelism. Programmers need to rely on an OpenMP compiler to automatically handle vectorization or they need to use vendor-specific extensions (e. g., vectorization directives) to express SIMD parallelization. Programmers need to trust the compiler on SIMD vectorization interacting correctly and optimally with the OpenMP constructs. This, unfortunately, is not the case across the board. Several commercial compilers (e. g., Cray's, IBM's, etc.) support directives that

B.M. Chapman et al. (Eds.): IWOMP 2012, LNCS 7312, pp. 59–72, 2012.

allow programmers to express independence between loop iterations which in turn enables vectorization. But these extensions are neither portable nor complete enough to handle more complex cases.

To alleviate the situation for programmers, we propose special SIMD constructs for OpenMP to extend parallelism from thread-level parallelism to instruction-level parallelism. The proposed constructs provide a standardized set of SIMD constructs for programmers who no longer need to use non-portable, vendor-specific vectorization intrinsics or directives. In addition, SIMD constructs provide additional knowledge about the code structure to the compiler and allow for a better vectorization that blends well with parallelization.

2 Related Work

Since the appearance of the traditional vector architectures, automatic vectorization of scalar code has become an outstanding topic in compiler research. The relatively recent introduction of short VPUs in the latest CPUs and accelerators, and the increasing role that these units are playing, are bringing vectorization into prominence again. To succeed in the auto-vectorization process, compilers need to deal with alignment constraints, control flow divergences, different memory access patterns, operations between data types with different length, loops with dynamic bounds, etc.

As a result, we find a lot of related work in that direction that comes up with promising techniques on auto-vectorization with alignment constrains and operations on mixed data lengths [5,17,23,24], vectorizing code with non-stride-one data accesses [15,16,18], and control flow divergences [4,10]. We can find even the definition of a new level of parallelism, called superword-level parallelism, focused on exploiting these short SIMD units in a different way to how data-level parallelism does [4,13].

However, these techniques are not always useful. To avoid poor performance it requires very sophisticated heuristics, analysis, and code transformations, which are usually not implemented in production compilers [14]. Even implementing them, compilers cannot always vectorize due to inter-procedural and inter-file analysis limitations, loops with dynamic/unknown compile-time bounds, complex memory accesses, and pointer arithmetic. All these characteristics may hinder the compiler ability to auto-vectorize. In some cases, we have different options of vectorization, as when both the inner and outer loops could be vectorized and the compiler cannot choose the right one [19].

As a result of these limitations, programmers are often forced to use low-level intrinsics to exploit the SIMD level of the architecture. This is an error-prone and time-consuming process for programmers who need to rewrite their code and that, also, reduces the portability of the programs. To ease this problem, OpenCL [11] introduced basic data types that represent vectors allowing the user to specify operations between them that will be in turn vectorized by the compiler. This approach still requires rewriting of the code but to a lesser and more portable extend. Others [2,12,22] have introduced a user-guided vectorization based on compiler directives that allow programmers to mark loops that should be vectorized. These last approaches require little effort by the programmer while still achieving very good performance across platforms.

We argue that it would be beneficial to OpenMP users that the OpenMP specification would provide support for user-directed vectorization in order to improve performance

```
1 #pragma omp parallel
2     {
3 #pragma omp for
4         for (i=0; i<N; i++) {
5             for (j=16; j<N-16; j++) {
6                 a[i][j] = a[i][j-16] + b[i][j];
7                 b[i][j] = b[i][j+16] + a[i][j];
8             }
9         }
10     }
```

Fig. 1. Parallel code fragment that cannot be vectorized automatically

portability of programs at the SIMD-parallel level. In the following sections we discuss why and how this support should be integrated into OpenMP.

3 Motivation

While the existing worksharing constructs of OpenMP already define loop-level parallelism on for (C/C++) or do loops (Fortran), re-using these existing constructs to describe vectorization does not work. The example in Fig. 1 shows a code fragment that can (partially) be executed in parallel, but cannot be vectorized by the compiler without additional knowledge about vectorization and the correct vector length.

In Fig. 1, two issues for the compiler arise that inhibit vectorization by the for construct. First, it cannot simply extend the for worksharing construct to the j-loop, since this would violate the OpenMP semantics. At the same time, it is not possible to nest a second for construct to indicate to the compiler that the inner-most loop is safe to parallelize or vectorize. Second, the j-loop contains a loop-carried dependency that prohibits the automatic vectorizer of the compiler to emit vectorized code. However, the code can be vectorized for any given vector length for array b and for vectors shorter than 16 elements for array a.

Also note that, in general, to maintain the OpenMP principle that "if the user cannot tell, then it is ok", compilers can only apply vectorization inside of each chunk of a for as otherwise there would be observable differences in the mapping of loop iterations to threads. As a result of this, the performance maybe hampered by the inefficient use of vector registers and because of alignment of the data of the different chunks. This is particularly true when the loop size is a small ratio of the vector length.

Our solution to the above issue is to extend OpenMP with a set of constructs and clauses that enable programmers to specify vectorization patterns in addition to the parallelization patterns. This completes OpenMP's support for multi-level parallelism, that is, both thread-level and instruction-level parallelism by exploiting SIMD instructions.

4 SIMD Extensions to OpenMP

To facilitate vectorization of OpenMP codes, we propose to extend the set of OpenMP directives by a new set of directives to handle vectorization. In the following we will describe the syntax and semantics of the proposed extensions.

```
1 #pragma omp parallel
2     {
3 #pragma omp for
4         for (i=0; i<N; i++) {
5 #pragma omp simd vectorlength(16)
6             for (j=16; j<N-16; j++) {
7                 a[i][j] = a[i][j-16] + b[i][j];
8                 b[i][j] = b[i][j+16] + a[i][j];
9             }
10        }
11    }
```

Fig. 2. Code of Fig. 1 with vectorization construct added

4.1   Vectorized Worksharing Construct

The basis of our extensions to OpenMP is the simd construct for for (C/C++) and do loops (Fortran). Fig. 2 shows how the proposed construct can be used to guide the compiler on vectorizing the code of Fig. 1 (we will cover the vectorlength clause later in this paper).

The syntax of the simd construct is as follows:

C/C++:
#pragma omp simd *[clause[[,] clause] ...] new-line*
    for-loops

Fortran:
!$omp simd *[clause[[,] clause] ...] new-line*
    do-loops
[!$omp end simd]

The simd construct closely follows the idea and syntax of the existing worksharing constructs. It supports several clauses that we will cover in Section 4.3. The loop header of the associated for or do loop must obey the same restrictions as for the existing worksharing constructs. These restrictions enable the OpenMP compiler to determine the iteration space of the loop upfront and distribute it accordingly to fit the vectorization.

4.2   Vectorization and Parallelization

In line with the existing combined parallel worksharing constructs, we define a set of combined simd constructs:

C/C++
#pragma omp simd for *[clause[[,] clause] ...] new-line*
    for-loops
#pragma omp parallel simd for *[clause[[,] clause] ...] new-line*
    for-loops

Fortran:
```
!$omp simd do [clause[[,] clause] ...] new-line
    do-loops
[!$omp end simd do ]
!$omp parallel simd do [clause[[,] clause] ...] new-line
    do-loops
[!$omp end parallel simd do ]
```

While the simd construct vectorizes sequential loops, the simd for construct combines the semantics of the for and simd constructs in a single construct. It vectorizes a loop and distributes it across the binding thread set. The simd for construct may appear anywhere the for worksharing construct may be and supports all clauses of the for worksharing construct.

The combined constructs go beyond mere syntactical sugar. The combined simd for slightly changes the semantics of the optional chunk size of the scheduling clause. In simd worksharing constructs, the chunk size refers to the chunk size after vectorization has been applied. That is, a loop chunk is created after the loop has been distributed across the SIMD registers.

4.3   Additional Vectorization Clauses

To further influence the behavior of the simd construct, we define clauses to control data visibility, vector length, induction variables, and memory alignment. All clauses are optional and only need to be used when the compiler does not recognize a vectorization pattern or if programmers want to override the defaults of the simd construct.

Data Sharing Clauses.   All OpenMP data-sharing clauses are available to control the visibility and sharing of variables for vectorized loops. We extend the semantics of the clauses to match the requirements of vectorization. The private clause creates an uninitialized vector for the given variables. The firstprivate clause promotes variables to private vectors that are initialized with values from outside the loop. With lastprivate, a private vector is created and the variable's value in the last loop iteration is retained. The reduction clause creates a private copy of the variable and horizontally aggregates partial values of a vector into a global, scalar reduction result.

Controlling the Vector Length.   The default vector length can be specified through the vectorlength and vectorlengthfor clauses. If the compiler cannot determine the correct vector length (e. g., due to loop-carried dependencies), the programmer may use vectorlength to enable vectorization. The value for vectorlength must be of an integral compile-time constant and depends on the data type used for computation and the distance of the loop-carried dependency (if any). It must also be a power of two (e. g., 2, 4, 8). For instance, a loop working on double values would select 4 as the vector length when compiling for a processor with support for Intel AVX. The vectorlengthfor clause helps identify the correct vector length for a given data type. It accepts a data type of the base language as its argument and automatically chooses the vector length to fit the machine architecture.

The vector length may be a multiple of the machine vector length. In this case, the compiler may apply double-pumping, triple-pumping, or quad-pumping that emulates longer vectors by fusing multiple vector registers into a larger logical vector register.

Induction Variables. Induction variables are variables whose value linearly depends on the loop counter of a loop. With the linear clause, a programmer can specify a set of variables that shall be considered induction variables across loop iterations. For each variable, the linear clause accepts the identifier and an increment:

simd-construct linear (*identifier[:increment] [, identifier[:increment] ...]*)

The increment can either be a compile-time constant or a variable. When the compiler vectorizes the loop, the compiler generates vectors that contain the induction values for the current loop chunk and makes sure that the vector is updated accordingly along the loop iteration space.

Data Alignment. Data alignment is important since most platforms can load aligned data much faster than unaligned data. This especially applies to vectors. Yet, compilers are in general not able to detect the alignment properties of data across all modules of a program. Compilers, thus, have to react conservatively and emit code that uses only unaligned loads and stores. Hence, we define the align clause to explicitly provide this knowledge to the compiler:

simd-construct align (*identifier[:alignment] [, identifier[:alignment] ...]*)

For each identifier in the list of the align clause, the programmer can specify the alignment properties. If the alignment is omitted, the default is the standard alignment for vectors on the target platform (e. g., 16 B for Intel SSE).

Forced Vectorization. The simd construct implies that the associated loop or function is always vectorized by the OpenMP compiler. If the compiler cannot vectorize the code for some reason (e. g., a too complex code pattern), it should abort compilation and emit a diagnostic message to inform the programmer. This can help programmers avoid an unexpected performance behavior and reduce the (performance) debugging effort. To further control this behavior, we define the noassert clause to specify that the programmer does not want to get notified about the vectorization process of the associated code in any case (e. g., if asserts have been turned on globally by means of a compiler switch). Simarly, the assert clause can be used by the programmer to turn on notifications if the compiler cannot vectorize a loop (or function) and notifications have been turned off on a global scale.

4.4   Vectorizing Functions

Functions that are called from a to-be-vectorized loop need special treatment to successfully vectorize the whole loop. Fig. 3 shows an example of a loop that calls into the functions min and distsq. Since the code will be vectorized over the arrays a, b, c, and d, the functions min and distsq can no longer have scalar arguments. They

```
1 #pragma omp simd(min) nomask
2 float min(float a, float b) {
3     return a < b ? a : b;
4 }
5
6 #pragma omp simd(distsq) nomask
7 float distsq(float x, float y) {
8     return (x − y) * (x − y);
9 }
10
11 void example() {
12 #pragma omp parallel simd for
13     for (i=0; i<N; i++) {
14         d[i] = min(distsq(a[i], b[i]), c[i]);
15     }
16 }
```

Fig. 3. Vectorization of a loop with calls into functions

instead need to accept arguments that constitute a full vector of input parameters. Similarly, functions can no longer return a scalar value but must return a vector of values.

To guide the compiler on which functions to vectorize, we allow the simd directive to also annotate function declarations and definitions. The directive instructs the compiler to create a scalar version of the function definition and to also create versions of the function that accept vector arguments and that return a vector of return values. The compiler must generate both versions as the scalar version could be used in a different compilation unit. Besides the vectorlength, vectorlengthfor, linear, and align clauses, the simd directive for function annotation accepts two additional clauses to guide the compiler on how to vectorize the function.

The default behavior when vectorizing a function is that a particular formal parameter of the function should be promoted to a vectorized function argument. For the example code in Fig. 3, the compiler would promote a and b of min to vector registers. In some cases, however, it might be desired to replicate a scalar parameter into the vector register during promotion. The uniform clause lets the programmer override the default behavior for a parameter and switch to (conceptual) replication.

To support conditionals in vectorized loops, two implementations of functions are provided: one especially suitable for conditional invocation (i. e., masked), and another especially suitable for unconditional invocation (i. e., unmasked). If all invocations at call sites of the function are conditional, generation of the unmasked implementation can be suppressed using the mask clause. Similarly, if all invocations are unconditional, generation of the masked implementation can be suppressed using the nomask clause. Using both clauses together has no effect: both implementations are provided in this case. With these clauses, programmers may reduce the code size of the application.

5   Implementation

The implementation of the SIMD directives for OpenMP is based on the existing implementation of Intel® Cilk™ Plus. Intel Cilk Plus defines a set of SIMD pragmas for

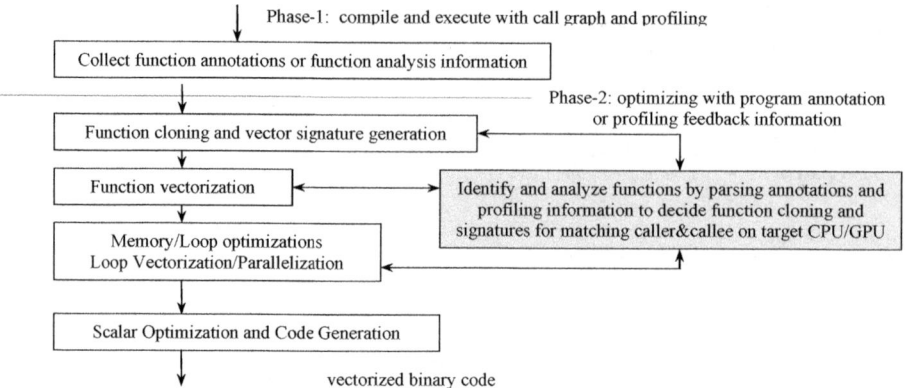

Fig. 4. Compilation infrastructure of the SIMD directives in ICC [22]

guided vectorization and the implementation can be reused for the OpenMP SIMD directives. We do not rely on anything that comes from the multi-threading features of Cilk Plus.

In addition to the implementation in the Intel® Composer, there exist two additional implementations. The Mercurium compiler [3] has been extended [2] with OpenMP SIMD directives and can be used as a research prototype. The Cilk Plus runtime has also been ported to the GNU Compiler Collection 4.7 [6] and can be used as the basis to adopt OpenMP SIMD directives in other compilers.

Since the details of the Cilk Plus implementation of SIMD pragmas can be found in [22], we restrict ourselves to sketch the ideas of the implementation and refer to [22] for the details.

For each vectorized function with a simd directive, the compiler applies multi-versioning and emits several variants of the function to support different vectorization schemes as well as the original scalar code. Creating the scalar code is important not to break (non-vectorized) code that imports symbols from other compilation units. A name-mangling scheme uniquely identifies the created variants so that they can safely be linked into the final executable. At the call site, the compiler searches for the function definition and recreates the mangled name from the usage in the vectorized code.

Masking support for a vector function is implemented by adding a hidden formal parameter that contains a boolean. An added if statement only performs the computation of the function when the boolean is *true*. During vectorization, this boolean is promoted to a vector of booleans to only apply the function to those vector elements for which the mask bit is set to *true*.

When a uniform or linear clause is present, the compiler does not promote the parameter to a vector, but instead keeps the scalar parameter. For uniform parameters, the compiler uses a scalar register to store the runtime value. If the uniform parameter is a pointer then the compiler can take this (scalar) address as the base address for vector loads and stores. A linear clause directs the compiler to use scalar loads/stores and to assume that data referenced by the `linear` parameter is stored in memory with the stride specified at the clause (unit stride by default).

The compiler can automatically determine the correct value for `vectorlength` in most cases. From the data type used in the computation and the target machine instruction set, the compiler can deduce the vector length (e. g., 2 for double-precision with SSE or 8 for single-precision with AVX). Specifying a `vectorlength` that is a multiple of a vector length instructs the compiler to use double-pumping or quad-pumping, that is, to fuse multiple physical registers into a single virtual register. For mixed-type computations, e. g., single-precision and double-precision, it needs to find a common virtual vector length that suits both data types. For instance, double-pumping might be applied to the double-precision registers, while a single physical register is used for single-precision values.

6 Evaluation

To document the benefits of adding the OpenMP SIMD directives, we conduct a series of benchmarks. The benchmarks have been selected to reflect different application domains and to correspond to typical HPC-type applications.

6.1 Methodology

We use the following experimental setup for our evaluation. The benchmarking system is a dual-socket Intel® Xeon® X5680 processor with 3.33 GHz, Hyper-Threading technology, and 24 GB main memory (at 1333 GHz). The machine runs RedHat* Enterprise Linux* 6.0 (kernel 2.6.32-71). We use the GNU Compiler Collection (GCC, version 4.6.2) and the Intel® C++ Composer XE for Linux (ICC, version 2011 SP1) with support for SIMD directives to compile the benchmarks.

To rule out machine effects and jitter, we run each benchmark ten times and take the average of the runs as the timing result. We use GCC as the baseline performance for the evaluation. The results are normalized against this baseline and we show the relative speed-up compared to the GCC baseline.

6.2 Benchmarks

We have evaluated our proposal using the following benchmarks from different application domains:

Mandelbrot computes the well-known mandelbrot set by testing a progression of complex numbers for convergence. The convergence test makes Mandelbrot a difficult code for an auto-vectorizer. The input size is 4,000x4,000.

Volume Rendering is a typical kernel from graphics processing. It contains several conditional tests, which inhibit optimal auto-vectorization. The benchmark uses 40,960 rays for rendering.

Blackscholes implements a version of the Black-Scholes model used in the financial sector for option pricing. Although it is a data-parallel problem, the auto-vectorizer

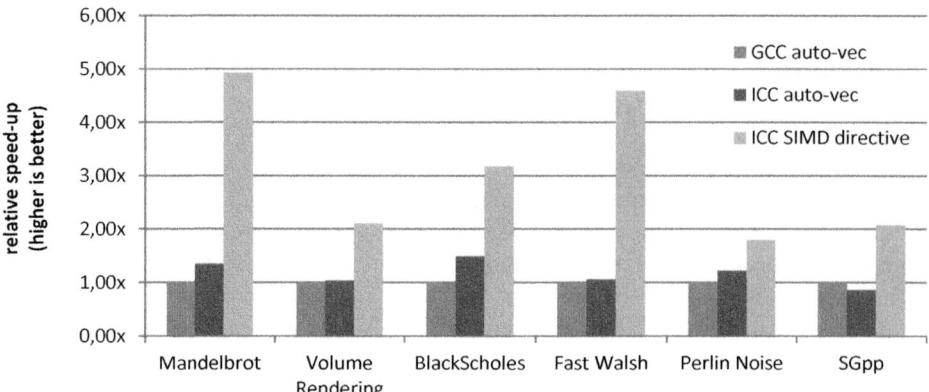

Fig. 5. Relative speed-up of the benchmarks over GCC auto-vectorization baseline

cannot properly vectorize the code because it suspects data dependencies. The benchmark is tested with an input data size of 16,000x16,000 SP floating-point elements.

Fast Walsh Transform performs a dyadic convolution, a transformation based on the Fourier transformation with applicability to electrical engineering and numerical theory. This benchmark is tested in single-precision using 67,108,864 elements as input data.

Perlin Noise is an image filter to increase realism in computer graphics. The computation is performed using SP floating-point numbers while the image is stored using unsigned-char data types. We use an image size of 10,240x10,240 pixels.

SG++ is a DP kernel that uses sparse adaptive grids [8] for data-mining to learn and predict properties of data. Due to the non-linear nature of the code, auto-vectorizers fail and manual vectorization becomes necessary. We use a 5-dimensional data set that consists of 10,000 training data points and 38,400 analysis data points.

6.3   Results

The normalized performance of the benchmarks is shown in Fig. 5. It compares GCC's and ICC's auto-vectorizer performance with the peformance of the OpenMP SIMD directives. Fig. 6 compares the performance of ICC only to rule out improvements because of different compiler optimizations.

Mandelbrot cannot be auto-vectorized by neither GCC nor ICC. The compilers are not able to properly detect the structure of the loop and to vectorize the function invocation for the convergence check. If the OpenMP SIMD directives are added to the code, the compiler receives enough knowledge about the code structure so that it can replicate the convergence check into a vectorized function. With the vectorized function body it becomes possible to vectorize the parallel loop. This immediately pays off in a 3.33x performance improvement over the non-vectorized version compiled by ICC.

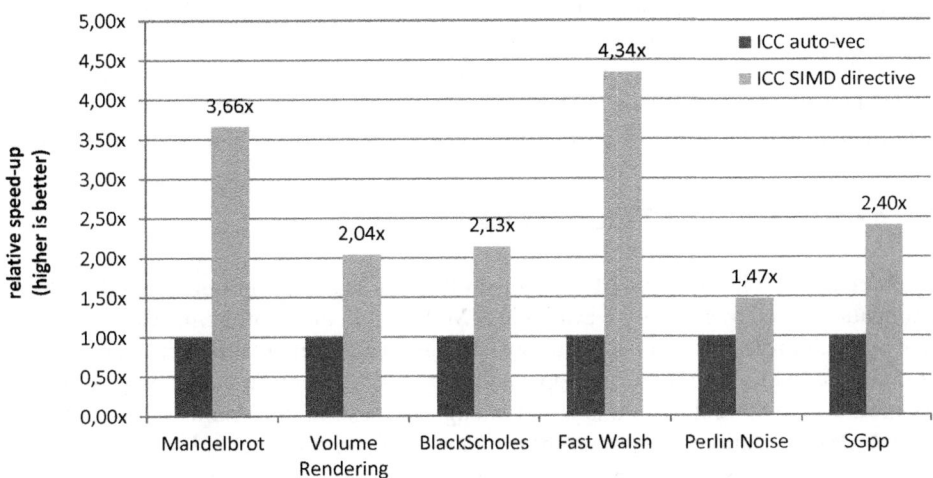

Fig. 6. Relative speed-up of the benchmarks over ICC auto-vectorization baseline

Volume Rendering suffers from the same auto-vectorizer problems. Due to the code structure with loops spread over different functions and the complex control flow, the compilers fail to auto-vectorize the code. Adding the OpenMP SIMD directives helps to gain about a 2x speed-up with vectorization.

Blackscholes contains two nested loops with calls into math functions (square root, exponentials, and logarithms). Because of the mathematical functions, GCC cannot auto-vectorize the code. ICC assumes data dependencies that inhibit auto-vectorization; the speed-up of 1.50x over GCC is due to the optimized mathematical functions that ship with ICC. Adding the SIMD directives to the non-vectorized loops overrules ICC's data dependency analysis and also enables the vectorized version of the mathematical functions. This yields a speed-up of 2.13x over the non-vectorized ICC version.

The *Fast Walsh Transform* contains a loop structure of three nested loops. The number of iterations of the outer-most loop decreases logarithmically; the middle loop is running with stride one but the upper bound depends on the outer loop. The inner-most loop runs backwards and the trip count also depends on the outer loop. The automatic vectorization fails to detect that the loop can be vectorized. Adding the SIMD directive to the inner-most loop enables ICC to vectorize and to achieve a 4x better performance.

Perlin Noise is the most complex benchmark. It contains SP and unsigned-char computation in the same loop. The mixture of data types makes it hard for the compiler to vectorize the code, since different data types correspond to different vector lengths. To equalize the vector length, virtual vector registers need to be used by fusing two or more physical registers (double pumping or quad pumping). Without SIMD directives, ICC only generated slightly better code than GCC. The SIMD directives enable ICC to generate better code, but still there is headroom for improvement, since ICC does not fully exploit double and quad pumping at present.

SG^{++} is too complex for the auto-vectorizers. The outer-most loop is well-suited for parallelization due to its large trip count. The trip count of the inner-most loop is too low for vectorization (number of dimensions). The middle loop is the best target for vectorization. However, the non-linear kernel prevents auto-vectorization; the compiler is not able to detect that a reduction variable across the non-linear kernel can be promoted to a vector. With the added SIMD directives, we can force the compiler to make this change and to gain a 2.08x speed-up over the ICC and GCC non-vectorized codes.

7   Conclusions and Future Work

In order to exploit all levels of parallelism that are available in current architectures applications need to exploit the available SIMD level in many of them. We have shown that while auto-vectorization technology has significantly improved over the years, it is still not possible to vectorize all loops. Although the `for` construct can help compilers to know where to vectorize, this is not enough because of constraints imposed by the OpenMP specification and because of limitations of compiler technology.

To overcome this limitation, we have presented a proposal for a new OpenMP directive: the `simd` directive. This directive allows the programmer to instruct the compiler which loops should be vectorized, and also give some other information by means of the clauses to allow for better vectorization. This directive can also be applied to function declarations so the compiler emits vector-enabled versions of those function to use them from vectorized loops.

Our evaluation with a set of benchmarks shows how the use of this directive can give significant improvements over the auto-vectorizer of a production compiler.

In the future, we expect to improve our vector code generation for different cases (such as when the loop uses different data types) and test the portability of the directive across different platforms. We also want to try different combinations on the order of cutting chunks and vectorization of loop iterations.

Acknowledgments.   * Other brands and names are the property of their respective owners.

Intel, Xeon, and Cilk are trademarks or registered trademarks of Intel Corporation or its subsidiaries in the United States and other countries.

We would like to acknowledge the support of the European Commission through the ENCORE project (FP7-248647), and the support of the Spanish Ministry of Education (contracts TIN2007-60625, CSD2007-00050), and the Generalitat de Catalunya (contract 2009-SGR-980).

References

1. Borkar, S., Chien, A.A.: The Future of Microprocessors. Communications of the ACM 54(5), 67–77 (2011)
2. Caballero, D.L.: User-directed Vectorization in OmpSs. Master's thesis, Universitat Politècnica de Catalunya, Barcelona, Spain (September 2011)
3. Barcelona Supercomputing Center. The NANOS Group Site: The Mercurium Compiler, http://nanos.ac.upc.edu/mcxx

4. Omer Cheema, M., Hammami, O.: Application-specific SIMD Synthesis for Reconfigurable Architectures. Microprocessors and Microsystems 30(6), 398–412 (2006)
5. Eichenberger, A.E., Wu, P., O'Brien, K.: Vectorization for SIMD Architectures with Alignment Constraints. In: Proc. of the ACM SIGPLAN 2004 Conf. on Programming Language Design and Implementation, Washington, D.C, pp. 82–93 (June 2004)
6. Free Software Foundation Inc. GCC 4.7 Release Series (March 2012), `http://gcc.gnu.org/gcc-4.7/`
7. Heinecke, A., Klemm, M., Bungartz, H.-J.: From GPGPUs to Many-Core: NVIDIA Fermi* and Intel® Many Integrated Core Architecture. Computing in Science and Engineering (to appear, 2012)
8. Heinecke, A., Pflüger, D.: Multi- and many-core data mining with adaptive sparse grids. In: Proc. of the 8th ACM Intl. Conf. on Computing Frontiers, New York, pp. 29:1–29:10 (May 2011)
9. Intel Corporation. Intel® Advanced Vector Extensions Programming Reference, Document number 319433-011 (June 2011)
10. Karrenberg, R., Hack, S.: Whole-Function Vectorization. In: Proc. of the 9th Intl. Ann. IEEE/ACM Symp. on Code Generation and Optimization, Charmonix, France, pp. 141–150 (April 2011)
11. Khronos OpenCL Working Group. The OpenCL Specification (February 2009), `http://www.khronos.org/registry/cl/`
12. Krzikalla, O., Feldhoff, K., Müller-Pfefferkorn, R., Nagel, W.E.: Auto-Vectorization Techniques for Modern SIMD Architectures. In: Proc. of the 16th Workshop on Compilers for Parallel Computing, Padova, Italy (January 2012)
13. Larsen, S., Amarasinghe, S.: Exploiting Superword Level Parallelism with Multimedia Instruction Sets. In: Proc. of the ACM SIGPLAN 2000 Conf. on Programming Language Design and Implementation, Vancouver, BC, Canada, pp. 145–156 (June 2000)
14. Maleki, S., Gao, Y., Garzarán, M.J., Wong, T., Padua, D.A.: An Evaluation of Vectorizing Compilers. In: Proc. of the 2011 Intl. Conf. on Parallel Architectures and Compilation Techniques, Galveston Island, TX, pp. 372–382 (October 2011)
15. Naishlos, D., Biberstein, M., Ben-David, S., Zaks, A.: Vectorizing for a SIMdD DSP architecture. In: Proc. of the 2003 Intl. Conf. on Compilers, Architecture and Synthesis for Embedded Systems, San Jose, CA, pp. 2–11 (October 2003)
16. Naishlos, D., Biberstein, M., Zaks, A.: Compiler Vectorization Techniques for a Disjoint SIMD Architecture. Technical Report H-0146, IBM Research Division, Haifa, Israel (November 2002)
17. Nuzman, D., Henderson, R.: Multi-platform Auto-vectorization. In: Proc. of the 4th Ann. IEEE/ACM Intl. Symp. on Code Generation and Optimization, New York, pp. 281–294 (March 2006)
18. Nuzman, D., Rosen, I., Zaks, A.: Auto-vectorization of Interleaved Data for SIMD. In: Proc. of the 2006 ACM SIGPLAN Conf. on Programming Language Design and Implementation, Ottawa, ON, Canada, pp. 132–143 (June 2006)
19. Nuzman, D., Zaks, A.: Outer-loop Vectorization: Revisited for Short SIMD Architectures. In: Proc. of the 17th Intl. Conf. on Parallel Architectures and Compilation Techniques, Toronto, ON, Canada, pp. 2–11 (October 2008)
20. OpenMP Architecture Review Board. OpenMP Application Program Interface, Version 3.1 (July 2011), `http://www.openmp.org/`
21. Sutter, H.: The Free Lunch Is Over—A Fundamental Turn Toward Concurrency in Software. Dr. Dobb's Journal 30(3) (March 2005)

22. Tian, X., Saito, H., Preis, S.V., Kozhukhov, S.S., Cherkasov, A.G., Nelson, C., Panchenko, N., Geva, R.: Compiling C/C++ SIMD Extensions for Function and Loop Vectorization on Multicore-SIMD Processors. In: Multicore and GPU Programming Models, Languages and Compilers Workshop (Submitted for peer review)
23. Wu, P., Eichenberger, A.E., Wang, A.: Efficient SIMD Code Generation for Runtime Alignment and Length Conversion. In: Proc. of the 3rd Ann. IEEE/ACM Intl. Symp. on Code Generation and Optimization, Jan Jose, CA, pp. 153–164 (March 2005)
24. Wu, P., Eichenberger, A.E., Wang, A., Zhao, P.: An Integrated Simdization Framework Using Virtual Vectors. In: Proc. of the 19th Annual Intl. Conf. on Supercomputing, Boston, MA, USA, pp. 169–178 (June 2005)

Introducing Task Cancellation to OpenMP

Oussama Tahan[1], Mats Brorsson[2], and Mohamed Shawky[1]

[1] Heudiasyc-UMR 7253 Université de Technologie de Compiègne, Compiègne, France
{oussama.tahan,shawky}@hds.utc.fr
[2] KTH Royal Institute of Technology, Stockholm, Sweden
matsbror@kth.se

Abstract. Multi-core processors are at the heart of current and future trends for computer architectures. The number of cores on a single chip is rapidly increasing, so as the need for simpler and more efficient programming models. OpenMP is a powerful programming model that has been adopted by a large spectrum of research and development teams to develop parallel applications on multi-core processors. To fully exploit the available cores in multi-cores chips, the latest versions of OpenMP specification marked a transition from a thread-centric to a task-centric programming model. Hence, tasks are used to express parallelism and to execute concurrent computations. However, this programming model suffers from the lack of a useful feature where created tasks can be explicitly cancelled. Task cancellation is considered an important aspect in programs based on speculative execution and search algorithms, where computation resources should be quickly released if not needed, yielding higher computation efficiency and lower power consumption. In this paper, we present a proposal and an enhancement to the OpenMP programming model that allows users to create special type of tasks called "cancellable tasks". New easy to use extensions are added in order to support both cooperative and forced cancellation of these special tasks through specific cancellation calls. We will show that these extensions reduce execution time and response delays of parallel applications that may need cancellation and prompt resources re-allocation compared to the user cancellation approach based on flags.

Keywords: Multi-Core Processors, Parallel Programming Models, OpenMP, Task Cancellation.

1 Introduction

Today, OpenMP is a widely used shared memory parallel programming model. In 2008 Ayguadé et al. [7] presented the design of adding a task-centric programming model to OpenMP. This model has given programmers the ability to explicitly create a task that can be immediately executed on one or several existing threads or it can be deferred for a later execution. This programming model has shown more flexibility and simplicity in expressing parallelism than the previous thread-centric model (OpenMP up to version 2.5). In addition, it

B.M. Chapman et al. (Eds.): IWOMP 2012, LNCS 7312, pp. 73–87, 2012.

turns out to be more efficient in many cases since unbalanced computations and workloads are simply and effectively dealt with when using tasks while dealing with these issues was not possible with the previous model.

However, an interesting aspect of task management has not yet been studied or taken into account in the task-based model which is task cancellation. Many programs are based today on parameter sweep applications, parameterized and search algorithms, N-version programming methodologies and application level speculative executions [10]; therefore, task cancellation is an essential feature to deal efficiently with this kind of algorithms.

We introduce in this paper a new compiler and runtime approach that adds extensions to the OpenMP tasking model in which programmers will have the ability to create applications containing cancellable tasks and group of tasks through specific constructs extensions. In addition, programmers will also be able to cancel these groups of tasks before they start their execution, immediately or at specific scheduling points. To present our contribution, this paper is structured as follows: In the following section we present some related work to task cancellation in other task-based programming models and in OpenMP. In Section 3 we present the OpenMP tasking model and the motivation behind building this extension. We then present our proposed extension in Section 4. In Section 5 we present an example and the evaluation of this extension while in Section 6 we conclude and present our future work.

2   Related Work

In order to program multi and many core chips, some other task-based parallel programming languages exist like Intel Cilk Plus, TBB (Intel's Threading Building Blocks), .Net TPL (Task Parallel Library) or PPL (Parallel Pattern Library), Chapel, X10 and Habanero-Java (HJ). Like OpenMP 3.0, these programming models are based on dynamic task parallelism where user defined tasks are used to run computations concurrently. Through our research, we found out that only two of these parallel programming languages have officially introduced task cancellation in their model. These two models are the TBB and the TPL/PPL libraries. However, Perez et al. [6] introduced task cancellation to Cilk++ (a predecessor to Intel Cilk Plus) by relying on the abort library already existing in the Cilk-5 programming model. When an abort procedure is called through a task, the subtree of tasks that has the calling task as root is cancelled; however, only tasks already spawned are cancelled but not future tasks to be spawned [1] and other subtrees spawned from other tasks are not affected.

As for the TBB, cancellation is based on defining and creating groups of tasks that can be cancelled [2]. When the TBB function `cancel_group_execution()` is called by a task, a request for cancellation will be sent for all not yet executed tasks in its own group and subordinate groups. Using the TBB and Cilk-5 cancellation schemes, a task can belong only to one group and when a task calls the cancellation request only tasks from the same group can be cancelled. Therefore, to cancel tasks not belonging to the same team, user-defined shared memory flags must be used. It means that a programmer should implement the comparison of the flags inside of a task and hence a thread has to switch its execution to the new task before cancelling it and the programmer has to explicitly protect the flag from concurrent accesses.

A similar approach has been implemented in the TPL/PPL library where groups of cancellable tasks are explicitly created and defined [3], but like in TBB, a task can only be part of only one user defined cancellable group and tasks already executing cannot be cancelled and hence they should continue their execution until completion or until cancellation is detected through user code. Wong et al. [14] presented an error model for OpenMP that extends the programming model with error handling features. They proposed the *done* construct that a programmer can use to cancel regions like parallel, worksharing and task regions. This approach seems to be useful when a programmer aims to terminate the whole subset of the region in which the cancellation request has been called including the caller itself, or only the innermost region. However, we believe that this model is not efficient for algorithms where only parts of the subset may be requested for cancellation or when tasks can be grouped for cancellation, neither in situations where some tasks should be protected from cancellation. In our work, we propose a cancellation model that takes into consideration these issues not dealt with in the previous proposal by offering several APIs that a programmer can use efficiently for tasks cancellation. In contrast to the cancellation features used in other programming models, we propose in this work an extension to the OpenMP tasking model that allows task cancellation in both cooperative and forced manners. In addition, using our approach, an OpenMP task can belong to one or several cancellable groups to manage task cancellation in a simpler way. Moreover, a task is able to cancel tasks belonging to other groups while avoiding the use of user-defined shared flags. On the other hand, user-level cancellation protection can be applied by an OpenMP programmer to protect portions of a task or the whole task from cancellation.

3   Task Cancellation in OpenMP

In the following sections, we briefly present the OpenMP tasking model and the motivation behind adding task cancellation to OpenMP.

3.1   The OpenMP Tasking Model

The tasking model was added to OpenMP as of specification version 3.0. When a thread encounters the "`#pragma omp task`" directive, a new task is created and immediately executed or pushed in a queue of tasks for later execution. In order to synchronize created tasks, a parent task can wait for its child tasks to finish execution by using the "`#pragma omp taskwait`" directive. The parent task will be stuck at this synchronization point until all child tasks have finished their execution. Different clauses are also used to define variables shared between tasks, or variables private for each task [4].

3.2   The Motivation behind Adding Task Cancellation to OpenMP

Today, many applications are based on algorithms where application level speculative execution is needed, or they rely on search and parameterized algorithms
[10]. All of these algorithms strongly depend on task cancellation in order to have
more efficient execution. Süß and Leopold [11] proposed a cancellation scheme
to OpenMP based on the thread-centric OpenMP model. In their proposal, they
introduced new directives to OpenMP that allow a programmer to simply cancel
threads in a parallel region. However, their method might not be efficient for the
task-centric programming model where only task cancellation may be needed
and not the whole parallel region. In [14], the *done* construct has been proposed
to terminate innermost OpenMP regions depending on the specified clause. This
proposal does not take into account the need to terminate groups of the running
or scheduled tasks neither the need to protect tasks from being cancelled. We
believe that adding task cancellation to OpenMP will improve the efficiency of
this kind of applications and it will allow programmers to easily develop these
programs. Task cancellation is important since first of all, execution time can be
reduced when cancelled tasks release the threads on which they were running
and these threads become available and ready to execute other tasks. On the
other hand, when tasks are cancelled, time spent on synchronization will become
smaller and hence a parent task may be released and may continue executing
sooner.

Moreover, reducing power consumption is increasingly important in order to
obtain good performance with low power consumption. Cancelling tasks can
reduce the power consumed by an application by avoiding unnecessary computations. In addition, cancelling a task can be used to free a thread from a task
that may take too much time to finish or from a task stuck in an endless loop.

Furthermore, when cancelling not yet executed or created tasks, and by detecting through the runtime if a cancellation is requested, we can reduce time
spent by a thread for tasks switching since cancelled tasks do not have to execute and they can be eliminated before being switched to the thread. Currently,
OpenMP programmers may express cancellation through user-defined shared
flags creation and communication; hence, they must ensure that these flags are
always updated in the memory in order to be read correctly by the other tasks
running on other threads to avoid possible deadlocks or extra unnecessary computation. However, using the flush directive is frequently missed by OpenMP
users with little experience [12]. In addition, since these flags are accessed in
both read and write modes in parallel, data races may occur and these latter
may cause incorrect results and unexpected application behavior. To avoid these
data races, atomic or critical accesses should be used. In [12], experiments showed
that the most frequent mistake in OpenMP programming is that programmers
do not take into account concurrent accesses to some variables and hence they
do not protect these shared variables. When implementing a cancellation scheme
within the compiler and the runtime, user-defined flags are not needed anymore
and since protecting and flushing the memory will be automatically done in the
runtime, no deadlocks or extra computation may take place. In addition, flag

polling overheads can be reduced by implicitly replicating the cancellation flag on the existing threads so each thread polls on its own flag. In the following section we present our idea to introduce task cancellation to the OpenMP tasking model.

4   Adding Cancellable Tasks to OpenMP

In our work, we introduced a new type of tasks to OpenMP, which is the cancellable type of tasks. These new cancellable tasks can be destroyed by the programmer during the execution of the program. Our aim is to give the programmer the ability to build in a flexible way, parallel programs containing two different types of tasks; cancellable and non cancellable tasks, and to easily cancel and stop the former ones from executing. Using our proposal, programmers can apply cancellation through either cooperative or non-cooperative way. In order to obtain cancellable tasks, we introduce a new specific type of group of tasks called cancellable group. In an OpenMP program containing more than one cancellable task, several cancellable groups may exist and cancellable tasks will belong to these groups. The programmer can allocate a group for one or several cancellable tasks and these latter can be created and assigned to a specific group anywhere in the program. When a group is cancelled, all tasks that belong to this group should be cancelled. In addition, unlike the cancellation schemes presented in Section 2, a cancellable task can be assigned to one or several cancellable groups at the same time.

4.1   Creating Cancellable Tasks

To create a cancellable task, we propose to add an extension to the OpenMP task creation directive. Through this extension, programmers will be able to specify if a task is cancellable and will assign it to a specific group. In addition, they will also be able to assign a task to several groups at the same time which means that this specific task will be cancelled if at least one of the groups to which it is assigned is cancelled. This will give a programmer the flexibility to cancel a task in several ways without having to assign a new special group for it. The proposed extension is: *cancellable (group #1, group #2, ...)*
Using this cancellable clause, the programmer will indicate if a task is cancellable and will specify the cancellable groups to which this task belongs. These groups are identified by a number specified by the programmer; hence each group will have its own user defined identification number. In a future implementation, we can add extensions to the current implementation to allow programmers easily define a group of tasks (taskgroup) and insert it within the proposed clauses.

The OpenMP directive for creating a cancellable task is proposed as follows:

```
#pragma omp task cancellable (group #1, group #2, ...)
{ do_work();}
```

4.2 Dealing with Nested Tasks

Since nested parallelism is frequent in OpenMP programs based on tasks, and since most applications contain nested tasks, our method should deal with this too; hence, when a parent task is cancelled, its child tasks are cancelled too. In general, when a programmer requests the cancellation of a task, it means that the whole parallel tree of work created by this task should also be cancelled. Therefore we introduced the groups' inheritance in our method which means that child tasks will automatically inherit their parent task's group or groups. The programmer does not have to insert and code this inheritance since it will be automatically detected by the runtime and a child task will inherit the cancellable groups of all its anterior tasks in the tree when created.

4.3 Cancelling Tasks

In order to cancel tasks during the program execution, a programmer must cancel the group in which these tasks have been assigned. Therefore, we propose a new OpenMP function that gives a programmer the ability to cancel the groups of tasks. When cancellation is requested by a task, the programmer should specify which groups of tasks should be cancelled. If no groups were specified for cancellation, all cancellable groups and tasks belonging to them will be cancelled. The programmer can also specify if the cancellation request should be done in a forced way (not finished tasks are forced to stop execution) or in a cooperative way (only not started or created tasks are cancelled). The proposed OpenMP function calls are respectively `int omp_forced_taskscancel (int group #1, int group #2, ...)` and `int omp_coop_taskscancel (int group#1, int group#2, ...)`.

If the return value of these functions is equal to 1, this means that cancellation is successful. If the return value is equal to 0, it means that at least one of the destination groups has already been cancelled while if the value is equal to -1, the cancellation cannot take place.

On the other hand, if a programmer wants to send a cancellation call to a specific group from a task that belongs to this same group, the calling task will also be cancelled with its cancellable group when the call is a forced cancellation. However, the programmer can specify if the task should still be alive and continue its normal execution by using another OpenMP function that we name forced cancellation with exclude. Using this cancellation with exclude, the calling task will ignore its own cancellation request only if the cancelled group or groups do not belong to the list of its inherited groups.

The forced cancellation function with exclude will be as follows:

`int omp_forced_taskscancel_exclude (int group#1, int group#2, ...)`

If the return value of this function is equal to 1, it means that cancellation has succeeded while if the value is equal to 0, it means that at least one of the destination groups has already been cancelled. However, if the return value is equal to -1, this will mean that cancellation cannot take place. This last return value can be obtained in a future implementation when taskgroups will be defined. Cancelling a taskgroup that does not exist may yield to this negative return value.

When a task calls its same group for cancellation we should notice that its child tasks (if there are any) will be belonging to the same group through inheritance, consequently they will be cancelled as well. In order to prevent this from happening when the cancellation with exclude is used, a programmer must ensure that already submitted child tasks have finished execution. If it is not the case, the runtime will implicitly force the task to wait for all its child tasks before sending the group cancellation request. After sending the cancellation call with the exclusion, the new created child tasks will not inherit the group requested to be cancelled and hence they will not be cancellable on that group.

4.4   Protecting Tasks from Cancellation

Using our approach, we allow tasks to be cancelled during their execution through forced cancellation, unlike TBB and TPL libraries where only not yet started tasks are cancelled. However, cancelling some tasks forcefully or even cooperatively may cause deadlocks in a program or prevent tasks from doing some important work like releasing locks, freeing resources or doing some critical functions etc. Therefore, we introduced in our approach a cancellation protection scheme that gives the programmer the ability to specify cancellable tasks or parts of them as unaffected by cancellation.

In order to protect a task from cancellation, we have taken two cases into account. The first one is where a cancellable task should not be cancelled before being created. Therefore, if a task encounters a cancellable task creation procedure, the new task will be created and submitted for execution even if it belongs to an already cancelled group. The second case is when a programmer needs to protect the whole body of a cancellable task or just a part of it from cancellation.

In order to protect a task from being banned from creation, we added another extension to the task creation directive called *locked-on-creation*. This clause will prevent the non creation of a task and it will also prevent the cancellation of the body of this cancellable task when this latter is submitted for execution or has started its execution. This extension can be useful if the child task belongs to a cancellable group but it does some important work like freeing memory resources or releasing a lock. A programmer can create this type of child tasks within a cancellable or non cancellable parent task. If the parent task is cancellable, usually the programmer should ensure that it cannot be interrupted during its execution. This can be done by guaranteeing that the parent task's group will not be forced for cancellation (through application specifications) or by manually locking the parent task from cancellation. However, using our implementation, if the parent task is cancellable and not already locked, it will automatically lock itself for cancellation when creating this type of tasks and it will release itself right after the child task submission. In its current stage, the runtime does not take into account orphaning issues but we intend to bring modifications to the implementation in the future to ensure that all child tasks finished their execution before cancelling the parent task.

In addition, programmers are able to lock cancellable tasks from cancellation within the body of a task through `int omp_cancellabletask_lock(void)` function call and release it through `int omp_cancellabletask_unlock(void)`.

The first function is used to lock and protect the task from cancellation. If the returned value is equal to 1 it means that locking was successful. If the value is equal to 0 it means that the task was already locked while the returned value is equal to -1 if the task could not be locked.

The second function is used to unlock the calling cancellable task. If the return value is equal to 1 it means that unlocking was successful and the task should be cancelled. If it returns 0 it signifies that the task has been unlocked successfully but no cancellation for the task is needed. However, if the return value is equal to -1 it indicates that the calling task was already unlocked while if the return value is equal to -2, it means that unlocking was not successful (e.g., if the calling task is not a cancellable task).When a task is being created inside a protected code, it will also inherit the protection status of its parent task and will be automatically defined as protected.

We also added a new OpenMP runtime function that allows programmers to detect if a task is requested to be cancelled. This extension is the following:

`int omp_iscancelled(int group)`

When a cancellation is requested for the group specified as a parameter of the function, the return value will be equal to 1. However, if the return value is equal to 0, it means that the specified group cancellation has not yet been requested. If the return value is equal to -1 it means that the calling task is not a cancellable type of task.

4.5   When Does Cancellation Take Place?

Our task cancellation method is a combined compiler and runtime system based approach. In order to obtain this new OpenMP feature, we made modifications to the Mercurium source to source compiler and to the Nanos++ runtime system [8][13]. Both the runtime and compiler are developed by the Barcelona Super Computing Center (BSC) and support OpenMP and OmpSs models. OmpSs is an extension to OpenMP that lets programmers express more fine-grained dependences between tasks than the taskwait construct and that supports heterogeneous devices [5]. However, in this paper we only consider the OpenMP model and we do not take into consideration the possible effects of OmpSs.

We have made some modifications to Mercurium in order to detect the new cancellation related directives, clauses and functions that we defined earlier in this paper. We also modified the runtime in order to handle the new functions generated by the source to source compiler.

During its lifetime, an OpenMP task can have one of these statuses:

1. a task may be not yet created or submitted for execution;
2. a task may be created and submitted for execution but not yet executed;
3. a task may be running and being executed by a thread;
4. a task may be synchronizing or sleeping in a queue waiting for a specific condition to release it (like a taskwait construct).
5. a task may already have finished execution;

When a task calls the groups cancellation request, the runtime will check if an older request has already been sent. If this is the first request, a cancellation flag will be enabled, and the requested cancellable groups are registered in the runtime. If no groups were specified through the call, a special flag is enabled to declare that all groups are requested for cancellation. The task cancellation procedure is protected through the runtime by locks and hence, cancellation cannot be done concurrently by more than one task.

When a task encounters a task creation procedure, it will check if the new task is considered as cancellable (user-defined, through inheritance or both), it will verify if the task is protected against cancellation and it will detect the groups to which it is assigned. If the cancellable task is not protected and at least one of its groups is cancelled, this task will not be created. However, if it is protected or none of its groups are cancelled, the task will be created and submitted and it will be assigned to its user defined groups and inherited groups if there are any.

As for the tasks currently running on threads, if the call is a forced cancellation, the calling thread will detect through the runtime if they are cancellable, if they are assigned to the called cancellable groups and if they are unlocked for cancellation. If all these conditions are met, a signal will be sent to the specific threads to stop executing these current running tasks. This signal is sent using the POSIX *pthread_kill* function and will be handled by the destination thread which is forced to discard the currently running task and to pick another task immediately from the tasks queue.

In addition, when at least one of the cancellation flags have been enabled, and if a forced cancellation is called, tasks that are synchronizing or waiting to be executed in the tasks pools and that met the cancellation conditions are removed from the queues and prohibited from execution when picked up by the threads. When a thread picks from the tasks pools a task that belongs to cooperatively cancelled group or groups, this task is cancelled only if it has not yet started.

Interrupting running tasks or cancelling those who already started execution and sleeping in the queues is considered as a forced non cooperative cancellation method and hence resources deallocation is difficult and it may lead to corrupted data. Therefore we consider that programmers should use this method only when they know for sure that applying this forced cancellation to their tasks will not generate faults or incorrect results and behavior in their application.

Algorithm 1. NQueens code using the proposed cancellation scheme

```
1. void find_queens (int size, int goal_number)
2.. { int number_of_solutions, depth=0;
3..    #pragma omp parallel
4.     {
5.       #pragma omp single
6.         {
7.           nqueens(size, &number_of_solutions, goal_number, depth, ...);
8.         } //end single
9.     } //end parallel
10.  } //end find_nqueens

11. void nqueens (int n, int *solutions, int goal, int depth, ... )
12. {
13.    if (depth==n) {
14.    int found_solutions=0;
15.      #pragma omp critical
16.        {
17.          *solutions=*solutions+1;
18.            found_solutions+=*solutions;
19.        } //end critical

20. if ((found_solutions >= goal) && (satisfy_conditions()) && (!omp_iscancelled(1))) {
21.      int cancellation_succeeded=omp_coop_taskscancel (1);
22.        if (cancellation_succeeded)
23.          {//this will execute only once
24.            do_some_work ();
25.            print_found_queens_positions();
26.          } //endif
27.    } //endif
28.    } //end if

29.   for (i=0; i<n; i=i+1) {
30.      #pragma omp task cancellable (1) shared (solutions, goal)
31.        {
32.          if (!omp_iscancelled(1)) {
33.          if (verify_good_position()) nqueens (n, soluttions, goal, depth+1, ...);
34.          } //endif
35.        } //end task
36.    } // endfor

37. #pragma omp taskwait
38. } //end nqueens
```

5   Evaluation of OpenMP Task Cancellation

We have made an initial evaluation of our proposal using the NQueens benchmark from BOTS (Barcelona OpenMP Tasks Suite) [9] developed by the Barcelona Super Computing Center. The benchmark is based on the NQueens problem where all solutions are computed. The purpose of this algorithm is to determine a placement for n queens on an $n \times n$ chessboard where the queens cannot attack each other. In Algorithm1, we show a part of the implementation code of the NQueens benchmark using the proposed OpenMP task cancellation approach. To test our approach, we considered that the benchmark should stop looking for placements when at least a certain number of solutions is found and a certain condition specified by the user is satisfied (line 20 in Algorithm 1). Therefore, when both conditions are satisfied, the rest of the computations should be aborted in order to save computation time and unnecessary power consumption.

In this implementation, we use the cooperative cancellation procedure and hence we do not force the tasks to be cancelled.

Algorithm 2. NQueens cancellation using user-defined flags

```
1. void find_queens (int size, int goal_number)
2..  { int number_of_solutions, depth=0;
3..    #pragma omp parallel
4.     {
5.       #pragma omp single
6.       {
7.         nqueens(size, &number_of_solutions, goal_number, depth, flag, ...);
8.       } //end single
9.     } //end parallel
10.  } //end find_nqueens

11. void nqueens (int n, int *solutions, int goal, int depth, int flag, ... )
12. {
13.    if (depth==n) {int cancellation_succeeded=0;
14.      #pragma omp critical
15.      {
16.        *solutions=*solutions+1;
18.      if ((*solutions >= goal) && (satisfy_conditions()) && (!flag)) {
19.      flag+=1; //conditions satisfied, raise flag
20.      cancellation_succeeded+=1;
21.      } //end if
22.      }//end critical, flushes are implicitly defined at entry and exit of the critical section

23.        if (cancellation_succeeded)
24.          {//this will execute only once
25.            do_some_work ();
26.            print_found_queens_positions();
27.          } //endif
28.      } //endif

29.    for (i=0; i<n; i=i+1) {
30.        int temp=0;
31.        #pragma omp critical
32.        temp=flag;
33.        if (temp!=1)
34.      #pragma omp task shared (solutions, flag)
35.      {
36.          int temp=0;
37.          #pragma omp critical
38.          temp=flag;
39.          if (temp!=1) {
40.          if (verify_good_position()) nqueens (n, soluttions, goal, depth+1, ...);
41.          } //endif
42.      } //end task
43.      } // endfor

44. #pragma omp taskwait
45. } //end nqueens
```

From an algorithmic point of view, using the cancellation scheme is considered more efficient than letting the user define and compare flags. When using flags, programmers should insert the flush directive in several parts of the code to make sure that the flag is updated in the shared memory and that other threads are reading the newest value from it. In addition, since the flag may be read and written in parallel, the programmer has to protect this variable from concurrent read/write accesses in order to prevent any race conditions. Locks, *atomic* or *critical* constructs should be used for this purpose. Our implementation offers these protections and flushes implicitly within the proposed extensions. In Algorithm2, we show the NQueens benchmark that uses a flag to enable cancellation and uses critical sections to protect this shared flag (flushing the memory is implicitly done in critical sections).

On the other hand, we have evaluated the performance of the approach by running NQueens on a Sun Fire X4600 server running Linux CentOS with 8 Dual Core AMD Opteron(tm) 8218 Processors at a clock speed of 2.6 GHz and employing a NUMA architecture with 32 GB of memory. We have tested our method on the *test* inputs of the NQueens benchmark using different numbers of threads (maximum 16) and by applying a breadth-first tasks scheduling policy. We compared the performance of the application to the intitial benchmark with the initial implementation where there are no checking for cancellation requests. Our implementation brought 4% overhead to the execution time. This overhead is mainly due to the costs of task groups' inheritance and to the overheads of polling of the cancellation flags. We noticed that this overhead tends to increase with larger input sets; studying in details the inputs size effect on performance and memory usage will be the subject of future works. However, compared to the user-defined cancellation approach, our method offers better performance and response time when cancellation is requested, with a speed-up that increases with the increasing number of threads and with the growing number of tasks to cancel.

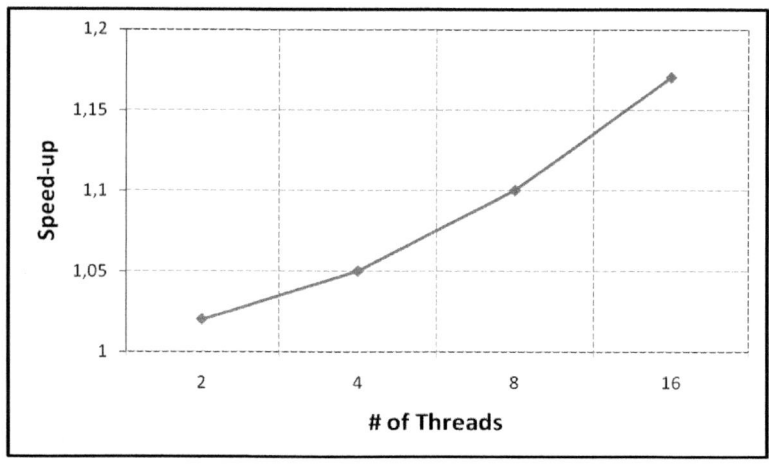

Fig. 1. NQueens speed-up using runtime cancellation over using user-defined flags

In Figure1, we can notice that execution time speed-up is almost 2% when running the benchmark on two threads, and it increases with the growing number of threads to achieve a 17% speedup on 16 threads. The proposed approach brought an improvement in performance because cancelling tasks waiting in the queue does not require tasks context switching before being cancelled, they are checked for cancellation and cancelled immediately when dequeued. On the other hand, when cancellation is requested, threads rush to pick tasks from the queue more frequently because the executed cancellable tasks become very fine grained and hence they lead to contention in the task queue which also causes a higher response time for cancellation. In addition, polling of one user-defined flag may also cause loss in performance specially when protecting the flag within a critical region. This overhead is reduced using the new implementation since each thread polls on its own flag. But in this study, we do not evaluate and compare the different overheads produced when inserting critical regions or any other memory protection mechanisms and we leave it for future work.

6 Conclusion and Future Work

In this paper, we presented new extensions to the OpenMP task-centric programming model that gives programmers the possibility to easily code parallel applications where task cancellation is necessary and where fast resource reallocation is important for better efficiency. This approach can also be used for applications where users can cancel work through an interface for example.

```
// create a cancelable task belonging to the list of groups specified between  parentheses
#pragma omp task cancellable groups(...)

// cooperatively cancel tasks and child tasks belonging to the list of groups specified between parentheses
int omp_coop_taskscancel (int group#1, int group#2, ...)

// force  the cancellation of tasks and child tasks belonging to the list of groups specified between parentheses
int omp_forced_taskscancel (int group #1, int group #2, ...)

// force cancellation of groups between parentheses and ignore the request of cancellation of the calling task
int omp_forced_taskscancel_exclude (int group#1, int group#2, ...)

// the locked-on-creation is used to protect the task from being canceled
#pragma omp task  locked-on-creation cancellable groups (...)

// protect the calling task from being forced for cancellation
int omp_cancellabletask_lock (void)

// allow the calling task to be forced for cancellation
int omp_cancellabletask_unlock (void)

// detect if a task has been requested to be canceled
int omp_iscancelled (int group)
```

Fig. 2. Suggested OpenMP Task Cancellation Directives

These extensions are based on several new directives and runtime functions that create cancellable protected and unprotected tasks, and assign them to cancellable groups of tasks that can be cooperatively or forcefully cancelled through runtime specific calls. The suggested directives and clauses are shown in Figure2. Our proposed method is simple and straightforward and easily understandable by programmers. We showed also its improvements compared to applying user defined flags.

In our future work, we would like to analyze more benchmarks using cooperative or forced cancellation scheme. We will study methods to enable resources deallocation and ensure clean region and program exit. We will also add extensions that allow tasks to dynamically switch groups of cancellation and to enable or disable task cancellation in parallel regions. We will also scrutinize the effects of the different input sizes on performances and we will analyze other tasks scheduling policies effects on the performance of our proposal.

References

1. The Cilk Project: Cilk5 Specifications (2010),
   http://supertech.csail.mit.edu/cilk/manual-5.4.6.pdf
2. Intel Threading Building Blocks for Open Source: TBB Specifications (2012),
   http://threadingbuildingblocks.org/documentation.php
3. Microsoft MSDN Library: Cancellation in the PPL (2012),
   http://msdn.microsoft.com/en-us/library/dd984117.aspx
4. OpenMP Architecture Review Board: OpenMP Specifications (2011),
   http://www.openmp.org/specs
5. Programming Models at BSC: The OmpSs Programming Model (2012),
   https://pm.bsc.es/content/ompss-programming-model
6. Perez, R., Malecha, G.: Speculative Parallelism in Cilk++ (2010),
   http://courses.csail.mit.edu/6.884/spring10/
   projects/rmperez-gmalecha_paper.pdf
7. Ayguadé, E., Copty, N., Duran, A., Hoeflinger, J., Lin, Y., Massaioli, F., Teruel, X., Unnikrishnan, P., Zhang, G.: The Design of OpenMP Tasks. IEEE Trans. Parallel Distrib. Syst. 20, 404–418 (2009)
8. Balart, J., Duran, A., Gonzàlez, M., Martorell, X., Ayguadé, E., Labarta, J.: Nanos Mercurium: a Research Compiler for OpenMP. In: European Workshop on OpenMP (EWOMP 2004), pp. 103–109 (2004)
9. Duran, A., Teruel, X., Ferrer, R., Martorell, X., Ayguade, E.: Barcelona OpenMP Tasks Suite: A Set of Benchmarks Targeting the Exploitation of Task Parallelism in OpenMP. In: Proceedings of the 2009 International Conference on Parallel Processing, ICPP 2009, pp. 124–131. IEEE Computer Society, Washington, DC (2009)
10. Prabhu, P., Ramalingam, G., Vaswani, K.: Safe Programmable Speculative Parallelism. In: Proceedings of the 2010 ACM SIGPLAN Conference on Programming Language Design and Implementation, PLDI 2010, pp. 50–61. ACM, New York (2010)
11. Süß, M., Leopold, C.: Implementing Irregular Parallel Algorithms with OpenMP. In: Nagel, W.E., Walter, W.V., Lehner, W. (eds.) Euro-Par 2006. LNCS, vol. 4128, pp. 635–644. Springer, Heidelberg (2006)

12. Süß, M., Leopold, C.: Common Mistakes in OpenMP and How to Avoid Them: A Collection of Best Practices. In: Mueller, M.S., Chapman, B.M., de Supinski, B.R., Malony, A.D., Voss, M. (eds.) IWOMP 2005 and IWOMP 2006. LNCS, vol. 4315, pp. 312–323. Springer, Heidelberg (2008)
13. Teruel, X., Martorell, X., Duran, A., Ferrer, R., Ayguadé, E.: Support for OpenMP Tasks in Nanos v4. In: Proceedings of the 2007 Conference of the Center for Advanced Studies on Collaborative Research, CASCON 2007, pp. 256–259. ACM, New York (2007)
14. Wong, M., Klemm, M., Duran, A., Mattson, T., Haab, G., de Supinski, B.R., Churbanov, A.: Towards an Error Model for OpenMP. In: Sato, M., Hanawa, T., Müller, M.S., Chapman, B.M., de Supinski, B.R. (eds.) IWOMP 2010. LNCS, vol. 6132, pp. 70–82. Springer, Heidelberg (2010)

Automatic OpenMP Loop Scheduling: A Combined Compiler and Runtime Approach*

Peter Thoman, Herbert Jordan, Simone Pellegrini, and Thomas Fahringer

University of Innsbruck,
Distributed and Parallel Systems Group,
A6020 Innsbruck, Austria
peter.thoman@uibk.ac.at

Abstract. The scheduling of parallel loops in OpenMP has been a research topic for over a decade. While many methods have been proposed, most focus on adapting the loop schedule purely at runtime, and without regard for the overall system state. We present a fully automatic loop scheduling policy that can adapt to both the characteristics of the input program as well as the current runtime behaviour of the system, including external load. Using state of the art polyhedral compiler analysis, we generate *effort estimation functions* that are then used by the runtime system to derive the optimal loop schedule for a given loop, work group size, iteration range and system state. We demonstrate performance improvements of up to 82% compared to default scheduling in an unloaded scenario, and up to 471% in a scenario with external load. We further show that even in the worst case, the results achieved by our automated system stay within 3% of the performance of a manually tuned strategy.

1 Introduction

OpenMP [1] is one of the most widely used languages for programming shared memory systems, particularly in the field of High Performance Computing (HPC). Despite the introduction of task-based parallelism in recent versions of the standard [5], loop parallelism remains a very important part of most OpenMP programs. Thus, the question of how to map parallel loop iterations to threads and cores has been continually investigated since the standards' inception. In Section 5 we provide an overview of some of this existing work, and describe how our approach improves upon previous methods.

Our loop scheduling system is built on the idea of *close integration between a state-of-the-art compiler providing in-depth analysis and a custom runtime library* that continuously monitors the overall system state while minimizing overhead. Such integration is realized by having the compiler generate a data

* This work was funded by the FWF Austrian Science Fund as part of project TRP 220-N23 "Automatic Portable Performance for Heterogeneous Multi-cores" and by the FFG Austrian Research Promotion Agency as part of the OpenCore project 824925.

B.M. Chapman et al. (Eds.): IWOMP 2012, LNCS 7312, pp. 88–101, 2012.

structure for each parallel loop in the original program which captures analysis-derived meta-information about the loop body in addition to the actual executable code. This approach is immediately applicable to existing programs without any code-level changes, a significant advantage considering the large number of OpenMP codes in active HPC use.

We have implemented this system and evaluated its performance. Our concrete contributions are as follows:

- A method using polyhedral model [16] based utilities to obtain effective estimates of OpenMP loop performance over all potential iteration ranges.
- A runtime scheduling algorithm that uses these estimators as well as current sytem state information to make loop scheduling decisions.
- An encoding of meta-information statically collected by the compiler into executable code usable at runtime.
- An implementation of this architecture in the Insieme compiler and runtime system [2].
- Evaluation and analysis of the actual performance of our scheduling algorithm in terms of program execution time. We compare our results to results obtained by the version of GOMP [3] included with GCC 4.5.3, using both its default scheduling policy and the best policy for each program determined by exhaustive search.

The remainder of this paper is structured as follows: The next section will provide some experimental results that motivate our work. In Section 3 we describe the architecture and implementation of our system, including the compiler analysis, the runtime scheduling system and their interaction. The results of experimental evaluation are presented in Section 4. Section 5 gathers some references to related work. Finally Section 6 presents a conclusion, and an outlook on potential future improvements.

2   Motivation

In this section we present some initial experiments using simple OpenMP kernels in a variety of settings. These results motivated our design of a unified

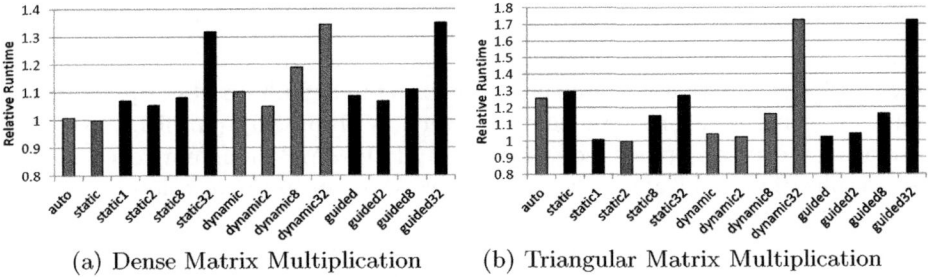

(a) Dense Matrix Multiplication   (b) Triangular Matrix Multiplication

Fig. 1. Initial Experiments, Impact of Program Characteristics

compiler/runtime approach to loop scheduling. They also demonstrate the importance of load awareness. For a complete description of the experimental setup and hardware used throughout this paper see Section 4. In all our figures the relative execution time normalized to the best performing configuration is shown.

Figure 1 illustrates results for two kernels, dense matrix multiplication with full and triangular matrices, using a variety of standard OpenMP loop scheduling policies. Clearly, the ideal loop schedule depends on the characterics of the program. The dense matrix multiplication requires an equal amount of work within each iteration of the parallel loop while for the triangular matrix, the effort per iteration depends on the iterator value. We say that the dense matrix multiplication has a *flat work profile* while the work profile for the triangular matrix is *slanted*.

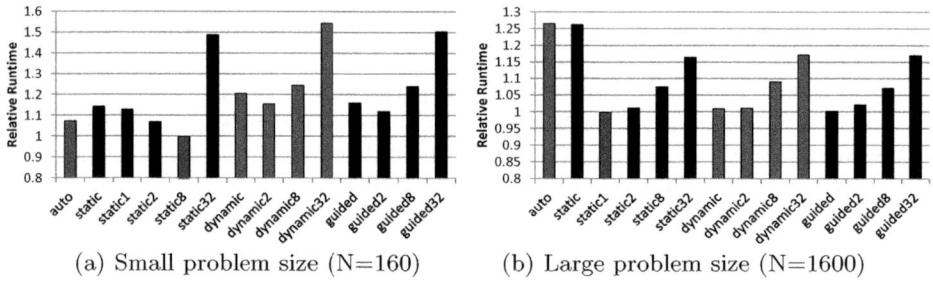

(a) Small problem size (N=160)   (b) Large problem size (N=1600)

Fig. 2. Initial Experiments, Impact of Problem Size

In the next experiment we investigated the impact of the problem size on the ideal loop schedule. In Figure 2 we see that with small problem sizes, the negative performance impact of scheduling policies with a runtime component (dynamic, guided) increases, most likely due to thread scheduling overhead. Also, the increase in workload per chunk mitigates the slightly worsened load balance for a static chunk size of 8, leading to this configuration showing the best result. With large problem sizes, the relative overhead of runtime scheduling is much smaller, tough still measureable. The round-robin static scheduling policy "static,1" features acceptable load balance with relatively low overhead, making it the best performing configuration.

Finally, we look at a scenario that has often been neglected in loop scheduling research: the impact of external system load on the execution of a program. While this is an unusual situation in traditional HPC, where a cluster of servers is reserved for exclusive use by one program, it is the default on desktops, workstations and some large shared memory servers. With on-chip parallelism steadily increasing – even on embedded systems – and OpenMP being employed in end-user applications and games [6], we believe that an automatic loop scheduler needs to take this scenario into account.

Figure 3 shows the same program configurations as Figure 1(b) in two distinct load scenarios (for information on how the load simulation is performed, see Section 4). With increasing system load more fine-grained runtime scheduling

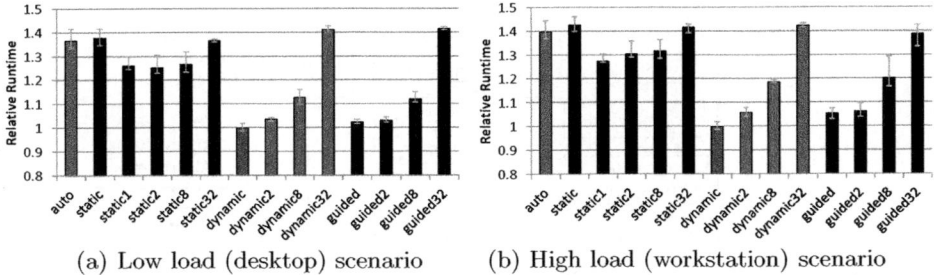

(a) Low load (desktop) scenario   (b) High load (workstation) scenario

Fig. 3. Initial Experiments, Impact of External Load

policies gain a significant advantage of up to 46% compared to the default policy. These figures contain error bars since there was a slightly larger variance in the measurements – particularly for static scheduling – as a result of operating system scheduling behaviour.

To summarize, these initial findings guided the design of our loop scheduling in the following ways:

– As per the first set of figures, the automatic loop scheduler clearly needs to be aware of the *program structure*. This is accomplished via compiler analysis.
– However, as the second set of examples shows, just having static information is insufficient. The *problem size* is usually only known at runtime, necessitating integration of statuc compiler analysis with a runtime system.
– Finally, when exclusive use cannot be assumed, being aware of *external system load* is of utmost importance when selecting a scheduling policy. Thus, the runtime needs to consider the system state.

3 Architecture

Our loop scheduling system consists of the following components:

– An advanced analysis component in the Insieme source-to-source compiler that generates a symbolic *effort estimation function* for each parallel loop in the target program, or a less accurate per-iteration effort value as a fallback.
– A backend extension to the compiler that allows forwarding of this meta-information from the compiler to the Insieme runtime system.
– A monitoring component that measures the current external system load.
– A custom runtime library implementing a loop scheduling algorithm based on the meta-information provided by the compiler, the exact iteration range of the current loop and the external load.

Figure 4 illustrates how these components interact on a high level. In the following subsections each component will be discussed in detail.

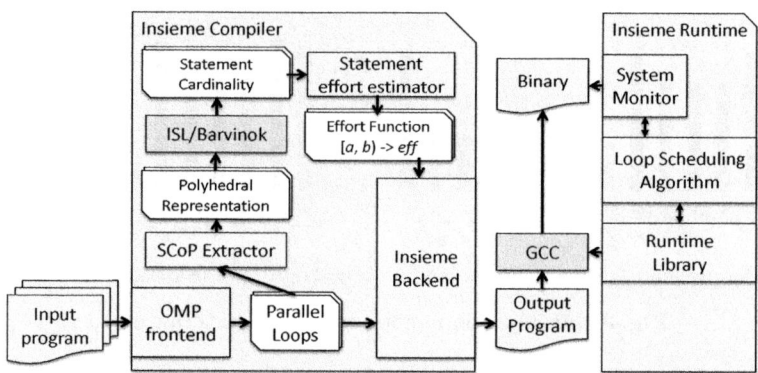

Fig. 4. An Overview of the Architecture of our System

3.1   Compiler Analysis

The main goal of our compiler analysis is to obtain, for each parallel loop, an *effort estimation function* $f_{\text{effort}} \in \mathbb{N}^2 \to \mathbb{N}$. Given lower and upper iteration bounds a and b, the evaluation of $f_{\text{effort}}(a, b)$ provides an estimate for the computational cost of the corresponding subrange of the covered loop.

This effort estimation function is derived in several steps, starting from the parallel loop body B:

1. Enclose B in a *for* loop iterating over the symbolic range $[a, b)$.
2. Extract a polyhedral representation of this parameterized loop.
3. Set the effort estimation function $f_{\text{effort}}(a, b) := 0$
4. For each statement $stmt \in B$:
   (a) Use the barvinok [17] library to obtain a piecewise affine function for the statement's cardinality $f_{\text{card}}(a, b)$
   (b) Weight this function with the effort estimation $\text{eff}(stmt)$ for the statement, computing $f_{\text{stmt}}(a, b) := f_{\text{card}}(a, b) * \text{eff}(stmt)$
   (c) Add the statement effort to the total effort function
   $f_{\text{effort}}(a, b) := f_{\text{effort}}(a, b) + f_{\text{stmt}}(a, b)$
5. Algebraically simplify $f_{\text{effort}}(a, b)$ using CUDD [18]

In step 2, the internal representation of the loop B is analyzed and a polyhedral representation is extracted. In-depth discussion of the polyhedral model and its application in compilers goes beyond the scope of this paper – a thorough introduction is provided by Bastoul [7]. For our purpose, it suffices to mention that the polyhedral model can be applied to Static Control Parts (SCoPs). SCoPs are program fragments that fulfill the following conditions: (1) all control structures are **for** loops or **if** statements with **affine** boundaries and conditions; (2) arrays are the only complex data structures, and are accessed with affine subscript expressions; (3) Subscripts, bounds and condition expressions depend only on loop iterators and symbolic constants.

The polyhedral model assigns to each statement an n-dimensional polytope describing how frequently it is processed within the modeled loop nest. Using this representation, a piecewise affine function expressing the number of executions of each statement can be calculated by computing its cardinality (4a). In step 4b we arrive at an effort estimation function for each such statement by weighting its cardinality function with an estimate for the cost of executing it once. The weighting factor eff(*stmt*) takes into account the expected number of CPU instructions and memory accesses required for the given statement. This estimation is rather simplistic in our current implementation: we count the number of memory accesses and floating point operations required to perform the statement in our internal representation, without taking into account any transformations performed by the back-end compiler.

Special considerations apply when performing the SCoP analysis for our use case. Generally, the polyhedral model is used to *transform* code fragments (see section 5), while we only use it to *estimate* effort. In the former case, the analysis needs to accurately cover all effects of the code to maintain the program semantics. For estimation, failing to fully analyze some statement means that the estimation function might be less accurate, potentially weakening the performance of the scheduling algorithm, but the program semantics are preserved. In practice, this allows us to extend the applicable range of our analysis by ignoring the side effects of external function calls, as long as we can provide an effort estimate for them (e.g. `printf`). We further extended the interprocedural applicability of our estimation by applying implicit inlining which does not affect the generated code.

In the case where a loop can still not be covered by the polyhedral model, as is the case when control flow depends on input data, we apply a rough estimate to loop boundaries and conditionals to generate a single scalar effort estimation representing one iteration of the parallel loop. Section 4.2 provides some experimental data on how commonly this fallback needs to be employed in real programs.

3.2   Compiler Backend

The Insieme compiler produces C code, which is in turn translated to a binary by a secondary compiler – typically GCC. The Insieme compiler backend enumerates all the parallel loops included in the program, and, for each of them, generates a *work item structure*. To pass loop-related meta-information from the compiler to the runtime, this structure includes an (optional) function pointer of type `uint64 effort_estimator(int64 lower, int64 upper)` and a scalar fallback value `uint64 iteration_effort`. For each loop where our analysis was successful, the function pointer is set to a compiler generated C implementation of the deduced effort estimation function.

3.3   Runtime Monitoring

The resource monitoring component of the runtime needs to measure the current *external load*, that is, CPU load generated by processes other than the managed parallel program. This is obtained by using the Linux `proc` filesystem. Specifically, the current processes' CPU usage values from `/proc/self/stat` are compared with the system-wide values obtained from `/proc/stat`, and a value between 0.0 and 1.0 representing the total external load across all cores is computed. To minimize the overhead of this method and to increase measurement reliability, this value is cached and updated at most ten times per second. Increasing the update frequency did not improve scheduling performance in our experiments.

3.4 Loop Scheduling Algorithm

All information gathered by the components outlined above is used by the runtime loop scheduler to make a scheduling decision for each individual execution of every parallel loop. The decision algorithm is outlined in Figure 5 and consists of four major steps:

1. Immediately schedule tiny loops if the estimated effort is small (lines 1-8)
2. Check the external load and use an adaptive dynamic schedule if it is greater than a threshold value (9-12)
3. If an effort estimator is available, use calculated balanced distribution (13-15)
4. Otherwise, assume irregular load and schedule dynamically (16-19)

lower, upper	lower and upper bound of iteration range
members	number of members in the current work group
estimator	effort estimation function for current loop
iter_effort	scalar per-iteration effort estimate for current loop
load	current external system load
MINEFF	minimum effort for consideration (constant per-system)
MINLOAD	minimum load for consideration (constant per-system)

```
 1: if estimator available then
 2:     estimate = estimator(lower, upper)
 3: else
 4:     estimate = (upper − lower) * iter_effort
 5: end if
 6: if estimate < MINEFF then
 7:     return  immediate
 8: end if
 9: if load > MINLOAD then
10:     chunk = max((MINEFF/iter_effort) * (1 − load), 1)
11:     return  dynamic(chunk)
12: end if
13: if estimator available then
14:     shares = compute_shares(lower, upper, members, estimator)
15:     return  balanced(shares)
16: else
17:     chunk = max(MINEFF/iter_effort, 1)
18:     return  dynamic(chunk)
19: end if
```

Fig. 5. Loop scheduling algorithm

The result of the algorithm determines the loop scheduling behaviour for the current loop execution instance. Three modes are available:

immediate no parameters. Immediately executes the whole loop on the first thread to encounter it.

dynamic one parameter, the chunk size. Works like the standard OpenMP policy of the same name, dynamically distributing chunks of the loop range to requesting threads.

balanced requires an array of floating point values determining the relative starting points of the shares for each member of the work group. For example, [0.0, 0.25, 0.5, 0.75] would implement an equal distribution amongst four threads, while [0.0, 0.6, 0.9, 0.96] assigns progressively smaller chunks to subsequent threads.

The algorithm makes use of the compute_shares(`lower`, `upper`, `members`, `estimator`) function. It generates a distribution that tries to assign approximately the same amount of work to each member of the current work group. It first estimates the total effort for the given range [`lower`, `upper`], divides it by the number of work group members, and then uses a binary search to find a suitable chunk for each thread using the estimation function. Though this is usually a very quick process since the estimation function only takes a few cycles to run, the result is cached and reused if the same loop is executed for the same range again. This is a very common occurance in HPC codes, and the caching minimizes overhead in this case.

The parameters MINEFF and MINLOAD need to be set once per system. We have not yet developed a rigorous method for deducing these automatically. Nevertheless, experience indicates that systems are relatively insensitive regarding the precise values of these parameters, making them easy to tune manually.

4   Evaluation

In this section our system and algorithm are evaluated, starting with small kernels designed to allow easy analysis of the behaviour of the algorithm, followed by tests in a real-world setting. All experiments were performed on a SuperMicro 7046GT-TRF server with two Intel Xeon 5650 processors, containing 6 cores (12 hardware threads) each. The system runs CentOS version 5 (kernel 2.6.18) 64 bits. To compile the reference version of the example programs and as a secondary compiler for the code produced by Insieme, GCC version 4.5.3 was used with the -O3 flag set to reflect a production environment. When we refer to a "default" scheduling policy, we specifically mean the default implementation of the version of GOMP [3] included with this version of GCC.

To ensure statistical significance each experiment was repeated five times, and the median result is reported. In cases where significant statistical variance occurred vertical error bars are used to show the standard deviation. We depict three values per configuration (combination of program and system load state): the default OpenMP behaviour, the best result obtained using OpenMP policies for each configuration, and the result obtained by our method. The "best" OpenMP policy is found by exhaustive search across the following settings: [(no change), auto, static, dynamic, guided]. The latter three are tested with the chunk sizes 1, 2, 8 and 32. All values are normalized to the execution time of the best performing version.

External load profiles were recorded by monitoring each indivual core of a reference system. During experiments, these profiles were replayed by a custom load generator. We used two separate load profiles, a "desktop" profile and a "workstation" profile. The former features generally lower load and short peaks of activity, while the latter shows a higher average load level and fully saturates some cores.

4.1   Kernel Experiments

For illustrative purposes, we will apply our method to three small kernels: a dense matrix multiplication, a triangular matrix multiplication, and a pendulum simulation. These represent three major classes of problems. Both the dense and triangular matrix multiplication satisfy the SCoP constraints and can therefore be rigorously analyzed. The former has a flat work profile and is thus ideally suited to static OpenMP scheduling, while the latter has a slanted work profile. Finally, the per-iteration work in the pendulum kernel strongly depends on the input data, hence it can not be covered by SCoP analysis.

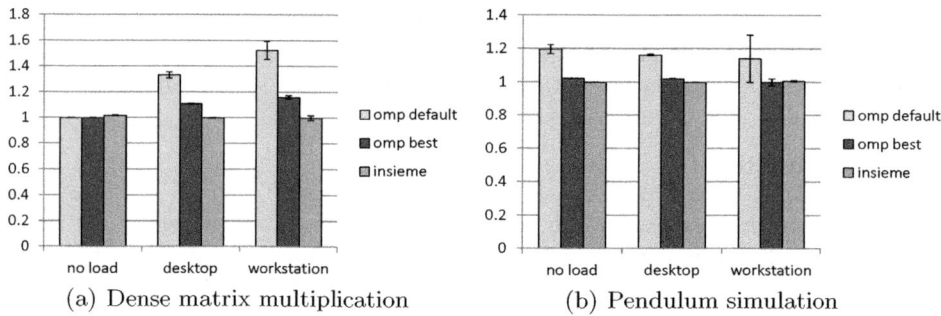

(a) Dense matrix multiplication   (b) Pendulum simulation

Fig. 6. Kernel experiment

Figure 6(a) shows the results for dense matrix multiplication. In the absence of external load, fully static scheduling is ideal for this kernel, and our implementation is 1.7% slower than the best (and default) OpenMP policy. With external load, the default policy is ineffective, and our result improves on the best OpenMP policy by 10% to 15%. The best policy found for desktop load is "dynamic,8" while the best policy for the workstation load profile is "dynamic". The reason for the good result demonstrated by our method is that due to the detection of external load the chunk size is adapted dynamically.

Next, we look at the triangluar matrix multiplication kernel, which has a more interesting load profile. As Figure 7(a) illustrates, the compiler-assisted workload distribution performed by our method in the unloaded case is very effective, improving performance by 82% compared to the default behaviour,

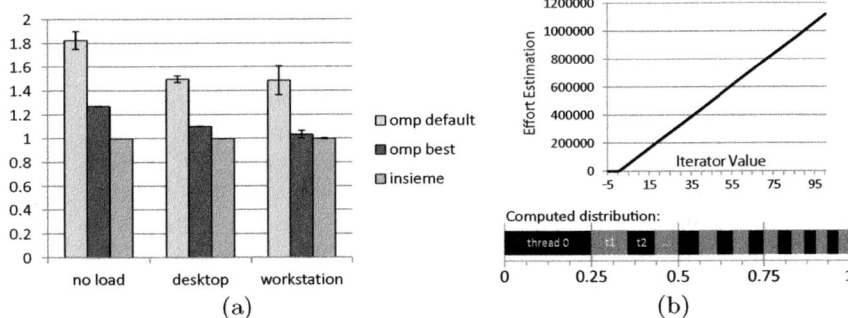

Fig. 7. Triangular matrix multiplication results

and by 27% compared to the best OpenMP scheduling policy, "static,2". This improvement over the block-cyclic scheduling can be explained by.

The effort estimation function generated by our analyis and the per-thread shares computed for 16 threads are shown in Figure 7(b). In the upper part, the effort estimation for each iterator value is plotted: iterations below zero perform no work, above that the amount of effort increases with the iterator value as the lower left triangular matrix rows become progressively wider. For this test case, the best scheduling policy with a loaded system is "dynamic" for both load profiles. Our scheduling is the fastest for both situations, though in the "workstation" case the difference is negligible (3%).

The performance results for the pendulum kernel are depicted in Figure 6(b). This benchmark computes the resting points of pendulae under the effect of magnetic fields, from many starting locations. It is communication-free but has an unpredictable, input data dependent, load imbalance, causing default scheduling to be sub-optimal. For the case with no load, the "dynamic,2" policy is best, while for the other two cases "dynamic" performs best. When the workstation external load profile is active, our method performs slightly (0.7%) worse than the "dynamic" OpenMP policy. For this load profile and the loop effort estimated for this kernel, our scheduler always decides to dynamically distribute a single loop iteration, thus performing exactly the same operation as the "dynamic" policy. The 0.7% difference can be explained by the overhead introduced by our scheduling process.

4.2   Real-World Applicability

While the results measured on small kernels are encouraging, methods based on extensive compiler analysis often fail when applied to larger code bases. However, the polyhedral model has been successfully used in production compilers [8], and, as described in Section 3.1, we were able to further relax some of its constraints for our use case.

In this section, we present an experimental analysis on some of the benchmarks contained in the NAS Parallel Benchmarks (NPB) [4] suite. As a first step we investigate the extent to which the parallel loops contained within these programs can be treated with our analysis method.

Table 1. Applicability of our analysis on NPB loops

State	Number of loops	% of loops
Total	465	100.0%
Fully analysed	373	80.2%
Non-affine expressions	57	12.3%
Data-dependent control flow	33	7.1%
Contain while loops	2	0.4%

Table 1 lists total number of loops contained within the NPB programs, the amount that were fully analysed, and groups those that could not be analysed into categories depending on the reason for the analysis failure. Note that the number of loops listed here is higher than the amount statically contained within the program source code, due to our method analysing each call site separately. More than 4 out of 5 of all parallel loops contained in the set of benchmarks can be analyzed. The most common reason for analysis failure are non-affine boundary, condition or subscript expressions, followed by data-dependent control flow. Two of the parallel loop nests contain *while* loops.

Table 2. Nas Parallel Benchmark performance results

Name	External Load	Gain Over Default	Best	Best Config
ft.B	none	4.2%	-0.2%	static,1
ft.B	desktop	21.8%	4.4%	dynamic,2
ft.B	workstation	59.9%	11.2%	dynamic
ep.B	none	14.0%	-1.9%	dynamic,8
ep.B	desktop	3.2%	-0.9%	dynamic
ep.B	workstation	19.7%	3.0%	dynamic,32
bt.B	none	-2.4%	-2.4%	static
bt.B	desktop	70.8%	65.2%	dynamic
bt.B	workstation	*	*	*
cg.B	none	8.4%	3.9%	guided,32
cg.B	desktop	113.4%	111.2%	guided,32
cg.B	workstation	471.3%	451.7%	guided,8
mg.B	none	51.7%	5.3%	dynamic
mg.B	desktop	56.1%	33.0%	dynamic
mg.B	workstation	157.4%	110.8%	dynamic,2
GM	none	13.7%	0.9%	
GM	desktop	48.2%	36.8%	
GM	workstation	94.9%	67.7%	

The results of our performance evaluation are summarized in Table 2. The "Default" and "Best" columns list the relative difference in execution time achieved by our scheduling system compared to default scheduling (as specified by the benchmarks) and the best scheduling policy found in the search space described earlier. For example, 4.2% in the ft.B/none/default cell means that executing the ft benchmark with no external load and the default scheduling policy took 104.2% of the time the same configuration took using our scheduling system. Predefined problem size B was chosen for all the benchmarks as a good compromise between realistic size and maintaining a feasible duration for the experiments. The **GM** values are the geometric means, for each configuration, across all benchmarks.

Some points that deserve particular attention are:

- The bt benchmark with workstation external load could not be completed due to time constraints – the execution time increased disproportionately with increased load across all scheduling policies.
- There is only a single case where our algorithm performs worse than the default: bt with no load. It is the only benchmark where the default scheduling (static) is also the best policy. For most loops within bt our method picks this optimum, but for one of them the analysis fails, causing a fallback to a slightly less efficient dynamic schedule.
- The best speedup in a load-free scenario occurs for mg. This is due to the nature of the algorithm implemented by this benchmark, which leads to some loops being executed with very small iteration domains. These are identified as low-effort by our method and immediately scheduled as a whole on the first thread available.
- Generally, higher levels of external load favour our system, which can effectively adapt to them.
- Even with no external load, our method tends to achieve a marked improvement over default scheduling due to the availablity of compiler-deduced meta-information. The average speedup obtained in this setting is 13%.

5   Related Work

Enhancing OpenMP loop scheduling is a topic that has been repeatedly investigated over the years. However, most research has focused on pure runtime solutions to the problem [11][12][10]. Conversely, our approach integrates an intelligent runtime system with meta-information provided by compiler analysis.

Recent work on compiler-based OpenMP loop scheduling by Wang et al. [9] uses machine learning to estimate the best loop scheduling policy at compile time. Since this is a pure compiler approach, it cannot deal with changing runtime conditions. Also, unlike the single-pass analysis of our approach, it requires an extensive training phase.

Some systems use OpenMP in conjunction with the polyhedral model to generate parallel code [13][14]. Other recent work investigates using information provided by polyhedral analysis of OpenMP programs to improve programmer error detection [15]. None of these works aim on improving loop scheduling by forwarding static analysis results to a runtime system.

6   Conclusion

This paper presents an automatic OpenMP loop scheduling method that combines advanced compiler analysis with a load-aware runtime system. Polyhedral analysis is used to calculate a parameterized *effort estimation function* for each parallel loop, based on the cardinality of all statements it contains. Executable code for this function is generated by the compiler backend, and invoked at runtime to calculate an ideal balanced schedule or estimate efficient chunk sizes for dynamic scheduling. Additionally, external CPU load is taken into account during the scheduling process.

We evaluated our system on small kernels as well as programs from the NAS Parallel Benchmarks suite, and achieved improvements of up to 82% in the unloaded state, and 471% with heavy external load, compared to default OpenMP scheduling. To estimate the absolute effectiveness of our approach, we performed an exhaustive search over a broad range of standard OpenMP scheduling policies and compared with the best results. Our scheduling frequently improves upon even this tuned result, particularly in scenarios featuring external load. The worst-case performance achieved by our system is within 3% of the best standard OpenMP policy.

References

1. OpenMP Architecture Review Board: OpenMP Application Program Interface. Version 3.1 (July 2011)
2. The Insieme Compiler Project, http://insieme-compiler.org/
3. GOMP – An OpenMP implementation for GCC, http://gcc.gnu.org/projects/gomp/
4. Bailey, D., Barton, J., Lasinski, T., Simon, H.: The NAS Parallel Benchmarks. NAS Technical Report RNR-91-002, NASA Ames Research Center, Moffett Field, CA (1991)
5. Duran, A., Corbalán, J., Ayguadé, E.: Evaluation of OpenMP Task Scheduling Strategies. In: Eigenmann, R., de Supinski, B.R. (eds.) IWOMP 2008. LNCS, vol. 5004, pp. 100–110. Springer, Heidelberg (2008)
6. Knafla, B., Leopold, C.: Parallelizing a Real-Time Steering Simulation for Computer Games with OpenMP. In: Proc. Parallel Computing (ParCo), pp. 219–226 (2007)
7. Bastoul, C.: Improving Data Locality in Static Control Programs. PhD thesis, University Paris 6, Pierre et Marie Curie, France (2004)
8. Trifunovic, K., Cohen, A., et al.: GRAPHITE Two Years After: First Lessons Learned From Real-World Polyhedral Compilation. In: GCC Research Opportunities Workshop (GROW) (2010)
9. Wang, Z., O'Boyle, M.: Mapping parallelism to multi-cores: a machine learning based approach. In: Proceedings of the 14th ACM SIGPLAN Symposium on Principles and Practice of Parallel Programming (PPoPP) (2009)
10. Zhang, Y., Burcea, M., Cheng, V., Ho, R., Voss, M.: An Adaptive OpenMP Loop Scheduler for Hyperthreaded SMPs. In: Proc. of PDCS 2004: International Conference on Parallel and Distributed Computing Systems (2004)

11. Tzen, T., Tzen, T.H., Ni, L., Ni, L.M.: Trapezoid Self-Scheduling: A Practical Scheduling Scheme for Parallel Compilers. IEEE Transactions on Parallel and Distributed Systems (1993)
12. Ayguadé, E., Blainey, B., Duran, A., Labarta, J., Martínez, F., Martorell, X., Silvera, R.: Is the *Schedule* Clause Really Necessary in OpenMP? In: Voss, M.J. (ed.) WOMPAT 2003. LNCS, vol. 2716, pp. 147–160. Springer, Heidelberg (2003)
13. Bondhugula, U., Ramanujam, J., et al.: PLuTo: A practical and fully automatic polyhedral program optimization system. In: Proceedings of the ACM SIGPLAN 2008 Conference on Programming Language Design and Implementation (PLDI) (2008)
14. Baskaran, M., Vydyanathan, N., Bondhugula, U., Ramanujam, J., Rountev, A., Sadayappan, P.: Compiler-assisted dynamic scheduling for effective parallelization of loop nests on multicore processors. In: Proceedings of the 14th ACM SIGPLAN Symposium on Principles and Practice of Parallel Programming (PPoPP) (2009)
15. Basupalli, V., Yuki, T., Rajopadhye, S., Morvan, A., Derrien, S., Quinton, P., Wonnacott, D.: ompVerify: Polyhedral Analysis for the OpenMP Programmer. In: Chapman, B.M., Gropp, W.D., Kumaran, K., Müller, M.S. (eds.) IWOMP 2011. LNCS, vol. 6665, pp. 37–53. Springer, Heidelberg (2011)
16. Benabderrahmane, M.-W., Pouchet, L.-N., Cohen, A., Bastoul, C.: The Polyhedral Model Is More Widely Applicable Than You Think. In: Gupta, R. (ed.) CC 2010. LNCS, vol. 6011, pp. 283–303. Springer, Heidelberg (2010)
17. Verdoolaege, S.: barvinok: User Guide, http://www.kotnet.org/~skimo/barvinok/barvinok.pdf
18. Somenzi, F.: CUDD: CU Decision Diagram Package, http://vlsi.colorado.edu/~fabio/CUDD/cuddIntro.html

LIBKOMP, an Efficient OpenMP Runtime System for Both Fork-Join and Data Flow Paradigms

François Broquedis[1], Thierry Gautier[2], and Vincent Danjean[3]

[1] INPG
[2] INRIA
[3] UJF,
MOAIS Team, LIG, Grenoble, France
{francois.broquedis,vincent.danjean}@imag.fr,
thierry.gautier@inrialpes.fr

Abstract. To efficiently exploit high performance computing platforms, applications currently have to express more and more finer-grain parallelism. The OpenMP standard allows programmers to do so since version 3.0 and the introduction of task parallelism. Even if this evolution stands as a necessary step towards scalability over shared memory machines holding hundreds of cores, the current specification of OpenMP lacks ways of expressing dependencies between tasks, forcing programmers to make unnecessary use of synchronization degrading overall performance. This paper introduces LIBKOMP, an OpenMP runtime system based on the X-KAAPI library that outperforms popular OpenMP implementations on current task-based OpenMP benchmarks, but also provides OpenMP programmers with new ways of expressing data-flow parallelism.

Keywords: OpenMP, data-flow programming, task parallelism, runtime systems.

1 Introduction

The architecture design of high performance computing platforms keeps getting more and more complex, widening the gap between the theoretical computing power of a given architecture and the performance parallel applications can achieve on it. HPC programmers have to express massive parallelism to occupy the constantly growing number of processing units contained in a multicore chip, and finely control the way parallel flows are executed to efficiently deal with memory affinity (shared cache memory, NUMA design, etc.). This burden will not get any lighter with the recent evolution of processor design, in which architects associate a few powerful cores with numerous, more simple cores. The success of this kind of design will rely on the ability for programmers to write applications with good performance at runtime, even for small problem instances.

Several libraries and programming environments [30,15,29,9,8] were proposed to improve the productivity of programmers by encouraging them to express all the potential parallelism in an application at fine grain, while delegating to the runtime system (or the compiler) the role to extract useful parallelism for the target multicore machine. They introduce high-level parallel constructs, such as Cilk `cilk_for`, X10

B.M. Chapman et al. (Eds.): IWOMP 2012, LNCS 7312, pp. 102–115, 2012.
© Springer-Verlag Berlin Heidelberg 2012

for_each or OpenMP parallel for, to easily describe potential parallelism in most of HPC numerical applications. In Cilk++, Intel Cilk+, Intel TBB, X-KAAPI and OpenMP (using the dynamic loop scheduler), the parallel loops generate internal tasks and rely on variations of a work stealing algorithm to deal with load balancing.

Tasks are now part of the OpenMP standard since version 3.0. To schedule task-based parallel applications, the work-stealing algorithm [6,3,16,20,26] is one of the most heavily-studied dynamic scheduler. Its biggest advantage lies in its simple predictive performance model. Several studies on OpenMP task scheduling have shown that work-stealing based algorithms seem to provide, on average, good speedup [11,27,28,1,23].

While we consider this evolution as a necessary step to exploit *manycore* computers efficiently, several studies have illustrated the limitation of the OpenMP *fork-join* task execution model [5,12,22] with respect to the data flow model, emphasizing that data flow applications are able to express more parallelism. The OpenMP ARB is already considering interesting possible extensions to the standard to deal with task/data dependencies [4,12], allowing OpenMP programmers to exploit accelerators in a unified model.

The X-KAAPI[1] library, a re-design in C of the Kaapi library [17] we develop, provides a runtime system that has proven to be efficient when it comes to scheduling data-flow parallel applications over multicore machines. X-KAAPI comes with very little task creation and scheduling overheads and implements recursive tasks in a very efficient way, making this runtime system a good candidate for both scheduling OpenMP 3.0 tasks, as the fork-join model can be seen as a particular case of the data-flow paradigm, and experiment with possible data-flow related extensions to the OpenMP standard.

This paper introduces LIBKOMP, an OpenMP runtime system based on the X-KAAPI library that performs well on current task-based OpenMP benchmarks and applications, but also emphasizes the interest of extending the OpenMP standard to express data-flow parallelism, presenting performance improvements for OpenMP benchmarks that were modified to express task/data dependencies.

The paper is organized as follows. Section 2 introduces the main assets of the X-KAAPI runtime system that the LIBKOMP library can rely on, and details the way we implement the OpenMP tasking model. Section 3 describes the evaluation of our runtime on the original BOTS benchmarks suite and modified versions of the SparseLU and NQueens kernels to benefit from the data-flow execution model while Section 4 presents some related work.

2 The LIBKOMP Runtime System

OpenMP tasks offer the application programmer new ways of expressing parallelism. This new paradigm will make OpenMP applications generate a great number of fine-grain tasks. The success of such an approach for parallelizing applications will greatly depend on the runtime system's ability to:

1. *Generate all these tasks with the smaller overhead possible:* the long term goal would be to let the runtime system decide how many tasks a parallel region should create considering both the application and the system current states.

---
[1] http://kaapi.gforge.inria.fr

2. *Provide efficient ways of performing load balancing to reach scalability:* a task-based application can dynamically generate tasks of different types and workloads.
3. *Implement recursive tasks in an efficient way:* recursive algorithms should be parallelized using recursive tasks, as it's most of the time the most convenient way to parallelize them, and not being penalized in terms of performance.

On top of focusing on these three aspects while implementing the OpenMP 3.0 libGOMP ABI, our LIBKOMP runtime system also provides the OpenMP programmer with new ways of expressing dependencies between OpenMP tasks, thanks to specific keywords provided by a source-to-source compiler we also develop, called *KaCC* [25]. So, LIBKOMP can be used either as a run-time replacement of the libGOMP runtime for OpenMP binaries compiled with GCC, or it can be used as a classical shared library for applications compiled with *KaCC* (allowing use of its extended features).

2.1 The LIBKOMP Execution Model

In LIBKOMP, each OpenMP thread corresponds to a X-KAAPI task. The number of kernel threads used to run an OpenMP program is controlled by the internal control variable called *nthreads-var* [29]. When the application reaches a scheduling point, a kernel thread is able to suspend the current task to execute another one, and resume execution of the previous task later. LIBKOMP takes advantage of such context switches to restore previous internal control variables (ICV), OpenMP thread number, *etc.*, if required. When the execution starts, the master thread of the current process starts to execute the main task. A thread creates tasks and pushes them on its own workqueue. The workqueue is represented as a stack. The enqueue operation is very fast, typically about ten cycles on current processors. As for Cilk, a running X-KAAPI task can create child tasks. Once a task terminates its execution, the thread that was executing it picks its children first, following the FIFO order of their creation.

2.2 Parallel Regions in LIBKOMP

A parallel region creates a set of implicit initial tasks, each of them being associated with a unique OpenMP thread number, which share team-related information. Tasks are pushed into the X-KAAPI stack of the running thread in a new activation frame. Tasks are not bound to kernel threads: it is the responsibility of the X-KAAPI work stealing scheduler to dynamically decide the mapping. LIBKOMP interprets a program specification of a number of threads num_threads in a *parallel* directive as the creation of num_threads X-KAAPI tasks. Several of these tasks may be scheduled on the same kernel thread, depending on the threads workload and the scheduling decisions taken by the X-KAAPI work-stealing scheduler. At the end of a parallel region, its master thread calls a LIBKOMP function to wait for the completion of all previously created tasks in the activation frame associated with this region.

2.3 Data Access Modes for Dependent Tasks

A X-KAAPI task is a function call that should return no value except through the shared memory and the list of its effective parameters. Tasks share data if they have access to

```
1  for  (k = 0;  k < NB;  ++k)
2  {
3  #pragma kaapi task readwrite (sli[k,k])
4     potrf (BS, sli[k,k]);
5
6     for (m = k+1; m < NB; ++m)
7     {
8        if (is_empty (sli[m,k])) continue;
9  #pragma kaapi task read (sli[k,k]) readwrite (sli[m,k])
10       trsm (BS, sli[k,k], sli[m,k]);
11    }
12
13    for (m = k+1; m < NB; ++m)
14    {
15       if (is_empty (m, k, &sli)) continue;
16 #pragma kaapi task read (sli[m,k]) readwrite (sli[m,m])
17       syrk (BS, sli[m,k], sli[m,m]);
18
19       for (n = k+1; n < m; ++n)
20       {
21          if ((is_empty (n, k, &sli) || (is_empty (m, n, &sli))) continue;
22 #pragma kaapi task read (sli[n,k], sli[m,k]) readwrite (sli[m,n])
23          gemm (BS, sli[n,k], sli[m,k], sli[m,n]);
24       }
25    }
26 }
27 #pragma kaapi sync
```

Fig. 1. Pseudo code for sparse Cholesky factorization

the same memory region. A memory region is defined as a set of addresses in the process virtual address space. With X-KAAPI, this set has the shape of a multi-dimensional array [25].

The user is responsible for indicating the mode each task uses to access the memory: the main access modes are *read, write, cumulative write* or *exclusive* [16,17,25,24]. The syntax to specify these access modes is very close to the directives proposed in StarSs meta model [5] and those defined by the OpenMP dependent tasks proposal [12].

Code of figure 1 illustrates the API provided by X-KAAPI along with the KaCC compiler [25] on a sparse Cholesky factorization used in the performance evaluation section. The matrix is composed of at most $NB \times NB$ blocks of size $BS \times BS$. The clauses *read* or *readwrite* specify access mode for variables following the structured block. True dependencies exist when a task read data produced by a previously created task. For instance, the task created at line 3 produces (read-write access) the diagonal block $[k, k]$ that will be consumed by tasks created at line 9. A variable that does not appear in any clause is passed by value.

OpenMP task model does not allow dependent tasks. The application programmer has to insert coarse grain synchronizations using the `taskwait` keyword to respect data flow dependencies, which can limit parallelism [22].

Tasks with data flow dependencies have already been cited to be important in linear algebra [22] or for managing multi-CPUs multi-GPUs computations [4,12,2,21] in a unified model. It could be used to avoid unnecessary synchronizations in recursive divide and conquer programs, such as the BOTS NQueens. Indeed, the number of solutions cumulated by each task only requires one final synchronization. Due to the limitations of the OpenMP tasking model, the BOTS NQueens implementation waits for the completion of all created child tasks at each level of the recursion. This synchronization allows to cumulate subresults but it also permits fast C stack allocation of chess board state for each child. Thanks to the cumulative access mode and the stack-based task management proposed by X-KAAPI, it is also possible to avoid these synchronization points by allocating a chess board state in the internal X-KAAPI stack, such that it is valid when a spawned task performs its computation [17].

A X-KAAPI task is a very light object. It basically holds a pointer to the main entry point function, its parameters and some flags set by the task scheduler. For each type of task, the runtime maintains a *format* object which is responsible to interpret the task: retrieve the access mode and type of each parameters, getting the implementation of the entry point of the task (CPU or GPU [21]). Such separation reduces the task size by factorizing common information.

2.4   Stack-Based Execution

At runtime, a X-KAAPI task generates a sequence of child tasks that access data in a shared memory area. Each task is pushed into the queue of the current thread. After a task finishes, its children tasks are executed with respect to the order of their creation. The local queue is managed as LIFO queue of activation frames. Each activation frame is a FIFO queue of tasks. This model implements a valid, highly efficient sequential execution order [16,17], as the runtime system only needs to compute data flow dependencies when the thread execution scheme reaches a task that has been stolen and not completed yet. The successors of the stolen task depend on its completion. So, all tasks following the first stolen task encountered, must require computation of data flow dependencies to detect whether they are ready or not. In order to keep fast stack-based execution without computation of data flow dependencies in X-KAAPI [17], a thread suspends its execution when it reaches the first stolen task in its stack and calls the work stealing scheduler to steal a new ready task.

2.5   Work Stealing and Data Flow Dependencies

Thanks to Cilk [6,15], the work stealing technique has become mainstream and is now often considered when it comes to dynamically balance the work load among processing units. The work stealing principle can be synthesized as follows. An idle thread, called a thief, initiates a steal request to a random selected victim. On reply, the thief receives one or more ready tasks.

At the startup time, only the main thread of X-KAAPI process performs tasks, all others threads are idle. This original idea in X-KAAPI follows the *work first principle* [15]; at the expense of a larger critical path, X-KAAPI moves the cost of computing ready tasks from the work performed by the victim during task's creations to the steal operations performed by thieves. Theoretical analysis of work stealing algorithms to schedule dependent tasks are studied in [16,18] and an elegant recent proof is written in [32] which considered specifics of the X-KAAPI work stealing protocol.

To compute a ready task, a thief thread iterates through the victim's queue from the last recent pushed task to the most recent one and it computes true data flow dependencies for each task. False dependencies are resolved through variables renaming. The iteration stops on the first task found ready.

The main difference between X-KAAPI and other software [5,2,34] is that X-KAAPI computes data flow dependencies only when idle thread search for a ready task.

2.6 Discussion

If a program is highly parallel, i.e. $T_\infty \ll T_1$, then the number of steal operations per thread remains in order $O(T_\infty)$ which is low. In that case, the cost of computing data flow, perhaps multiple times if several idle threads iterate over the same queue, is negligible with comparison to systematic computation on task creation. Otherwise, if the frequency of steal operations increases, X-KAAPI tries to aggregate multiple requests to the same victim. Our protocol elects the thieves to reply to all of the victim's requests. This aggregation strategy permits the combination of k searches of ready tasks in a less costly operation to one search of k ready tasks [19]. In [32], a theoretical analysis shows it can reduce the total number of steal requests.

Nevertheless, the overhead to manage tasks and computing data flow graph could remain important. Also, X-KAAPI implements an original optimization. It is applied when the cost of computing ready tasks becomes important, especially when the victim's stack contains many tasks. The user may annotate code or the scheduler automatically detects such situation. Then, the scheduler computes, and attaches to the stack, an accelerating data structure to make faster steal operations. The structure maintains the list of ready tasks. When a task completes and activates dependent tasks, the runtime pushes them directly into list (of ready tasks). The capacity of X-KAAPI to pass from workqueue' stack representation to this accelerating data structure makes it unique. It allows to move overhead in computing ready tasks during steal operation to the computation of accelerating data structure with low cost steal operation.

2.7 Parallel Loops in LIBKOMP

The parallel loop support in GCC/OpenMP relies on three main functions to initialize the iteration space, get the next slice for local computation and a function call at the end of the loop. Static scheduling may inline some of them. LIBKOMP follows the same ABI and relies on the X-KAAPI loop support [24]. Loop support in X-KAAPI is based on adaptive algorithms [33,31] to dynamically adapt the parallelism grain (number of tasks, number of iterations per task, etc.) considering the current system state. The LIBKOMP loop port on X-KAAPI is only required to decompose the original X-KAAPI parallel loop in order to fit the parallel work share construct of the libGOMP ABI.

3 Performance Evaluation

This section presents our evaluation on the BOTS benchmarks suite and two versions of the Cholesky factorization to compare the performance obtained by our solution with respect to two other OpenMP implementations: the original libGOMP that comes with version 4.6.2 of the GCC compiler and version 12.1.2 of the Intel C OpenMP compiler. LIBKOMP is based on version 1.0.2 of the X-KAAPI runtime system.

We conducted our experiments on CC-NUMA 48 cores AMD Magny Cours. There are three levels of cache memory. L1 (64 KB) and L2 (512 KB) are per core, whereas L3 (5 MB) is shared by 6 cores. This configuration provides a total of 256 GB (32 GB per NUMA node) of main memory. We will refer to this configuration as **AMD48** in the following of the paper.

3.1   Task Management Overhead

This section compares the overhead of task creation and execution with respect to the sequential computation. The experiment evaluates the time to execute the KaCC/LIBKOMP program of figure 2 for computing the 35-th Fibonacci number using the fast task creation protocol. Equivalent programs in term of task creations and synchronizations are written in Intel Cilk+, Intel TBB 4.0 and GCC/libGOMP. Sequential time is $0.091s$. Figure 2 reports times using 1, 8, 16, 32 and 48 cores from our *AMD48* configuration. On 1 core, LIBKOMP has the smallest overhead with respect to the sequential computation (slowdown of about 8). This overhead can easily be absorbed by increasing the task granularity, but at the expense of increasing the critical path, thus reducing the available parallelism [15,11]. The grain is too fine for OpenMP/libGOMP (computation was stopped on 32 and 48 cores after 5 minutes). For one core execution, libGOMP never creates tasks and makes function calls as sequential execution does.

```
void fibonacci(long* result,
     const long n)
{
  if (n<2)
    *result = n;
  else
  {
    long r1,r2;
#pragma kaapi task write(&r1)
    fibonacci( &r1, n-1 );
    fibonacci( &r2, n-2 );
#pragma kaapi sync
    *result = r1 + r2;
  }
}
```

(a) LIBKOMP benchmark using KaCC

#cores	Cilk+	TBB	LIBKOMP	libGOMP
1	1.063	2.356	0.728	2.429
(slowdown)	(x 11.7)	(x 26)	(x 8)	(x27)
8	0.127	0.293	0.094	*51.06*
16	0.065	0.146	0.047	*104.14*
32	0.035	0.072	0.024	*(no time)*
48	0.028	0.049	0.017	*(no time)*

(b) Time (second) on the AMD48 configuration for fibonacci(35). Sequential time is 0.091 s.

Fig. 2. Fibonacci micro benchmark

3.2   Parallel Loops

In this section, we compare the performance obtained by both the libGOMP runtime system and LIBKOMP on a parallel version of EUROPLEXUS [14], an industrial application that computes finite element simulation of fluid-structure systems, exposing a single OpenMP parallel loop. Because work per iteration is lightly irregular, we tested both static and dynamic scheduling for libGOMP. We use the MAXPLANE instance as input of the EUROPLEXUS application. Figure 3 reports the obtained speedup of parallel implementations with respect to the sequential version. The same cores was used in both libGOMP or LIBKOMP using the environment variable GOMP_CPU_AFFINITY. Overall speedups are very close, but LIBKOMP scales better for a larger number of cores (>25).

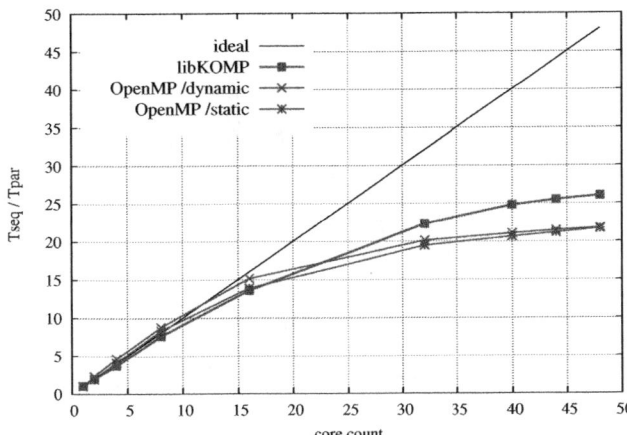

Fig. 3. EUROPLEXUS parallel loop speedup, libGOMP (static, dynamic) VS LIBKOMP (xkaapi)

3.3   Barcelona OpenMP Tasks Suite (BOTS)

The Barcelona OpenMP Tasks Suite has been introduced to test the behavior of 3.0-compatible OpenMP runtime systems regarding tasks implementation. It provides several kernels inspired from real-life OpenMP applications and projects. Each kernel, detailed in [13], comes with different implementations relying on different aspects/keywords of the OpenMP 3.0 tasks model (tied/untied tasks, controlling the cut-off using the if clause, etc.). We ran all these kernels on the AMD48 platform using a varying number of cores to experiment with each kernel's scalability, and kept the best implementation for each runtime system. Figure 4 shows the corresponding results.

Executing some of these kernels may lead to the creation of a great number of tasks. For instance, the execution of the NQueens algorithm on a 14x14 chessboard generates more than 370M of tasks. Creating such a number of tasks comes with overheads on any tested runtime systems, the worst ones being observed from libGOMP. Determining the *right* number of tasks to instanciate from an application may be really challenging. Some runtime systems like libGOMP implements a threshold heuristic that limits tasks creation when the number of tasks is greater than k times the number of threads. It has the advantage of limiting the number of tasks but may limit the parallelism of the application, as observed on the FFT benchmark performance on figure 4b in which creating all the 2M tasks expressed in the application allows both the LIBKOMP and Intel runtime systems to perform better load balancing. Some of these embarassing applications comes with implementations in which the application programmer can define the maximum depth from which new tasks will be executed sequentially, taking the number of creating tasks from 370M for NQueens to 2394 for example, thus explaining the better performance obtained by libGOMP on the these kernels.

More generally, these experiments show LIBKOMP obtains performance that is comparable to other OpenMP runtime systems (sometimes being even better!) on fork-join applications exposing a reasonable number of tasks, and outperforms libGOMP

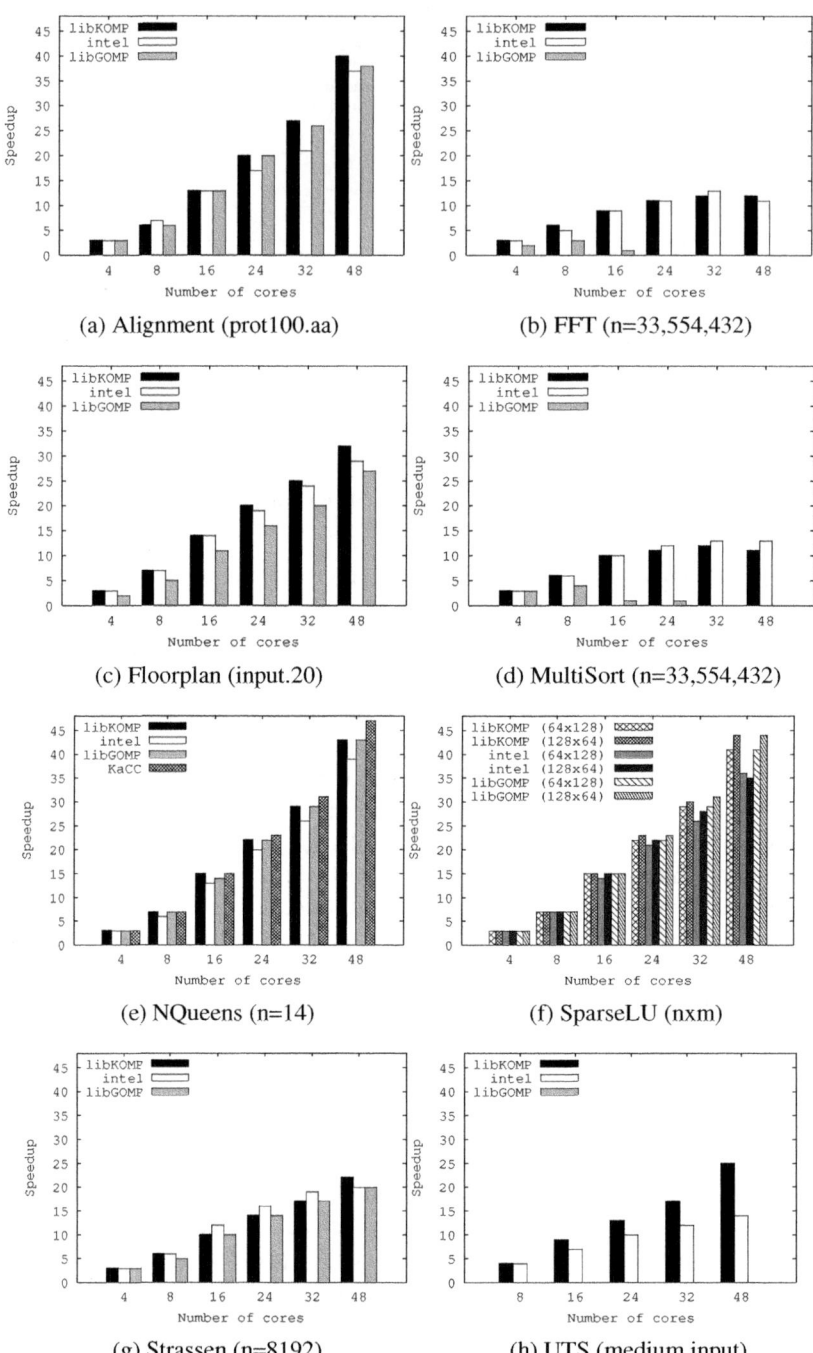

Fig. 4. Speedups of the BOTS benchmarks suite scheduled by the LIBKOMP, libGOMP and Intel runtime systems on a varying number of cores from the AMD48 platform with respect to the GCC-compiled sequential version

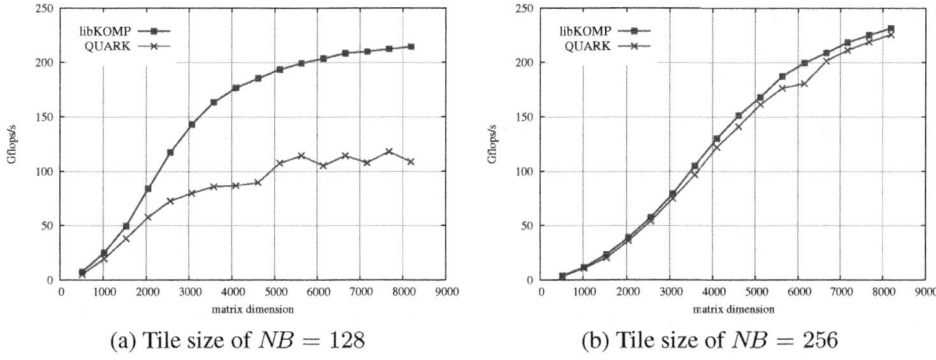

(a) Tile size of $NB = 128$ (b) Tile size of $NB = 256$

Fig. 5. Gflops on Cholesky algorithm with QUARK and LIBKOMP

and Intel on applications creating a great number of tasks, thanks to its efficient management of recursive tasks.

To conclude this section, reported experiments have demonstrated that LIBKOMP has almost the same performance as libGOMP or Intel ICC for a moderate number of tasks and a moderate number of cores. For tasks-intensive computations, such as UTS, LIBKOMP outperforms the other two OpenMP implementations. LIBKOMP is designed to schedule data-flow graphs.

Mixing tasks with declaration of memory access modes allows a finer resolution of synchronizations. It also provides valuable information on memory accesses to the runtime system. The implementation of BOTS NQueens has been modified as described at the end of section 2.4 and compiled with KaCC/LIBKOMP. Letting the runtime system deal with fine-grain sychronizations allows to significantly improve the overall performance here, as this version of NQueens reaches a speedup of 47.8 over 48 cores of the AMD48 machine (KaCC performance reported on figure 4e).

3.4 Data Flow Tasks versus Fork-Join Tasks

We evaluate the potential gain offered by data-flow tasks over OpenMP 3.0 fork-join tasks executing two different versions of the Cholesky factorization, a widely-used linear algebra algorithm.

LIBKOMP versus QUARK. The first one relies on the `PLASMA_dpotrf_Tile` algorithm coming from version 2.4.2 of the PLASMA [7] library that comes with a runtime system, in charge of scheduling PLASMA tasks, called *QUARK*. We implemented the QUARK [34] ABI for dependent tasks on top of LIBKOMP to compare our implementation with the original version of QUARK.

Figure 5 reports the performance, in GFlop/s, for different matrix sizes on the *AMD48* machine. One can observe that LIBKOMP outperforms QUARK for fine grain tasks ($NB = 128$). The main reasons are: 1/ QUARK implements a centralized list of ready tasks; 2/ Creating QUARK tasks comes with bigger overheads. We can expect this contention point to become more severe as the number of cores increases with next generation machines, affecting PLASMA performance. When the grain increases, LIBKOMP remains better but the difference decreases because of the relatively small impact of the task management with respect to the whole computation. One can also note that increasing the grain size reduces the average parallelism and limits the speedup. For a matrix size of 3000, the performance for $NB = 128$ reaches $150 GFlops$, while for $NB = 256$, it drops to about $75 GFlops$.

LIBKOMP versus OMP. The second version of the Cholesky factorization we studied here is a sparse factorization (LDL^t) coming from the industrial code EURO-PLEXUS [14]. We compare a data flow program on top of LIBKOMP with respect to the original EUROPLEXUS code using OpenMP 3.0 task. The two code structures are similar to Cilk and SMPSs codes presented in [22] for the dense case. Management of sparsity is done in the same way as in the BOTS SparseLU code. Figure 6 reports speedup using a matrix used by the MAXPLANE simulation in EUROPLEXUS [14].

The dimension of the matrix is 59462 with 3.59% of non zero elements. The block size with the best sequential time is $BS = 88$ and is used for parallel versions. The sequential time is $47.79s$. LIBKOMP version outperforms lib-GOMP version, for the same reasons as for the dense case [22]: thanks to the knowledge of data dependencies, independent tasks between outer loop iterations can be executed concurrently.

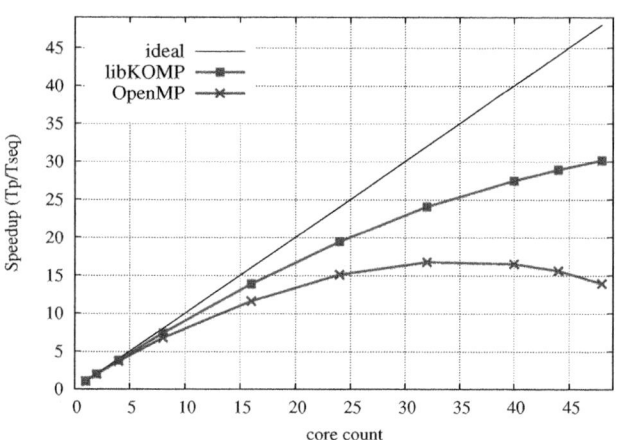

Fig. 6. Speedups on sparse Cholesky

4   Related Work

Kaapi [17] was designed in our group after our preliminary work on Athapascan [16,10]. X-KAAPI keeps definition of access modes to compute data flow dependencies between a sequence of tasks. StarSs/SMPSs [5], QUARK [34], StarPU [2] follow the same design. We can still note differences in the kind of access modes and the shape of the memory region that are defined : StarSs/SMPSs, QUARK have similar access mode but only consider unidimensional arrays. QUARK comes with an original `scratch` access mode to reuse thread-specific temporary data. StarPU [2] has a more complex way to split data and define sub-views of a data structure. X-KAAPI has a direct support for multi-dimensional arrays [25].

The data flow task model is flat in StarSs/SMPSs, QUARK and StarPU while X-KAAPI also allows recursive tasks creation. The fork-join parallel paradigm is only supported by X-KAAPI, Intel TBB [30], Cilk [6,15] and Cilk+ (Intel version of Cilk). The X-KAAPI performance for fine grain recursive applications is equivalent, and sometimes better, than Cilk+ and Intel TBB, that only allow the creation of independent tasks.

In TBB, Cilk or X-KAAPI, task creation is several order of magnitude cheaper than in StartSs/SMPSs, QUARK or StarPU. Scalability of the QUARK and StarPU runtime system is limited due to their central list scheduling. SMPSs seems to support a more distributed scheduling.

X-KAAPI has a unique model of adaptive task that allows a runtime adaptation of tasks creation when a resource turns idle. The OpenMP runtime of GCC 4.6.2, lib-GOMP, implements a threshold heuristic that limits tasks creation when the number of tasks is greater than k times the number of threads ($k = 64$). It has the advantage of limiting the number of tasks [11] (max-task strategy) but may limit the parallelism of the application, as observed on the FFT benchmark performance [11]. TBB, with an autopartitionner heuristic, is able to limit the number of tasks without *a priori* limiting the application parallelism.

Intel TBB, Cilk+, OpenMP and X-KAAPI support parallel loops which are not available in StarSs/SMPSs, QUARK or StarPU. Our comparison with OpenMP/GCC 4.6.2 shows that for benchmarked instances on real EUROPLEXUS code, OpenMP loop scheduling strategy is not an important feature.

From all of the tested softwares, X-KAAPI is the only runtime system that allows to mix in a unified framework data-flow tasks, fork-join tasks and parallel loops with at least equivalent performance (sometimes even better!) than specific softwares for each paradigm.

5 Conclusion

Computer architects keep designing more and more complex platforms embedding an almost constantly increasing number of processing units. To deal with these so-called manycore architectures, OpenMP had to evolve to allow the application programmer to express finer-grain parallelism. The 3.0 version of the OpenMP standard has layed the fundations of a fine-grain environment, introducing the task construct to generate fine-grain tasks, either explicitly or out of OpenMP 2.5 parallel regions. We proposed in this paper a runtime system, called LIBKOMP, that efficiently implements the OpenMP task model and is binary compatible with existing OpenMP applications built against GCC's libGOMP. LIBKOMP outperformed popular OpenMP implementations like GCC's libGOMP and ICC's KMP runtime systems on several benchmarks of the Barcelona OpenMP Tasks Suite. We also showed the interest of taking OpenMP task proposal one step further, proposing extensions to deal with data dependencies. We implemented these extensions inside a source-to-source compiler obtaining better performance using data-flow tasks compared to OpenMP 3.0 fork-join tasks. From our point of view, many of the characteristics of the LIBKOMP runtime system, and more generally the X-KAAPI runtime system LIBKOMP is based on, like adaptive loops scheduling, moldable tasks and also unified CPU/GPU programming are interesting to discuss as possible OpenMP evolutions.

Acknowledgement. The authors would like to thank Fabien Le Mentec for providing results on EUROPLEXUS code. Work on EUROPLEXUS have been partially supported by CEA and by the 09-COSI-011-05 REPDYN ANR Project. This work has been partially supported by the ANR-11-BS02-013 HPAC ANR Project.

References

1. Agathos, S.N., Hadjidoukas, P.E., Dimakopoulos, V.V.: Design and implementation of openmp tasks in the ompi compiler. In: Angelidis, P., Michalas, A. (eds.) Panhellenic Conference on Informatics, pp. 265–269. IEEE (2011), http://dblp.uni-trier.de/db/conf/pci/pci2011.html#AgathosHD11
2. Agullo, E., Augonnet, C., Dongarra, J., Ltaief, H., Namyst, R., Roman, J., Thibault, S., Tomov, S.: Dynamically scheduled Cholesky factorization on multicore architectures with GPU accelerators. In: Symposium on Application Accelerators in High Performance Computing (SAAHPC), Knoxville, USA (July 2010)
3. Arora, N.S., Blumofe, R.D., Plaxton, C.G.: Thread scheduling for multiprogrammed multiprocessors. Theor. Comp. Sys. 34(2), 115–144 (2001)
4. Ayguade, E., Badia, R.M., Cabrera, D., Duran, A., Gonzalez, M., Igual, F., Jimenez, D., Labarta, J., Martorell, X., Mayo, R., Perez, J.M., Quintana-Ortí, E.S.: A Proposal to Extend the OpenMP Tasking Model for Heterogeneous Architectures. In: Müller, M.S., de Supinski, B.R., Chapman, B.M. (eds.) IWOMP 2009. LNCS, vol. 5568, pp. 154–167. Springer, Heidelberg (2009), http://dx.doi.org/10.1007/978-3-642-02303-3_13
5. Badia, R.M., Herrero, J.R., Labarta, J., Pérez, J.M., Quintana-Ortí, E.S., Quintana-Ortí, G.: Parallelizing dense and banded linear algebra libraries using smpss. Concurr. Comput.: Pract. Exper. 21, 2438–2456 (2009)
6. Blumofe, R., Joerg, C., Kuszmaul, B., Leiserson, C., Randall, K., Zhou, Y.: Cilk: An efficient multithreaded runtime system. Journal of Parallel and Distributed Computing 37(1), 55–69 (1996), citeseer.nj.nec.com/article/blumofe95cilk.html
7. Buttari, A., Langou, J., Kurzak, J., Dongarra, J.: A class of parallel tiled linear algebra algorithms for multicore architectures. Parallel Comput. 35, 38–53 (2009)
8. Chamberlain, B., Callahan, D., Zima, H.: Parallel programmability and the chapel language. Int. J. High Perform. Comput. Appl. 21, 291–312 (2007), http://dl.acm.org/citation.cfm?id=1286120.1286123
9. Charles, P., Grothoff, C., Saraswat, V., Donawa, C., Kielstra, A., Ebcioglu, K., von Praun, C., Sarkar, V.: X10: an object-oriented approach to non-uniform cluster computing. SIGPLAN Not. 40, 519–538 (2005)
10. Dumitrescu, B., Doreille, M., Roch, J.L., Trystram, D.: Two-dimensional block partitionings for the parallel sparse cholesky factorization. Numerical Algorithms 16, 17–38 (1997)
11. Duran, A., Corbalán, J., Ayguadé, E.: Evaluation of OpenMP Task Scheduling Strategies. In: Eigenmann, R., de Supinski, B.R. (eds.) IWOMP 2008. LNCS, vol. 5004, pp. 100–110. Springer, Heidelberg (2008)
12. Duran, A., Perez, J.M., Ayguadé, E., Badia, R.M., Labarta, J.: Extending the OpenMP Tasking Model to Allow Dependent Tasks. In: Eigenmann, R., de Supinski, B.R. (eds.) IWOMP 2008. LNCS, vol. 5004, pp. 111–122. Springer, Heidelberg (2008)
13. Duran, A., Teruel, X., Ferrer, R., Martorell, X., Ayguade, E.: Barcelona openmp tasks suite: A set of benchmarks targeting the exploitation of task parallelism in openmp. In: International Conference on Parallel Processing, ICPP 2009, pp. 124–131. IEEE (2009)
14. Faucher, V.: Advanced Parallel Computing for Explosive Fluid-Structure Interaction. In: COMPDYN 2011, Corfu, Greece (May 2011)
15. Frigo, M., Leiserson, C.E., Randall, K.H.: The implementation of the cilk-5 multithreaded language. In: Proceedings of the ACM SIGPLAN 1998 Conference on Programming Language Design and Implementation, PLDI 1998, pp. 212–223. ACM, New York (1998)
16. Galilée, F., Roch, J.L., Cavalheiro, G.G.H., Doreille, M.: Athapascan-1: On-line building data flow graph in a parallel language. In: Proceedings of PACT 1998, p. 88. IEEE Computer Society, Washington, DC (1998)

17. Gautier, T., Besseron, X., Pigeon, L.: Kaapi: a thread scheduling runtime system for data flow computations on cluster of multi-processors. In: PASCO 2007 (2007)
18. Gautier, T., Roch, J.L., Wagner, F.: Fine grain distributed implementation of a dataflow language with provable performances. In: Workshop PAPP 2007 - Practical Aspects of High-Level Parallel Programming in (ICCS2007). IEEE, Beijing (2007)
19. Hendler, D., Incze, I., Shavit, N., Tzafrir, M.: Flat combining and the synchronization-parallelism tradeoff. In: Proceedings of the 22nd ACM Symposium on Parallelism in Algorithms and Architectures, SPAA 2010, pp. 355–364. ACM, New York (2010)
20. Hendler, D., Shavit, N.: Non-blocking steal-half work queues. In: PODC 2002: Proceedings of the Twenty-First Annual Symposium on Principles of Distributed Computing, pp. 280–289. ACM, New York (2002)
21. Hermann, E., Raffin, B., Faure, F., Gautier, T., Allard, J.: Multi-GPU and Multi-CPU Parallelization for Interactive Physics Simulations. In: D'Ambra, P., Guarracino, M., Talia, D. (eds.) Euro-Par 2010. LNCS, vol. 6272, pp. 235–246. Springer, Heidelberg (2010)
22. Kurzak, J., Ltaief, H., Dongarra, J., Badia, R.M.: Scheduling dense linear algebra operations on multicore processors. Concurr. Comput.: Pract. Exper. 22, 15–44 (2010)
23. LaGrone, J., Aribuki, A., Addison, C., Chapman, B.: A Runtime Implementation of OpenMP Tasks. In: Chapman, B.M., Gropp, W.D., Kumaran, K., Müller, M.S. (eds.) IWOMP 2011. LNCS, vol. 6665, pp. 165–178. Springer, Heidelberg (2011), http://dl.acm.org/citation.cfm?id=2023025.2023042
24. Le Mentec, F., Danjean, V., Gautier, T.: X-Kaapi C programming interface. Tech. Rep. RT-0417, INRIA (December 2011)
25. Le Mentec, F., Gautier, T., Danjean, V.: The X-Kaapi's Application Programming Interface. Part I: Data Flow Programming. Tech. Rep. RT-0418, INRIA (December 2011)
26. Michael, M.M., Vechev, M.T., Saraswat, V.A.: Idempotent work stealing. SIGPLAN Not. 44, 45–54 (2009)
27. Olivier, S.L., Porterfield, A.K., Wheeler, K.B., Prins, J.F.: Scheduling task parallelism on multi-socket multicore systems. In: Proceedings of the 1st International Workshop on Runtime and Operating Systems for Supercomputers, ROSS 2011, pp. 49–56. ACM, New York (2011), http://doi.acm.org/10.1145/1988796.1988804
28. Olivier, S.L., Porterfield, A.K., Wheeler, K.B., Spiegel, M., Prins, J.F.: Openmp task scheduling strategies for multicore numa systems. International Journal of High Performance Computing Applications (2012)
29. OpenMP Architecture Review Board (1997-2008), http://www.openmp.org
30. Robison, A., Voss, M., Kukanov, A.: Optimization via reflection on work stealing in TBB. In: IPDPS (2008)
31. Tchiboukdjian, M., Danjean, V., Gautier, T., Le Mentec, F., Raffin, B.: A Work Stealing Scheduler for Parallel Loops on Shared Cache Multicores. In: Guarracino, M.R., Vivien, F., Träff, J.L., Cannataro, M., Danelutto, M., Hast, A., Perla, F., Knüpfer, A., Di Martino, B., Alexander, M. (eds.) Euro-Par-Workshop 2010. LNCS, vol. 6586, pp. 99–107. Springer, Heidelberg (2011)
32. Tchiboukdjian, M., Gast, N., Trystram, D., Roch, J.-L., Bernard, J.: A Tighter Analysis of Work Stealing. In: Cheong, O., Chwa, K.-Y., Park, K. (eds.) ISAAC 2010, Part II. LNCS, vol. 6507, pp. 291–302. Springer, Heidelberg (2010)
33. Traoré, D., Roch, J.-L., Maillard, N., Gautier, T., Bernard, J.: Deque-Free Work-Optimal Parallel STL Algorithms. In: Luque, E., Margalef, T., Benítez, D. (eds.) Euro-Par 2008. LNCS, vol. 5168, pp. 887–897. Springer, Heidelberg (2008), http://www.caos.uab.es/europar2008/
34. YarKhan, A., Kurzak, J., Dongarra, J.: Quark users' guide: Queueing and runtime for kernels. Tech. Rep. ICL-UT-11-02. University of Tennessee (2011)

A Compiler-Assisted Runtime-Prefetching Scheme for Heterogeneous Platforms

Li Chen[1], Baojiang Shou[1], Xionghui Hou[1], and Lei Huang[2]

[1] State Key Laboratory of Computer Architecture,
Institute of Computing Technology, Chinese Academy of Sciences
No.6 Kexueyuan South Road,Beijing 100190, China
{lchen,shoubaojiang,houxionghui}@ict.ac.cn
[2] Department of Computer Science, Prairie View A&M University,
Prairie View,TX 77446, USA
lhuang@pvamu.edu

Abstract. GPGPU has been widely used in recent years in both academia and industry. Many research for benchmarks on GPUs were reported to achieve over 100 times speedup, however, due to the high overhead of data transfer between GPU and CPU in real-world applications, the achievements are dramatically limited. In the case of using multiple GPUs, the situation is even worse. Another difficulty raised by the GPGPUs is the programming productivity.

In this work, we introduce a new language extension to the easy-to-use programming model OpenMP, implement a runtime and a prefetching mechanism to further extend our work in support of OpenMP on heterogeneous platforms. The new language extension allows the OpenUH compiler to generate efficient code for heterogeneous platforms with multiple GPUs included. To improve the performance of applications with lots of data transfer, we implement runtime inter-thread dataflow analysis and a runtime-prefetching mechanism with the help of compiler analysis, making the data transfer overlap with the computation as much as possible. We have evaluated our prefetching system using benchmarks including NPB SP, kmeans and nbody. In these experiments, we achieve speedups of 1.23, 1.4 and 1.32 respectively compared with the versions without prefetching support.

1   Introduction

Within recent years, GPGPUs have been widely used in both academia and industry. Significant research has been carried out in optimizing programs running on a single GPU, and some of them have reported to achieve great speedup [19][14][23][2][26]. However, for the real-world applications, the data transfers between CPUs and GPUs have typically slowed down the performance [6][25] dramatically. The situation becomes more complicated in the latest heterogeneous systems since they are typically equipped with multicores and multiple GPUs together. The common practice of GPU programming on a single GPU, to offload the most compute-intensive kernel completely to it is not the most

B.M. Chapman et al. (Eds.): IWOMP 2012, LNCS 7312, pp. 116–129, 2012.

efficient [25][13][22] [11] in the latest heterogeneous systems anymore. It is necessary to offload works to multiple GPUs [18][10] and multicores instead of to a single GPU. Research [4] shows the importance of maintaining cross-device data mappings with a case study of concurrent CPU-GPU execution. In order to achieve satisfied performance on real-world applications on today's heterogeneous systems, it is critical to solve the bottleneck of the data transfer among these devices.

Some latest architecture such as AMD Fusion integrates CPU and GPU cores together to share the main memory. Although these architectures make the explicit data transfers unnecessary, the data placement and cache coherence is still a key factor that affects application performance. For the existing disjoined CPU and GPU systems, as well as to software managed scratch memory/cache architectures, the data transfer optimization is still critical to performance. In order to optimize data transfer, it is worth revisiting the achievements of reducing data communication on Distributed Memory Systems (DSM) on last decades. Researchers optimized the data transferring in such systems using data distribution, compiler optimizations and software DSM runtime support. In heterogeneous systems, it would also achieve better performance if the programming models support data distribution to allow users to specify how data is distributed on different devices. It will reduce large amount of unnecessary data transfer specified by the developers who know the best for where/how the data will be used in the program. Compiler optimizations are essential to reduce data transfer by analyzing data access patterns and further optimizing them by performing code motion and instruction scheduling. However, the compiler optimizations are limited to many unknown factors at compile time. We believe that it has more space to perform aggressive optimizations if we can apply the compiler analysis at the runtime.

In this paper, we made the following contributions. Firstly we proposed a new method of static task partition. Secondly we provided a runtime inter-thread use-def analysis; Thirdly we proposed a prefetching scheme based on the result of data-flow analysis and we implemented it in the OpenUH compiler system. This paper is organized as follows. Section 2 discusses the language extension, section 3 gives the related compiler supports, and section 4 contains the details of the prefetching scheme. Section 5 talks about the implementation and evaluation of our work. Related work is in section 6 and conclusion is given in section 7.

2   Language Extensions

We make several extensions to OpenMP to support work distribution among CPUs and GPUs. In concept, we separate the OpenMP threads and GPU threads. For a worksharing construct in OpenMP, we keep the OpenMP threads intact, while introduce additional GPU agent threads that manages GPU kernels and handles data transfers. Similar to setting up the number of OpenMP threads, the number of GPU agent threads can be defined using an environment variable *OMP_NUM_ACCS*, a *num_accs(integer-expression)* clause for the *parallel* construct, and a function *omp_set_num_accs*. In a parallel region, thread order is like this, GPU threads always have larger thread number than OpenMP threads, and this is compatible to the OpenMP semantics.

The following is the syntax to extend the *static* schedule in *omp for* to control the work distribution among multiple GPUs and CPUs.

```
#pragma omp for schedule (static [,cchunck] [,gchunk] [<C_ratio:G_ratio>])
```

With the new extended schedule, loop iterations are divided hierarchically among CPUs and GPUs. The iterations of a parallel loop is divided into two consecutive parts based on the two ratios *C_ratio* and *G_ratio*, of which the first part is mapped to the CPUs, while the remainder part is assigned to GPUs. The default ratio is 1:0. The distribution between CPUs and GPUs allows users to control the load balance. Each partition is further divided into small chunks, whose size is specified by *cchunk* on the CPU side and *gchunk* on the GPU part. These chunks are statically assigned to the related computing devices in a round-robin fashion in the order of the thread number. When any of the chunk size values is not specified, the related partition space is divided into chunks that are approximately equal in size, with one chunk assigned to one computing device. We call it a *heterogeneous schedule* if the ratio description is specified.

The work distribution between CPU and GPU leads to a data distribution by a compiler. Typically, data partitioning can be carried out by splitting the arrays either in strips or in chessboard blocks, generating different communication topologies. When using chessboard partitioning, every GPU has two indistinct neighbors, and this incurs more communication overhead, so we only consider strip-based partitioning currently.

Currently, *omp master*, *omp critical*, *omp atomic* and *omp ordered* are not allowed in the loop body decorated with heterogeneous schedule clause. Because on GPGPUs, it's usually hard and expensive to run a parallel loop with fine-grained synchronizations in it with out-of-order multithreaded execution model (such as CUDA).

The heterogeneous schedule can be used by an expert programmer or by a performance tuning system.

3   Compiling Supports

On heterogeneous platforms, data prefetch is asynchronous data transfer overlapped with kernel computation. Compared with multicore prefetching, longer prefetch distance is usually needed since the *cache* (global memory of GPUs) here has longer latency and more data may be needed to transfer for a kernel computation. And this calls for inter-procedural code motion. So, effective compile-time prefetch further needs accurate control flow information and accurate dataflow information. To overcome the limitation of compiler analysis, we use execution-based prefetch.

Prefetch region is a loop that has a large iteration count and contains parallel loops with heterogeneous schedule. The codes of prefetching threads are actually another multi-threaded program. Through team collaboration, these prefetching threads can go multiple parallel regions ahead of the computing threads making enough room for communication scheduling.

Before code generation, static loop partitioning and array region analysis are applied, and runtime calls are inserted to describe array access information of each structured code block. After that, prefetching codes can be generated in three steps. Firstly, each prefetch region is cloned and placed in a separate procedure, and live-in variables are identified and passed as parameters. Each callee in the dynamic scope of the prefetch region should also be cloned. Thread forking codes are inserted before the prefetch region, and *kill* is inserted after the region to terminate prefetching threads. Secondly, inter-procedural program slicing is applied in the cloned prefetch region where slicing seeds are the data access expressions in the runtime calls. Thirdly, store removal should be applied to those assignment statements to statically allocated global variables and heap variables, since prefetching codes cannot modify those global data. Although store removal can lead to a different control flow path in the prefetching code from the original program, but it is usually not the case.

In the generated prefetch codes, most of the statements are just data access descriptions. OpenMP runtime calls (such as *barrier* and *ompc_fork*) are also reserved as they are in the original program, but act differently since they are called by a prefetch thread not by a computing thread.

4   Runtime Use-Def Analysis and Prefetch Scheduling

In our prefetcing scheme, there are two kinds of threads for data prefetching. The prefetch inspection threads are responsible for gathering data access information, while the prefetch execution threads see to issuing prefetches and synchronizing with the corresponding computing threads. In fact, there are one prefetch inspection thread and one working thread for each separated memory, i.e. the number of prefetch inspection threads is larger than the number of current active accelerators by one, since the CPU side also need to apply data prefetching for the existence of separate memories. These prefetch threads are forked on the entry of each parallel region in the prefetch code.

To temporarily store data access information, an internal data structure called DFTrace is introduced and shared by these threads. DFTrace is a queue, and new items are pushed into the tail by the prefetch inspection thread, and the front item is popped out by the prefetch execution thread. There are two kinds of items in the DFTrace, barrier routine calls and structured code blocks (mostly are loops). For each code block entry in the DFTrace, only data access information of the related computing thread (local information) are recorded. Due to the OpenMP memory model, local modifications to shared data cannot be seen by other threads before the next flush. In our system, local definitions can only be seen by other threads after the next barrier. For each barrier entry in the DFTrace, there are a dynamic counter, a compile-time assigned tag, a prefetching queue and data regions that need to be flushed. In the barrier operation of each prefetch inspection thread, local definitions during this barrier phase will be merged by the prefetch inspection thread and exchanged with other prefetch inspection threads of the same team, to build up global definition information and to record them in the barrier entry.

Pending prefetches and instant prefetches are two kinds of prefetches that will be generated by prefetch inspection thread. The instant prefetch can be carried out immediately, because its reaching definition has been finished and the data have been flushed. A pending prefetch is hung upon a future barrier which is the reaching definition of the data, and is triggered on when the corresponding barrier has finished execution. Prefetching threads keep pace with the computing threads through barrier matching, which is realized by matching the barrier counter from different threads.

For each use region in a newly generated DFTrace entry, its use-def chain is built using set operations on the fly. The following algorithm describes how to generate prefetches from this analysis. As we have pointed out, there are three kinds of definitions during the analysis, barrier operations recorded in the DFTrace, data prefetches recorded on certain barrier entries, and past definitions that are not recorded in the DFTrace. To apply data flow analysis, barrier entries are visited in reverse order. Each single datum has only one reaching definition at runtime, while data region may have several reaching definitions, and each corresponds to one sub- data region. If the reaching definition is in the DFtrace, the related prefetch is a pending prefetch at the related barrier. Otherwise,the reaching definition is a past definition in this thread or in some other thread. If the related data does not present in the local memory, an instant prefetch can be generated.

```
Algorithm. Prefetch generation for a use region
Input: u is the USE region of a newly generated DFTrace item
Output: Pending prefetches and instant prefetches
1. for (each barrier of DFTrace in reverse order, from the tail on){
2. let the local def region of the item be ldef, and its global def
      region be gdef
3. u=u-ldef;
4. if(u==null) break;
5. if (meet(u,gdef)!=null) {
6. pf1=meet(u,gdef);
7. pf1 is a pending prefetch, and is hung at this barrier;
8. }
9. u=u-gdef;
10. for (each pending prefetch, p_pf, at this barrier)
11. u=u-regions(p_pf);
12. }
13. u_remote=u-local_memory;
14. if (u_remote!=null)
15. u_remote is an instant prefetch;
```

Fig. 1. Runtime data flow analysis and prefetch generation

Figure 2 illustrates the prefetching scheme with a snapshot of a simple code. The code structure of a computing thread is given on the left, which is comprised of four parallel loops and four barriers, and the second loop (L2 for short) is being executed right now. In this code, there are definitions to array A in both loop1 and loop2, *output* is a runtime call to describe DEF array regions while *input* describing USE array regions. Helper code of the prefetch inspection thread is outlined on the right, in which kernel calls have been cut away and the fourth loop is now being inspected. The DFTrace is shown in the middle, for the use region A[0-74] in the fourth loop, we find two reaching definitions using use-def analysis. A[50-74] is a remote definition in B2, so a pending prefetch is generated there. A[0-49] is a past definition, and since part of it hits in local memory, an instant prefetch A[25-49] is generated.

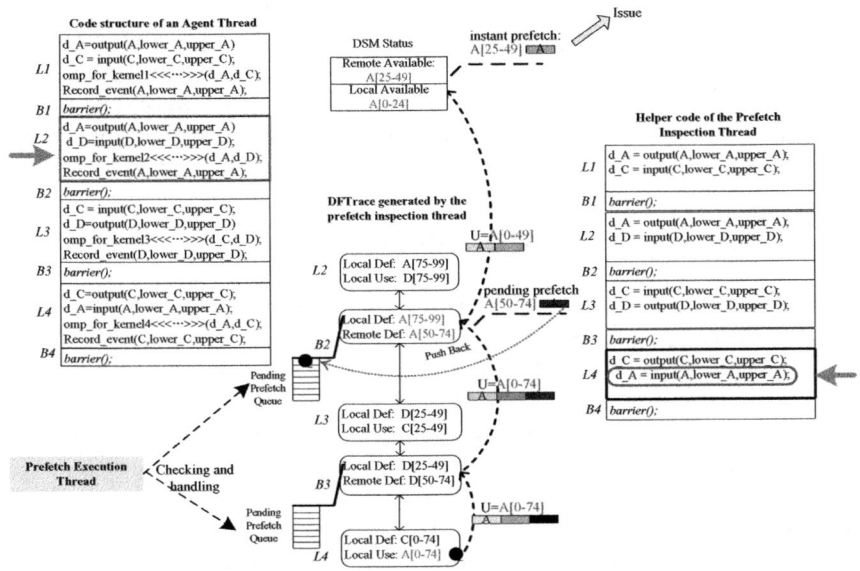

Fig. 2. Snapshot of the prefetching scheme

The thread relationship between computing threads and prefetching threads is set up through message exchange on the entry of the first encountered parallel region. Prefetch execution threads keep pace with the computing threads to update their memory status through barrier matching. To support barrier matching, a separate barrier counter is maintained for each computing thread and its prefetch inspection thread, with the initial value being 0. Each prefetching inspection thread acts exactly the same as its computing thread in aspect of control flows when store removal does not change the control flow of prefetching codes, Or else, prefetch inspection thread may generate irrelevant prefetches, but this is very rare.

4.1   Adaptive Scheduling

The above scheduling strategy is to launch the data transfer as early as possible. But it is not optimal, if data transfer needed by a computing thread is hindered by a un-related data prefetch. This means that the corresponding prefetch of the former data transfer should have been scheduled ahead of the ongoing prefetch. In many scientific applications, communication patterns are repetitive and keep stable for a relative long time, so an adaptive method can be adopted. Runtime system monitors such violations, and will adjust the prefetch placement in the next iteration.

To discriminate different data transfers, each barrier call is assigned a compile-time tag and each data transfer shares the same tag as its reaching definition (the barrier call). At runtime, if an agent thread is hindered by an un-related data prefetch when it tries to launch new data transfers, a new scheduling rule will be generated and sent to the corresponding prefetching thread. The rule is a binary tuple (pf_tag, wt_tag), where pf_tag is the tag of the ongoing prefetching operation and wt_tag is the tag of the waiting data transfer. This binary tuple indicates that in the next loop iteration, the scheduling order of the two prefetches should be exchanged. After adaptation, the tag of each involved prefetch operation may be changed to the tag of the barrier that it attaches to currently.

5   Implementation and Evaluation

Our compiler is based on the OpenUH compiler which is built by the University of Houston focusing on OpenMP research. We uses its source-to-source functionality to translate OpenMP codes into hybrid codes of pthreads and CUDA. We developed a runtime library called OMPH, which is built upon the traditional OpenMP runtime, supports collaboration between different prefetch inspection threads and supports the communication between prefetch inspection threads, prefetch execution threads and the agent threads. An intelligent software distributed shared memory system (DSM) is also realized including data layout transformation functionality and heap management. After the source-to-source compilation, the compiler invokes native NVCC compiler to compile the hybrid code of pthreads and CUDA. At last, it links the pthreads library, CUDA library, object files, OMPH library and the DSM library together to get the executables.

Translator. Our compiler supports the heterogeneous *static* schedule of *omp for*. Heterogeneous loop tiling is applied in the LNO phase, which is realized through loop index splitting according to the partitioning ratio values, thread divergence generation and loop tiling according to different chunk sizes on different computing devices. For each array reference, the array region is computed and its halo width is also computed in order to simplify runtime management. Array region information of each structured block is used to generate data description DSM calls. Currently, only the rectangular array region is supported, and the non-rectangular region will be conservative to the entire array.

The generation of prefetching codes is comprised of two phases. In the ipa phase, prefetch region is identified and procedure cloning is annotated for all callsites in the dynamic scope of the prefetch region. And then an interprocedural slicing is applied, where slicing seeds include subscript expressions of each array reference, *if* clause expression and *num_threads* clause of each *omp for*. The latter two kinds of expressions are considered because they impact the control flow of each parallel loop but are not executable WHIRL statement yet before OpenMP transformation. Slicing annotations are marked in WHIRL statements. During the LNO phase, loop partitioning for heterogeneous schedule is applied and slicing annotations are perserved during that time. After loop partitioning and OpenMP code transformation, procedure cloning is performed and irrelevant codes are cut away according to slicing annotation, and prefetching codes are generated.

Target Machine. We evaluation our prefetch scheme on a system with two Tesla C2050 cards, figure 3 gives the layout of the motherboard and the two GPU cards are in slot4 and slot8. There are two Intel Xeon E5620 qual-cores CPUs which support two SMT threads per core and there were 12GB DDR3 main memory. Each Tesla C2050 card has 3GB global memory, 14 stream multiprocessors and 32 stream processors per stream multi-processor run at a frequency of 1.15GHz. Tesla C2050 uses PCI-E 2.0 x16 bus to connect with the system and has two DMA engines to transfer data in uplink and downlink simultaneously. The operating system is SUSE Linux 11.2 and CUDA SDK 4.0 is used in the following experiments. Since the distance between different CPUs and GPUs is inconsistent, agent threads and prefetching inspection threads are bound to the nearest cpu cores with respect to the related GPUs in the following experiments. We found that the worst binding will lead to 9.4% performance decrease for SP's static prefetching version.

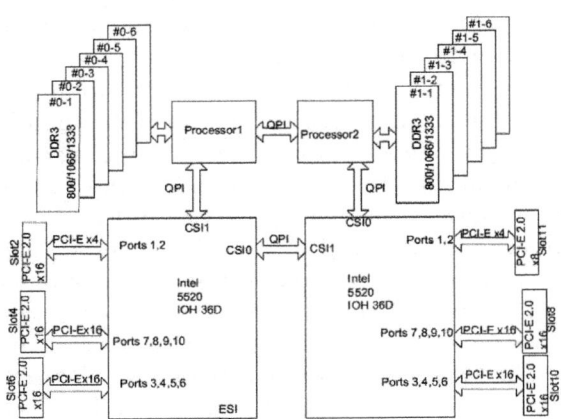

Fig. 3. The motherboard layout of the GPU platform

Benchmarks. We evaluated our prefetching scheme with three benchmarks, SP from NPB-3.3/OMP, kmeans and nbody. For all the parallel loops in these program, the partitioning ratio between CPUs and GPUs is 0:1. We rewrite SP in C language since our compiler system only supports C language at present and add heterogeneous schedule clause for each parallel loop. In SP, there are multiple parallel regions, and some of the parallel loops are partitioned along

Table 1. Ideal prefetching: communication times and the maximal overlapped ratios

Benchmark	Computation Time(s)	Data Transfer Time(s)	Overlapped Time(s)	Overlapped Percentage(%)
SP (CLASS C)	124.26	85.8	49.40	57.6
Kmeans (16M)	6.47	5.65	3.70	65.5
Nbody (32K)	22.45	15.9	10.65	47.44

different array dimensions, leading to a large amount of data transfer (data redistributions on several main large arrays) between the two GPUs. Kmeans is a popular algorithm used in data mining. The input of SP is class C, while nbody runs with an input of 32K nodes. The input of Kmeans is 16M nodes, 32 features per node and 10 clusters. All these benchmarks are compute intensive, and better kernel speedups can be achieved using more than one GPUs.

An ideal static prefetching version is constructed for each benchmark, and related data are collected in Table 1. Not all the data transfer time listed in the table can be overlapped with kernel computing. In SP, some newly generated data will be used immediately in the next kernel, so such communication cannot be hiden by data prefetching. For SP, optimal communication placement is achieved with the help of profiling, casual placement of the data transfers will not lead to maximum overlap. Insufficient global memory problem is encountered in both kmeans and nbody, and memory replacement incurs data transfer between CPUs and GPUs. Nbody has less overlapped percentage than kmeans, because the prefetch distance in nbody is just several small loop tiles while in kmeans it is one entire outer loop iteration.

Figure 4 gives the results of the three benchmarks. In all these tests, OMP_NUM_ACCS is set to be 2. And execution times are shown in Figure 4a. In the figure, standard version is a hand-tuned hybrid program of pthreads and CUDA, without special communication code motion or runtime support. In the DSM version, all the communication is realized using DSM routine calls, and it has no prefetching optimization either. The execution times are normalized to that of the standard version. Figure 4c shows the speedups of different prefetching schemes according to standard versions, while Figure 4d shows the percentage difference. In SP, the reason of less speedup of eager policy than static prefetching is due to the blindness of the prefetch placement. In fact, a certain data prefetch takes long time, and during that time several kernels finished running and a follow-up kernel is hindered since it needs some halo-region data transfer before launching. When using adaptive placement policy, the placement of the prefetch will be adjusted in the first two outer-loop iterations, and after that the related prefetch arrives at its optimal position, so a better speedup is achieved. For kmeans and nbody, due to the relative simple behaviors of the applications, runtime-prefetching scheme almost achieved the same speedup as the static prefetching version.

Figure 4b shows the runtime overhead of the DSM system which is relatively small. Many of the overhead comes from locking operations for accessing shared

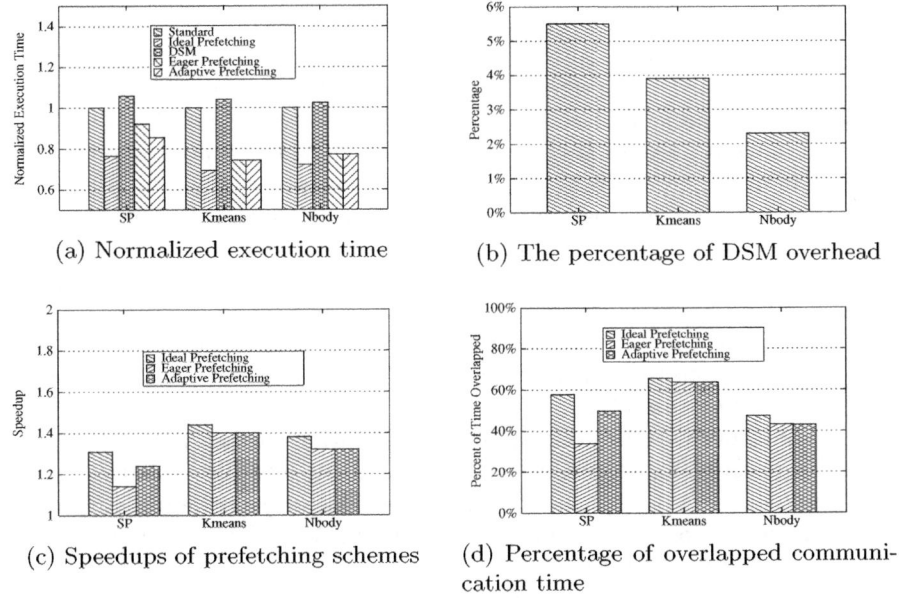

(a) Normalized execution time   (b) The percentage of DSM overhead

(c) Speedups of prefetching schemes   (d) Percentage of overlapped communication time

Fig. 4. Effects of prefetching schemes and overhead of the DSM system

data objects such as software DSM items. To minimize the cost of heap allocation on GPU, a heap manager with a caching policy is realized. The heap manager will not actually free a memory block when the user frees it. Instead, the base address of the data block will be stored into a reclaim buffer along with its size. For each heap allocation request, the reclaim buffer is searched for a data block with the same size. Only when not found, a new data block will be allocated. And the manager will not free any data block in the reclaim buffer unless a new allocation request can not be satisfied. The prefetch inspection threads run very fast unless memory allocation cannot be satisfied by the reclaim buffer.

The experimental results show that the proposed runtime-prefetching scheme can achieve comparable speedup to hand-tuned, static prefetching.

6   Related Work

Heterogeneous architecture has been a hot research topic in computer architectures. Many work has been done on improving the programming productivity and program optimizations on such systems. We compare our work with some of them in the areas of programming interface, optimizations, compiler and runtime support.

OpenCL [7] attempts to provide a common programming interface for multi-core and many-core platforms. However, its programming level is relatively low, especially in the complicated data management part, which has significant performance impact. There are many tools such as [21] [8] developed to simplify programming on accelerators. Several language extensions are put forward to porting legacy codes to heterogenous platforms efficiently. OpenACC [15] is an open standard for offloading codes in standard C, C++ and Fortran from a host CPU to an attached accelerator. It allows the programmer to specify guidance on how to map parallel loops onto accelerators, to describe data layout and optimize data movement in an abstract way, so as to help compiler generate efficient codes. It is quite similar in syntax to PGI Accelerator [20]. These extensions provide users high level abstractions for optimizations. A different approach is adopted in [9] to optimize a certain type of data transfer among CUDA kernels (cyclic data communication), which combines compiler analysis and runtime optimizations and does not depend on the strength of static compile-time analyses or on programmer-supplied annotations. Compared with the above works, our work proposed a moderate extension to the standard API OpenMP to support heterogeneous programming.

There are many studies on synergistic execution on heterogeneous processors, taking workload balancing and data transfer into consideration. Among them, some of the works focus on dynamic workload partitioning and scheduling. Task-driven execution model is used in [12][13] [1] [16], where high level APIs are put forward to describe data parallelism and tasks are organized into DAGs at runtime for adaptive mapping on heterogeneous platforms. Besides, StarPU [1] also provides data prefetching for future tasks. An OpenCL framework is proposed [10] to provide a single compute device image for systems with multiple GPUs, where the OpenCL runtime maintains a virtual device memory, and identifies an optimal workload distribution by applying a run-time memory access range analysis and a sampling run to each kernel. For optimal workload mapping, data transfer between CPUs and GPUs is deferred until necessary [3]. Many of the above works take data transfer into consideration when scheduling tasks, and some of them even realize data preloading. However, these approaches are not suitable for general OpenMP programs. There are also many works on static workload partitioning. A combination of thread mapping and subteam is proposed [24] to let programmers control over how work is allocated on these architectures statically. Automatic static approach is adopted in [17] for MATLAB programs. This work maintains resource vectors, uses a variant of list scheduling and tries to minimize the amount of data transfer needed in workload mapping. Another purely static approach [5] is developed based on predictive modeling and program features to find the best partitioning on heterogeneous systems. Our approach handles the data transfer optimization in a generic and integrated way that combines OpenMP extension, compiler analysis and runtime support. It can handle complicated control flows and data flows.

7   Conclusion and Future Work

In this paper, we present a compiler-assisted runtime prefetching scheme to overlap the data transfer on heterogeneous systems. In order to achieve the goal, we first extend OpenMP with a heterogeneous schedule clause to enable static task partition among CPUs and GPUs. The new extension enables programmers to fully control the load balance on such a system. We then implement the extension in the OpenUH compiler to generate hybrid codes of Pthreads and CUDA, as well as software DSM to support data communications. To cut down the overhead of data transfer between device memories and the main memory, we demonstrated a runtime-prefetching scheme that leverages compile-time analysis information and code generation support. Prefetching codes are simply another OpenMP program, in which prefetching threads can collaborate with each other and go multiple parallel regions ahead of computing threads, and this provides the long prefetching distance needed in the GPU scenario. Runtime inter-thread dataflow analysis is used to overcome the limitations of compiler analysis. To optimize communication placement, an adaptive scheduling policy is given. We test our compiler and runtime system with three benchmarks, and the results show that runtime-prefetching scheme can have similar performance as its hand-coded counterparts.

For the future work, we plan to further optimize the prefetching scheme by exploiting additional compiler analysis, and evaluating them using more benchmarks and applications. We would like to discuss the language extensions with OpenMP ARB to seek a unified solution for keeping load balance among different devices.

Acknowledgement. This research is supported in part by the National Hi-Tech Research and Development 863 Program of China (2012AA010902), the National Fundamental Research Program of China (2011CB302504), the National Natural Science Foundation of China (60970024 and 60925009) and the Innovation Research Group of NSFC (60921002).

We would like to thank the reviewers for valuable comments and suggestions.

References

1. Augonnet, C., Thibault, S., Namyst, R., Wacrenier, P.A.: Starpu: a unified platform for task scheduling on heterogeneous multicore architectures. Concurr. Comput.: Pract. Exper. 23, 187–198 (2011)
2. Barrachina, S., Castillo, M., Igual, F., Mayo, R., Quintana-Orti, E.: Evaluation and tuning of the level 3 cublas for graphics processors. In: IEEE International Symposium on Parallel and Distributed Processing, IPDPS 2008, pp. 1–8 (April 2008)
3. Becchi, M., Byna, S., Cadambi, S., Chakradhar, S.: Data-aware scheduling of legacy kernels on heterogeneous platforms with distributed memory. In: Proceedings of the 22nd ACM Symposium on Parallelism in Algorithms and Architectures, SPAA 2010, pp. 82–91. ACM, New York (2010), http://doi.acm.org/10.1145/1810479.1810498
4. Che, S., Sheaffer, J.W., Skadron, K.: Dymaxion: optimizing memory access patterns for heterogeneous systems. In: Proceedings of 2011 International Conference for High Performance Computing, Networking, Storage and Analysis, SC 2011, pp. 13:1–13:11. ACM, New York (2011)

5. Grewe, D., O'Boyle, M.F.P.: A Static Task Partitioning Approach for Heterogeneous Systems Using OpenCL. In: Knoop, J. (ed.) CC 2011. LNCS, vol. 6601, pp. 286–305. Springer, Heidelberg (2011)
6. Gelado, I., Kelm, J.H., Ryoo, S., Lumetta, S.S., Navarro, N., Hwu, W.M.W.: Cuba: an architecture for efficient cpu/co-processor data communication. In: Proceedings of the 22nd Annual International Conference on Supercomputing, ICS 2008, pp. 299–308. ACM, New York (2008)
7. Group, K.O.W.: The opencl specification (2011), http://www.khronos.org/registry/cl/
8. Han, T.D., Abdelrahman, T.S.: /hi/cuda: a high-level directive-based language for gpu programming. In: GPGPU-2: Proceedings of 2nd Workshop on General Purpose Processing on Graphics Processing Units, pp. 52–61. ACM, New York (2009)
9. Jablin, T.B., Prabhu, P., Jablin, J.A., Johnson, N.P., Beard, S.R., August, D.I.: Automatic cpu-gpu communication management and optimization. In: Proceedings of the 32nd ACM SIGPLAN Conference on Programming Language Design and Implementation, PLDI 2011, pp. 142–151. ACM, New York (2011)
10. Kim, J., Kim, H., Lee, J.H., Lee, J.: Achieving a single compute device image in opencl for multiple gpus. In: Proceedings of the 16th ACM Symposium on Principles and Practice of Parallel Programming, PPoPP 2011, pp. 277–288. ACM, New York (2011)
11. Lee, V.W., Kim, C., Chhugani, J., Deisher, M., Kim, D., Nguyen, A.D., Satish, N., Smelyanskiy, M., Chennupaty, S., Hammarlund, P., Singhal, R., Dubey, P.: Debunking the 100x gpu vs. cpu myth: an evaluation of throughput computing on cpu and gpu. In: Proceedings of the 37th Annual International Symposium on Computer Architecture, ISCA 2010, pp. 451–460. ACM, New York (2010)
12. Linderman, M.D., Collins, J.D., Wang, H., Meng, T.H.: Merge: a programming model for heterogeneous multi-core systems. In: Proceedings of the 13th International Conference on Architectural Support for Programming Languages and Operating Systems, ASPLOS XIII, pp. 287–296. ACM, New York (2008)
13. Luk, C.K., Hong, S., Kim, H.: Qilin: exploiting parallelism on heterogeneous multiprocessors with adaptive mapping. In: Proceedings of the 42nd Annual IEEE/ACM International Symposium on Microarchitecture, MICRO 42, pp. 45–55. ACM, New York (2009)
14. Meng, J., Skadron, K.: Performance modeling and automatic ghost zone optimization for iterative stencil loops on gpus. In: Proceedings of the 23rd International Conference on Supercomputing, ICS 2009, pp. 256–265. ACM, New York (2009)
15. Org., O.S.: The openacc application programming interface (2011), http://www.openacc-standard.org/Downloads/OpenACC.1.0.pdf?attredirects=0&d=1
16. Planas, J., Badia, R.M., Ayguadé, E., Labarta, J.: Hierarchical task-based programming with starss. Int. J. High Perform. Comput. Appl. 23, 284–299 (2009), http://dl.acm.org/citation.cfm?id=1572226.1572233
17. Prasad, A., Anantpur, J., Govindarajan, R.: Automatic compilation of matlab programs for synergistic execution on heterogeneous processors. In: Proceedings of the 32nd ACM SIGPLAN Conference on Programming Language Design and Implementation, PLDI 2011, pp. 152–163. ACM, New York (2011), http://doi.acm.org/10.1145/1993498.1993517
18. Strengert, M., Müller, C., Dachsbacher, C., Ertl, T.: Cudasa: Compute unified device and systems architecture. In: Favre, J.M., Ma, K.L. (eds.) EGPGV, pp. 49–56. Eurographics Association (2008)

19. Sung, I.J., Stratton, J.A., Hwu, W.M.W.: Data layout transformation exploiting memory-level parallelism in structured grid many-core applications. In: Proceedings of the 19th International Conference on Parallel Architectures and Compilation Techniques, PACT 2010, pp. 513–522. ACM, New York (2010)
20. The Portland Group: PGI Fortran & C Accelator Programming Model. White Paper (2010)
21. Ueng, S.-Z., Lathara, M., Baghsorkhi, S.S., Hwu, W.-m.W.: CUDA-Lite: Reducing GPU Programming Complexity. In: Amaral, J.N. (ed.) LCPC 2008. LNCS, vol. 5335, pp. 1–15. Springer, Heidelberg (2008)
22. Venkatasubramanian, S., Vuduc, R.W., none, n.: Tuned and wildly asynchronous stencil kernels for hybrid cpu/gpu systems. In: Proceedings of the 23rd International Conference on Supercomputing, ICS 2009, pp. 244–255. ACM, New York (2009)
23. Vineet, V., Harish, P., Patidar, S., Narayanan, P.J.: Fast minimum spanning tree for large graphs on the gpu. In: Proceedings of the Conference on High Performance Graphics 2009, HPG 2009, pp. 167–171. ACM, New York (2009)
24. White, L.: OpenMP Extensions for Heterogeneous Architectures. In: Chapman, B.M., Gropp, W.D., Kumaran, K., Müller, M.S. (eds.) IWOMP 2011. LNCS, vol. 6665, pp. 94–107. Springer, Heidelberg (2011),
    http://dl.acm.org/citation.cfm?id=2023025.2023036
25. Yang, C., Wang, F., Du, Y., Chen, J., Liu, J., Yi, H., Lu, K.: Adaptive optimization for petascale heterogeneous cpu/gpu computing. In: Proceedings of the 2010 IEEE International Conference on Cluster Computing, CLUSTER 2010, pp. 19–28. IEEE Computer Society, Washington, DC (2010)
26. Yang, Y., Xiang, P., Kong, J., Zhou, H.: A gpgpu compiler for memory optimization and parallelism management. In: Proceedings of the 2010 ACM SIGPLAN Conference on Programming Language Design and Implementation, PLDI 2010, pp. 86–97. ACM, New York (2010)

Experiments with WRF on Intel® Many Integrated Core (Intel MIC) Architecture

Larry Meadows

Intel Corporation, Hillsboro OR, USA
lawrence.f.meadows@intel.com

Abstract. WRF is a well-known weather code with a hybrid OpenMP and MPI implementation. This paper investigates the performance of WRF on heterogeneous hardware consisting of Intel® Xeon® processors and Intel MIC Architecture co-processors, using offload, OpenMP, and MPI.

1 Introduction

The Intel Many Integrated Core (MIC) architecture[1] was originally announced in May of 2010. The Knights Ferry design and development kit will be followed with the Knights Corner product. The Intel MIC architecture combines many Intel Architecture CPU cores on a single chip. This architecture is very different from the GPGPU architectures in that it can execute a full operating system and entire programs, rather than just kernels. In particular, it is possible to run one or more ranks of an MPI program on an Intel MIC chip.

The Weather Research and Forecasting (WRF) Model[2] is a widely respected weather prediction system developed by a collaborative partnership among NCAR, NOAA, and several other agencies. A version of WRF was included in the retired SPEC HPC2002 benchmark suite and is included in the SPEC MPI2007 benchmark suite. WRF has a hybrid MPI and OpenMP parallel model, and comes with benchmark data sets that represent real problems and include verification tests, making it an excellent code for studying and tuning performance on heterogeneous parallel systems.

Section 2 describes the Intel MIC hardware architecture. Section 3 describes the Intel OpenMP and MPI implementations for Intel MIC architecture. Section 4 describes WRF, its parallel model, and the benchmark data set. Section 5 presents results for compiler offload. Section 6 presents results for hybrid MPI+OpenMP runs on heterogeneous hardware.

2 Intel MIC Architecture

2.1 Hardware Architecture

The results in this paper were obtained on a Knights Ferry (KNF) PCI-Express card. The KNF processor consists of 32 in-order cores running at 1200MHz,

B.M. Chapman et al. (Eds.): IWOMP 2012, LNCS 7312, pp. 130–139, 2012.

each with four hardware thread contexts. Each core has 256KiB of shared L2 cache, 32KiB of L1 data cache, and 32Kib of L1 instruction cache. The cores are interconnected to each other and to memory controllers by a ring bus. All caches are coherent with each other and with main memory. Each core has a 512-bit vector floating point unit that is able to operate on 16 single precision floating point values per cycle.

The hardware thread contexts each have their own set of scalar Intel64 registers as well as 512-bit vector floating point registers. The four hardware threads help to cover latency as is usual in SMT architectures.

Fig. 1 is a block diagram of the Intel MIC architecture.

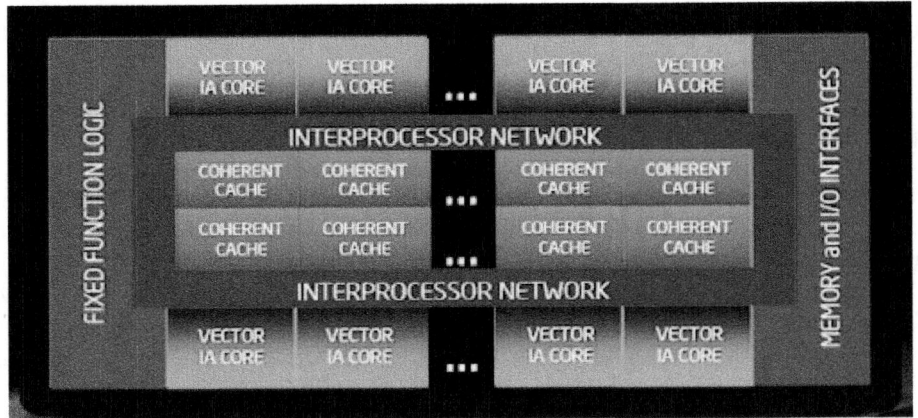

Fig. 1. Intel MIC Architecture Block Diagram

KNF is limited to 2GiB of GDDR5 memory.

Multiple KNF cards can communicate with each other and with the host over the PCI express bus. A DMA engine supports asynchronous data movement between cards and between a card and the host.

The host hardware used in this paper is a dual socket Intel Xeon X5680 running at 3.33GHz. Each socket is a 6 core part, and each core has two hardware thread contexts, for a total of 24 hardware thread contexts. The system has 24GiB of memory and runs Red Hat EL6.

2.2   System Software Architecture

KNF runs a version of the Linux kernel with a Busybox[3]environment. The device has a ramdisk to hold the kernel and the command environment. A virtual ethernet driver and NFS support is provided, so host file systems can be mounted on the card, or native executables and shared objects can be copied to the ramdisk.

Both the host kernel and the device kernel support DMA through a kernel driver. DMAs can be initiated from either the host or the device and can be reads or writes. The hardware DMA engine requires 64-byte alignment of source and destination addresses. It is also possible to map remote memory across the PCI-Express bus so that writes from one side are visible to the other side.

For memory to be mapped or DMAd, the physical memory must first be registered (and the virtual addresses pinned) so that it isn't paged out. Registration is a relatively expensive operation, and there is a limit to the amount of memory that can be registered, so careful management of memory registration is required.

3   Software Stack Implementation

The work described here uses three major pieces of software: OpenMP, MPI, and compiler-assisted offload.

3.1   OpenMP

Intel's OpenMP implementation fully supports the OpenMP 3.1 specification[4]. OpenMP annotations are recognized by the compiler, which then generates code and calls to the OpenMP runtime library to realize the OpenMP parallelism[5].

Since Intel MIC is an implementation of Intel64 Architecture, it is able to use substantially the same compiler and runtime as Xeon. There are two differences between Intel MIC and Intel Xeon that affect the runtime implementation or the optimal use of OpenMP: thread yielding and affinity.

The Intel MIC core is a 4-thread implementation of simultaneous multithreading (SMT)[6]. When a thread is stalled the core executes another thread that is able to execute. The OpenMP runtime often uses busy wait loops for synchronization. It is important that the thread executing the busy wait loop yield the core so that other threads on the same core can execute. Intel MIC provides the delay instruction for this purpose. The delay instruction causes the hardware thread picker to advance to the next thread on the core. This instruction takes an integer argument giving the number of cycles for which the thread should be skipped.

Each hardware thread on Intel MIC is represented by an OS CPU number. By default, the OS can schedule OpenMP threads on any available CPU, and can change the CPU on which an OpenMP thread is executed at any time. It is often useful to restrict the sets of CPUs on which an OpenMP thread can execute, and also to place particular OpenMP threads on the same core as other threads.

Intel provides the KMP_AFFINITY environment variable (as well as an API) for this purpose[7]. OpenMP threads can be bound to individual OS CPUs or to cores, and can be placed according to a policy, or explicitly placed on a given core or OS CPU. The policies are called compact, to place threads in order on cores; scatter, to place threads round-robin on cores; and balanced, to place threads in order on cores but to use as many cores as possible.

3.2   MPI

One of the major differences between Intel MIC and GPGPU is that Intel MIC supports a full OS environment. Entire programs, not just kernels, can execute on Intel MIC. Intel provides an implementation of MPI-2[8] based on MPICH2[9] that supports MPI communication between process on the devices and processes on the host, and will support clusters of such nodes. The implementation uses a combination of mapped memory and DMA for host-device communication, and shared memory for intra-device and intra-host communication.

3.3   Compiler Offload

Intel MIC can be used in two ways: as a platform for native execution, and as an offload platform to run portions of a computation. The latter is the way in which GPGPUs are used as accelerators today. Intel's compiler provides the ability to offload essentially arbitrary sections of code to the device from a program executing on the host using directives (in Fortran) and pragmas (in C/C++). The offload directives typically specify the data to be transferred between the host and the device and delimit the code to be executed on the device. The actual code that is executed on the device can use OpenMP directives or any other model of parallelism, make system calls, do I/O, and anything else a native program can do on the device.

Section 5 has an example of offloading a computation from WRF onto the device (in Fortran).

Offload directives exist for Fortran, C, and C++. The remainder of this section describes some of the directives for Fortran.

It is possible to offload an OpenMP parallel region to the device with the !DEC$ OMP OFFLOAD directive followed by an OpenMP parallel construct. This results in an offload region consisting of the body of the parallel construct:

```
!DEC$ OMP OFFLOAD
!OMP PARALLEL

. . .

!$OMP END PARALLEL
```

The combined parallel workshare constructs may also be used. It is also possible to offload a block of code or a call statement.

Attributes following the offload directive tell the compiler which variables are input to the device (IN), output from the device (OUT), or both input and output (INOUT). The compiler generates code to transfer the input data before executing the offload region, execute the offload region, and transfer the data back after executing the offload region. The compiler attempts to automatically transfer data that is used in the offload region, but it is often necessary and/or more efficient to explicitly specify the data to be transferred. There are also mechanisms to transfer data asynchronously and to start an offload region and later wait for its completion.

It is also possible to place persistent data, for example, Fortran common blocks, on both the device and the host. Such data can be updated independently by both the device and the host, and can also be transferred to and from the host with the appropriate offload attributes.

Finally, if a subprogram is called from within an offload region, it is necessary to annotate the subprogram definition so that a device version of the subprogram is created. This is done with the !DEC$ ATTRIBUTES OFFLOAD: MIC:: *subprogram-name* directive.

When an OpenMP offload region is created on the device, it is completely independent from any OpenMP region on the host. The number of threads, thread affinity, and any other attributes of the region are determined from device-specific environment variables or OpenMP API calls. However, OpenMP thread teams persist from one offload region to another on the device, so any thread creation cost is incurred only once.

4   WRF Benchmark

WRF can be run as a single OpenMP process or as multiple MPI+OpenMP processes. The MPI implementation decomposes the domain and exchanges the boundaries of the grid at each timestep. The OpenMP implementation further decomposes the grid into a set of tiles with one tile per OpenMP thread. Each set is computed in parallel using the OpenMP PARALLEL DO construct. The implicit barrier at the end of each construct is used for synchronization.

The benchmark data set used in this paper is the single domain 12km Continental U.S. (CONUS) dataset with a simulation time step of 72 seconds over a three hour simulated time period. This benchmark is from the WRF V3 benchmark page[10]. Version 3.0 of the WRF code was used.

The majority of the execution time is spent in the solve_em subroutine and in subroutines it calls. This subroutine contains 38 PARALLEL DO constructs. Thus there is overhead for starting and ending each construct, as well as some serial time outside of the constructs.

We used Vtune Amplifier XE to profile serial execution of the code on the host. The top 20 functions accounted for 69% of the execution time. The microphysics routine wsm52d took 11.6% of the time.

5   WRF Offload

Reference [11] describes work done to offload the wsm5 microphysics routine to an Nvidia accelerator. Since this function takes only 11.6% of the serial time, this work did not result in significant overall performance improvement. However, it is a good way to demonstrate the offload capabilities of different compilers and hardware, so we performed a similar experiment.

The outer loop for this region is show in Fig.2. The NVIDIA offload involved substantial code restructuring to better match the device's characteristics. Since Intel MIC is a general purpose CPU architecture, we were able to offload this region by simply placing an appropriate directive identifying the offload region and data to be transferred before the outermost DO loop, as seen below:

```
DO j=jts ,jte
        DO k=kts ,kte
        DO i=its ,ite
            t(i ,k)=th(i ,k,j)*pii(i ,k,j)
            qci(i ,k,1) = qc(i ,k,j)
            qci(i ,k,2) = qi(i ,k,j)
            qrs(i ,k,1) = qr(i ,k,j)
            qrs(i ,k,2) = qs(i ,k,j)
        ENDDO
        ENDDO
        CALL wsm52D(t ,  q(ims ,kms,j ),  qci ,  qrs           &
                    ,den(ims ,kms,j )                          &
                    ,p(ims ,kms,j ),  delz(ims ,kms,j )        &
                    ,delt ,g,  cpd,  cpv ,  rd ,  rv ,  t0c    &
                    ,ep1 ,  ep2 ,  qmin                        &
                    ,XLS,  XLV0,  XLF0,  den0 ,  denr          &
                    ,cliq ,cice ,psat                          &
                    ,j                                         &
                    ,rain(ims ,j ),rainncv(ims ,j )            &
                    ,sr(ims ,j )                               &
                    ,ids ,ide ,  jds ,jde ,  kds ,kde          &
                    ,ims ,ime ,  jms ,jme ,  kms ,kme          &
                    ,its ,ite ,  jts ,jte ,  kts ,kte          &
                    ,snow(ims ,j ),snowncv(ims ,j )            &
                                                               )

        DO K=kts ,kte
        DO I=its ,ite
            th(i ,k,j)=t(i ,k)/ pii(i ,k,j)
            qc(i ,k,j) = qci(i ,k,1)
            qi(i ,k,j) = qci(i ,k,2)
            qr(i ,k,j) = qrs(i ,k,1)
            qs(i ,k,j) = qrs(i ,k,2)
        ENDDO
        ENDDO
        ENDDO
```

Fig. 2. wsm5 outer loop

```
!dec$ omp offload target(mic:0) in(delt ,g ,cpd ,cpv ,t0c ,  &
!dec$& den0 ,rd ,rv ,ep1 ,ep2 ,qmin ,XLS ,XLV0 ,XLF0 ,cliq ,      &
!dec$& cice ,psat ,denr ,jts ,jte ,kts ,kte ,its ,ite ,ims ,      &
!dec$& kms ,ids ,                                                 &
!dec$& ide ,jds ,jde ,kds ,kde ,ime ,jms ,jme ,kme )             &
!dec$& in(t ,qci ,qrs) in(delz ,p ,den ,pii )                     &
!dec$& inout(snowncv ,rainncv )                                   &
!dec$& inout(qs ,qr ,qi ,qc ,th ,q ,snow ,rain )                  &
!$omp parallel do private(i ,j ,k ,t ,qci ,qrs)
```

This tells the compiler which variables to transfer in to, out from, or both in to and out from the card, and further to create an OpenMP PARALLEL DO to run on the card. The compiler creates variable descriptors and a function (encapsulated in a shared object). When the first offload region is encountered, the offload runtime on the card loads the shared object into memory; then the offload runtime on the host and the card cooperate to exchange the data and call the offload function.

It is also necessary to ensure that persistent data on the card is properly initialized. The routine wsm5init must be called on the card. Finally, the routine rgmma is called from wsm52D and the compiler must be told that a device version of that routine is required. The following additional directives, and one additional subroutine call, were required in module_mp_wsm5.F and module_physics_init.F:

```
module_mp_wsm5.F:
!dec$ attributes offload: mic:: wsm52D
!dec$ attributes offload: mic:: rgmma
!dec$ attributes offload: wsm5init
module_phsics_init.F:
!dec$ offload target(mic:0) &
!dec$ in(rhoair0 ,rhowater ,rhosnow ,cliq ,cpv ,allowed_to_read )
         call wsm5init(rhoair0 ,rhowater ,rhosnow ,cliq ,cpv , &
                       allowed_to_read )
```

Offloading wsm5 to the Intel MIC card decreased the time spent in wsm5 by a factor of 4.4. This includes the time for data transfer to and from the card. This speedup is comparable to the speedup quoted in [11].

It does not appear that WRF has any other obvious offload opportunities, at least on this benchmark data set. The other high profile routines are not as compute intensive relative to the amount of data that would have to be transferred. Conceivably the offload could be performed at the level of the OpenMP parallel regions in solve_em, but this would involve moving almost all the data to the card and would require a substantial number of offload directives. Therefore, we took advantage of the general purpose abilities of Intel MIC and used MPI to move an entire subdomain of the model to the card. This is described in the next section.

6 MPI Implementation

WRF supports parallelism at two levels. The problem can be decomposed into MPI ranks (processes), and then each rank can use OpenMP for parallelism within the process. This made it easy to run part of the benchmark on the MIC card and part of the benchmark on the host.

Normally we would have started by running a single process on the MIC card, tuning for OpenMP and serial performance, and then adding MPI. However, the benchmark data set is too large to fit in the 2GiB memory of the KNF card. Measurements on the host indicate that the benchmark requires more than 3GiB of memory.

The bulk of the WRF data goes on the main thread's stack. Each OpenMP thread also requires a stack. Since Intel MIC uses lots of threads, the per-thread stack size becomes significant. After experimentation we determined that one MPI rank would fit on the card if the problem was decomposed into four MPI ranks. This resulted in a main thread stack size of 450MiB and per-thread stack sizes of 7MiB for a total of 898MiB on 64 threads. Together with the code size, other internal memory usage, and the ramdisk holding the OS and the images, and memory usage by the kernel and other processes, this resulted in 100% memory usage on the card.

Running 4 ranks, with three on the host and one on the card, resulted in a simulation time speedup of 3.29x over the serial code. The remainder of this section analyzes the various bottlenecks.

6.1 Timing Model

The OpenMP regions all have implicit barriers at the end. There are no MPI calls in the OpenMP regions. The MPI exchanges also result in implicit synchronization. Each simulation timestep consists of a number of OpenMP regions with MPI exchanges and some serial code in between. So the timing model is relatively simple: $T_{step} = T_{omp} + T_{mpi} + T_{serial}$. T_{serial} includes both serial computation time and serial OpenMP overhead (such as loop setup and fork-join overhead). T_{omp} can be further divided into true parallel time and load imbalance: $T_{omp} = T_{par} + T_{imb}$. Load imbalance occurs when one thread has less work than another thread, and shows up as more time spent by a thread in the implicit barrier.

6.2 Timing Measurement and Results

Vtune has two different kinds of profiling collectors. The software stack sampling collector uses posix timers to generate periodic interrupts to each thread. It records the stack at each sample and then provides a breakdown by callstack. This collector was used on the host to collect the initial profile mentioned in Section 4. The second collector uses hardware Performance Monitoring Unit (PMU) events. The events are programmed to interrupt after a certain count threshold is reached. This collector does not provide a callstack but it does provide the IP of the instruction that was executing when the interrupt occured. The software stack sampling collector is not yet available on Intel MIC so we used the PMU collector. We used the hardware event CPU_CLK_UNHALTED which increments on every clock cycle with an overflow threshold of 2,000,000, which results in an effective sample rate of 600 HZ. Using the IP associated with the sample we can get a statistical profile of the application.

The OpenMP runtime library is instrumented to record the entry and exit to each parallel region. The entry is recorded on each thread, and the exit is recorded by the main thread after the parallel region completes (immediately after the master thread returns from the barrier).

Both the runtime instrumentation points and the PMU samples use the high-resolution Time Stamp Counter (TSC) available on the Intel MIC. The TSCs are synchronized between the cores and their resolution is the clock frequency; furthermore the instruction (RDTSC) that is used to read the TSC has very low overhead.

Thus we have two data sources that we can accurately correlate: the beginning and end of each parallel region, and the samples themselves. This gives us estimates of T_{omp} and of $T_{mpi} + T_{serial}$ as follows: when a sample for a thread falls within a parallel region for that thread, it is labeled as T_{omp}; when it falls outside a parallel region, it is labeled as T_{serial}.

We can further segregate the T_{serial} samples by looking at the shared object (module) in which the IP for the sample resides. For example, the OpenMP runtime and the MPI runtime are implemented as shared objects; further the WRF code itself is a separate module (the main program wrf.exe).

We tried to measure MPI time directly using mpiP[12]. The tool worked, but it increased execution time by more than 10%, so the results were inconclusive. Ideally we could get T_{mpi} from the samples that fall into the MPI module; however, much of the MPI time is spent doing DMA in the kernel.

The following table shows T_{par} and T_{imb} statistics per thread, and T_{omp}, T_{serial}, and T_{mpi} (estimated) as percentages of the total simulation time.

	Average	Stddev	Overall
T_{par}	45.17	7.97	
T_{imb}	17.03	7.35	
T_{omp}			64.64
T_{serial}			7.70
T_{mpi}			27.56

7   Conclusions and Future Work

This paper describes the results of running one of the standard WRF benchmarks on Intel MIC KNF hardware using both compiler offload and heterogeneous MPI. A very low overhead method of determining OpenMP load imbalance is presented. The design and development KNF kit exhibits respectable performance.

Some of the methods used in this paper provide implementation ideas for future tools. Future areas for investigation include finer-grained characterization of OpenMP and MPI overheads and analysis of core-level performance on specific WRF subroutines.

References

1. Intel Corporation,
   http://www.intel.com/content/www/us/en/architecture-and-technology/
   many-integrated-core/intel-many-integrated-core-architecture.html
2. NCAR, et al.: The Weather Research and Forecasting Model,
   http://www.wrf-model.org
3. http://busybox.net/about.html
4. The OpenMP ARB, Inc., OpenMP Application Program Interface Version 3.1,
   http://www.openmp.org
5. Tian, X., et al.: Intel OpenMP C++/Fortran Compiler for Hyper-Threading Technology: Implementation and Performance. Intel Technology Journal 6(1) (February 2002)
6. Eggers, S.J., Emer, J.S., Levy, H.M., Lo, J.L., Stamm, R.L., Tullsen, D.M.: Simultaneous Multithreading: A Platform for Next-Generation Processors. IEEE Micro, 12–19 (October 1997)
7. Intel Corporation, Intel® Fortran Compiler XE 12.1 User and Reference Guides, Document number 323276-121US
8. Message Passing Interface Forum, MPI: A Message-Passing Interface Standard, Version 2.2, http://www.mpi-forum.org
9. Argonne National Laboratories,
   http://www.mcs.anl.gov/research/projects/mpich2/
10. WRF WG2, WRF V3 Parallel Benchmark Page,
    http://www.mmm.ucar.edu/wrf/WG2/benchv3/
11. Wolfe, M., Toepfer, C.: PGI Insider, The PGI Accelerator Programming Model on NVIDIA GPUS Part 3: Porting WRF (October 2009)
12. Vetter, J., Chambreau, C.: mpiP: Lightweight, Scalable MPI Profiling, Version 3.3, June 23 (2011), http://mpip.sourceforge.net

Optimizing the Advanced Accelerator Simulation Framework Synergia Using OpenMP

Hongzhang Shan[1], Erich Strohmaier[1], James Amundson[2], and Eric G. Stern[2]

[1] Future Technology Group
Computational Research Division
Lawrence Berkeley National Laboratory
Berkeley, CA 94720
{hshan,estrohmaier}@lbl.gov
[2] Fermi National Accelerator Laboratory
Batavia, IL 60510
{amundson,egstern}@fnal.gov

Abstract. Synergia is an advanced accelerator simulation framework widely used in the accelerator community. Unfortunately, its performance and scalability suffers significantly from very high communication requirements. In this paper, we address this issue by replacing the flat MPI programming model with the hybrid OpenMP+MPI programming model. We describe in detail how the code has been parallelized in OpenMP and what the challenges are. The improved hybrid code can perform over 1.7 times better than the original program for a realistic benchmark problem.

1 Introduction

Synergia [1] is an open source framework developed by the accelerator community to simulate beam dynamics with fully three dimensional space-charge capabilities and a higher order optics implementation. It can be used to predict the motion of high energy particles in a beam (bunched or continuous) in 6D phase space. The electric and magnetic fields are expressed on a 3D rectangular grid, and, at any given time, both longitudinal and transverse motions are treated consistently. It is designed to be run efficiently on parallel computers and the ultimate design goal is to run accelerator simulations on the largest available leadership class computing platforms. However, due to the substantial difficulties in performance optimization of tightly coupled 6D particle-in-cell (PIC) simulations, the near-term goal in code development is to enable efficient code execution on medium size clusters.

The most difficult obstacle to high performance or scalability is the high communication requirement of the current flat MPI implementation. Synergia uses the particle-in-cell (PIC) [8] method to simulate the beam dynamics. The interactions between the particles and the fields cause a large amount of data to be communicated globally between involved processes. Figure 1 shows the scaling behavior of the benchmark problem used with Synergia for this study.

B.M. Chapman et al. (Eds.): IWOMP 2012, LNCS 7312, pp. 140–153, 2012.

With increasing number of MPI processes, the communication time (MPI time) increases steadily. When the number of processes reaches 256, over 70% of the running time has been spent on MPI communication and the total running time no longer declines. In this paper, we will discuss in detail why and how using OpenMP can improve the performance of our applications. In addition, we will also discuss the choices, problems and limitations we face during our optimizing process.

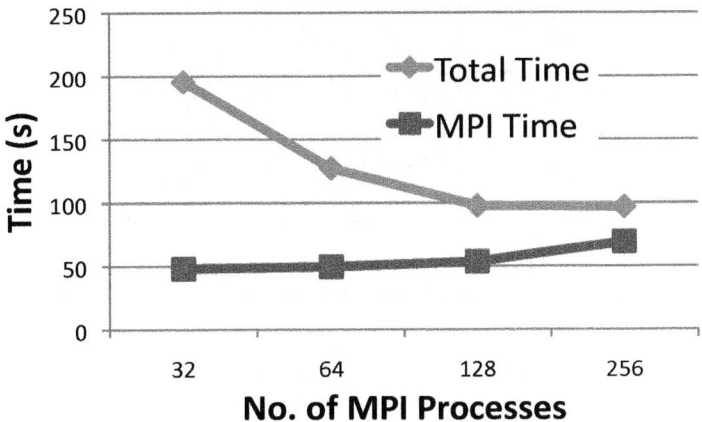

Fig. 1. The scalability of Synergia on the Cray XE6

Using a hybrid MPI+OpenMP programming model fits naturally with the trend in in computer architectures towards the ubiquitous use of multicore or manycore technology in current high-performance computing (HPC) platforms. MPI is used for inter-node communication while OpenMP is used for intra-node computation and communication between cores on the same node. Compared with the flat MPI programming model, using OpenMP enables the potential for a reduction of the amount of memory needed by applications due to its global shared address space. This advantage will become increasingly important as the amount of memory per core will decline on future petascale or exascale architectures.

The rest of the paper is organized as follows. First, Section 2 describes the algorithms and communication patterns of the benchmark application for Synergia. Section 3 describes the experimental platform. The detailed optimization process using OpenMP is discussed in Section 4. Related work is discussed in Section 5. Finally, we summarize our conclusions and future work in Section 6.

2   Benchmark Application

Synergia is a multi component, multi language framework. It provides a straightforward user interface through Python classes. The benchmark application used

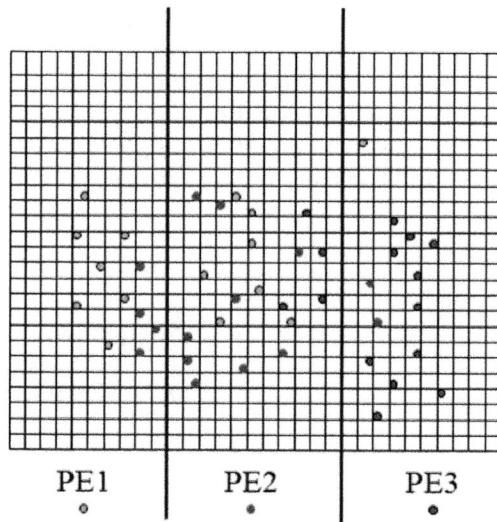

Fig. 2. A schematic plot of the particle-field decomposition method, source from [8]

in this study is contained in the subdirectory cxx_test in the file cxx_example.cc. It is build as part of the normal Synergia build process.

The code simulates the beam dynamics with full 3D space-charge effects using the particle-in-cell algorithm [8]. The charged particles interact via magnetic and electric fields and for its simulation the code has to go through several performance critical subroutines. The field is modeled by a 3D computational grid which is partitioned uniformly among all the processes. Similarly, the charged particles are also evenly partitioned among the processes. However, the dynamics of moving particles does not preserve physical locality and as a consequence particles assigned to a process may be scattered across the whole physical field rapidly. Figure 2 shows a schematic plot of the particle-field decomposition among three processors. The major algorithmic steps performed by the benchmark are:

1. **Get Local Charge Density (RHO):** The charge of the particles are deposited onto the computational grid to obtain the charge density distribution. Due to the non-local distribution of the particles, a copy of the whole computational grid is needed locally. (Local operation)
2. **Get Global Charge Density (RHO):** The local charge densities have to be summed up by calling MPI_Allreduce. (Global operation)
3. **Get PHI2:** Solving the Poisson equation on the global grid using the FFT-based Green function method. The FFT is performed using the FFTW [5] software package. The communication in the transpose step is implemented using pairwise MPI_Sendrecv. (Local + global operations)
4. **Get PHI:** Communicate with neighbors to get data for the boundary of the subdomain. (Global operation)
5. **Sort:** Sort the local particles based on position in Z direction. This is a function periodically invoked to improve the data locality. (Local operation)

6. **Get Local En:** Calculate the local electric field by differentiating the scalar field. All three spatial field components are calculated. (Local operation)
7. **Get Global En:** All processes gather the entire electric field data using MPI_Allgather. (Global operation)
8. **Apply Kick:** The electric field is interpolated to the position of individual particles and the particles are advanced using the self-consistent electromagnetic field and the external maps. (Local operation)

The code contains three major communication operations. The first is the MPI_Allreduce operation in *Get Global Charge Density* phase to sum up all local charge density. The second is the MPI_Sendrecv operation in *Get PHI2* phase for the matrix transpose in the solution of the Poisson equation using the FFT-based method. The third is the MPI_Allgather operation in the process of gathering the electric potential from the subdomain of each processor after the solution of the Poisson equation. The total communication volume is proportional to the number of computational grid points. Furthermore, the communication volumes of the first and the third operations are also proportional to the number of MPI processes. With shared data arrays some of the communication in these steps can be avoided. Therefore, using OpenMP can potentially reduce the total communication volume and improve application performance.

3   Platforms

Our work has been performed on a Cray XE6 platform, called Hopper, which is located at NERSC and consists of 6,384 dual-socket nodes each with 32GB DDR3 1,333-MHz memory and 24 cores. The peak Gflops rate is 8.4 Gflops/core and 201.6 Gflops/node. Each socket within a node contains an AMD "Magny-Cours" processor at 2.1 GHz with 12 cores. Each Magny-Cours package is itself

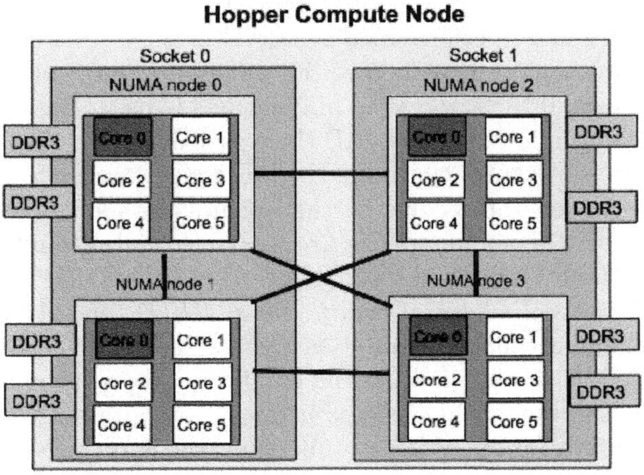

Fig. 3. The node architecture of Hopper

a MCM (Multi-Chip Module) containing two hex-core dies connected via hyper-transport. (See Figure 3.) Each die has its own memory controller that is connected to two 4-GB DIMMS. This means each node can effectively be viewed as having four chips and there are large potential performance penalties for crossing the NUMA domains. Each core has its own L1 and L2 caches, with 64KB and 512KB respectively. One 6-MB L3 cache is shared between 6 cores on the Magny-Cours processor. Every pair of nodes is connected via hypertransport to a Cray Gemini network chip, which collectively form a 17x8x24 3-D torus.

The compilation of Synergia is through an automatic build system based on CMake [4]. The software packages we used include the GNU gcc compiler (SUSE Linux) 4.3.4, Python 2.6, and CMake version 2.8.2.

4   Improving the Performance Using OpenMP

In this section, we will focus on improving the benchmark performance using OpenMP. The computational grid size is set as 64, 64, and 256 in X, Y, and Z direction, respectively. There are 10 particles per cell and a total of about 10 Million particles. In total 256 time steps have been simulated.

4.1   Parallelizing the Loops

The first step is straightforward. Finding those loops which have no data dependence across iterations and using "omp parallel for" pragma to parallelize the work, including the loops which perform reductions at the end. Data placement requires special attention when using OpenMP on systems with non-uniform memory access (NUMA) node architecture. Since a first touch policy is used on Hopper, in which the data will be allocated in the memory associated with the first thread to access it, we intentionally touch the data immediately after memory allocation so that an OpenMP thread and the data it will work on have the same core affinity. Otherwise, accessing data across the NUMA domains inside a node will cause a large performance penalty.

Figure 4 displays the time breakdowns for different number of OpenMP threads per MPI process when the same total of 256 cores is used. Based on the default thread deployment policy, the OpenMP threads spawned by the same MPI process are assigned to the cores continuously. Since each node has 24 cores, a total of 11 nodes are needed and 8 cores on the last node are left unused.

The top five time-consuming phases are shown (from bottom to up). They are for *Get Global Charge Density (Global RHO), Get PHI2 (PHI2), Get Global EN (Global EN), Get Local Charge Density (Local RHO), and Apply Kick (Apply Kick)*. The remaining time is counted as *Others*. The bottom three phases are totally dominated by communication and can be treated as communication time. The other three can be roughly treated as local computation time. For the flat MPI implementation (#OpenMP=1), the time spent on these three phases is around 73 seconds. It drops to 43 seconds when two OpenMP threads per MPI process are used and drops further to 37 seconds when four OpenMP threads per

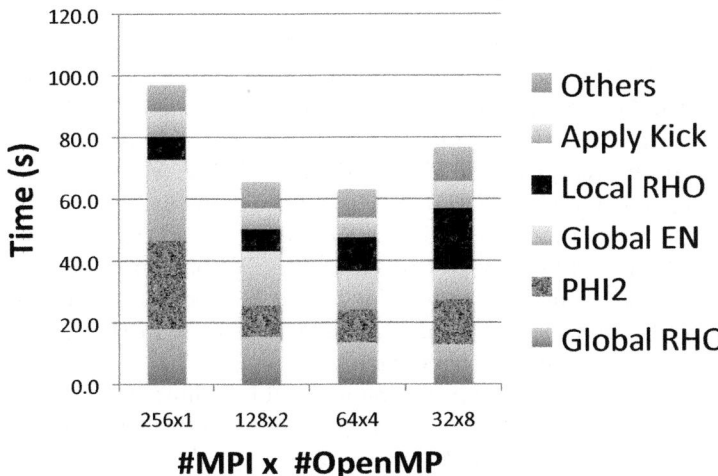

Fig. 4. The time breakdowns for different number of OpenMP threads

MPI process are used. For *Global RHO* and *Global EN*, the better performance is mainly due to the reduced total communication volume as the number of MPI processes goes down. For *PHI2*, the communication is dominated by the matrix transpose needed by the FFT operation. The communication volume is constant. The transpose time drops significantly when switching from the flat MPI to using two OpenMP threads per MPI process. This is probably because of the larger message sizes. However, further increasing #OpenMP does not improve the performance. Instead when #OpenMP=8, the time for *PHI2* goes up, causing the total communication time to increase accordingly.

Local RHO, is responsible for depositing the local particles onto a local auxiliary grid and involves no MPI communication. Its time goes down slightly when #OpenMP=2 and then goes up when higher number of OpenMP threads are used. Due to the data dependence across iterations, this phase can not be easily parallelized using OpenMP "parallel for" pragma. Currently only one OpenMP thread executes during this phase. When the number of MPI processes goes down, the number of local particles assigned to an MPI process becomes larger, leading to higher depositing time. The time does not go up when #OpenMP=2 is due to reduced memory contention within the node. The time of *Apply Kick* is mainly related to the number of particles assigned to each OpenMP thread. When the loop is perfectly parallelized with OpenMP, the number of particles per OpenMP thread remains constant if the total number cores stays at 256. Therefore, the execution time of this phase should be constant. The small variation is caused by the differences in the memory performance.

Overall, the best performance is obtained when four OpenMP threads per MPI process are used. The total running time has been reduced over from 97 to 63 seconds. In the next two sections, we will investigate the performance of phase *PHI2* and phase *Local RHO*.

4.2   Using OpenMP for FFTW

FFTW [5] is used in Synergia to perform the FFT to solve the Poisson equations in phase *Get PHI2*. The computational domain used for FFT is a doubled domain padded on the boundary. The actual size is 128, 128, and 512 for X, Y, and Z directions, respectively. By default, only MPI processes are involved. We changed the initialization process for FFTW3 and enabled OpenMP so that all OpenMP threads can participate in the FFT process. The results using only MPI processes (the case in above section) and using all OpenMP threads are shown in Figure 5. Using more than one OpenMP threads for FFTW helps the performance. But the improvement is only minor for the 2 and 4 OpenMP thread cases; it only becomes significant when 8 OpenMP threads are used. In the latter case, more than 20% of FFTW time has been saved.

To understand whether the performance could be improved further, we isolate the code related to FFTW from Synergia and develop an independent micro benchmark based on it. We find that the micro benchmark results match those of Synergia very well, indicating further improvement dependent solely on future optimizations of FFTW or the MPI implementation. The best result for this phase is obtained with #OpenMP=2.

4.3   Parallelizing Deposit

During the stage of computing the local charge density, the particles are deposited onto a computational grid to obtain the charge density distribution. Due to the spatial distribution of the particles, the grid size should cover the whole field instead of only the subdomain assigned to a process. As we mentioned earlier, due to the data dependence, this section can not be easily parallelized using "pragma omp parallel for".

Naive Approach. The naive approach is to allocate an auxiliary copy of the global grid for each OpenMP thread so that each thread can directly deposits its particles onto it. The particles assigned to an MPI process will be evenly partitioned among all the OpenMP threads spawned by the process. After the deposition, the charge density stored on the auxiliary grid will be summed up by a reduction operation. There are a lot of algorithms to perform this reduction operation. In this study, we examined three implementations: Critical, Slicing, and BinaryTree.

- **Critical.** Critical depends on "pragma omp critical" statement to perform the reduction. As soon as an OpenMP thread finishes its particle deposition, it starts to compete for the critical section to add its particle contributions to the final field. This serializes access to the final field array.
- **Slicing.** In Slicing, each OpenMP thread is responsible for a fixed slice of the final field and fetches the data from all other OpenMP threads to perform the reduction.
- **BinaryTree.** The reduction among the OpenMP threads will be carried out according to a binary tree structure from bottom to top. At the bottom, the

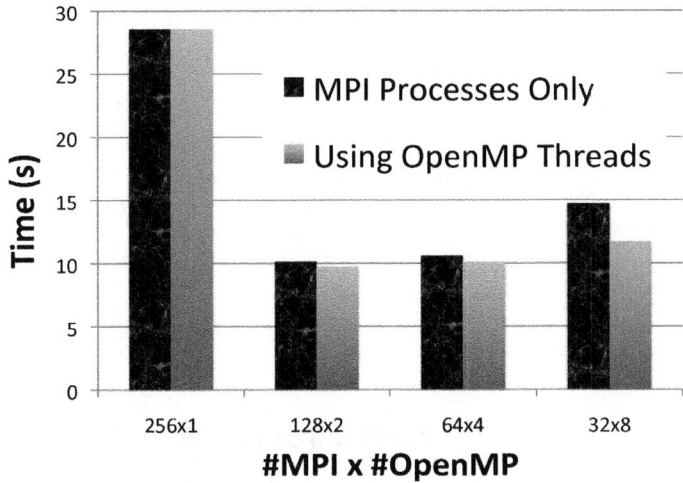

Fig. 5. The times for FFTW when one OpenMP thread and more threads are used

reduction will be done in pairs. Only one thread of a pair will be responsible to perform this reduction. In the next step, the participating number of OpenMP threads will be reduced to half, only including those threads which performed the reduction operation in the last step. This process will be repeated $\lceil \log_2 n \rceil$ times (n is the number of OpenMP threads spawned by the same MPI process).

The timing results for phase *Get Local Charge Density* for different algorithms are shown in Figure 6. The *Base* times are those measured in Section 4.1. None of the new algorithms performs better than the *Base*. The advantage of using more OpenMP threads is overshadowed by the overhead to access extra memory and perform the reduction operation. We also tried to use the reduction operation supported by OpenMP itself. However, we did not see better performance results either.

Lock Approach. Another strategy is to use omp_locks instead of allocating extra amount of memory. The whole field domain will be partitioned along the Z direction among all the OpenMP threads spawned by the same MPI process. Each OpenMP thread will be only responsible to compute the charge density for its assigned subdomain. All the particles assigned to an MPI process, no matter which OpenMP thread they are assigned to, as long as they fall into the same subdomain, will be deposited onto the field by the same thread which owns the subdomain. However, the particles near subdomain boundaries will not only affect the charge density of its own subdomain. They will also affect the charge density of neighboring subdomains. Therefore, for boundary positions omp_locks are needed to assure result correctness. Different locks will be allocated for different positions to maximize concurrency. The number of locks allocated is proportional to the number of OpenMP threads.

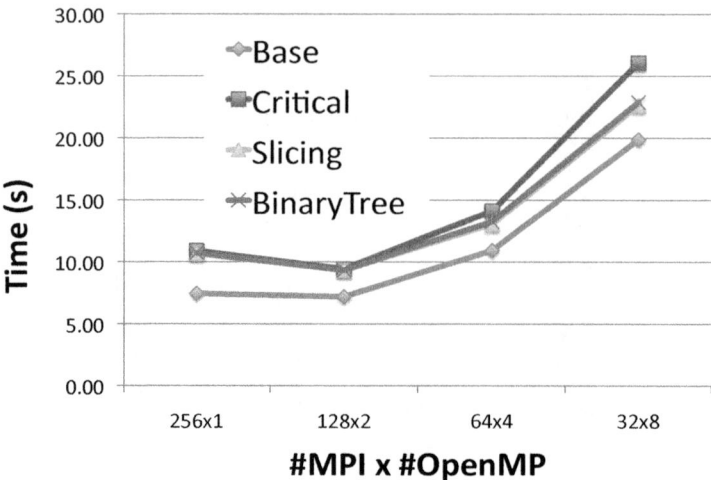

Fig. 6. The times for computing local charge density for different algorithms

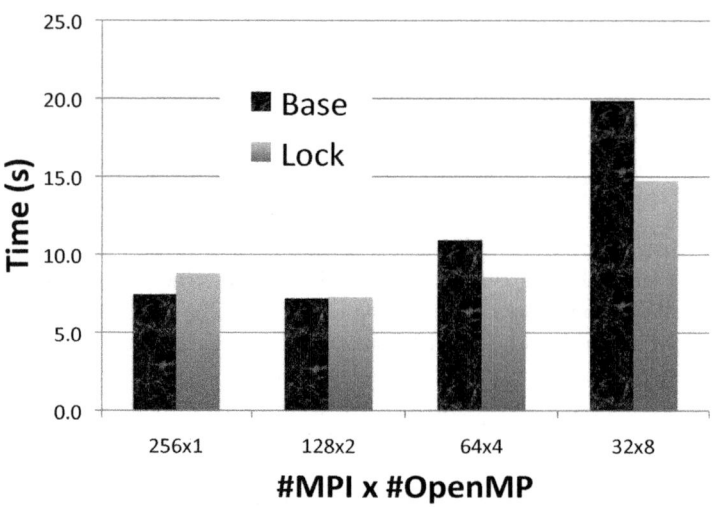

Fig. 7. The times for computing local charge density using omp_lock

The remaining question is how each thread will find those particles for which it should be responsible. The OpenMP thread can not afford going through all the particles to find the ones within their subdomain. One possible solution is to allow the MPI process to sort the particles first based on their positions in Z direction and then partition the particles among the OpenMP threads. However, the sorting turns out to be very expensive. Even worse, the time goes up when more OpenMP threads per MPI process are used. Therefore, sorting can only be done periodically to improve data locality.

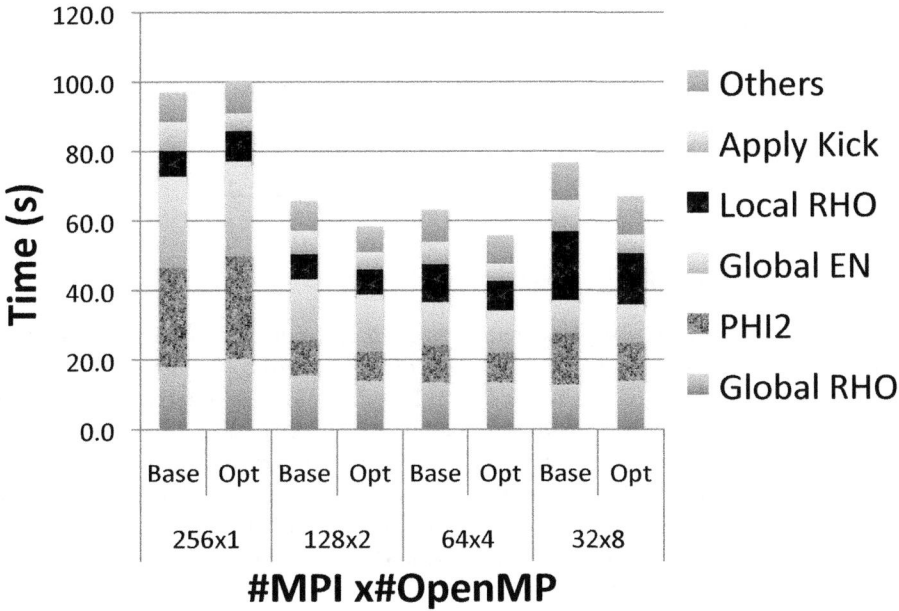

Fig. 8. The time breakdowns before and after optimization

Instead, we partition the particles first among the OpenMP threads and allow each OpenMP thread to perform a sort on its own particles. We add a function called subsort in the Synergia source code for this purpose. The results is that all the particles assigned to an MPI process are now divided into n (n = #OpenMP) sorted sections. For each section, an OpenMP thread can use binary search to find the first particle it should work on and move left and right to get other particles as the particles it will work on should be continuous. This process will be repeated for every section.

Figure 7 shows the new results using omp_lock. When one OpenMP thread is used, the time becomes slightly higher due to the extra sorting work. When two threads are used, it is similar to the *Base* case. However, when four or eight threads are used, the performance becomes better. Over 30% of the time has been saved in the eight-thread case.

The final breakdown of execution times is shown in Figure 8 when both optimizations for FFTW and charge deposition have been applied (labeled as OPT and comparing with the Base). The best performance is obtained when four OpenMP threads per MPI process are used. Compared with the flat MPI results, the performance become more than 1.7 times better when 256 cores are used. Using a hybrid OpenMP+MPI programming model has significantly improved the performance. Another advantage of using OpenMP is the memory usage. Substantial amount of memory could be saved due to the shared address space supported by OpenMP. Table 1 shows the memory footprints when different number of OpenMP threads are used. As the growth in memory capacity is not keeping track with the growth in the number of cores on future architectures, memory considerations are becoming much more important.

Table 1. The memory footprints for different MPI x OpenMP configurations (GB)

#MPI x #OpenMP	256x1	128x2	64x4	32x8
Memory (GB)	12.06	6.50	3.80	2.23

4.4 Performance Discussion

In Section 3, we mentioned that each node on Hopper can be viewed as having four chips and each chip has six cores. The default computational grid sizes (used above) are 64, 64, and 256 in X, Y, and Z direction, respectively. Currently, Synergia can only partition the workloads along Z direction. The size 256 in Z direction prevents us from testing the performance for six or twelve OpenMP threads per MPI process. In this section, we use a slightly different domain size to measure the OpenMP effect for cases where the number of OpenMP threads is a multiple of 6. Figure 9 shows the performance for different number of OpenMP threads for a grid size 64x64x264[1].

The shortest running time is obtained when six OpenMP threads per MPI process are used. For cases with more than six OpenMP threads, the *Local* time (the upper three components) increase substantially and rapidly as more and more data need to be accessed across chip boundaries. Surprisingly, the *Comm* time also increases when more than six OpenMP threads are used. This is mainly due to the matrix transpose to perform the global FFT.

Since the main performance bottleneck of Synergia is the global communication and using fewer MPI processes can reduce the total amount of communicated data and improve the performance, one interesting question is how the performance changes with the number of OpenMP threads for a constant number of MPI processes running on a fixed configuration of cores. In Figure 9, we show the running timing results using 44 MPI processes (labeled as 44x1). We still request 264 cores but use only 4 cores (one on each NUMA chip) on a node. This is the identical arrangement of MPI thread as on the case 44x6. Comparing the performance results for the cases 44x1 and 44x6, the global *Comm* time

---

[1] Due to a recent system software upgrade during the preparation of the final version of this paper, the MPI_Allreduce performance deteriorated under the GNU compiling environment. This is caused by a potential performance bug in the new MPI implementation. We isolated the MPI_Allreduce functions used and compiled it with the alternate Cray compiler. The performance results of this isolated benchmark match our earlier results with GNU compiler very well. In order to be consistent with our earlier results, we replace in this figure the time spent in MPI_Allreduce in Synergia with those measured independently using the Cray compiler. The time for all other code phases is based on the GNU compiler to ensure comparability with results elsewhere in this paper.

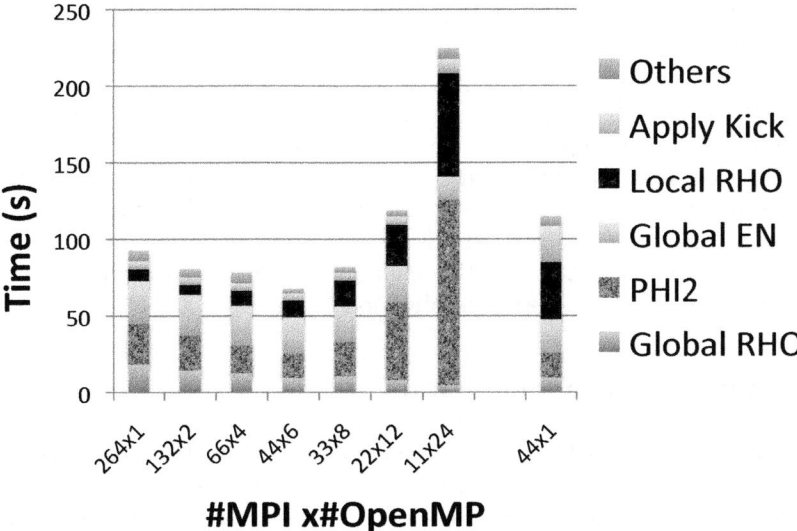

Fig. 9. The time breakdowns for different number of OpenMP threads

is similar, but *Local* time is substantially higher. The additional parallelization with OpenMP does not materially affect the MPI communication time but is (obviously) needed to help lowering the *Local* computation time.

As we noted from both Figure 4 and Figure 8, using more than six OpenMP threads per MPI process will substantially increase the local computation time compared with cases using fewer OpenMP threads per MPI processes. The current trend in architectures is to use more and more cores on a node. The number of cores will reach several hundreds or even a thousand within a few years. Using OpenMP to scale complex applications like Synergia to a full node scale is extremely challenging. Some tools, such as [2,10], need to be developed to automatically optimize data placement and thread affinity. If not impossible, it will be very challenging for developers to perform such kind of task for complex applications as the number of OpenMP regions and related number of variables become very large. To improve the data locality for the NUMA architecture inside a node, some optimization techniques developed in the last decade for MPI may need to be applied to OpenMP also.

To further improve the scalability of Synergia, we can use more particles per cell. Using more particles will only increase the local computation time without affecting global communication. Currently, we use 10 particles per cell and a total of about 10 Million particles.

5   Related Work

Using OpenMP or hybrid MPI+OpenMP to improve the performance has been studied by many researchers. To name a few, Nakajima [7] described how to use a three-level hybrid programming model (vectorization, OpenMP, and MPI) to program efficiently on Earth Simulator. Shan et al. [9] discussed the advantage of using hybrid MPI+OpenMP programming model for NAS parallel applications. Kaushik et al. [6] investigated the performance of implicit PDE simulations for hybrid MPI+OpenMP programming model on a multicore architecture. Brunst and Mohr [3] introduced a tool to analyze the performance for hybrid OpenMP and MPI programs. Recently, some tools have been developed to improve the OpenMP performance for NUMA architectures [2,10]. The main difference to our work is that we focus on a specific application Synergia and on a new architecture, the Cray XE6. But the technologies for our optimization can be generalized and applied to other applications.

6   Summary and Conclusions

In this paper, we describe in detail how to use OpenMP to improve the performance of the accelerator simulation code Synergia. Using up to six OpenMP threads per MPI process, the performance can be improved significantly. In the best case, the performance has increase over 1.7 times for our test-case using 256 cores. However, using more than six OpenMP threads per MPI process does not improve the performance further. Performance improvements stall as memory contention becomes more severe. To address this challenge, we are currently working on a tool that can optimize the data placement and dynamically schedule the OpenMP threads inside a node to improve data locality. We are also planning on changing the workload partition method for Synergia. Currently, it only partitions the grid along Z direction, which limits the scalability of the code.

References

1. Amundson, J., Spentzouris, P., Qiang, J., Ryne, R.: Synergia: An accelerator modeling tool with 3-d space charge. J. Comp. Phys. 211, 229 (2006)
2. Broquedis, F., Furmento, N., Goglin, B., Namyst, R., Wacrenier, P.-A.: Dynamic Task and Data Placement over NUMA Architectures: An OpenMP Runtime Perspective. In: Müller, M.S., de Supinski, B.R., Chapman, B.M. (eds.) IWOMP 2009. LNCS, vol. 5568, pp. 79–92. Springer, Heidelberg (2009)
3. Brunst, H., Mohr, B.: Performance Analysis of Large-Scale OpenMP and Hybrid MPI/OpenMP Applications with Vampir NG. In: Mueller, M.S., Chapman, B.M., de Supinski, B.R., Malony, A.D., Voss, M. (eds.) IWOMP 2005 and IWOMP 2006. LNCS, vol. 4315, pp. 5–14. Springer, Heidelberg (2008)
4. CMAKE: the cross-platform, open-source build system, http://www.cmake.org
5. Frigo, M., Johnsoni, S.G.: The design and implementation of fftw3. Proceedings of the IEEE 93(2), 216–231 (2005)
6. Kaushik, D., Keyes, D., Balay, S., Smith, B.: Hybrid Programming Model for Implicit PDE Simulations on Multicore Architectures. In: Chapman, B.M., Gropp, W.D., Kumaran, K., Müller, M.S. (eds.) IWOMP 2011. LNCS, vol. 6665, pp. 12–21. Springer, Heidelberg (2011)

7. Nakajima, K.: Three-level hybrid vs. flat MPI on the Earth Simulator: parallel iterative solvers for finite-element method. Applied Numerical Mathematics 54(2) (July 2005)
8. Qiang, J., Li, X.: Particle-field decomposition and domain decomposition in parallel particle-in-cell beam dynamics simulation. Computer Physics Communications 181, 2024 (2010)
9. Shan, H., Blagojevic, F., Min, S.J., Hargrove, P., Jin, H., Fuerlinger, K., Koniges, A., Wright, N.J.: A programming model performance study using the nas parallel benchmarks. Scientific Programming-Exploring Languages for Expressing Medium to Massive On-Chip Parallelism 18(3-4) (August 2010)
10. Su, C., Li, D., Nikolopoulos, D., Grove, M., Cameron, K., de Supinski, B.: Critical path-based thread placement for NUMA systems. In: 2nd International Workshop on Performance Modeling, Benchmarking and Simulation of High Performance Computer Systems (2011)

Using Compiler Directives for Accelerating CFD Applications on GPUs

Haoqiang Jin, Mark Kellogg, and Piyush Mehrotra

NAS Division, NASA Ames Research Center, Moffett Field, CA 94035-1000 USA
{haoqiang.jin,mark.kellogg,piyush.mehrotra}@nasa.gov

Abstract. As the current trend of parallel systems is towards a cluster of multi-core nodes enhanced with accelerators, software development for such systems has become a major challenge. Both low-level and high-level programming models have been developed to address complex hierarchical structures at different hardware levels and to ease the programming effort. However, achieving the desired performance goal is still not a simple task. In this study, we describe our experience with using the accelerator directives developed by the Portland Group to port a computational fluid dynamics (CFD) application benchmark to a general-purpose GPU platform. Our work focuses on the usability of this approach and examines the programming effort and achieved performance on two Nvidia GPU-based systems. The study shows very promising results in terms of programmability as well as performance when compared to other approaches such as the CUDA programming model.

Keywords: GPU Programming, Accelerator Directives, Performance Evaluation.

1   Introduction

The current trend of parallel systems for exascale computing is towards a cluster of multi-core nodes enhanced with accelerators such as general-purpose graphics processing units (GPGPUs). Thirty-nine systems in the most recent Top 500 list [14] use an accelerator-based hybrid architecture. They take advantage of the ability of accelerators to execute large numbers of threads while maintaining high levels of power efficiency. However, software development for such systems has become a major challenge. The popular programming models for GPGPU, CUDA [8] and OpenCL [6], support high performance computing at different hardware levels but often require a substantial rewrite of users' codes. Several compiler directive-based approaches, notably Portland Group (PGI)'s Accelerator model [11], CAPS' HMPP language [3], and the recent OpenACC standard [9], have been developed as a way to ease the programming effort. Extensions for the OpenMP model have also been proposed to support accelerators [2]. However, achieving the desired performance goal is still not a simple task.

In this study, we describe our experience using the PGI's accelerator (ACC) directives to port a computational fluid dynamics (CFD) application SP benchmark from the NAS Parallel Benchmarks (NPBs) [1] to GPGPU-based platforms. Our work focuses on the usability of this ACC directive-based approach and examines the programming effort and achieved performance in comparison with the CUDA approach on two Nvidia

B.M. Chapman et al. (Eds.): IWOMP 2012, LNCS 7312, pp. 154–168, 2012.
© Springer-Verlag Berlin Heidelberg 2012

GPU-based systems. There are quite a few previous studies on porting CFD applications to accelerators (for example, Overflow [4], NPB-LU [10], NPB-OpenCL [13]). This study is the first attempt to utilize the directive-based approach for the selected benchmark and to understand the performance impact of different implementations of a single benchmark.

The rest of the paper is organized as follows. We give a brief overview of GPU programming in Section 2. Section 3 describes the different implementations of the SP benchmark. In Section 4 we first present performance results from two small kernels for matrix transposition and matrix multiplication, and then examine performance impact of different approaches in implementing the SP benchmark. We conclude our study in Section 5 and also elaborate on future work.

2   GPU Programming

A GPU device consists of a set of multiprocessors, each containing multiple streaming processing cores. Logically, the device is organized as an array of thread blocks partitioned in a multidimensional manner. Execution of thread blocks is carried out by the multiprocessors independently. Each thread block is executed by the cores on a specific multiprocessor. Thread synchronization is only possible within a thread block. A small fast memory, called "shared memory," is accessible to threads in a given multiprocessor. All threads can also access a global memory that is large, but with high latency. One can improve bandwidth to global memory by coalescing accesses. For comprehensive information on GPU computing, a good reference is [7].

The CUDA (Compute Unified Device Architecture) approach was developed by Nvidia [8] as both a hardware and a software solution for supporting general-purpose GPUs. The CUDA programming model uses a set of extensions to Fortran and C to describe how codes or "kernel" functions can be "offloaded" to the device for execution and to specify where data reside. The user has to define an explicit layout of the threads on the GPU (number of blocks, number of threads) for each kernel function.

The PGI's Accelerator model [11] is a high-level approach using compiler directives for GPU programming. The key to this approach is that the user specifies high-level constructs and the compiler translates them into appropriate low-level calls. This preserves the original code structure and simplifies the code development substantially. In this model, the "acc region" construct defines the code segment to be executed on the device. Additional clauses can be used to specify data transfers between the host and the device. The "acc do" loop directive can be used to map loop nests to thread blocks on the device. The user can fine-tune the mapping with loop scheduling clauses, but for many cases, the compiler can automatically place the loop directives as well as data transfer clauses for the ACC region. This is a descriptive approach used by the PGI model, as opposite to prescriptive approaches like OpenMP where the compiler interprets user-inserted high-level instructions and translates them into proper low-level codes without further analysis. For performance consideration, several directives are provided for allocating device-resident data within a scope (data region) or throughout the program (global data). One can use the "acc mirror" directive to create duplicated copies of a variable on both device and host, and the "acc update" directive to synchronize the copies.

Sample codes for a matrix transposition implemented using different approaches are illustrated in Fig. 1. The ACC directive version (*b*) differs from the serial version (*a*) only by the additional "acc region" and "acc do" directives. The CUDA version, shown in (*c*) for kernel code and (*d*) for host code, in contrast is much more complex.

a) Serial (CPU) code	c) CUDA kernel
1 `real(8)::a(m,n),b(n,m)`	1 `attributes(global) subroutine &`
2 `do i = 1,m`	`mt_kernel(m,n,a,b)`
3 `  do j = 1,n`	2 `real(8) :: a(m,n),b(n,m)`
4 `    b(j,i) = a(i,j)`	3 `integer,parameter :: bsize = 16`
5 `  end do`	4 `j = (blockidx%x-1)*bsize + threadidx%x`
6 `end do`	5 `i = (blockidx%y-1)*bsize + threadidx%y`
	6 `b(j,i) = a(i,j)`
	7 `end subroutine mt_kernel`
b) ACC directive code	**d) CUDA host code**
1 `real(8)::a(m,n),b(n,m)`	1 `real(8),device,allocatable,dimension(:,:) &`
2 `!$acc region`	`:: a_dv,b_dv`
3 `!$acc do`	2 `integer,parameter :: bsize = 16`
4 `do i = 1,m`	3 `type(dim3) :: dgrid,dblock`
5 `  !$acc do`	4 `allocate(a_dv(m,n),b_dv(n,m))`
6 `  do j = 1,n`	5 `a_dv = a     !copy data to device`
7 `    b(j,i) = a(i,j)`	6 `dblock = dim3(bsize,bsize,1)`
8 `  end do`	7 `dgrid = dim3(m/bsize,n/bsize,1)`
9 `end do`	8 `call mt_kernel<<<dgrid,dblock>>> &`
10 `!$acc end region`	`(m,n,a_dv,b_dv)`
	9 `b = b_dv     !copy data back to host`
	10 `deallocate(a_dv, b_dv)`

Fig. 1. Sample codes for matrix transposition: *a*) serial version, *b*) ACC directive version, and *c*,*d*) CUDA kernel and host codes

When developing GPU codes, a few optimization techniques should be kept in mind: use lots of parallelism to hide memory latency, maximize memory bandwidth via memory coalescing, and cache frequently accessed data in fast memory (such as shared memory). The last method is analogous to cache blocking, a common optimization technique for the CPU. Figure 2*a* shows the CUDA kernel code using shared memory (variable `asub`) for matrix transposition where a call to `syncthreads` is used to synchronize the update of `asub` in a thread block. Figure 2*b* shows the corresponding cache blocked code for the CPU.

3   Benchmark Implementations

This section describes several approaches of using the PGI Accelerator directives to implement the SP application benchmark. For comparison, we also include a CUDA implementation of this benchmark.

```
a) CUDA kernel, cached
1   attributes(global) subroutine mt_kernel(m,n,a,b)
2     real(8) :: a(m,n),b(n,m)
3     integer,parameter :: bsize = 16
4     real(8),shared :: asub(bsize+1,bsize)
5     ix = threadidx%x; iy = threadidx%y
6     i = (blockidx%x-1)*bsize + ix
7     j = (blockidx%y-1)*bsize + iy
8     asub(ix,iy) = a(i,j)  ! cache sub block
9     call syncthreads()
10    i = (blockidx%x-1)*bsize + iy
11    j = (blockidx%y-1)*bsize + ix
12    b(j,i) = asub(iy,ix)  ! copy data back
13  end subroutine mt_kernel
```

```
b) Host CPU code, blocked
1   integer,parameter :: bsize=64
2   real(8) :: asub(bsize,bsize),bsub(bsize,bsize)
3   do ii = 1,m,bsize
4   do jj = 1,n,bsize
5     asub = a(ii:ii+bsize-1,jj:jj+bsize-1)
6     do i = 1,bsize
7       do j = 1,bsize
8         bsub(j,i) = asub(i,j)
9       end do
10    end do
11    b(jj:jj+bsize-1,ii:ii+bsize-1) = bsub
12  end do
13  end do
```

Fig. 2. Sample codes for matrix transposition: *a*) CUDA kernel with data cached via shared memory, *b*) host CPU code with cache blocking

SP is one of the application benchmarks in the NAS Parallel Benchmarks (NPBs) suite [1]. The benchmark mimics the computation, memory access and communication patterns found in many NASA computational fluid dynamics (CFD) codes. It has a larger surface-to-volume ratio and less computation per grid point compared to other application benchmarks in the NPBs. Thus, it should give us a bottom line on how well CFD applications might perform on a GPU platform.

The core of SP is a scalar penta-diagonal solver for a 3-dimensional (3D) grid with five elements at each grid point. The flow of the benchmark is illustrated in Fig. 3. The solver alternates an implicit scheme in each of the three dimensions (x/y/z_solve) iteratively for a designed number of time steps. The implicit scheme contains data flow dependences in the sweeping dimension, and is fully independent in the other two dimensions. Computation in compute_rhs (for the right-hand side calculation) and other smaller routines is explicit and can be performed concurrently in 3D. The benchmark reports the timing of the iteration loop without initialization and final verification.

3.1 Baseline Code

The starting point for our study is the serial version of SP written in Fortran from the recent NPB 3.3.1 release. This *original* version employed several 4-dimensional (4D) arrays for solution and working space in a (m,i,j,k) form that was designed for better CPU cache performance [5]. In all of the 4D arrays, m is always of size 5, but i, j, and k vary according to the problem size and are always much larger than m. Fortran arrays follow column-major order, which means the leftmost index changes most rapidly in memory. For programming on GPU architectures, such a data layout is not ideal and memory access patterns in many cases may not be stride-1, which reduces opportunities for memory coalescing. This could lead to a serious performance bottleneck. To mitigate the issue we applied a couple of transformations to the original code. The first change involves array dimension swapping from (m,i,j,k) to (i,j,k,m) so that memory accesses can coalesce along the inner dimension of the arrays. The second change includes the use of Fortran allocatable arrays in a module for those working arrays specified in common blocks. This change is necessary to use the PGI "`acc mirror`" directive (see next section). The modified code is our *baseline* for developing different implementations for the GPU.

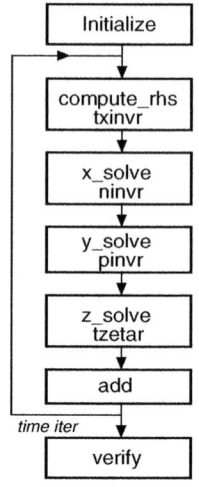

Fig. 3. Schematic diagram of the SP benchmark control flow

3.2 Implementations Using ACC Directives

Applying ACC directives to the serial code to get an initial port for the GPU is straightforward. However, achieving the desired performance on the GPU requires careful consideration of several issues. It is important to minimize the data transfer between host and device, maximize parallelism across all levels, and use fast memory and stride-1 memory accesses for computation. We relied on feedback from the PGI compiler at compile time and profile information at run time for the development and optimization process.

In the SP implementation, we elected to have the GPU device perform the full computation of the time iteration loop with only the initialization and verification being executed on the host. Using device-resident arrays reduces data transfer between host and device. In fact, in our final version, only the initial data from initialization and the solution data for verification are transferred between the host and the device (via the "`acc update`" construct). The benchmark time includes the time spent on data transfer. Although overlapping host and device computations can hide data transfer latency, this technique was not tested in this study.

When developing codes using the ACC directives, we wanted to examine the performance impact from different approaches. Here we summarize five versions produced at different stages of the code development, varying in complexity from very simple to substantially optimized.

simple – This initial version applies the "acc region" directive to the outermost parallel loops in all routines. The compiler identified many parallel loops and automatically generated "acc do parallel" and "acc do vector" constructs with the proper width factor at different loop nesting levels. Only a few loops required manual insertion of the "acc do parallel" directive with necessary data scoping clauses, mainly in the three solve routines. The compiler was able to generate "copyin" and "copyout" clauses automatically for global data transferred in and out of ACC regions.

mlocal – The second version pays more attention to the location of data. Specifically, the "acc mirror" directive was used for three global arrays (u,rhs,forcing) to indicate the "mirroring" of data on both the host and the device. Other working arrays were declared with "acc local" for device-only allocation. As a result, the compiler suppressed many copyin and copyout clauses for the mirrored arrays, but data copy clauses were still added for device-local variables. We used the "acc update device(u,forcing)" and "acc update host(u)" directives explicitly for copying the initialization data to the device before the time iteration loop and the solution data to the host after the iteration loop.

mirror – The third version uses "acc mirror" for all working arrays previously declared as local. Use of the directive eliminates all the unnecessary data transfers between ACC regions. As in the *mlocal* version, the "acc update" directive is used for transferring global data between the host and the device. The only drawback is that the host has to keep unused copies of the working arrays.

Another approach is to use a single "acc data region" to contain all ACC regions at a higher level, and then use the "acc device present" directive to list all global variables that do not need to be copied. But for the current code where ACC regions are spread across many routines, we decided to use the declarative approach with the "acc mirror" directive for simplicity.

dim-prom – The next version includes dimension promotion for the working arrays (lhs,lhsp,lhsm) from 3D to 4D in routines x/y/z_solve as

```
lhs(i,j,m) -> lhs(i,j,k,m).
```

This increases the ability to achieve stride-1 memory access and allows exploitation of parallelism in multiple dimensions.

data-trans – The last version applies data transposition to the rhs residual array in routine x_solve from rhs(i,j,k,m) to rhsx(j,i,k,m). The computation is then applied to the new array and the results are copied back to the original array at the end. Because of data dependence in the *i* dimension, we can only parallelize loops associated with the *j* and *k* dimensions. This transformation allows stride-1 memory access in the *j* dimension and improves GPU memory bandwidth utilization via memory coalescing. A similar transposition was also applied to the lhs, lhsp, and lhsm arrays.

3.3 CUDA Implementations

For comparison purposes, we developed CUDA implementations of the SP benchmark based on the CUDA Fortran programming model [12]. The development consisted of two phases.

Phase I represented a first attempt at CUDA parallelization based on the *original* SP code. All the program semantics and data structures in the code were transferred to the CUDA version with as little alteration as possible. The main task involved mapping loop nests to CUDA kernels with proper thread blocks. Converting multidimensional array indices to use thread block id's and thread id's was a tedious process. As mentioned in Section 3.1, because of the small size of m in the 4D arrays, proper memory coalescing was awkward and difficult to achieve. Additionally, and more importantly, the original layout of the arrays resulted in the need for large amounts of shared memory on the GPU to facilitate coalesced accesses to the arrays in GPU global memory.

The use of shared memory became a problem because it limited thread occupancy, i.e., the efficiency of multiprocessor usage. On the Nvidia Tesla M2090, a much smaller amount of shared memory (48 KB per multiprocessor) is available compared to global memory. Many of the CUDA kernels required over 12 KB of shared memory per thread block. This severely limited the number of kernel blocks that could be simultaneously executed, and therefore the overall thread occupancy. This limitation was ultimately a serious impediment to the performance gains achieved in Phase I.

In Phase II, we addressed the issue of excessive shared memory usage by realizing that memory coalescing can be easily achieved if we use a modified array structure via the transformation:

```
rhs(m,i,j,k) -> rhs(i,j,k,m).
```

This essentially followed the same code modification for the *baseline* version described in Section 3.1. The advantage of this transformation was that accesses to the transformed arrays in GPU global memory can be easily coalesced since CUDA threads map naturally to unique values of i. So we achieved memory coalescing without the usage of shared memory, which resulted in a significant performance increase in Phase II over Phase I. Detailed discussion of the CUDA implementations of SP will be presented in a separate publication. The rest of the paper focuses on this final CUDA version only.

The Phase II CUDA code performs several data transpositions, which require additional working arrays. As a result, the overall memory usage increases. Table 1 summarizes the memory requirements of different SP versions for various problem sizes. The first three ACC directive-based versions are not listed in the table since they have memory requirements similar to the *baseline* version. Versions employing data transpositions require significantly more memory.

Table 1. Memory usage (MB) of different versions of the SP benchmark

Problem Size	baseline	dim-prom	data-trans	cuda
CLASS A ($64 \times 64 \times 64$)	48.1	80.0	90.9	129.8
CLASS B ($102 \times 102 \times 102$)	191.7	320.3	363.6	519.4
CLASS C ($162 \times 162 \times 162$)	760.7	1274.0	1446.2	2066.0
CLASS D ($408 \times 408 \times 408$)	12032.1	20202.2	22932.2	32760.3

4   Performance Study

Our performance study was conducted on two types of GPU-enabled compute nodes installed at NASA Ames Research Center. Table 2 summarizes the main characteristics of these nodes. The *Pleiades-GPU* node is part of the Pleiades supercomputer for high performance computing. Each node contains two Intel six-core Westmere processors and one Nvidia Tesla M2090 GPU. The Tesla M2090 is the best performing Fermi-based T20-series GPGPU, capable of 665 Gflops in double precision and 177 GB/s memory bandwidth (ECC off). The *hyperwall-GPU* node is part of a visualization cluster. Each node contains two AMD quad-core Opteron processors and two Nvidia GTX 480 GPUs. The GTX 480 is based on the same Fermi architecture as the Tesla M2090 except that it has a smaller non-ECC memory. The 64 KB configurable memory on both GPUs can be configured as either 16 KB of shared memory with 48 KB of L1 cache, or 48 KB of shared memory with 16 KB of L1 cache. We used version 11 of the PGI compiler for compiling both accelerator directive codes and CUDA-Fortran codes. The compiler sets aside 16K of shared memory space for accelerator directive codes.

Table 2. Summary of machine characteristics

Machine Name	Pleiades-GPU	hyperwall-GPU
CPU Type	Intel Xeon X5670	AMD Opteron 2354
CPU Speed	2930 MHz	2200 MHz
L3 Cache	12 MB	2 MB
#Cores / Socket	6	4
#Cores / Node	12	8
Node Memory	48 GB	16 GB
GPU Type	Tesla M2090	GeForce GTX 480
Clock Rate	1301 MHz	1451 MHz
Configurable Memory	64 KB	64 KB
Global Memory	5375 MB	1535 MB
ECC	Enabled	N/A
#Multiprocessors	16	15
#CUDA Cores	512	480
Compute Capability	2.0	2.0
NVRM Version	275.09	290.10
OS	SUSE Linux 11.1	CentOS Linux 6.0
Compiler	PGI 11.9	PGI 11.10

In the remainder of this section, we first present results from two small kernels for matrix transposition and matrix multiplication. We then examine the performance impact of different approaches in parallelizing the SP benchmark on the GPUs and compare that with a single core of the hosts.

4.1 Matrix Transposition

Matrix transposition is a common operation in many applications and appears in several implementations of the SP code. Study of this kernel can give us some insights into the performance characteristics of SP. Figure 4 compares both GPU and CPU performance of matrix transposition implemented in several ways, three of which (*host simple*, *acc directive*, and *cuda simple*) were shown in Fig. 1. The *cuda cached* version uses shared

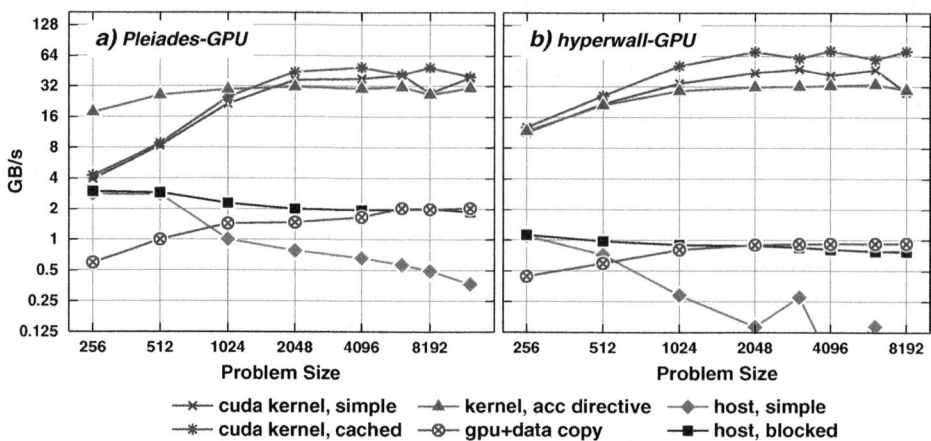

Fig. 4. Performance comparison of matrix transposition (64-bit words) on both GPUs and CPUs

memory to improve memory coalescing, while the *host blocked* version applies cache blocking on the CPU, as shown in Fig. 2. The GB/s rates for GPU kernels were computed from execution times spent on the device, excluding data transfers from/to the host. The timing profiles were obtained with the PGI `pgcollect` tool.

As the problem size increases, the CUDA-based codes show a gradual increase in performance and the *cached* version gains an additional benefit from using shared memory. It is interesting to note that the ACC directive version performed very well for all problem sizes and even outperformed the CUDA versions for smaller problem sizes on the Tesla M2090 used in *Pleiades-GPU*. The CUDA version performed slightly better (10-15%) on the GTX 480 compared to the Tesla M2090, which can be attributed to the use of ECC memory on the Tesla processor. When comparing GPU with CPU, we observe that the performance difference is about 16X on *Pleiades-GPU* and 32X on *hyperwall-GPU*, partly due to a weaker CPU on the latter system. However, when considering communication between device and host, the GPU versions are dominated by data transfers and the net results, labeled "gpu+data copy" for one case in Fig. 4, become similar to or even worse than the cache-blocked host version. The simple-minded host version suffers from poor cache utilization at larger problem sizes.

4.2   Matrix Multiplication

Matrix multiplication can demonstrate the upper bound of performance that is achievable on GPUs. Figure 5 compares the performance of this kernel code implemented in the same five ways as outlined for matrix transposition in the previous section. The performance of the GPU versions includes the data transfer time between the host and the device. As shown in the figure, the performance of the properly cache-blocked host code is invariant with respect to the problem size, while the unblocked simple version suffers from poor cache performance. On the other hand, the GPU versions (both CUDA and ACC directive) show increased performance as problem size increases. The highest Gflop/s rates achieved from the CUDA, ACC directive, and host versions are

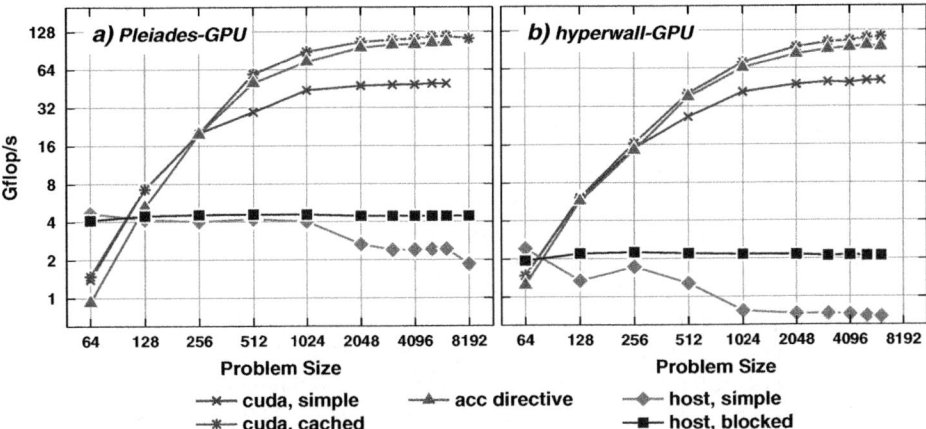

Fig. 5. Performance comparison of matrix multiplication (64-bit words) on both GPUs and CPUs

117.8, 105.3, and 4.6, respectively. Although the CUDA cached version with shared memory has shown the best performance, the ACC directive version has similar performance but with much less programming effort, which indicates the great potential of this programming model.

4.3   SP Benchmark

The study of the SP benchmark focused on the performance impact of the programming efforts described in Section 3. We conducted a set of runs for the CLASS A problem size and collected routine-level timing data for each of the approaches. We also obtained time spent by GPU kernels using the pgcollect tool. The results on the two GPU systems are summarized in Table 3 together with total benchmark time, GPU kernel time, and GPU communication time between the host and the device. Performance improvements from different approaches using the *baseline* version of SP as a reference are shown in Fig. 6 for both systems.

Several observations can be made from these results. Compared to the *original* version, the *baseline* host version is about 20% slower on the older AMD Opteron processor, but performs comparably on the newer Intel Westmere processor where vectorization helps. Faster CPU speed and larger L3 cache of the Westmere processor contribute to the better host performance of the *baseline* version on this platform. It is not surprising that the *simple* ACC directive version, without paying any attention to data transfers, is 3X-8X slower than the *baseline* and is dominated by data transfers between the device and the host. Use of the "acc mirror" suppresses many of the unnecessary data transfers and improves performance substantially, as seen for routines using explicit schemes (e.g., 36X speedup for compute_rhs). Among the three solve routines, x_solve performs the best on the CPU due to efficient cache utilization, but the worst on the GPU because of the non-stride-1 memory access in the parallel dimensions. The first three ACC directive codes show no difference in GPU kernel time.

Table 3. Timing profile (in seconds) of different implementations of the SP benchmark (CLASS A) on the two GPU systems

Pleiades-GPU	original	baseline	simple	mlocal	mirror	dim-prom	data-trans	cuda
compute_rhs	16.21	15.82	126.84	38.37	3.47	3.47	3.41	1.72
x_solve	6.08	6.90	35.91	25.77	22.48	7.56	3.09	2.55
y_solve	6.20	6.26	34.39	20.51	17.27	2.07	2.11	1.74
z_solve	6.35	6.99	32.33	20.78	17.46	2.45	2.49	1.71
add	1.09	0.76	16.56	0.20	0.20	0.20	0.20	0.15
rest	3.88	2.49	57.89	5.30	0.94	0.94	0.95	0.18
total	39.81	39.22	302.58	110.56	61.65	16.63	12.22	8.03
GPUkrnl	0.00	0.00	59.37	59.60	59.78	15.14	10.32	7.34
GPUcomm	0.00	0.00	243.21	50.96	1.87	1.49	1.90	0.69
hyperwall-GPU	original	baseline	simple	mlocal	mirror	dim-prom	data-trans	cuda
compute_rhs	32.58	42.71	122.78	36.55	2.94	2.89	2.48	1.43
x_solve	10.32	9.34	28.59	17.07	14.06	5.51	2.61	3.06
y_solve	11.61	19.09	26.62	13.69	10.63	1.96	1.98	1.32
z_solve	11.90	17.83	25.55	13.83	10.72	2.19	2.19	1.33
add	2.37	2.30	15.88	0.14	0.14	0.14	0.14	0.11
rest	10.22	6.98	56.56	4.50	0.67	0.68	0.67	0.38
total	79.01	98.25	275.97	85.79	39.16	13.37	10.08	7.25
GPUkrnl	0.00	0.00	36.71	37.01	37.10	12.08	8.72	7.18
GPUcomm	0.00	0.00	239.26	48.78	2.06	1.30	1.37	0.07

Array dimension promotion for the working arrays in the solve routines is a key transformation for speeding up these routines by 3X-5X on the GPU. Data transposition for better memory coalescing produces an additional performance gain in x_solve and to some extent in compute_rhs, although such a code transformation will likely worsen performance on the CPU because of cache unfriendliness. The final ACC directive version (*data-trans*) resulted in a performance improvement over the host *baseline* version by a factor of 3.2X on the Westmere core and 9.7X on the Opteron core. Compared to the CUDA code, the best ACC directive version is only 30-40% slower, which is very acceptable given the fact that programming effort for the directive-based codes is considerably less.

To scale up the problem size, we used the best ACC directive version and compared it with the *cuda* version and the host *baseline* version. The total benchmark times are summarized in Table 4 for CLASS A, B, and C. As noted in Table 1, the *cuda* code requires 2 GB of memory for the CLASS C problem, which is more than the available GPU memory on *hyperwall-GPU*. For the sake of completeness of our performance study, we created another CUDA version of SP with reduced memory requirements by removing some of the working arrays used for improving memory coalescing. The timing results from this version are marked as "(mr)" for CLASS B and CLASS C in Table 4. Figure 7 presents the performance for different data sizes using the *baseline* results on *Pleiades* as a reference. We observe further performance improvement on the GPUs when scaling up to larger problems.

An interesting observation from Table 3 is that the performance of the ACC directive versions is consistently lower on *Pleiades-GPU* (Tesla M2090) than on *hyperwall-GPU*

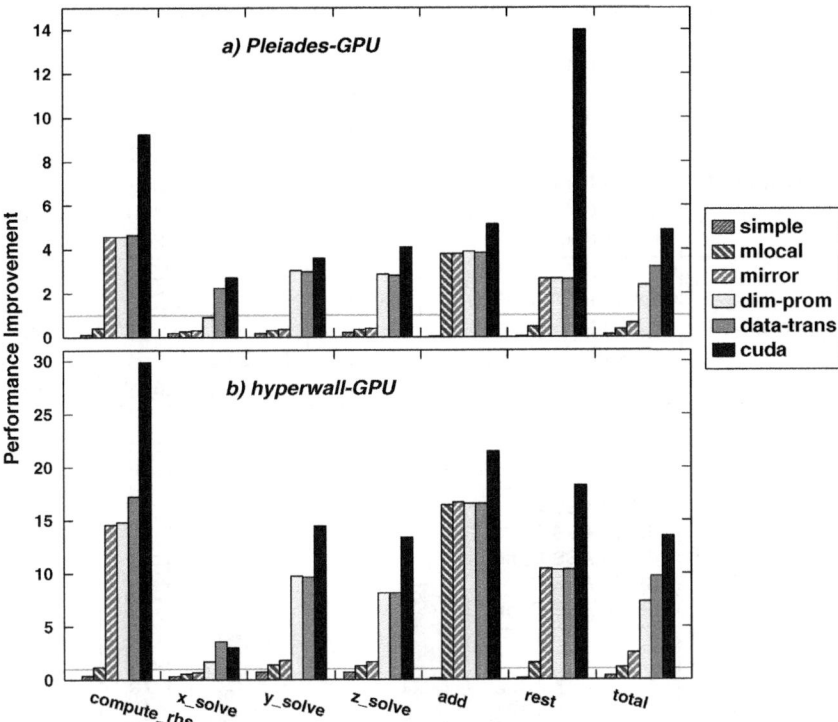

Fig. 6. Performance improvement of the SP benchmark (CLASS A) relative to the *baseline* on *a*) *Pleiades-GPU*, *b*) *hyperwall-GPU*

(GTX 480). The GPU communication time on the two systems is similar. The main difference comes from time spent on executing GPU kernels. For the *simple, mlocal,* and *mirror* versions, the slowdown in kernel performance is as much as 60%, which cannot be solely attributed to the use of ECC memory in the Tesla M2090. As a comparison, the performance difference of the *cuda* version on the two systems is only about 10%. As the problem size scales up as shown in Fig. 7, the performance difference of the CUDA version on the two GPUs is no more than 15%, but the ACC directive version again shows consistently better results on the GTX 480 GPU, with performance increasing by as much as 60%. It is interesting to note that the memory-reduced CUDA version suffered substantial performance degradation on the Tesla M2090 but less so on the GTX 480. This indicates the sensitivity of the Tesla M2090 to performance tuning. It also suggests that the ACC directive version still has room for further improvement.

One explanation of the decreased ACC directive performance on the Tesla GPU is related to how the PGI accelerator compiler treats shared memory. For a Fermi-based GPU, each streaming multiprocessor (MP) has 64KB of configurable local memory, which can be set to 48KB as hardware cache and 16KB as shared memory, or 16KB as hardware cache and 48KB as shared memory. The compiler uses the default setting of 16KB as shared memory, set on a per kernel basis, which cannot be adjusted by the user. The Fermi GPU has 16 MPs, each with two SIMD units, and each SIMD unit has 16

Table 4. Timing results (in seconds) of the SP benchmark for different problem classes

Machine	Problem Class	baseline Total Time	acc-directive (best) Total Time	acc-directive (best) GPUkrnl	cuda Total Time	cuda GPUkrnl
Pleiades-GPU	CLASS A	39.22	12.22	10.32	8.03	7.34
	CLASS B	157.78	56.73	54.76	31.49	30.56
	CLASS B(mr)				52.09	51.18
	CLASS C	646.49	231.19	228.75	122.27	120.18
	CLASS C(mr)				208.50	205.72
hyperwall-GPU	CLASS A	98.25	10.08	8.72	7.25	7.18
	CLASS B	358.74	36.67	35.10	26.34	25.97
	CLASS B(mr)				31.74	31.46
	CLASS C	1728.97	143.60	141.23	–	–
	CLASS C(mr)				126.49	125.61

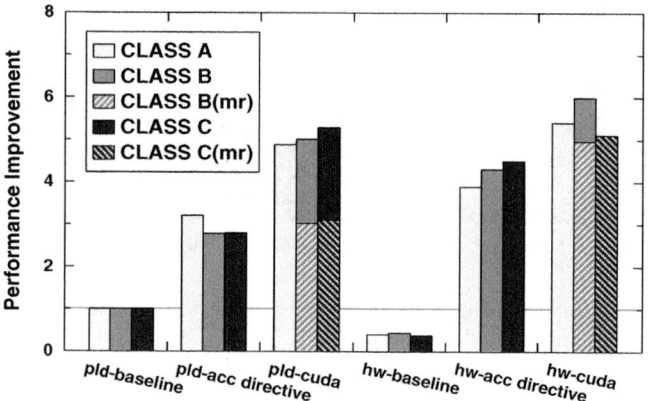

Fig. 7. Comparison of GPU performance of SP implementations with the *baseline* for different data sizes

CUDA cores. The two SIMD units share the same shared memory. Compiler feedback indicates that many of the kernels in SP require 10-14KB of shared memory. With the 16KB limitation of shared memory, the kernel launch can only run one instance (one thread block) of the kernel on each MP, since two thread blocks would require more than 20KB of shared memory. So for this case, the kernel is running only 16 thread blocks in parallel. There seems to be not enough parallelism within the thread block to keep the 32 CUDA cores in the two SIMD units in each MP busy.

5   Conclusions

In this paper we presented our efforts to port the SP benchmark to GPU-based platforms using the directive-based PGI accelerator model. We showed that this approach achieved decent performance with much less programming effort when compared to the low-level CUDA approach. The descriptive approach used by this model is convenient for users as they can gradually optimize performance based on compiler feedback. The GPU performance of SP is about a factor of 3X-10X when compared with a single CPU core, which is far from satisfactory given the fact that we have not considered multicore CPU performance.

We examined the performance impact of different programming efforts in the development process. Minimizing data transfer between the device and the host, and optimizing memory accesses are the keys for achieving desired performance. This often requires changes to the code structure, which may not always be portable. Certain optimizations, such as cache blocking via fast memory, work well on both CPUs and GPUs. In other cases, data transposition is required for better memory coalescing on the device, which does not necessarily translate into a performance gain on the host.

There are several areas of interest for further study. The impact of GPU shared memory size on application performance needs further study, in particular as a possible tunable parameter for the compiler and its runtime support. It is not clear how different loop schedules would affect performance. This study relies on the compiler to set the loop schedules automatically. Determining an optimal loop schedule is not easy, and may require an auto-tuning tool. Another area is to study the effectiveness of overlapping work on the host and the device to hide data transfer latency. Support of directive-based programming for multiple GPUs is a challenging task since overhead from data communication between GPUs could be overwhelming. For future work, we would like to extend our study to these areas as well as to other applications and platforms.

Acknowledgments. The authors would like to acknowledge fruitful discussions with Dennis Jespersen and Dale Talcott of the NAS Division on many experiments we conducted, and Michael Wolfe for providing valuable insight of the PGI compiler.

References

1. Bailey, D.H., Barszcz, E., Barton, J.T., Browning, D.S., Carter, R.L., Dagum, L., Fatoohi, R.A., Frederickson, P.O., Lasinski, T.A., Schreiber, R.S., Simon, H.D., Venkatakrishnan, V., Weeratunga, S.K.: The NAS Parallel Benchmarks. International Journal of Supercomputer Applications 5(3), 63–73 (1991)
2. Beyer, J.C., Stotzer, E.J., Hart, A., de Supinski, B.R.: OpenMP for Accelerators. In: Chapman, B.M., Gropp, W.D., Kumaran, K., Müller, M.S. (eds.) IWOMP 2011. LNCS, vol. 6665, pp. 108–121. Springer, Heidelberg (2011)
3. CAPS: HMPP Programming Model, http://www.caps-entreprise.com/hmpp.html
4. Jespersen, D.C.: Acceleration of a CFD code with a GPU. Scientific Programming 18, 193–201 (2010)
5. Jin, H., Frumkin, M., Yan, J.: The OpenMP Implementation of NAS Parallel Benchmarks and Its Performance. NAS Technical Report NAS-99-011, NASA Ames Research Center (October 1999)
6. Khronos Group, The OpenCL Standard, http://www.khronos.org/opencl/
7. Kirk, D.B., Hwu, W.W.: Programming Massively Parallel Processors: A Hands-on Approach. Morgan Kaufmann Publishers (2010)
8. NVIDIA CUDA Architecture, http://www.nvidia.com/object/cuda_home.html
9. The OpenACC Standard, http://www.openacc-standard.org/

10. Pennycook, S.J., Hammond, S.D., Jarvis, S.A., Mudalige, G.R.: Performance Analysis of a Hybrid MPI/CUDA Implementation of the NAS-LU Benchmark. ACM SIGMETRICS Performance Evaluation Review - PMBS 10 38(4), 23–29 (2011)
11. The Portland Group, PGI Accelerator Programming Model for Fortran and C, v1.3 (November 2010), http://www.pgroup.com/resources/accel.htm
12. The Portland Group, PGI CUDA Fortran Programming Guide and Reference, http://www.pgroup.com/resources/cudafortran.htm
13. Seo, S., Jo, G., Lee, J.: Performance Characterization of the NAS Parallel Benchmarks in OpenCL. In: IEEE International Symposium on Workload Characterization (IISWC), Austin, TX, pp. 137–148 (2011)
14. The Top 500 Supercomputer List (November 2011), http://www.top500.org/lists/2011/11

Effects of Compiler Optimizations in OpenMP to CUDA Translation

Amit Sabne, Putt Sakdhnagool, and Rudolf Eigenmann

Purdue University, West Lafayette IN 47907, USA

Abstract. One thrust of the OpenMP standard development focuses on support for accelerators. An important question is whether or not OpenMP extensions are needed, and how much performance difference they would make. The same question is relevant for related efforts in support of accelerators, such as OpenACC. The present paper pursues this question. We analyze the effects of individual optimization techniques in a previously developed system that translates OpenMP programs into GPU codes, called OpenMPC. We also propose a new tuning strategy, called *Modified IE (MIE)*, which overcomes some inefficiencies of the original OpenMPC tuning scheme. Furthermore, MIE addresses the challenge of tuning in the presence of runtime variations, owing to the memory transfers between the CPU and GPU. MIE, on average, performs 11% better than the previous tuning system while restricting the tuning system time complexity to a polynomial function.

Keywords: GPU, CUDA, Tuning System, Compiler Optimizations.

1 Introduction

OpenMP has established itself as a standard in parallel programming and is of particular interest for today's and future multicores. There is a large and growing code base, the standard is well understood and documented, and there exists a multitude of compilers and supporting tools. These features are of paramount importance to the programmer. They help significantly reduce the difficulty and the cost of developing parallel software.

The number of new parallel languages that have been proposed in even just the past two decades is massive. The question of cost versus benefit arises with every such proposal. Unfortunately, few quantitative analyses are available that would allow one to find out if the same objective could have been achieved with an existing language standard and what are costs and benefits of new versus old, in terms of performance and productivity. Obviously, any new language will start from zero in building a code base, compilers, tools, and programming experience.

* This work was supported, in part, by the National Science Foundation under grants No. CNS-0720471, 0707931-CNS, 0833115-CCF, and 0916817-CCF.

B.M. Chapman et al. (Eds.): IWOMP 2012, LNCS 7312, pp. 169–181, 2012.

A new language development has emerged in the context of new graphics processing units, or accelerators. These devices offer promising avenues towards low-energy, highly parallel computation for a class of applications. Among the proposed programming languages are CUDA and OpenCL, both of which allow the programmer to access architecture-specific features. These architecture-specific interfaces, however, significantly depart from the parallel programming semantics offered by standards, such as OpenMP. The cost/benefit question arises anew.

In previous work, we have addressed this cost/benefit question. We have provided quantitative comparisons of hand-written CUDA programs versus equivalent programs written in OpenMP and translated to CUDA [1]. Using an automatic translator and tuning system, called OpenMPC, we were able to achieve performance results that came close to hand-coded CUDA on a large set of benchmarks. The contribution of the present paper is to address three open issues of that work.

- The previous work provided overall performance numbers. The breakdown into individual techniques was not yet available. In the current paper, we quantify the contributions of each individual technique. Of particular interest in this analysis is also the importance of CUDA-specific OpenMP extensions, which are generated automatically in the OpenMPC system.
- A key component of the OpenMPC is its tuning system, which empirically searches through a large space of optimization variants and tries to find the best. The initial OpenMPC system used an inefficient exhaustive search mechanism. In this work, we use an improved navigation algorithm, significantly reducing tuning time.
- A problem faced by all empirical tuning systems is the variability of execution times, even for the same program executed repeatedly on the same platform in single-user mode. This effect makes it difficult to correctly measure the impact of an optimization technique. A common method is to average over multiple runs, increasing tuning time. We have developed a new method that identifies optimizations that are vulnerable to runtime variation and uses increased measuring time only for those.

The remainder of the paper is organized as follows. Section 2 describes Open-MPC and its available optimization options. It also identifies opportunities for improvement in the present OpenMPC tuning system. Section 3 explains our tuning mechanism for finding the best tuning options. Individual performance analysis is shown in Section 4. Section 5 makes concluding remarks and mentions ongoing work.

2   Overview of OpenMPC System

OpenMPC [1] is a programming framework that generates CUDA programs from OpenMP programs. The framework includes an extended OpenMP programming interface, a source-to-source translator, and an automatic tuning system.

The programming interface extends OpenMP with a new set of directives and environment variables (henceforth referred to as CUDA extensions[1]) for controlling CUDA-related parameters and optimizations. OpenMP translates standard OpenMP programs by applying a set of program transformations and by inserting CUDA extensions. OpenMPC includes an empirical tuning system that automatically generates, prunes, and searches the optimization space and determines the best combination of optimizations. Fig. 1 shows the workflow of the OpenMPC translator. Fig. 2 displays a small example of the OpenMPC translated CUDA code for Jacobi benchmark.

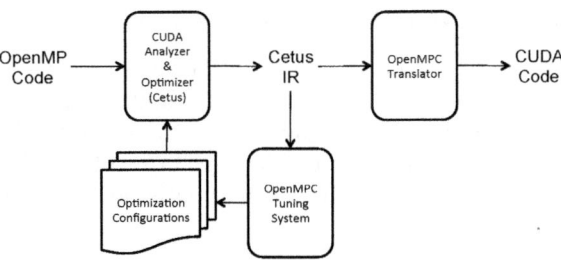

Fig. 1. OpenMPC workflow

```
#pragma omp parallel for private(i, j)
for (i = 1; i <= SIZE; i++){
  for (j = 1; j <= SIZE; j++){
    a[i][j]=(b[i-1][j]+b[i+1][j]+b[i][j-1]+b[i][j+1])/4.0f;
}}
```

(a)

```
__global__ void kernel(...){

  int _bid = (blockIdx.x+(blockIdx.y*gridDim.x));
  int _gtid = (threadIdx.x+(_bid*blockDim.x));
  tid=(_gtid+1);

  if (tid<=SIZE){
    for (i=1; i<=SIZE; i ++ ){
      a[i][j]=(b[i-1][tid]+b[i+1][tid]+b[i][tid-1]+b[i][tid+1])/4.0F;
}}}
```

(b)

Fig. 2. OpenMPC translation example. (a) source code in OpenMP (b) result CUDA kernel from OpenMPC translation.

---

[1] Our CUDA extensions are not meant to be a proposal for extending the OpenMP standard. They represent a research framework for exploring questions such as those addressed in this paper.

2.1   Optimization Options

There are 18 optimization options available in OpenMPC, grouped into 4 categories: (1) Program environment configuration, (2) Data caching strategy, (3) Data offloading optimizations, and (4) Code transformation. Table 1 shows all optimization options in OpenMPC that are considered for individual optimization analysis. The first three groups are supported by our CUDA extensions. The fourth group is applied through source-to-source transformation in the OpenMPC compiler.

2.2   Improving the OpenMPC Tuning System

To analyze the effects of individual tuning options, we make use of the OpenMPC system, which allows us to implement the method in [2]: Using the highest-optimized program variant as a baseline, this method iteratively switches off one optimization at a time, to measure its effect in terms of the slowdown incurred. To this end, we have identified a number of open issues in OpenMPC, which we address in the present work.

Advanced Optimization Space Navigation: The goal of an empirical tuning system is to generate a set of optimizations that yield best performance. In OpenMPC, 18 optimizations are available as compiler flags. Finding the best combination from these flags is non-trivial, because each optimization can improve or worsen the performance of a program, depending upon its characteristic and depending on other present optimizations.

The initial OpenMPC system uses simple *exhaustive search* to navigate the space of optimization variants. This space can be very large (for n on-off optimization options, the size is 2^n). OpenMPC reduces this space using aggressive tuning heuristics, which we refer to as *pruned exponential search (PE)*. PE does the program analysis to prune the tuning space by removing the inapplicable or non-beneficial tuning options for the particular program. It then runs exhaustive search over the remaining tuning options. However, two issues remain: The resulting search space can still be large (which was acceptable for obtaining the original research results [1], but can be too long for end users). In addition, sometimes the aggressive pruning heuristics may eliminate the best optimization combination.

Runtime Variations – A Key Problem of Auto-Tuning Systems: In computer systems, unpredictable system variations during program execution are usual. They arise due to OS overheads, other running processes, or underlying hardware operations. Although these variations do not affect the correctness of the program, they can impact its execution time. We define this type of variation as *runtime variation*. Although runtime variation does not disrupt program execution, in auto-tuning system, runtime variation can be problematic. Since the auto-tuning systems improves the program based on execution time, the variation can cause some beneficial optimizations to be removed from the tuning result and vice versa.

Table 1. Optimization options in OpenMPC

Program Environment Configuration

Compiler Flags	Description
cudaThreadBlockSize=N	Set the default CUDA thread block size
assumeNonZeroTripLoops	Assume that all loops have non-zero iterations

Data Caching Strategy

Compiler Flags	Description
shrdSclrCachingOnReg	Cache shared scalar variables onto GPU register
shrdArryElmtCachingOnReg	Cache shared array elements onto GPU register
shrdSclrCachingOnSM	Cache shared scalar variables onto GPU shared memory
prvtArryCachingOnSM	Cache private array variables onto GPU shared memory
shrdArryCachingOnTM	Cache 1-dimensional, R/O shared array variables onto GPU texture memory
shrdSclrCachingOnConst	Cache R/O shared scalar variables onto GPU constant memory
shrdArryCachingOnConst	Cache R/O shared array variables onto GPU constant memory

Data Offloading Optimization

Compiler Flags	Description
useMallocPitch	Use cudaMallocPitch() for 2-dimensional arrays
useGlobalGMalloc	Allocate GPU variables as global variables which provides more scope for reducing memory transfers
globalGMallocOpt	Apply CUDA malloc optimization for globally allocated GPU variables
cudaMallocOptLevel=N	Set CUDA malloc optimization level for locally allocated GPU variables
cudaMemTrOptLevel=N	Set CUDA CPU-GPU memory transfer optimization level

Code Transformation

Compiler Flags	Description
localRedVarConf=N	Configure how local reduction variables are generated for array-type variables
useMatrixTranspose	Apply Matrix Transpose optimization
useParallelLoopSwap	Apply Parallel Loop Swap optimization
useUnrollingOnReduction	Apply Loop Unrolling for in-block reduction

One of the significant observations made during our study was the fact that most of the variations on GPU programs are due to the variations in memory transfer times. Since GPU and CPU do not share a common address space, memory transfers form an essential part of GPU programs. GPUs are generally connected to the CPU using a PCIe bus, thereby leading to a variability in the memory transfer times. Table 2 compares the relative standard deviation in computation time and the memory transfer time. Relative standard deviation is a percentage of the ratio of standard deviation to the mean of the sample. It acts as an indicator as of how the variations relate to the average. From Table 2, we can see that the relative standard deviations in memory transfer can be as much as 7000 times the relative standard deviations in computation time.

Table 2. Variations on GPU Programs

Benchmark	Relative Standard Deviation for Memory Transfer Time (A)	Relative Standard Deviation for Computation Time (B)	Ratio (A/B)
NW (8192)	0.2395	0.0128	18.71
Jacobi (12288)	0.7394	0.0001	7394
CG (W)	0.2562	0.0706	3.63
FT (W)	0.1521	0.0112	13.58

To alleviate runtime variations, one can average execution times across multiple runs. However, multiple executions can increase the tuning time significantly. The PE algorithm does not take runtime variations into consideration, and therefore is more prone to erroneous final option combinations on GPU programs.

Objectives of This Work: Our goal is to determine the impact of individual optimization techniques in the OpenMP to CUDA translator. To this end, we use the improved OpenMPC translation and tuning system, which can find the best combination of optimization techniques for each program. In doing so, it also reports the performance difference made by individual optimizations. We proceed as follows.

- We modify a previously described *Iterative Elimination (IE)* [3] tuning algorithm to make it applicable to GPU programs.
- We describe a generic tuning methodology to deal with memory transfer time based variations of GPU applications.
- With the best tuning option combination generated by the above tuning system, we analyze the impact of each tuning option or compiler flag.

The next section presents the new tuning algorithm. Section 4 presents results obtained using this methodology.

3   Modified IE (MIE) Algorithm for OpenMPC

To address the issues presented in Section 2.2, we propose a *Modified IE (MIE)* algorithm, which is a tuning algorithm based on *Iterative Elimination (IE)* [3]. In this section, we briefly describe IE and then present our MIE algorithm.

3.1   Iterative Elimination

The IE algorithm is shown in Algorithm 1. IE begins by switching on all optimization options, and then iteratively measures their effect by switching off one tuning option at a time. Next, it removes the one with the most negative effect. The process repeats until all remaining optimizations show non-negative effects. The complexity of IE is $O(n^2)$, compared to $O(2^n)$ of the PE algorithm.

Algorithm 1. Iterative Elimination Algorithm

Require: n = Number of Tuning Options $(F_1, F_2, ... F_n)$
Ensure: $B = \{F_1 = 1, F_2 = 1, ..., F_n = 1\}$ B is a set of combination options
$\quad i \leftarrow 1; NextB \leftarrow B;$ $\quad\triangleright NextB$ stores the fastest combination in every iteration
$\quad$**for** $i = 1 \to n$ **do**
$\quad\quad$**for** $j = 1 \to n$ **do**
$\quad\quad\quad$**if** $F_j \neq 0$ **then**
$\quad\quad\quad\quad NextB = \min(NextB, B$ with $F_j = 0);$ $\quad\triangleright$ Compares the runtimes
$\quad\quad\quad$**end if**
$\quad\quad$**end for** $\quad\quad\quad\quad\quad\quad\triangleright$ Termination: No F_i has changed from 1 to 0
$\quad\quad$**if** $NextB = B$ **then**
$\quad\quad\quad$**break;** $\quad\quad\quad\triangleright$ None of the switched on options has a negative impact
$\quad\quad$**end if**
$\quad\quad B \leftarrow NextB;$ $\quad\quad\quad\quad\quad\triangleright$ Start next iteration with a new baseline $NextB$
$\quad$**end for** $\quad\triangleright$ Creates set of best tuning options e.g $B = \{F_1 = 1, F_2 = 0, ., F_n = 1\}$

Another tuning method, *Combined Elimination (CE)* [3] performs the option removal in a more aggressive fashion, under the assumption that some interferences between options are negligible. The tuning time of CE is known to be shorter than IE. However, since the performance of IE is known to be the best amongst the available tuning algorithms [3], we chose IE as our base algorithm. Other algorithms could be adapted in place of IE in our system [4,5]. Unlike the work in [6], which uses optimal ordering of compiler flags, IE tries to find the best tuning options set, irrespective of the order.

3.2   Grouping of Different Optimization Options

To deal with the problem of runtime variations, a direct implementation of IE would require multiple runs and averaging before eliminating an optimization option. This would lead to high tuning times, because the runtime variations of GPU programs can be large.

Comparing only the computation runtime instead of the total execution time can eliminate the effect of memory transfer variations on tuning. To achieve that, the behavior of memory transfers must be the same between two comparable candidate combinations of IE. If this invariant is maintained, the memory transfer time can be subtracted from total execution time (e.g., by obtaining these times from available hardware profilers) an optimization technique is evaluated by IE.

An intuitive strategy would be to apply techniques that affect memory transfers (i.e. data offloading optimizations shown in Table 1) in a first tuning phase, averaging the results over multiple runs. In a second phase, the remaining optimization options are tuned, whereby transfer times are removed from execution times. In this way, most of the runtime variations in the GPU program can be filtered out; a single run suffices.

The split into the two phases is beneficial only when the data offloading optimizations do not interfere with other. That is not always the case. For example, *useMallocPitch*, which manages 2D array allocation and transfer, may or may not be beneficial depending on the stride of 2D array accesses. Since *useParallelLoopSwap* transforms the array accesses in the code, *useMallocPitch* may improve performance if *useParallelLoopSwap* is applied.

To address this problem, *MIE* uses a third phase, in which memory transfer optimizations that are affected by computation optimization options are placed. This phase also averages runtimes over multiple runs. In a fourth phase, MIE tunes separately those optimizations that do not interact with others. It uses a simple, fast tuning algorithm for this phase.

Phase 1 contains all memory transfer-based (data offloading) optimizations, except useMallocPitch. *Phase 2* contains program environment configuration and code transformation options that impact the computation. *Phase 3* contains dependent optimizations. With the currently available tuning options in OpenMPC, *Phase 3* contains only *useMallocPitch*. This technique impacts the data offloading (memory transfers), but is dependent upon computation technique *useParallelLoopSwap*. *Phase 4* contains data caching optimizations. They are independent of the techniques in the other groups.

Table 3. Grouping of OpenMPC Options for Tuning (MemTR = Memory Transfer Optimization, Comp = Computation Optimization). Options in paranthesis imply multi-values options.

Phase	Type	Tuning Options
1	MemTR	useGlobalGMalloc, globalGMallocOpt, cudaMallocOptLevel=1, cudaMemTrOptLevel=2
2	Comp	useUnrollingOnReduction, useLoopCollapse, useMatrixTranspose, useParallelLoopSwap, prvtArryCachingOnSM, localRedVarConf=0, assumeNonZeroTripLoops
3	Dependent	useMallocPitch
4	Independent	ArrayCache = {shrdArryElmtCachingOnReg, shrdArryCachingOnTM, shrdArryCachingOnConst} ScalarCache = {shrdSclrCachingOnReg, shrdSclrCachingOnSM, shrdSclrCachingOnConst}

3.3   MIE Running Strategy

With the above groups of optimizations in place, we now describe the MIE run strategy.

1. **Data Offload Optimizations**: First the algorithm runs IE with the *Phase 1* optimizations as the input set. Since these options all impact memory transfers, they are vulnerable to high runtime variations. The MIE algorithm runs each IE stage multiple times and considers the average execution times for making elimination decisions.
2. **Computation Optimizations**: The configuration formed in *Phase 1* is the baseline configuration. MIE now appends *Phase 2* options to this configuration and runs IE over all new options. While making comparisons between two combinations, the memory transfer time is removed from the comparison, effectively considering only the computation time. This helps reduce the effect of variations to a large extent. This stage requires calculation of the time spent in copying the data between CPU and GPU memories. This is accomplished by using the CUDA profiler. Using this method, MIE avoids averaging over multiple runs, substantially reducing the time required.
3. **Dependent Optimizations**: In the combination formed after *Phase 2*, MIE includes *Phase 3* option i.e. *useMallocPitch* and averages the runtimes over multiple executions to see if this option is beneficial and should be included. (Should there be more tuning options added in *Phase 3*, MIE would run IE on this group, with averaging runtimes over multiple executions.)
4. **Independent Optimizations**: Since this group does not depend upon other options, MIE iteratively runs each *Phase 4* option on top of the configuration formed in *Phase 3*, and adds the best value of each multi-valued option to the final optimization configuration.

4 Performance Analysis

4.1 Setup

We ran both the PE and the MIE algorithm on NVIDIA Quadro FX 5600 GPU device, which has 16 multiprocessors (SMs) clocked at 1.35GHz and 1.5 GB of memory. Each SM consists of 8 SIMD processing units (SPs) and has 16 KB of shared memory. The host CPU is a 3-GHz AMD dual-core processor with 12 GB memory. The OpenMPC generated CUDA programs were compiled using the NVIDIA CUDA Compiler (NVCC) with option -O3.

We demonstrate the effectiveness of our tuning system on NAS OpenMP Parallel benchmarks, Rodinia OpenMP benchmarks and some scientific computation applications. As described in 3.3, we run *Phase 1* and *Phase 3* options 5 times each and use the average runtimes for IE. For other groups, we compare only the computation times for IE runs.

4.2 Performance Comparison between Pruned Exhaustive and Modified IE Algorithms

To evaluate the performance of the MIE algorithm, we show in Figure 3 the speedup of benchmarks achieved with MIE, normalized with respect to the PE algorithm. MIE performs better than the PE algorithm in most of the cases,

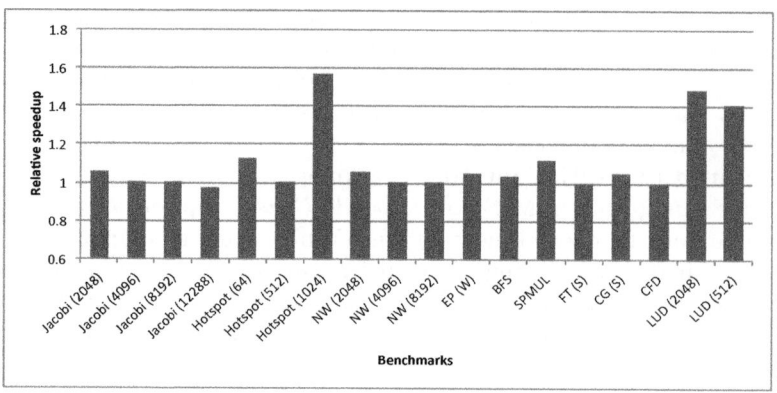

Fig. 3. Program Speedups of Modified IE relative to Pruned Exhaustive Algorithm

averaging to a 11% performance improvement over PE. In fact, MIE outperforms Pruned Exhaustive method substantially for the Hotspot and LUD benchmarks. This effect is due to the over-pruning occurring in the PE method, thereby missing out on the best option combination.

Another important observation is the fact that MIE performs marginally better (2 to 5 %) compared to Pruned Exhaustive method on most other programs where over-pruning does not happen. This is counter-intuitive since PE is expected to search through all possible choices. It is explained due to the excessive memory transfer based variations, wherein the best option combination produced by the Pruned Exhaustive method may not be the optimal, rather it is the one that suffered the least.

Table 4 compares the tuning time required by the Pruned Exhaustive algorithm against the tuning time required by the MIE algorithm. The advantage of IE in terms of tuning time is evident from this table.

Table 4. Tuning Time Comparison of Pruned Exhaustive Vs. Modified IE Algorithm

Benchmark	Tuning Time (mins)	
	Pruned Exhaustive Tuning	Modified IE Tuning
SRAD	538	23
FT (S)	2345	23
CG (S)	1108	17
CFD (97k)	1083	210
FT (A)	3680	97
Jacobi (12288)	98	55

4.3   Impact of Individual Optimization Options

As stated earlier, to analyze the effect of individual tuning options in OpenMPC, we follow the method from [2], wherein we turn off one optimization at a time

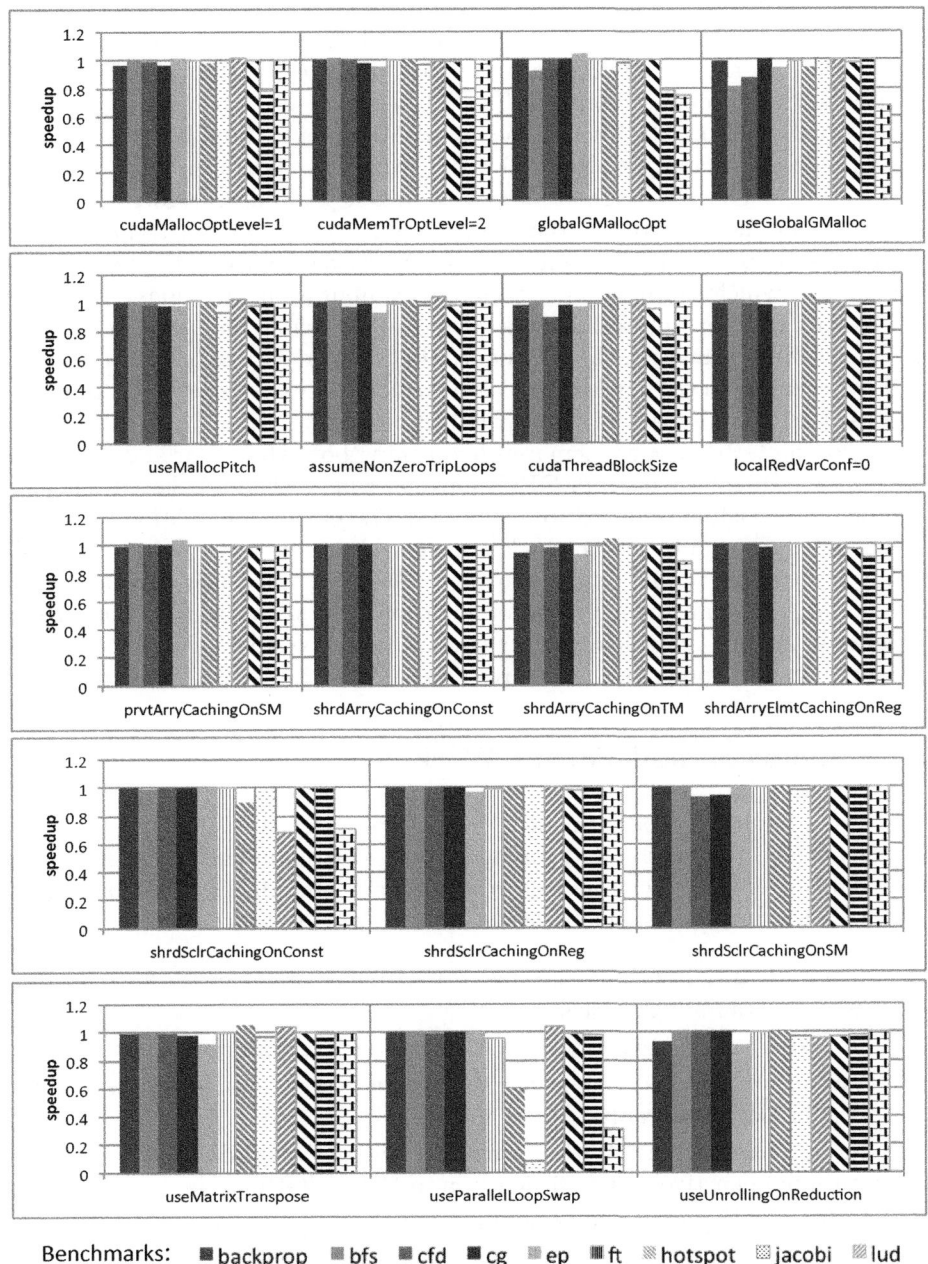

Benchmarks: ■ backprop ▨ bfs ■ cfd ■ cg ▨ ep ▥ ft ▨ hotspot ▨ jacobi ▨ lud
▨ nw ≡ spmul ⊞ srad

Fig. 4. Individual impacts of the 18 optimizations. Bars show normalized performance of the benchmarks after disabling the selected optimization. A large drop in performance indicates high impact.

from the best tuning options set, so as to understand the effects of the individual optimization in terms of the slowdown incurred. The bigger the slowdown, the larger is the benefit of the optimization. We analyze the results in Fig 4 with respect to the techniques shown in Table 1.

Some benchmarks like SRAD, Jacobi, SPMUL depict high benefits obtained due to compiler techniques. However, some others like Backprop show relatively small effects. The effectiveness of our Modified IE tuning algorithm can be gauged from the observation that switching off an individual technique with respect to the best tuning optimization set has never improved the performance beyond 3%, which can be attributed to the computation variations.

Memory transfer optimization-based techniques show high impact on many GPU programs. Similarly, the techniques that change data access strides can be highly beneficial since they help coalesce memory accesses. *useParallelLoopSwap* and *useMatrixTranspose* are some such techniques.

Exploiting GPU specific memories for caching both the scalar and array variables can be highly beneficial. GPUs have on-chip cache and shared memories and off-chip constant and texture memories. The current OpenMPC setup tries to put all the variables (either scalar or arrays) on one of these memories, depending upon the tuning option provided. However, since these memories may not be large enough to hold the complete data sets, the compilation of such programs may fail (in which case the current tuning system ignores the option). We foresee a methodology to adaptively exploit all the GPU specific memories.

5   Conclusion and Future Work

We have analyzed the performance of GPU optimization techniques present in the OpenMPC translation and tuning system. Our main findings indicate that the compiler engineer who wishes to translate a program in a given language into a CUDA program should consider the following optimizations:

1. Memory transfer optimization-based techniques are essential for offloading-based programming models.
2. Exploiting special memories on GPUs can yield significant speedups.
3. Transformations that change the memory access strides are of great importance in GPU programs.
4. Tuning is important. With its help, *standard* OpenMP programs can be translated effectively and efficiently into CUDA/GPU code.
5. Explicit GPU programming (without tuning support) needs to make use of CUDA-extensions (above items 1, 2) for best performance. It is important for emerging standards, such as OpenMP (3.1) [7] and OpenACC [8] to support these features. Above items 1 and 3 should be applicable to a wide range of accelerators. Item 2, however, is CUDA specific, but is necessary to obtain best performance.

We also proposed a new empirical tuning algorithm for GPU programs called Modified IE (MIE), which significantly reduces tuning time. MIE addresses and is able to tolerate runtime variations caused by memory transfer between GPU and CPU. As a result, MIE performs 11% better, on average, than the original OpenMPC tuning system [1], while maintaining polynomial tuning time.

Ongoing work: The presented analysis of different techniques has provided us with intuitions as of what kind of compiler techniques are useful on GPUs. We did not implement some of the *unsafe options* [1] in MIE, the application of which may provide larger benefits. We plan to extend the tuning system into automatically incorporating such options, with the programmer's help in understanding correctness of the output. Furthermore, best performance is achieved by inserting certain CUDA-extension directives in the OpenMP source program [1]. Our ongoing work includes the extension of the translation and tuning system to automate these modifications as well.

References

1. Lee, S., Eigenmann, R.: Openmpc: Extended openmp programming and tuning for gpus. In: Proceedings of the 2010 ACM/IEEE International Conference for High Performance Computing, Networking, Storage and Analysis, SC 2010, pp. 1–11. IEEE Computer Society, Washington, DC (2010)
2. Blume, W., Eigenmann, R.: Performance analysis of parallelizing compilers on the perfect benchmarks programs. IEEE Transactions on Parallel and Distributed Systems 3, 643–656 (1992)
3. Pan, Z., Eigenmann, R.: Fast and effective orchestration of compiler optimizations for automatic performance tuning. In: Proceedings of the International Symposium on Code Generation and Optimization, CGO 2006, pp. 319–332. IEEE Computer Society, Washington, DC (2006)
4. Triantafyllis, S., Vachharajani, M., Vachharajani, N., August, D.I.: Compiler optimization-space exploration. In: Proceedings of the International Symposium on Code Generation and Optimization: Feedback-Directed and Runtime Optimization, CGO 2003, pp. 204–215. IEEE Computer Society, Washington, DC (2003)
5. Pinkers, R.P.J., Knijnenburg, P.M.W., Haneda, M., Wijshoff, H.A.G.: Statistical selection of compiler options. In: Proceedings of the IEEE Computer Society's 12th Annual International Symposium on Modeling, Analysis, and Simulation of Computer and Telecommunications Systems, MASCOTS 2004, pp. 494–501. IEEE Computer Society, Washington, DC (2004)
6. Cooper, K.D., Subramanian, D., Torczon, L.: Adaptive optimizing compilers for the 21st century. J. Supercomput. 23, 7–22 (2002)
7. OpenMP 3.1: Openmp 3.1 released (July 2011), http://openmp.org/wp/openmp-31-released/
8. OpenACC (November 2011), http://www.openacc-standard.org/

Assessing OpenMP Tasking Implementations on NUMA Architectures

Christian Terboven, Dirk Schmidl, Tim Cramer, and Dieter an Mey

JARA, RWTH Aachen University, Germany
Center for Computing and Communication
{terboven,schmidl,cramer,anmey}@rz.rwth-aachen.de

Abstract. The introduction of task-level parallelization promises to raise the level of abstraction compared to thread-centric expression of parallelism. However, tasks might exhibit poor performance on NUMA systems if locality cannot be maintained. In contrast to traditional OpenMP worksharing constructs for which threads can be bound, the behavior of tasks is much less predetermined by the OpenMP specification and implementations have a high degree of freedom implementing task scheduling.

Employing different approaches to express task-parallelism, namely the single-producer and parallel-producer patterns with different data initialization strategies, we compare the behavior and quality of OpenMP implementations with task-parallel codes on NUMA architectures. For the programmer, we propose recipies to express parallelism with tasks allowing to preserve data locality while optimizing the degree of parallelism. Our proposals are evaluated on reasonably large NUMA systems with both important application kernels as well as a real-world simulation code.

1 Introduction

The availability of cost-efficient two- and quad-socket compute nodes with large memory made non-uniform memory access (NUMA) architectures omnipresent. In a NUMA architecture, the memory is partitioned and the latency and bandwidth of memory access depend on the distance to the core from which the access occurs. The thread-centric expression of parallelism, like worksharing in OpenMP[13], works fine on such machines for well-structured code and evenly-balanced algorithms, but it often is unsuitable for recursive algorithms, unbounded loops, or irregular problems in general. Task-level parallelism provides solutions for these applications, but while threads can be bound to cores, the OpenMP specification leaves a high degree of freedom regarding the behavior of tasks to the implementation. If tasks are executed on a NUMA node remote from the data, it has to be transferred first, leading to poor performance.

In this work, we compare the behavior and quality of OpenMP tasking implementations on recent NUMA architectures of different sizes. While detailed descriptions on the inner workings of research OpenMP implementations can be found in the literature (e.g.[14] or [10]), this information is not available for commercial ones, thus we created several experiments to analyze their behavior. We observed significant differences both in the overhead of task creation as well as in the task scheduling on NUMA architectures for the four implementations from Intel, GNU, Oracle and PGI. By analyzing how

B.M. Chapman et al. (Eds.): IWOMP 2012, LNCS 7312, pp. 182–195, 2012.
© Springer-Verlag Berlin Heidelberg 2012

the implementations execute tasks, we derived strategies for task-parallel programming that take the data allocation and work scheduling into account. For implementations that exhibit reliable and consistent behavior, we show that our strategies are successful for compute kernels as well as real-world applications.

This paper is structured as follows: the next chapter discusses related work. Chapter 3 contains our observations on how current OpenMP implementations execute tasks on NUMA architectures. In Chap. 4 we exploit this to express several compute kernels with tasks instead of employing worksharing constructs. Following in Chap. 5 we transfer our strategies to two real-world applications. Chapter 6 contains the summary of our findings.

2   Related Work

Tasking[1] has been introduced in OpenMP 3.0 and has been shown to be able to deliver comparable performance to OpenMP worksharing implementations[2]. The Barcelona OpenMP Task Suite[7] can be employed to compare the efficiency of tasking implementations for several kernels, but in contrast to this work it does not highlight differences in behavior on NUMA machines.

Several articles deal with the efficient scheduling of OpenMP tasks on multi-core multi-socket (NUMA) machines [12,3]. The main challenge is to reflect the system's memory hierarchy in the execution of the OpenMP tasks, while little or no knowledge is present of how tasks are being executed inside the application. Furthermore, task-stealing has to be applied in order to perform load balancing, which means the assignment of tasks from an overutilized thread to an underutilized thread. However, if tasks are moved to a different NUMA node, data of 'stolen' tasks remain on the NUMA node of the initialization, which then leads to remote memory accesses during task execution, as the Linux operating system with a standard kernel does not perform any auto-migration of memory pages.

3   Monitoring Task Execution

The OpenMP runtime has a lot of freedom in how to schedule tasks, providing both opportunities to optimize load balancing via 'task-stealing' and challenges to maintain data locality on NUMA architectures. Ideally tasks are distributed among the threads in a way that no thread is under- or overutilized and tasks are still close to their data, i.e. on the same NUMA node. While this goal is not achievable for any arbitrary workload and data access pattern, differences in especially the task-stealing have significant impact on the overall performance, depending on the pattern of task creation:

- *single-producer multiple-executors*: This pattern is popular for that it often requires little changes to code and data structures. The `single` construct ensures that a code region is executed by one thread only and thus avoids data races. The thread executing the `single` construct is responsible for creating all tasks of appropriate *task chunk size (tcs)* and all data necessary for the computation inside the tasks can be packed up at creation time using the `firstprivate` clause. The implicit barrier at the end of the `single` construct waits for the termination of all tasks.

- *parallel-producer multiple-executors*: A parallel OpenMP `for` worksharing construct loops over the outer iteration space with an increment specified as *task chunk size (tcs)*. In every iteration a task is spawned, performing the iteration over a range of size *tcs*. Thus, all threads of the team executing the worksharing construct create multiple tasks in parallel. The implicit barrier at the end of the `for` construct waits for the termination of all tasks. This pattern can also be expressed without any worksharing construct at all, as the content of a parallel region is executed by all threads of the corresponding team and thus a task construct encountered by all threads creates multiple tasks. Then the synchronization is performed at the end of the parallel region, or by appropriate task synchronization constructs or an explicit `barrier`.

Experiment Setup. We selected the Intel C/C++ 12.1.2, the Oracle Studio C/C++ 12.2 and 12.3, the GNU 4.5 and 4.6 and the PGI C/C++ 11.7-0 compilers for our comparisons, as they represent the most widely used OpenMP-enabled compilers on x86-compatible architectures. Two different machines were used to carry out our experiments:

- **4-sockets:** The bullx s6010 compute node is equipped with four Intel Xeon X7550 processors running at 2.0 GHz, thus offering 32 physical cores and 64 logical cores with hyper-threading, and 64 GB of main memory. The Intel Quickpath Interconnect (QPI) used to connect the four sockets with each other and with I/O facilities creates a system topology with four NUMA domains, with every NUMA node being separated from any other by just one hop. The system is running Scientific Linux 6.1.
- **16-sockets:** The Bull BCS system consists of four bullx s6010 systems as described above. The four systems are equipped with Bull's proprietary BCS cards providing a cache-coherent and high performant interconnect, running a single system image Scientific Linux 6.1 on 128 physical cores with 256 GB of main memory. It is important to notice that not only the BCS interconnect imposes a NUMA topology consisting of the four nodes, but still every node consists of four NUMA nodes connected via the QPI, thus this system exhibits two different levels of NUMAness.

3.1   Load Balancing vs. Data Locality

Load balancing and data locality are performance-critical aspects in shared memory parallel programming. To analyze the general behavior of OpenMP task implementations on a NUMA system, we created an artificial benchmark. It executes $128,000$ work packages, each of which reads an (inner) array with a constant value. To simulate load imbalance, the (inner) arrays differ in size: the first packages are much smaller than the last ones, so that the work is linearly increasing with steps of $128,000/n$ packages where n denotes the number of threads. The first $128,000/n$ packages consists of arrays of size $200,000/n$, the next $128,000/n$ packages read arrays of size $2 * (200,000/n)$, and so on. This benchmark allows to investigate load balancing capabilities as well as data locality effects very well: the data is distributed among the NUMA nodes using a chunk size of $128,000/n$ elements of the outer array, the first chunk of work packages reside on the NUMA node that thread 0 has been bound to, the next chunk is on NUMA node of thread 1, and so on. Thus, 'perfect' data locality would lead to weak load balance, and vice versa, a compromise has to be found. Figure 1 exemplary shows the size of work items and how they are initialized when using 8 threads.

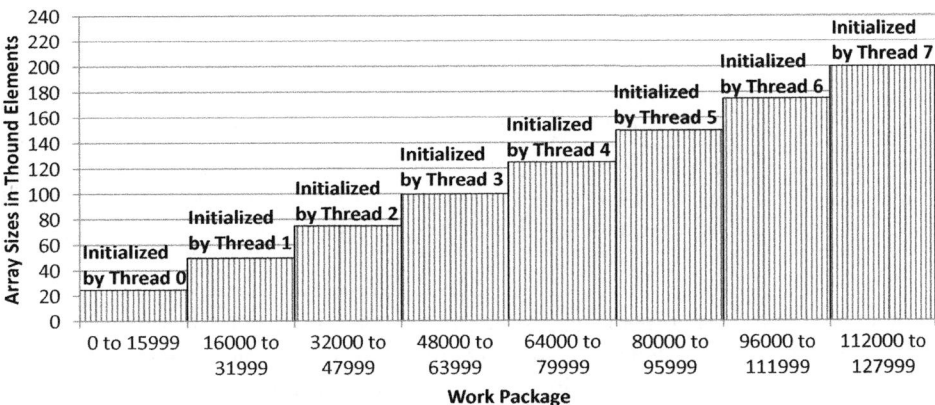

Fig. 1. Size of work packages when 8 threads are used in the load balancing experiment. Each chunk of work packages has been initialized by a different thread.

Linearly increasing load is the 'worst case' for a `for` worksharing construct with a `static` schedule and can be addressed by using a `dynamic` schedule, in which the (outer) iterations are distributed among the threads in the order in which they complete their previous work. In order to compare the behavior of the tasking implementations, we used the parallel-producer pattern along the (outer) iterations with one iteration per task. The work is measured as the total number of assignments to an inner array element. The goal is to achieve a work distribution close to 100 %, which means that every thread has to execute the same amount of work. The minimum, maximum and standard deviation of the average work per thread is shown in Table 1. Considering the 4-sockets system first, the Intel compiler distributes work almost evenly: all threads execute between 97 % and 101 % of the average work. The GNU and PGI compilers perform slightly worse, here all threads execute between 80 % and 115 % of the average work. The Oracle Studio compiler distributes work even more unbalanced over the threads, as we observed a range from 76 % to 161 %.

The load balancing on the 16-sockets machine is much worse than on the 4-sockets machine. Obviously it is harder to perform the task scheduling for 128 threads on 16 sockets than for 32 threads on 4 sockets. Thus, we expected a slightly worse result, in the order as shown by the Intel compiler: 85 % to 121 %. However, for the PGI, GNU and the Oracle Studio compilers, the distributions became extremely imbalanced. In the worst case, with the Oracle Studio Compiler, one particular thread only gets 0.09 % of the average work, whereas another thread gets 566.60 %.

Table 1. Minimum, maximum and standard deviation of the work done by a thread and percentage of local iterations for the load balancing kernel benchmark on the 4-socket and on the 16-socket machine

		4-sockets				16-sockets		
Tasking	MIN	MAX	STDV	local	MIN	MAX	STDV	local
Intel	97.65 %	100.43 %	0.51	79%	84.38 %	121.28 %	8.53	80%
GNU	81.53 %	114.15 %	5.60	80%	66.93 %	271.019 %	41.30	69%
Oracle Studio	76.02 %	161.52 %	17.68	60%	0.09 %	566.60 %	152.93	29%
PGI	83.41 %	106.56 %	5.04	82%	25.00 %	199.84 %	27.78	79%
Worksharing	MIN	MAX	STDV	local	MIN	MAX	STDV	local
Intel static	6.06 %	193.94 %	55.96	100%	1.55%	198.45%	57.29	100%
Intel dynamic	83.08 %	109.98 %	5.17	3.12%	8.61%	522.42%	148.99	0.82%

Using the same experiment again, now we shift focus on data locality. Again, we expect, that tasks are executed where they are created as long as enough work is available locally, so that there is no motivation for task-stealing. Only after all local work is complete, work from a remote location should be picked up. Table 1 also shows the results of this experiment for all investigated compilers for tasking and as well as a reference values for the Intel compiler using a `for` worksharing construct with a `dynamic` and a `static` schedule. These reference values indicate that there is an obvious trade of between load balancing and locality. The `static` schedule archives 100% locality on both systems, but the load balancing is poor. The `dynamic` schedule achieves better load balancing, but the data locality is about 3% (1%) on the 4-socket (16-socket) system. The Intel, GNU and PGI compilers achieve a local work rate of 70 − 80 % on both machines with tasks. The Oracle compiler archives a local access rate of 60 % on the 4-sockets and 29 % only on the 16-sockets system. Although this is slightly worse than the other compilers, it is still much better than the result of the `for` worksharing loop with `dynamic` schedule. We conclude that for computations which exhibit a load imbalance and are sensitive regarding data locality, tasks offer a better alternative to traditional worksharing constructs. However, the performance depends on the task scheduling mechanisms of the OpenMP runtime, and in this experiment Intel provided the best compromise.

3.2   Task Overhead

Overhead of task construction is an important factor for the performance of OpenMP implementations. The basic measurement technique of our experiment is based on the EPCC OpenMP benchmarks [4], where the time taken for a section of sequential code is compared to the time taken for the same code enclosed in a given directive. We extended the original implementation by two new methods. In the first case only one thread generates the tasks (single-producer, left) and in the second case we create tasks with the parallel-producer pattern (right):

```
#pragma omp parallel private(j)
#pragma omp single
  for (j=0; j<innerreps* \
    omp_get_num_threads(); j++)
#pragma omp task
    delay(delaylength);
```

```
#pragma omp parallel private(j)

  for (j=0; j<innerreps; j++)

#pragma omp task
    delay(delaylength);
```

The variable innerreps denotes the number of repetitions and is chosen so that the execution time is significantly larger than the costs of the enclosing single directive. The number of generated tasks is the same for both cases and increases with the number of threads. Table 2 shows that the overhead on the 4-sockets system for all compilers is much bigger for the single-producer (*sin-pro*) pattern than the for the parallel-producer (*par-pro*) pattern: for single-producer the overhead increases with the number of tasks. While the PGI runtime has a maximum overhead of approximately 58 μs, the GNU runtime levels out at more than 1, 100 μs. Compared to that, the parallel-producer pattern incurs much less overhead. Again the Intel and PGI runtime (0.3 μs and 3.3 μs with 32 threads, respectively) deliver outstanding results. The overhead increase with the GNU an the Oracle Studio compilers is much more moderate compared to the single-producer pattern, but still an order of magnitude higher than for the other two runtime implementations.

The experiments on the 16-sockets machine presented in Table 3 show the same trends concerning the two patterns. However, it also shows that with the single-producer pattern the absolute overhead rises sharply with 128 threads for all implementations and with the GNU and Oracle Studio runtime for the parallel-producer pattern as well. The overhead of the task generation for the single-producer with the GNU compiler is more than 40, 000 μs while it is less than 900 μs with the PGI compiler. In summary the Intel runtime generates tasks with least overhead of only 1.7 μs (128 threads) using the parallel-producer pattern.

Table 2. Overhead of task creation on 4-sockets in μs

	Threads	1	2	4	8	12	16	24	32
Intel	sin-pro	0.23	1.20	1.36	1.75	59.05	156.12	560.40	764.85
	par-pro	0.11	0.19	0.36	0.24	0.27	0.17	0.30	0.26
GNU	sin-pro	2.21	2.04	6.88	83.66	185.04	304.44	652.26	1126.18
	par-pro	1.86	2.09	2.92	5.86	10.11	14.28	27.05	44.22
ORACLE	sin-pro	0.09	1.05	9.24	59.89	139.49	211.27	299.22	424.22
STUDIO	par-pro	0.09	1.32	3.43	4.33	8.47	14.06	18.55	39.65
PGI	sin-pro	0.03	2.98	2.66	2.69	4.43	9.36	34.22	57.79
	par-pro	0.03	1.26	1.37	0.95	1.69	1.90	2.49	3.26

4   Task Behavior on NUMA Architectures

In this chapter we exploit the insights gathered in the previous one to create task-parallel implementations of two compute kernels, namely STREAM[11] and a

Table 3. Overhead of task creation on 16-sockets in μs

	Threads	1	2	4	8	16	32	64	128
Intel	sin-pro	0.12	1.89	187.68	199.57	492.64	2440.62	2432.05	5656.16
	par-pro	0.12	0.32	0.93	0.17	0.72	1.11	1.32	1.69
GNU	sin-pro	1.75	1.80	14.57	209.79	785.69	1361.50	11938.48	40555.73
	par-pro	1.74	1.98	2.89	34.76	324.20	401.80	1870.33	9908.19
ORACLE	sin-pro	0.09	3.52	37.02	176.28	643.73	1534.76	3571.80	7440.76
STUDIO	par-pro	0.09	1.89	5.95	18.42	88.01	235.51	505.06	1183.10
PGI	sin-pro	0.69	5.25	4.77	14.10	62.57	160.95	367.81	892.55
	par-pro	0.02	2.68	2.35	3.45	6.94	23.58	51.35	357.38

Sparse-Matrix-Vector-Multiplication in a CG-method[9], which both are very sensitive regarding the memory access pattern.

4.1 STREAM

For the sake of brevity we only examine results from the triad operation, they are consistent with the other ones. Figure 2 shows the results for the Intel, Oracle and GNU compilers only, as the PGI compiler failed to compile our experiment framework correctly (Internal error: assertion failed). The arrays have a dimension of $256, 435, 456$ `double` elements, which results in 1.96 GB of memory consumption per array, or 5.87 GB of total kernel size in the triad operation. This kernel size is much larger than the accumulated cache size and thus we achieve reliable measurements of the memory bandwidth of the system.

Considering the 4-sockets machine first, all three compilers deliver roughly the same performance for the traditional worksharing-based parallelization, which we refer to as *workshare: static-init for-loop* and regard as a reference. In this variant, a `static` schedule is employed both during data initialization and the actual computation, meaning that for t threads the arrays are divided into t parts of approximately equal size. Given four NUMA nodes in the system and a *scatter* thread binding, meaning threads are spread as far apart as possible, $\frac{t}{4}$ threads will be bound to each NUMA node, resulting in an even data distribution over all NUMA nodes in the system. We compared this to the following task-parallel variants, for which we found a task chunk size of $65, 536$ iterations per task to be optimal, although it does not have a significant influence on the performance as long as enough tasks are spawned to generate enough parallelism and as long as the work per task is computationally expensive enough compared to the task creation and scheduling overhead:

- *tasks: static-init single-producer*: The data initialization is performed in the same way as in the original parallel version. The generation of tasks is performed by one thread only (*single-producer multiple-executors* pattern).
- *tasks: static-init parallel-producer*: Again the data initialization is performed in the same way as in the original parallel version, but now the creation of tasks is performed in parallel (*parallel-producer multiple-executors* pattern).

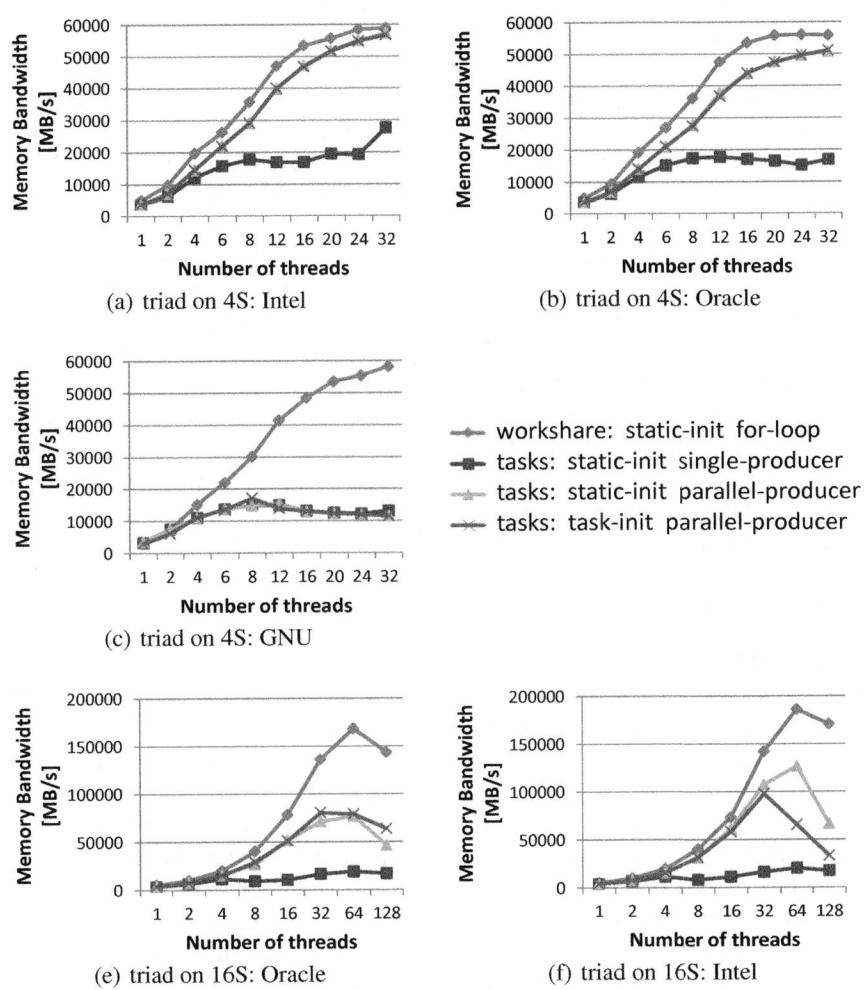

(a) triad on 4S: Intel

(b) triad on 4S: Oracle

(c) triad on 4S: GNU

→ worksafe: static-init for-loop
■ tasks: static-init single-producer
▲ tasks: static-init parallel-producer
✕ tasks: task-init parallel-producer

(e) triad on 16S: Oracle

(f) triad on 16S: Intel

Fig. 2. STREAM triad operation on the 4-sockets and 16-sockets system

– *tasks: task-init parallel-producer*: The data initialization and the computation is performed task-parallel by applying the same pattern to both code regions.

Still examining the 4-sockets (4S) machine in Fig. 2(a)-(c), for the Intel and the Oracle compiler, the worksharing version outperforms the best task-parallel version by just 3 % to 5 %. Regarding these runtimes, the two task-parallel variants employing the parallel-producer pattern deliver approximately the same performance, as both distribute the data in a nearly optimal fashion over the NUMA nodes. If the parallel-producer pattern is used in the data initialization and the computation, the OpenMP runtimes of Intel and Oracle are able to maintain data affinity. However, this does not work with the GNU compiler, for which all three tasking variants deliver about the same performance - the base performance that can be achieved on this machine for random memory access. For all three compilers, the single-producer tasking version clearly suffers from two effects: (1) the runtime cannot maintain data affinity, as all tasks are created from a single NUMA node and the work-stealing will just pick arbitrary tasks from the queue; and (2) the single thread responsible for creating the tasks cannot completely keep the other threads executing the tasks busy. If only one thread creates all the tasks, the runtime's task-stealing mechanism cannot take the data distribution into account during the 'stealing' and thus the performance on NUMA systems obviously suffers.

The situation looks different on the 16-socket (16S) machine, where the peak performance of the task-parallel versions is significantly below the `for` workshare version with a `static` schedule. Interpreting comments from the Intel OpenMP runtime, the system topology is assumed to consist of 16 packages (= processor sockets), the two levels of NUMAness are not respected. Corresponding to the observations in Chap. 3.1, with higher numbers of threads the task-to-thread affinity is not 'strong' enough to prevent disadvantageous task-stealing. The single-producer variant is far behind, as the 4S results already implied. Futhermore, employing 128 threads on that machine is not profitable, similar to experiences made with other big SMPs in the past. For the final paper we will investigate measurements with 120 or 124 threads.

4.2 SMXV in a CG Kernel

While STREAM served our purpose as a benchmark indicating fine differences in the memory access pattern, the Sparse-Matrix-Vector-Multiplication (SMXV) in a CG-Method [9] much more resembles a real-world compute kernel as part of many PDE solvers. Depending on the problem the matrix for the system of linear equations can be very irregular. In this case the sparse matrix vector product is a typical example of the importance of adequate load balancing. Especially in cases where the optimal work distribution cannot be calculated in advance, we expect task-parallel implementations to help avoiding performance issues. On the one hand the programmer has to ensure that a sufficient number of tasks is used to avoid load imbalance, on the other hand too many tasks introduce additional overhead. In our CG implementation all vector operations and the dot-product are parallelized with OpenMP `for` constructs. Only the SMXV is parallelized with tasks. The work is distributed by chunks of rows and the chunk size is the same for each task, calculated as

$$chunk\_size(tasks) = \begin{cases} \lfloor N/tasks \rfloor, & \text{if } N\%tasks = 0 \\ \lfloor N/tasks \rfloor + 1, \text{otherwise} \end{cases} \tag{1}$$

where N is the dimension of the square matrix and $tasks$ the number of tasks. The matrix used here represents a computational fluid dynamics problem (Fluorem/HV15R) and is taken from the University of Florida Sparse Matrix Collection [5]. The dimension is $N = 2,017,169$ and the number of nonzero values is $nnz = 283,073,458$, which results in a memory footprint of approximately 3.2 GB, so that the data set is big enough to not fit into the caches, even on the 16-sockets machine. The data is initialized using a `for` worksharing construct with a `static` schedule.

Figure 3 shows the performance of the SMXV when executing 1000 CG iterations. We compare the performance of the different OpenMP implementations on both machines. In almost all cases the Intel compiler delivers the best performances. For both machine types the parallel-producer pattern reaches a significantly higher performance than the single-producer pattern when using the Intel or the Oracle Studio implementation. In contrast, the peak performance achieved with the GNU compiler is below 9 GFLOPS (see 3(a)/3(b)) or rather below 5 GFLOPS (see 3(c)/3(d)) independent of the pattern. The figure also shows that even with more than 100,000 tasks the performance of the Intel compiler for the parallel-producer variant is stable in contrast to the single-producer pattern. The behavior for the other compilers is similar in this point, although the performance decrease becomes visible with lower amount of tasks already.

Figure 3(c) shows that all implementations do not scale on the 16-sockets system when the tasks are created by one single thread. In contrast to that the Intel compiler reaches up to 21 GFLOPS on the same system (see 3(d)) in the parallel-producer variant. Task-stealing done by the OpenMP runtime to perform load balancing by the assignment of tasks from an overutilized to an underutilized thread. Table 4 shows the percentage of tasks which are executed by a different thread than it was created from. As expected, for the single-producer pattern more than 90 % of the tasks are not executed by the same thread. Furthermore, for the parallel-producer pattern only 2.9 % or rather 8.6 % of the tasks are executed by a thread which did not create this task. This means that the amount of remote data accesses introduced due to task-stealing is very low, which results in much better performance. However, Table 4 also shows that there is no difference for the GNU runtime in all cases, meaning that this kernel does not benefit from the parallel producer pattern. The Oracle Studio runtime is almost as good as the Intel runtime on the 4-sockets system, but the amount of remote accesses increases to over 40 % on the 16-socket system.

Table 4. Percentage of remote data accesses for the single- and parallel-producer pattern on the 4-sockets and 16-sockets systems using the CG kernel with 1024 tasks

	4-sockets		16-sockets	
	single	parallel	single	parallel
Intel	96.21 %	2.87 %	99.22 %	8.61 %
GNU	96.87 %	96.90 %	99.04%	99.14 %
ORACLE STUDIO	95.97 %	4.04 %	98.24 %	41.02 %

5   Application Case Studies

Finally, we compare the different compilers for two real-world applications. Both codes have been parallelized with nested parallel regions and we added a new version utilizing OpenMP tasks. In both versions the parallelism is expressed in exactly the same way.

FIRE: The Flexible Image Retrieval Engine (FIRE) [6] was developed at the Human Language Technology and Pattern Recognition Group[1] of RWTH Aachen University. The retrieval engine takes a set of query images and for each query image it returns a number of similar images from an image database.

---

[1] http://www-i6.informatik.rwth-aachen.de

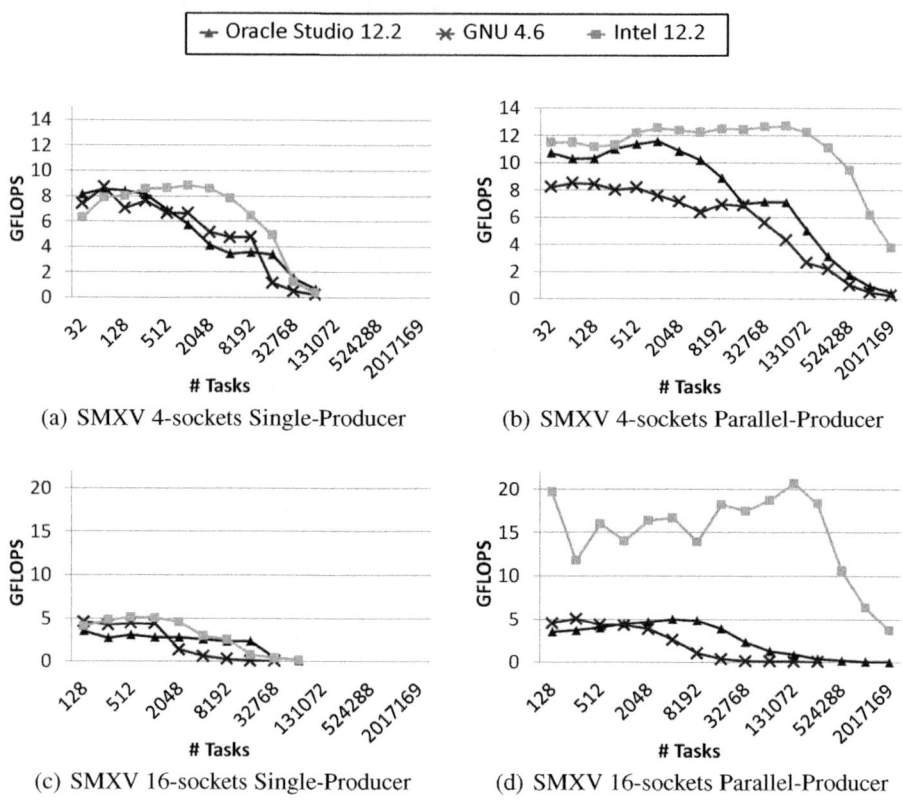

Fig. 3. Performance of SMXV for different Implementations

NestedCP: NestedCP [8] is developed at the Virtual Reality Group of the RWTH Aachen University[2] and is used to extract critical points in unsteady flow field datasets. Critical points are essential parts of the velocity field topologies and extracting them helps to interactively visualize the data in virtual environments.

Figure 4 shows the runtime and speedup of the FIRE and the NestedCP codes on the 16-sockets machine comparing the tasking version to the one with nested parallel regions. Only the Intel, GNU and Oracle Studio compilers have been investigated, as the PGI compiler failed to compile any of the two codes successfully.

Two observations are important for our discussion. Firstly, the best results for both codes are achieved using the tasking version with the Intel compiler. For the FIRE code a speedup of 127 is reached and for NestedCP a speedup of about 33, both on 128 cores. This version outperforms in both cases the nested parallel version, if the machine is fully utilized. This fact shows that the tasking paradigm works well for both applications and that the superior load balancing behavior of tasks compared to parallel regions can improve the programs performance.

---

[2] http://www.vr.rwth-aachen.de

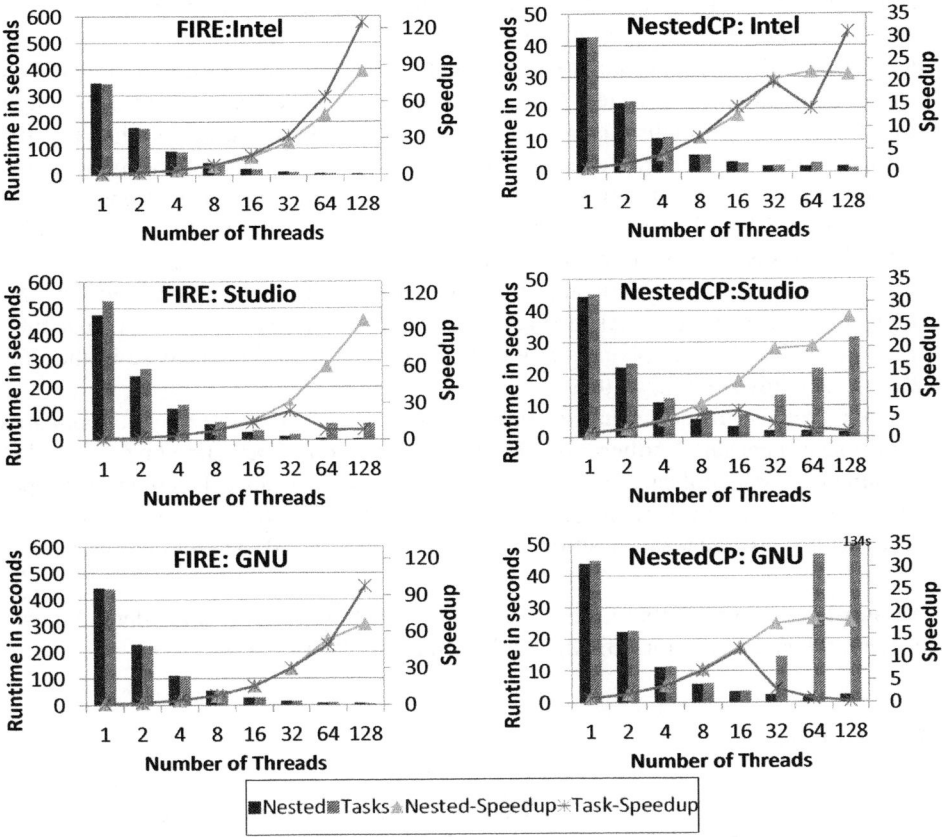

Fig. 4. Performance of the FIRE and NestedCP codes. A task-parallel version is compared to a nested variant.

Secondly, the behavior differs a lot between the compilers. With the GNU and Oracle Studio compilers, NestedCP does not scale to more than 16 threads at all with the tasking version. The FIRE code scales up to a speedup of 100 with the GNU compiler, with the Oracle compiler the performance drops down, when more than 32 threads are used. However, the FIRE version using nested parallel regions delivers the best speedup using the Oracle Studio compiler. These differences in the performance behavior of compilers and/or runtimes makes it nearly impossible to write code that performs equally well on a variety of platforms, meaning different hardware architectures and different OpenMP implementations.

6   Summary

The introduction of task-level parallelism in OpenMP raised the level of abstraction compared to thread-centric worksharing models, by delegating the responsibility of distributing the work among the threads to the runtime. On hierarchical NUMA architectures, tasks might exhibit poor performance if remote data is accessed frequently, that means if the runtime cannot maintain data locality when selecting a thread to execute a given task. If the system topology is not too complex, and if thread binding is used and the task-parallelism is expressed using an appropriate pattern, such as parallel-producer, OpenMP runtimes can maintain data affinity and thus achieve performance on par with or even better than state-of-the-art worksharing implementations. Comparing the OpenMP implementations on the 4-socket system, particularly the Intel runtime showed consistent behavior and incurs little overhead in task creation.

However, there were significant differences in behavior between the four OpenMP implementations on the 4-sockets machine and especially on the 16-sockets machines. In all kernels with all implementations the performance did not increase in the same way as the hardware's capabilties.

If the behavior of an OpenMP runtime differs a lot from another one, application performance gets hurt. Furthermore, the expectations from observation on the 4-sockets machine were not applicable on the 16-sockets machine, because the complexer topology was mostly not correctly respected. If a weak implementation does not offer reliable behavior, this also weakens the attractivity of the OpenMP tasking programming model.

Acknowledgement. Parts of this work were funded by the German Federal Ministry of Research and Education (BMBF) under Grant No. 01IH11006.

References

1. Ayguadé, E., Copty, N., Duran, A., Hoeflinger, J., Lin, Y., Massaioli, F., Teruel, X., Unnikrishnan, P., Zhang, G.: The Design of OpenMP Tasks. IEEE Transactions on Parallel and Distributed Systems 20(3), 404–418 (2009)
2. Ayguadé, E., Duran, A., Hoeflinger, J., Massaioli, F., Teruel, X.: An Experimental Evaluation of the New OpenMP Tasking Model. In: Adve, V., Garzarán, M.J., Petersen, P. (eds.) LCPC 2007. LNCS, vol. 5234, pp. 63–77. Springer, Heidelberg (2008)
3. Broquedis, F., Furmento, N., Goglin, B., Wacrenier, P.-A., Namyst, R.: ForestGOMP: An Efficient OpenMP Environment for NUMA Architectures. International Journal of Parallel Programming 38, 418–439 (2010) 10.1007/s10766-010-0136-3
4. Bull, J.M.: Measuring Synchronisation and Scheduling Overheads in OpenMP. In: Proceedings of First European Workshop on OpenMP, pp. 99–105 (1999)
5. Davis, T.A.: University of Florida Sparse Matrix Collection. NA Digest, 92 (1994)
6. Deselaers, T., Keysers, D., Ney, H.: Features for image retrieval: an experimental comparison. Information Retrieval 11(2), 77–107 (2008)
7. Duran, A., Teruel, X., Ferrer, R., Martorell, X., Ayguade, E.: Barcelona OpenMP Tasks Suite: A Set of Benchmarks Targeting the Exploitation of Task Parallelism in OpenMP. In: Parallel Processing, (ICPP 2009), pp. 124–131 (September 2009)
8. Gerndt, A., Sarholz, S., Wolter, M., Mey, D.A., Bischof, C., Kuhlen, T.: Nested OpenMP for Efficient Computation of 3D Critical Points in Multi-Block CFD Datasets. In: Proceedings of the ACM/IEEE, SC 2006 Conference, p. 46 (November 2006)
9. Hestenes, M.R., Stiefel, E.: Methods of Conjugate Gradients for Solving Linear Systems. Journal of Research of the National Bureau of Standards 49(6), 409–436 (1952)

10. LaGrone, J., Aribuki, A., Addison, C., Chapman, B.: A Runtime Implementation of OpenMP Tasks. In: Chapman, B.M., Gropp, W.D., Kumaran, K., Müller, M.S. (eds.) IWOMP 2011. LNCS, vol. 6665, pp. 165–178. Springer, Heidelberg (2011)
11. McCalpin, J.: STREAM: Sustainable Memory Bandwidth in High Performance Computers (1999), http://www.cs.virginia.edu/stream (accessed March 29, 2012)
12. Olivier, S.L., Porterfield, A.K., Wheeler, K.B., Prins, J.F.: Scheduling task parallelism on multi-socket multicore systems. In: Proceedings of the 1st International Workshop on Runtime and Operating Systems for Supercomputers, ROSS 2011, pp. 49–56. ACM, New York (2011)
13. OpenMP ARB. OpenMP Application Program Interface, v. 3.1, http://www.openmp.org
14. Teruel, X., Martorell, X., Duran, A., Ferrer, R., Ayguadé, E.: Support for OpenMP tasks in Nanos v4. In: Lyons, K.A., Couturier, C. (eds.) Proceedings of the 2007 Conference of the Centre for Advanced Studies on Collaborative Research, pp. 256–259. IBM (October 2007)

Performance Analysis Techniques for Task-Based OpenMP Applications*

Dirk Schmidl[1], Peter Philippen[2], Daniel Lorenz[2], Christian Rössel[2],
Markus Geimer[2], Dieter an Mey[1], Bernd Mohr[2], and Felix Wolf[1,2,3]

[1] RWTH Aachen University, 52056 Aachen, Germany
[2] Jülich Supercomputing Centre, 52425 Jülich, Germany
[3] German Research School for Simulation Sciences, 52062 Aachen, Germany

Abstract. Version 3.0 of the OpenMP specification introduced the task construct
for the explicit expression of dynamic task parallelism. Although automated
load-balancing capabilities make it an attractive parallelization approach for programmers, the difficulty of integrating this new dimension of parallelism into
traditional models of performance data has so far prevented the emergence of
appropriate performance tools. Based on our earlier work, where we have introduced instrumentation for task-based programs, we present initial concepts for
analyzing the data delivered by this instrumentation. We define three typical performance problems related to tasking and show how they can be visually explored
using event traces. Special emphasis is placed on the event model used to capture
the execution of task instances and on how the time consumed by the program is
mapped onto tasks in the most meaningful way. We illustrate our approach with
practical examples.

1 Introduction

To harness the available performance of today's multi-core systems, applications need
to make efficient use of the available parallelism. Cores sitting idle, for example in
communication calls waiting for data to arrive or in synchronization operations due to
load imbalance, waste resources and reduce the overall performance of the application.
However, optimizing load balance is often a non-trivial undertaking, especially since
the behavior of the application may change when ported to a different architecture or
executed on a different number of processor cores.

To address this situation, the tasking construct was introduced with OpenMP 3.0 [3].
Using tasks, the programmer is able to express parallelism in his code at a much finer
level of detail. Instead of specifying a single command stream per thread, as with the
traditional parallel and work-sharing constructs, the programmer can now decompose
his program into smaller tasks and specify dependencies between creator tasks and their
children. The defined tasks are assigned to the available threads by the runtime system.
This approach is supposed to automatically improve load balancing, although it incurs

---

* This material is based upon work supported by the German Federal Ministry of Research and
Education (BMBF) under Grant No. 01IS07005 and by the Department of Energy under Grant
No. DE-SC0001621.

B.M. Chapman et al. (Eds.): IWOMP 2012, LNCS 7312, pp. 196–209, 2012.

additional overhead in the runtime system. Moreover, it poses new challenges not only for developers, but also for performance-analysis tools used for tuning applications.

In our earlier work, we introduced a portable method to distinguish individual task instances and to track their suspension and resumption using event-based instrumentation [12]. A prerequisite for this approach is that tied tasks are used or untied tasks which are only suspended at task scheduling points. Based on this method, we present initial performance-analysis concepts in a trace-based analysis workflow. Specifically, we make the following contributions:

- We define three performance problems related to tasking.
- We describe an extension of the Open Trace Format 2 (OTF2) [6] event model to record constituents of these performance problems in event traces. This determines how task instances are represented in the control flow of individual threads.
- We show how time or other performance-related metrics are attributed to tasks and threads.
- We demonstrate our concepts using benchmarks and a real-world application.

The paper is organized as follows: We review related work in Section 2. After discussing typical performance problems in Section 3, we cover the OTF2 event model in Section 4. Next, we explain the representation of task instances and the attribution of execution time in Section 5. Practical examples follow in Section 6. Finally, in Section 7, we discuss progress and limitations, and present future work.

2 Related Work

Since OpenMP is such a commonly used parallel programming interface, there is already a body of work addressing performance analysis and optimization. Many current performance analysis tools support the measurement and analysis of performance data related to OpenMP constructs. Tools based on instrumentation, such as Scalasca [8], TAU [14], and Vampir [10], utilize the source-to-source instrumenter OPARI [13] to capture OpenMP-specific events. However, currently none of them provides support for tasks, mainly because the event stream of a thread may result in a sequence of task-instance fragments, which can only be analyzed if the overall task instance to which those fragments belong can be identified.

Fürlinger et al. [7] were the first who profiled tasks using instrumentation. However, their initial work provides no mechanism to identify task instances. Lorenz at al. [12] presented an instrumentation mechanism to identify task instances via source-code instrumentation of task-related constructs. This mechanism was demonstrated via a prototypical extension of OPARI. In the meantime, the successor OPARI2 [2] was released, which—among other improvements—contains a production version of this instrumentation mechanism. Our work builds upon the OPARI2 instrumentation and uses it as a prerequisite for performance measurements.

Instead of instrumenting the code directly, other tools such as HPCToolkit [1] apply statistical sampling. In this way, they obtain the call-stack and hardware counters in regular intervals. Moreover, Sun proposed a compiler interface [9] to obtain

OpenMP-related data for performance analysis. Lin and Mazurov [11] extended this proposal to support tasking and implemented a prototype based on the Sun Studio Performance Analyzer. However, whereas they focus on the acquisition of performance data, our work focuses on their analysis.

3   Performance Problems Related to Tasking

In task-parallel programs, typically many more task instances than compute resources exist. Consequently, we cannot expect all task instances to be executed in parallel. Tasks which have to wait at a synchronization point do therefore not necessarily indicate a performance drawback. In most HPC applications, the number of active threads is a good indication for the number of available compute resources, as most applications start one thread per core they want to use. Accordingly, all threads can be active at the same time. What needs to be investigated, even in tasking programs, is whether all threads are doing useful work all the time. Here, useful work means everything except spending time in the OpenMP runtime or doing nothing. The following three performance problems related to tasking can lead to situations where threads waste compute resources.

Too Finely Grained Task Parallelism. Overhead spent in the OpenMP runtime to create a task or to suspend and resume it should be avoided if possible. If the execution time of a task is very small, this overhead can consume more CPU cycles than the task's actual execution. In this case, it would be more efficient to execute the task's body immediately without separating it into a task. The overhead to create and manage a task, of course, depends on many different factors, such as the hardware, the compiler, the data-sharing attributes of the task, and so on. Thus, we cannot quantify precisely when it is beneficial to create a task.

Too Coarsely Grained Task Parallelism. In contrast to the previous situation, creating only a few very large tasks may result in load imbalance. For example, if 12 equally sized large tasks are created and eight threads are used, half of the threads will execute two tasks and the rest will only execute one. Even if there is a task for every thread, sometimes there might not be enough to smooth differences in the runtime of individual tasks, which can depend on dynamic conditions.

Task-Creation Bottleneck. When a lot of threads execute tasks while only a few threads create them, the creation of tasks can become the bottleneck. This can happen, for example, when tasks are created in a `single` region by just one thread. For n worker threads, the master thread must produce the tasks at least $(n-1)$ times faster than they are executed by workers. This situation is commonly known in master-worker approaches where the master can become the performance bottleneck if the number of workers is too large. Another reason why not enough tasks are created might be a shortage of available parallelism in dynamic algorithms.

4   The OTF2 Task Event Model

Before any performance analysis of an application can be done, information about its runtime behavior has to be collected. For this purpose, the work presented in this paper leverages the Score-P [2] instrumentation and measurement system. To instrument OpenMP directives, Score-P utilizes the source-to-source instrumenter OPARI2, using the technique presented in [12] for task-related constructs. In tracing mode, which forms the basis of this work, the instrumentation hooks inserted by OPARI2 trigger the generation of events in the Open Trace Format 2 (OTF2) [6]. But before describing its task-specific details, we first give a brief overview of OTF2.

OTF2 stores concurrent events in separate event streams per thread of execution, representing its runtime behavior. Common event types are entering/leaving a function, sending/receiving a message, or creating/destroying an OpenMP thread team. Each event includes a timestamp as well as additional event-specific data, such as the source-code region being entered or the number of bytes being transferred. To avoid redundancy in the data being stored, static entities (so-called definitions) such as information about source-code regions are stored only once and referenced using numerical identifiers. In addition, OTF2 uses an efficient encoding scheme for these identifiers and other attributes to compress the event data on-the-fly.

To encode task-specific behavior, the "traditional" records provided by OTF2, for example, `Enter/Leave` for entering or leaving a source-code region and `OmpFork/OmpJoin` for creating or destroying an OpenMP thread team, do not suffice. Therefore, new event types need to be introduced. A careful analysis of the performance deficiencies presented in Section 3 reveals that two types of actions are relevant to analyze the efficiency of task parallelism: the creation as well as the execution of a task. In the following, we describe which events are generated by those actions and which event attributes are required for our analyses.

When a task is created, the OpenMP runtime system basically has two choices: the task can either be executed immediately or queued for later execution. In both cases, it is essential for a measurement system to be able to identify each task instance. That is, for each task being created, we generate a corresponding `OmpTaskCreate` event and attach a unique numerical task identifier to it. The task identifier zero is reserved for the implicit task for which no `OmpTaskCreate` event is generated.

When a task starts its execution—either immediately or when dequeued from the task queue—the measurement system needs to be notified in order to be able to map all following events onto the task which generates them. For this purpose, we use the task identifier assigned during task creation. Obviously, the same notification is required when the execution of one task is suspended and another task is resumed, that is, a task switch occurs. As the begin of a task's execution is basically also a task switch (either switching from the implicit task or from another task which was suspended or finished its execution), we use only a single event to encode this behavior. As the identifier of the task previously being executed is implicitly known, the `OmpTaskSwitch` event carries only the task ID of the task being started or resumed, respectively.

Finally, to allow the measurement system to clean up its internal task-specific data structures, the completion of a task needs to be identified. For this reason, the

```
1   Enter("OMP task", metrics, timestamp);
2   OmpTaskCreate(new_task_id, timestamp);
3
4   #pragma omp task
5   {
6       OmpTaskSwitch(new_task_id, timestamp);
7       Enter("OMP task structured block", metrics, timestamp);
8
9           // Do some useful work...
10
11      Leave("OMP task structured block", metrics, timestamp);
12      OmpTaskComplete(new_task_id, timestamp);
13  }
14
15  if (current_task_id != old_task_id)
16      OmpTaskSwitch(old_task_id, timestamp);
17  Leave("OMP task", metrics, timestamp);
```

Fig. 1. OTF2 events generated for an OpenMP task construct

OmpTaskComplete event is introduced, also providing the task identifier of the task that has just finished its execution.

As can be seen, the identification of task instances via task identifiers is essential for our event model. However, the OpenMP standard does not yet require runtime systems to provide such identifiers. We therefore rely on the task instrumentation provided by OPARI2, which implements a portable method to track task identifiers for tied tasks, as well as untied tasks that are suspended only at implied scheduling points.

Figure 1 illustrates when the different events will be generated for an OpenMP task construct. As can be seen, task creation is surrounded by a conventional Enter/Leave event pair (lines 1 and 17). Inside, the task creation is recorded by the generating task, assigning a new task identifier (line 2). The OmpTaskSwitch event before leaving the creation region is only generated in the case one or more tasks have been executed at the implicit task scheduling point during creation (lines 15/16). The task execution itself is surrounded by an (unconditional) OmpTaskSwitch and an OmpTaskComplete event (lines 6 and 12), as well as an Enter/Leave pair for the task's structured block (lines 7 and 11).

For other task switching points (i.e., taskwait as well as implicit and explicit barriers) the event generation is depicted in Figure 2, using the taskwait directive as an example. Here, a conventional region is created for the construct itself (lines 1 and 7), and optionally an OmpTaskSwitch event is generated in case another task was executed in between (lines 5/6).

Note that time spent in either a task creation, barrier, or taskwait region is not necessarily a bottleneck, as these regions can also include the execution of tasks. Therefore, the time spent executing other tasks needs to be subtracted from the total time spent in these regions to compute the real waiting time.

5   Task Interruption

During the analysis of tasks, special care has to be taken when tasks are suspended and resumed. In this section, we discuss how analysis tools can handle OmpTaskSwitch events. The example code in Figure 3 illustrates problems regarding task suspension and resumption. Note that the taskwait statements in Figure 3 serve only as additional task scheduling points.

Both functions f1 and f2 in the example do exactly the same, they call do_work and run into a taskwait statement. A thread executing this code could create both tasks and push them into the task queue. At the barrier it might execute them in the order shown in Figure 3. First, it starts the execution of task1 and suspends it in the taskwait statement, then completely executes task2 before it resumes task1.

The rectangles in Figure 3 illustrate the times spent in every function. The length of the rectangles is directly proportional to the time spent in the region. Although both tasks actually do the same, the execution of task1 and f1 takes much longer than the execution of task2 and f2, because task1 was suspended in between. This is misleading to the programmer. Actually, the suspension of task1 also suspended the execution of f1, so the time for f1 should not include the execution of task2. We decided to virtually suspend all functions and regions in the task when the task is suspended and resume them later along with the task. Figure 4 shows the resulting event stream. Task1 is split in two intervals by the suspension. This clearly shows that task2 is not part of task1.

As a proof of concept, we implemented a post-processing tool to apply this approach to OTF2 traces. The tool duplicates the trace and inserts at task switch regions corresponding leave events for the suspended task and region enter events for the resumed task. Of course, rewriting the trace is too much overhead for traces of realistic size but it is sufficient to further investigate the concept. Later on, an analysis tool can generate the events on-the-fly when reading the trace.

6   Evaluation

As mentioned earlier, the tracing capabilities described in this paper were implemented as part of Score-P, while the handling of task switches was implemented in a post-processing tool for OTF2 traces generated by Score-P. Here, we demonstrate that our

```
1  Enter("OMP taskwait", metrics, timestamp);
2
3  #pragma omp taskwait
4
5  if (current_task_id != old_task_id)
6      OmpTaskSwitch(old_task_id, timestamp);
7  Leave("OMP taskwait", metrics, timestamp);
```

Fig. 2. OTF2 events generated for an OpenMP taskwait construct

event model is adequate to allow the identification of the performance problems introduced in Section 3. Our evaluation is based on both kernel benchmarks as well as a real-world application.

Kernel-Benchmarks. To show that the performance problems outlined ealier can be detected, we wrote artificial test programs for all three performance problems:

- A program that creates 10 very large tasks and represents the problem of coarsely grained tasks.
- A program that creates many finely grained tasks.
- A program that uses a master-worker approach. Here the master produces tasks sufficiently fast for a few threads but becomes a performance bottleneck for a larger number of threads.

After instrumenting these kernels and measuring their execution behavior using Score-P configured in tracing mode, we applied our post-processing tool to the generated OTF2 traces. The resulting modified trace files were then visualized using the graphical trace

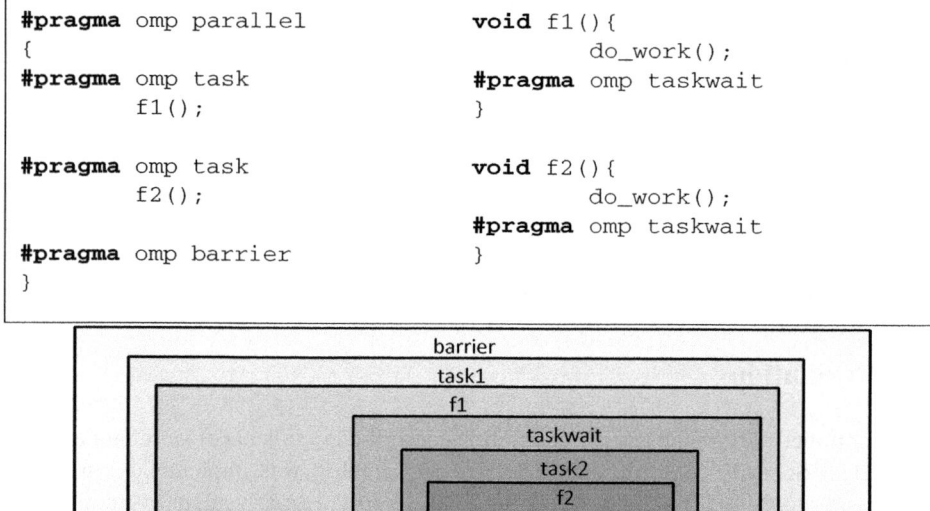

```
#pragma omp parallel          void f1(){
{                                     do_work();
#pragma omp task              #pragma omp taskwait
        f1();                 }

#pragma omp task              void f2(){
        f2();                         do_work();
                              #pragma omp taskwait
#pragma omp barrier           }
}
```

Fig. 3. Top: Code to generate two tasks, one calling f1 and the other one calling f2. Both functions do exactly the same. Bottom: Example execution sequence for this code with active functions shown as rectangles. Task1 is interrupted when task2 begins. The rectangles indicate, that task1 and f1 have a much longer execution time than task2 and f2.

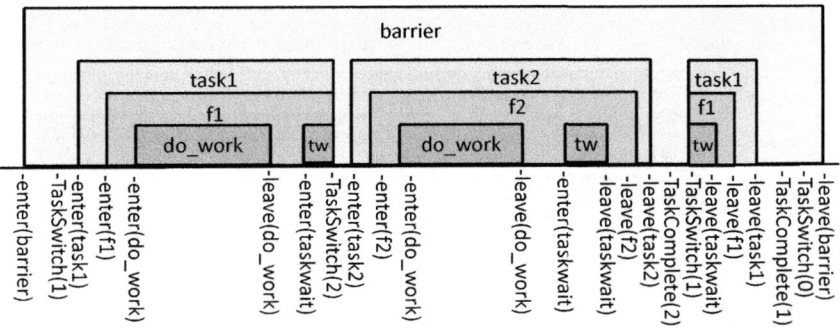

Fig. 4. Execution sequence of the above-mentioned example code with one thread only. Here all functions are interrupted when `task1` is interrupted. `Task1` and `task2` seem to take the same time, now.

browser Vampir [10]. In the following, regions called `task_X_Y` indicate a task that was created by thread X and whose identifier is Y. Regions named `!$omp task` indicate task creation overhead.

Figure 5 shows a Vampir screenshot for the first test program creating very large tasks. In the timeline view at the top, it is clearly visible that two threads execute two tasks, whereas the rest of the threads only execute a single task. Therefore, six threads spend a significant amount of time in the `!$omp implicit barrier` region, waiting for the two remaining threads to finish. The function summary view at the bottom displays the exclusive execution time spent in different regions, highlighting the performance bottleneck of this kernel. The program spends 0.6 seconds from a total of 1.6 seconds in the barrier which can be considered substantial overhead.

The corresponding displays for the second test program generating many finely grained tasks is shown in Figure 6. Here, we zoomed in on a smaller interval to see more details. The function summary chart gives again a first indication of suboptimal performance. It can be seen that a significant fraction of the wall-clock time is used for task creation (i.e., spent in `OMP_TASK`), while the fraction of actual workload execution seems to be minor. Looking closer at the timeline view, we can see that the individual tasks take about 50 μs, while the creation of one task takes about 5 ms or more. The program could therefore be optimized since immediate execution of the task body would be much faster than creating separate tasks.

The third kernel implements a master-worker approach where one thread creates many tasks and all other threads execute them. Figure 7 shows the timeline views for two different thread-team sizes. At the top, the timeline of an execution with four threads is shown. Thread 0 is continuously creating tasks and the other threads are executing them. Since threads 1-3 are busy executing the tasks and spend only a very small fraction of time in the barrier between task executions, the overhead spent in the OpenMP runtime is quite low.

At the bottom, the timeline of an execution with 16 threads is shown. Here, a different behavior can be observed. Thread 0 is still creating tasks all the time, but many of the other threads are waiting in the barrier without executing any tasks. Immediately

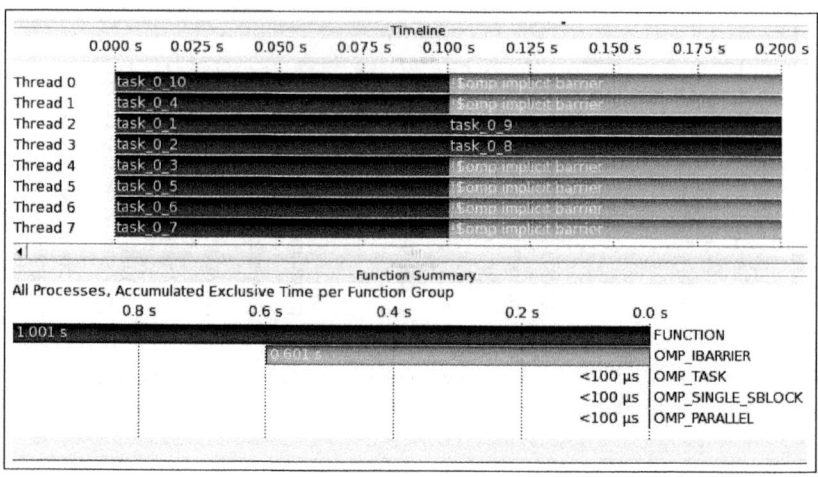

Fig. 5. Vampir screenshot illustrating how too coarsely grained tasks can be detected. In the time-line view two threads execute two task whereas the other threads execute only one task and wait in the barrier.

after a task has been created, a thread starts executing it. For example, after thread 0 fin-ished creating task_0_102, thread 10 stops idling and executes it. Shortly afterwards, thread 6 picks up task_0_103 and thread 4 executes task_0_104. This demonstrates that there are not enough tasks available for all threads. In this situation, the developer should think about a different task-creation approach, such as creating tasks in parallel or switching to larger tasks to fully utilize all available threads.

FIRE. Finally, we want to examine how our approach allows task execution to be rep-resented in call trees using a real-world example. The Flexible Image Retrieval Engine (FIRE) [4] was developed by the Human Language Technology and Pattern Recogni-tion Group of RWTH Aachen University. FIRE is used to compare k query images to an image database, identifying those images that are close to the query images. The first parallelization of the FIRE code used nested parallelism with two levels [15]. Here, we are using a modified version using tasking instead. For every query image, a separate task is created. Inside these tasks, every comparison of a query picture and one ele-ment of the database constitutes another task. This approach is a bit more flexible than the nested OpenMP version since every thread can work on any task. For nested par-allelism, it was necessary to assign a fixed number of threads to the inner regions. Our test case requires searching for two query images in a database of 1000 images.

Similar to the approach used for the kernel benchmarks, we instrumented the task-based FIRE code and generated an OTF2 trace using Score-P. After applying our post-processing tool, however, we analyzed the resulting trace files using a prototype of the automatic trace analyzer of Scalasca [8] which is capable of handling OTF2 traces. The analysis result is shown in the CUBE display in Figure 8. The left column shows

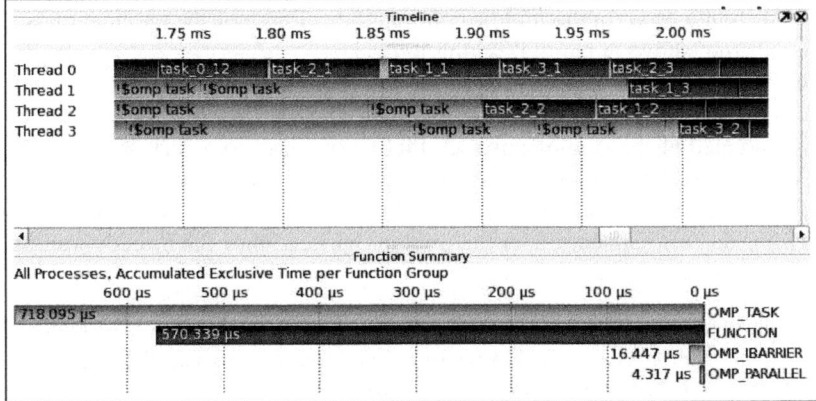

Fig. 6. Vampir screenshot illustrating how too finely grained tasks can be detected. The task creation (!$omp task) regions consume more time than the task execution (task_X_Y) regions.

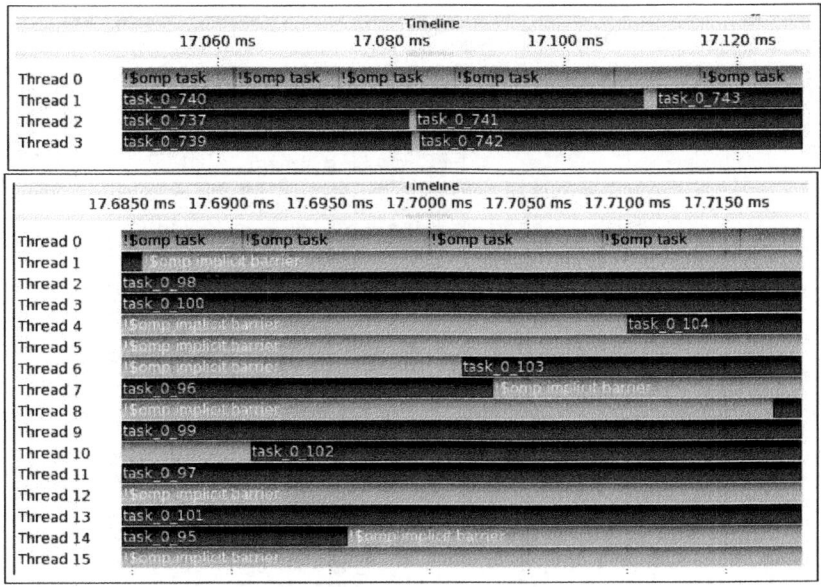

Fig. 7. Vampir screenshot illustrating how a task-creation bottleneck can be detected. Both timelines show the same program where a single thread creates tasks for all other threads. Top: With four threads every worker thread is busy, executing tasks. Bottom: With 16 Threads some threads are idle and wait for tasks from the master thread.

different metrics derived from the trace data, with the visit count being selected, whereas the right column shows the system tree, i.e., the machine, the process, and all the threads being used. In the middle column, the call tree of the application is shown.

The call tree shows a parallel region in `main -> Server::batch`. Inside the parallel region, there is a `single` construct where tasks are created and an implicit barrier at the end where the tasks are executed. The visit count indicates that only two tasks are created in the single construct, that is, one task for every query image. If we take a closer look at the tasks executed in the implicit barrier, we can identify these two tasks there (`task_0_1` and `task_0_2`). All the other subtasks, which were created by these two tasks, also appear under the implicit barrier, since the threads waiting in this barrier executed them.

Overhead Analysis. After having shown that our approach is capable of identifying the performance problems discussed in Section 3 and that it is also applicable to real-world application codes, we now examine the measurement overhead introduced by our instrumentation. For this purpose, we use the Barcelona OpenMP Task Suite (BOTS) [5], a set of benchmark codes for OpenMP tasking developed by Duran et al. We performed

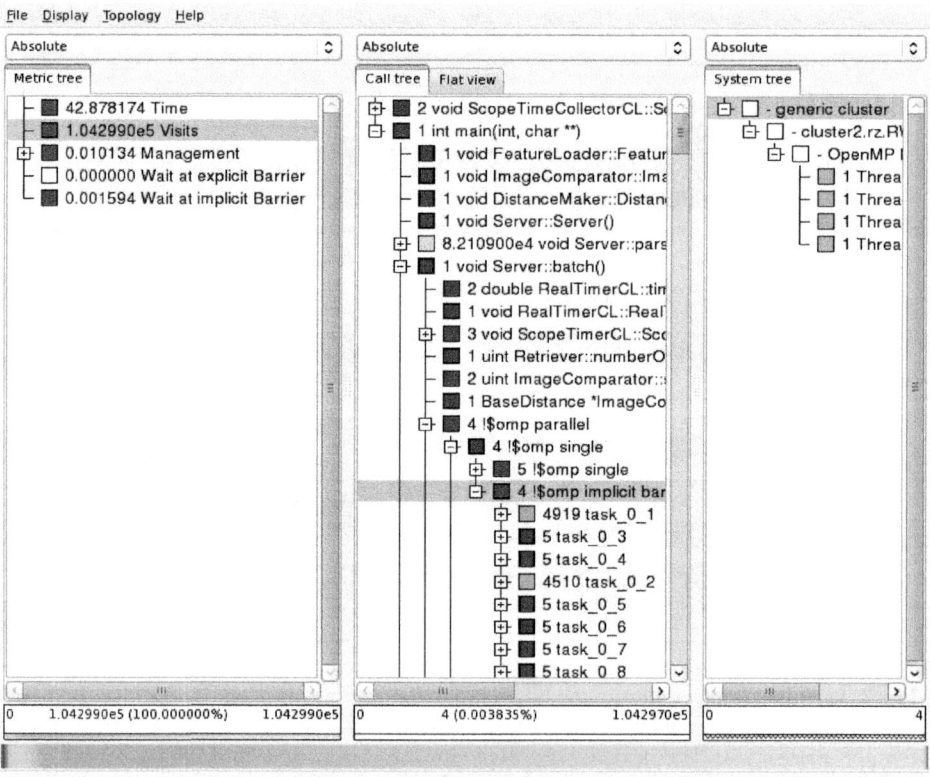

Fig. 8. Scalasca analysis result of the FIRE code. The middle column shows the call tree of the program run, with tasks being executed inside the implicit barrier at the end of a parallel region.

several test runs of these benchmarks on the Juropa[1] cluster at Jülich Supercomputing Centre, consisting of dual-socket boards with Intel Xeon X5570 quad-core processors. We compared the runtime of the instrumented and uninstrumented versions of the BOTS benchmark codes using eight threads and determined the overhead introduced. The runtime of each benchmark was measured 10 times and the minimum runtime out of these runs is shown in Table 1.

Obviously, there are differences in the overhead observed. Some tests show nearly no overhead, for example the `strassen` or `sparselu` benchmarks. Others, like `sort`, `floorplan` of `fft`, show an overhead of 5-25%. This overhead can still be considered acceptable, since the measurements provide very detailed information on the runtime behavior of the program. For some of the benchmarks, a negative overhead of up to -9% (`fib.omp-tasks-tied`) was observed. Since this phenomenon was consistent across all ten test runs, it is unlikely to be an artifact of run-to-run variation. Our current assumption is that for very small tasks, the executing threads are competing for some shared data structures in the OpenMP runtime. Since our instrumentation enlarges the computational part of the task, lock competition effects might diminish, leading to a reduction of the overhead time spent in the OpenMP runtime. However, since we cannot investigate runtime internals, we are unable to proof this assumption.

As an exception, we observed an overhead of roughly 500% for the `fib.omp-tasks-if_clause-tied` benchmark. The tasks executed by the `fib` code recursively spawn two child tasks, perform a `taskwait`, and then add the two

Table 1. Runtime of the BOTS benchmarks with eight Threads. The original runtime and the runtime of the instrumented benchmark, when only OpenMP constructs were instrumented (no function instrumentation by the compiler) is shown as well as the overhead due to instrumentation in percent.

	Original Runtime	Instrumented Runtime	Overhead
alignment.omp-tasks-tied	2,77 sec.	2,77 sec.	-0,08%
fft.omp-tasks-tied	5,49 sec.	6,25 sec.	13,77%
fib.omp-tasks-if_clause-tied	0,12 sec.	0,75 sec.	525,81%
fib.omp-tasks-tied	36,29 sec.	32,97 sec.	-9,16%
floorplan.omp-tasks-if_clause-tied	2,89 sec.	3,10 sec.	7,22%
floorplan.omp-tasks-tied	43,04 sec.	41,21 sec.	-4,25%
health.omp-tasks-if_clause-tied	3,24 sec.	4,00 sec.	23,51%
health.omp-tasks-tied	23,01 sec.	22,30 sec.	-3,05%
nqueens.omp-tasks-if_clause-tied	5,82 sec.	6,58 sec.	13,04%
nqueens.omp-tasks-tied	270,69 sec.	294,45 sec.	8,78%
sort.omp-tasks-tied	3,09 sec.	3,28 sec.	6,14%
sparselu.single-omp-tasks-tied	14,74 sec.	14,74 sec.	0,00%
strassen.omp-tasks-if_clause-tied	25,85 sec.	25,76 sec.	-0,36%
strassen.omp-tasks-tied	25,85 sec.	26,03 sec.	0,72%

---

[1] http://www.fz-juelich.de/ias/jsc/EN/Expertise/Supercomputers/JUROPA/JUROPA_node.html

values returned by the child tasks. In the if_clause variant, tasks are only spawned up to a fixed recursion depth, reducing the task creation overhead enormously. Our measurement approach does not instrument tasks not being spawned, but we still instrument and record all the `taskwait` statements for all recursion levels. However, the ratio of one `taskwait` statement for one addition in the code is quite artificial and unrealistic for real-world applications.

7   Conclusion

In this paper, we described potential performance problems that might emerge when utilizing OpenMP tasks. To capture the constituents of these performance problems in event traces, we presented the event model developed for OTF2, and described its implementation as part of the measurement infrastructure Score-P. Furthermore, a mechanism to attribute performance metrics to tasks taking their possible interruption into account has been prototyped as a post-processing tool which rewrites OTF2 event traces. With this infrastructure in place, we were able to detect the previously specified performance problems in synthetic benchmarks. Applying our approach to a real-world code like FIRE, we could show how tasks can be represented in more complex call trees.

In the future, we plan to integrate our concepts fully into Score-P, omitting the trace rewriting step, and into the supported performance analysis tools Vampir, Scalasca, TAU and Periscope. By gaining experience with our approach, for example, by analyzing real-world user codes, we will look out for typical task-related performance problems that have not been addressed yet and whose detection and analysis might be of value to the user.

References

1. Adhianto, L., Banerjee, S., Fagan, M., Krentel, M., Marin, G., Mellor-Crummey, J., Tallent, N.R.: HPCToolkit: Tools for performance analysis of optimized parallel programs. Concurr. Comput.: Pract. Exper. 22, 685–701 (2010), http://hpctoolkit.org
2. An Mey, D., Biersdorff, S., Bischof, C., Diethelm, K., Eschweiler, D., Gerndt, M., Knüpfer, A., Lorenz, D., Malony, A.D., Nagel, W.E., Oleynik, Y., Rössel, C., Saviankou, P., Schmidl, D., Shende, S.S., Wagner, M., Wesarg, B., Wolf, F.: Score-P–A unified performance measurement system for petascale applications. In: Proc. of the CiHPC: Competence in High Performance Computing, HPC Status Konferenz der Gauß-Allianz e.V., Schwetzingen, Germany, pp. 1–12. Springer (June 2010) (to appear)
3. OpenMP Architecture Review Board. OpenMP application progam interface version 3.0. Technical report, OpenMP Architecture Review Board (May 2008)
4. Deselaers, T., Keysers, D., Ney, H.: Features for Image Retrieval: A Quantitative Comparison. In: Rasmussen, C.E., Bülthoff, H.H., Schölkopf, B., Giese, M.A. (eds.) DAGM 2004. LNCS, vol. 3175, pp. 228–236. Springer, Heidelberg (2004)
5. Duran, A., Teruel, X., Ferrer, R., Martorell, X., Ayguadé, E.: Barcelona OpenMP Tasks Suite: A Set of Benchmarks Targeting the Exploitation of Task Parallelism in OpenMP. In: 38th International Conference on Parallel Processing (ICPP 2009), pp. 124–131. IEEE Computer Society, Vienna (2009)

6. Eschweiler, D., Wagner, M., Geimer, M., Knüpfer, A., Nagel, W.E., Wolf, F.: Open Trace Format 2 - The next generation of scalable trace formats and support libraries. In: Proc. of the Intl. Conference on Parallel Computing (ParCo), Ghent, Belgium (2011) (to appear)
7. Fürlinger, K., Skinner, D.: Performance Profiling for OpenMP Tasks. In: Müller, M.S., de Supinski, B.R., Chapman, B.M. (eds.) IWOMP 2009. LNCS, vol. 5568, pp. 132–139. Springer, Heidelberg (2009)
8. Geimer, M., Wolf, F., Wylie, B.J.N., Ábrahám, E., Becker, D., Mohr, B.: The Scalasca Performance Toolset Architecture. Concurrency and Computation: Practice and Experience 22(6), 702–719 (2010)
9. Itzkowitz, M., Mazurov, O., Copty, N., Lin, Y.: An OpenMP runtime API for profiling. Technical report, Sun Microsystems, Inc. (2007)
10. Knüpfer, A., Brunst, H., Doleschal, J., Jurenz, M., Lieber, M., Mickler, H., Müller, M.S., Nagel, W.E.: The Vampir Performance Analysis Tool Set. In: Tools for High Performance Computing, pp. 139–155. Springer (July 2008)
11. Lin, Y., Mazurov, O.: Providing Observability for OpenMP 3.0 Applications. In: Müller, M.S., de Supinski, B.R., Chapman, B.M. (eds.) IWOMP 2009. LNCS, vol. 5568, pp. 104–117. Springer, Heidelberg (2009)
12. Lorenz, D., Mohr, B., Rössel, C., Schmidl, D., Wolf, F.: How to Reconcile Event-Based Performance Analysis with Tasking in OpenMP. In: Sato, M., Hanawa, T., Müller, M.S., Chapman, B.M., de Supinski, B.R. (eds.) IWOMP 2010. LNCS, vol. 6132, pp. 109–121. Springer, Heidelberg (2010)
13. Mohr, B., Malony, A.D., Shende, S.S., Wolf, F.: Design and prototype of a performance tool interface for OpenMP. The Journal of Supercomputing 23(1), 105–128 (2002)
14. Shende, S., Malony, A.D.: The TAU Parallel Performance System. International Journal of High Performance Computing Applications 20(2), 287–331 (2006)
15. Terboven, C., Deselaers, T., Bischof, C., Ney, H.: Shared-Memory Parallelization for Content-based Image Retrieval. In: ECCV 2006 Workshop on Computation Intensive Methods for Computer Vision (CIMCV), Graz, Austria (May 2006)

Task-Based Execution of Nested OpenMP Loops*

Spiros N. Agathos**, Panagiotis E. Hadjidoukas,
and Vassilios V. Dimakopoulos

Department of Computer Science, University of Ioannina
P.O. Box 1186, Ioannina, Greece, GR-45110
{sagathos,phadjido,dimako}@cs.uoi.gr

Abstract. In this work we propose a novel technique to reduce the overheads related to nested parallel loops in OpenMP programs. In particular we show that in many cases it is possible to replace the code of a nested parallel-for loop with equivalent code that creates tasks instead of threads, thereby limiting parallelism levels while allowing more opportunities for runtime load balancing. In addition we present the details of an implementation of this technique that is able to perform the whole procedure completely transparently. We have experimented extensively to determine the effectiveness of our methods. The results show the actual performance gains we obtain (up to 25% in a particular application) as compared to other OpenMP implementations that are forced to suffer nested parallelism overheads.

Keywords: OpenMP, nested parallelism, runtime system, tasks, work-sharing constructs.

1   Introduction

OpenMP has become one of the most popular models for programming shared-memory platforms and this is not without good reasons; just to name a few, the base language (C/C++/Fortran) does not change, high-level abstractions are provided, most low-level threading details need not be dealt with and all these lead to ease of use and higher productivity. At the same time significant performance benefits are possible. While the initial target of OpenMP was mostly loop-level parallelism, its expressiveness expanded significantly with the addition of tasks in V3.0 of the specifications [8], making it now suitable for a quite large class of parallel applications.

Among the important features included from the very beginnings of OpenMP was nested parallelism, that is the ability of any running thread to create its own team of child threads. Although actual support for nested parallelism was

---

* This work has been supported in part by the General Secretariat for Research and Technology and the European Commission (ERDF) through the Artemisia SMECY project (grant 100230).
** S.N. Agathos is supported by the Greek State Scholarships Foundation (IKY).

B.M. Chapman et al. (Eds.): IWOMP 2012, LNCS 7312, pp. 210–222, 2012.
© Springer-Verlag Berlin Heidelberg 2012

slow to appear in implementations, nowadays most of them support it in some way. However, it is well known that nested parallelism, while desirable, is quite difficult to handle efficiently in practice, as it easily leads to processor oversubscription, which may cause significant performance degradation.

The addition of the `collapse` clause in V3.0 of the specifications can be seen as a way to avoid the overheads of spawning nested parallelism for certain nested loops. However, it is not always possible to use the `collapse` clause since:

- the loops may not be perfectly nested
- the bounds of an inner loop may be dependent on the index of the outer loop
- the inner loop may be within the extend of a general parallel region, not a parallel-loop region.

The nature of OpenMP loops is relatively simple; they are basically DO-ALL structures with independent iterations, similar to what is available in other programming systems and languages (e.g., the FORALL construct in Fortran 95, the `parallel_for` template in Intel TBB [10], or `cilk_for` in Cilk++ [7]). What is interesting is that some of these systems implement DO-ALL loops without spawning threads; they are mostly creating some kind of task set to perform the job. Can an OpenMP implementation do the same? While this seems rather useless for first-level parallel-for loops (since there is no team of threads to execute the tasks; only the initial thread is active), it may be worthwhile in a nested level.

What we propose here is a novel way of avoiding nested parallel loop overheads through the use of tasks. In particular, as our first contribution, we show that it is possible to replace a second-level loop by code that creates tasks which perform equivalent computations; the tasks are executed by the first-level team of threads, completely avoiding the overheads of creating second-level teams of threads and oversubscribing the system. We use the proposed method to show experimentally the performance improvement potential.

At the same time we observe that our techniques require sizable code changes to be performed by the application programmer, while they are not always applicable for arbitrary loop bodies. Our second contribution is then to automate the whole procedure and provide transparent tasking from the loop nests, which, except the obvious usability advantages, does not have the limitations of the manual approach. We present the implementation details of our proposal in the context of the OMPi [4] compiler. Finally, we perform a performance study using synthetic benchmarks as well as a face-detection application that utilizes nested parallel loops; all experimental results depict the performance gains attainable by our techniques.

The rest of the paper is organized as follows: in Section 2 we present the necessary code transformations that a programmer must perform in order to produce tasking code equivalent to a nested loop region, for cases where this is indeed possible. In Section 3 we discuss the transparent implementation of the proposed methodology, which is applicable for general loops and schedules.

```
                                    #pragma omp parallel num_threads(M)
                                    {
                                      for (t=0; t<N; t++)
#pragma omp parallel num_threads(M)    #pragma omp task
{                                      {
  #pragma omp parallel for\             calculate(N,LB,UB,&lb,&ub);
    schedule(static) num_threads(N)     for (i=lb; i<ub; i++)
  for (i=LB; i<UB; i++) {                 <body>
    <body>                            }
  }                                   #pragma omp taskwait
}                                   }
```

Fig. 1. Nested parallel loop example   **Fig. 2.** Transformation outline of Fig.1

Section 4 contains our performance experiments and finally Section 5 concludes this paper.

2   Proof of Concept: Re-writing Loop Code Manually

Consider the sample OpenMP code shown in Fig. 1. There exists a nested parallel for-loop which will normally spawn a team of N threads for each of the M (first-level) threads that participate in the outer parallel region[1]; a total of $M \times N$ threads may be simultaneously active executing second-level parallelism, leading to potentially excessive system oversubscription.

Fig. 2 illustrates how the code of Fig. 1 can be re-written so as to make use of OpenMP tasks instead of nested parallelism. The idea is conceptually simple: each first-level thread creates N tasks (i.e. equal in number to the original code's second-level threads), and then waits until all tasks are executed. The code of each task contains the original loop body; in order to perform the same work the corresponding thread would perform, it is necessary to calculate the exact iterations that should be executed, hence the calculate() call. In essence, the user code must perform the same calculations that the runtime system would perform for the case of Fig. 1 when handing out the iterations for the static schedule.

Why does it work? The answer is that the original code creates *implicit* tasks, according to OpenMP terminology, while the code in Fig. 2 emulates them through the use of *explicit* tasking. Also, while implicit tasks may contain barriers (which are not allowed within explicit tasks), there is no such a possibility here since the implicit tasks in Fig. 1 only execute independent loop iterations, and within the loop body there can not exist a barrier closely nested.

---

[1] Even if num_threads(M) is absent from the outer parallel construct, the standard practice is to produce as many threads as the number of available processors. Assume, without loss of generality, that they are equal to M.

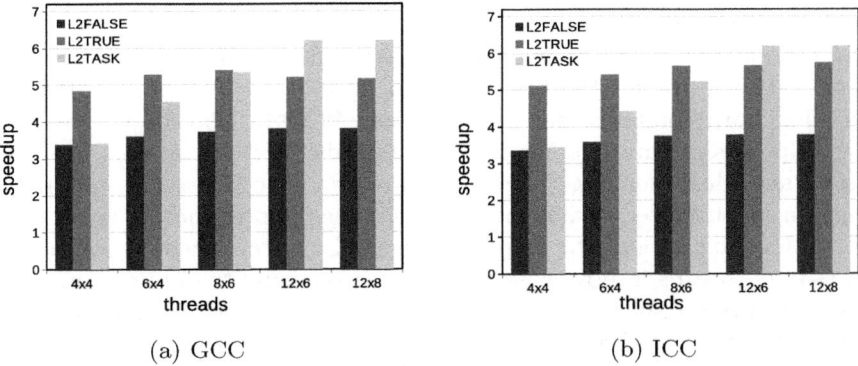

Fig. 3. Performance of the proposed technique; speedup for a face detection algorithm applied on an test image with 57 faces

As a result, the programs in Figs. 1 and 2 are equivalent, and no other changes are required[2], (we will return to this in the next section).

The important difference is that the code in Fig. 2 does *not* generate a second level of parallelism. It utilizes the tasking subsystem of the compiler and uses only the available M threads to execute the $M \times N$ tasks generated in total, allowing for improved load balance opportunities. While task creation and execution is not without overheads, it remains mostly in the realm of the OpenMP implementation to deal with it efficiently. On the other hand controlling a large amount of threads resulting from nested parallel regions may not be possible, especially when the OpenMP runtime relies on kernel-level threads (such as POSIX threads, which is a usual case).

We applied the above technique to the parallel version of a high-performance face detection application. The application itself, the 16-core system as well as the software configuration we used for our experiments are described in more detail in Section 4 so we will avoid repeating it here. The important issue is that the application contains a first-level parallel loop with unbalanced iteration load. The number of iterations depends on the image size and is usually less than 14. Inside this loop, there exist multiple second-level parallel for-loops, which clearly need to be exploited in order to increase performance. We re-wrote these second-level loops according to the method described above. We compiled the code with various OpenMP compilers and in Fig. 3 we show the execution results obtained using GNU GCC and Intel ICC on a particular image containing 57 faces; similar results were observed with other compilers, too. In the figure, the new application code is designated as L2TASK. The original code which utilized nested parallelism is the L2TRUE part. For comparison, we include the L2FALSE

---

[2] Actually one more change may be needed. Because in task regions the data sharing attributes of referenced variables default to `firstprivate` while in parallel regions they default to `shared` the user must explicitly set the data sharing attributes of all referenced variables in the new task-based code.

bars which represent the original code executed with nested parallelism disabled (i.e. the environmental variable OMP_NESTED was set to false).

In the plots we vary the number of participating threads per level using up to $M = 12$ threads for the first level and up to $N = 8$ threads in the second level. For both compilers nested parallelism (L2TRUE) boosts performance as long as processors are not heavily oversubscribed. It can be seen that GCC's performance drops for large number of threads, while ICC seems to handle the situation much better, although its performance approximately levels off after the 8×6 configuration. Our approach results in better speedups for more than 8 first-level threads in both cases, confirming the validity of our approach. The lower performance shown in smaller configurations is expected since we only rely on the few first-level threads while nested parallelism is able to utilize all the 16 processors in the system. Finally, in the larger configurations, notice that while the L2TRUE code utilizes all the 16 available processors (albeit with increased overheads), we obtain better speedups with only 12 threads.

3   Overcoming Limitations by Automatic Transformation

In the previous section we presented the core idea behind our method. The proposed code transformation was exemplified using a loop with a static schedule. A similar approach can be used for any schedule type, e.g. dynamic or guided. In these cases, however, the new code does not execute just one chunk of iterations; it should rather be enclosed within another loop that asks continuously for chunks of iterations. Calculating the iteration bounds becomes considerably more complicated as it has to take into account the competition / synchronization among tasks and keep some kind of state in order to hand out the iterations in accordance to the loop schedule. In essence, the user has to re-implement a mini worksharing runtime subsystem in order to cover all possible schedule configurations. This is clearly both undesirable for the user and redundant as far as the compiler is concerned, since all this functionality is already present in its OpenMP runtime library.

Another important issue is that even if the user is determined to do all this work, this will not be enough to make it applicable to all possible cases. The reason is that within the loop body there may exist references to thread-specific quantities, for example,

- the loop body may contain calls to omp_get_thread_num() and utilize the thread's ID in computations, or,
- the loop body may access threadprivate variables.

The above makes it almost impossible to move the loop's body to independent tasks, as there is no guarantee as to which threads will execute what tasks.

In conclusion, the manual code transformations need extensive programmer involvement and are not applicable in the general case. On the other hand, all the required functionality is already implemented within the runtime library of the OpenMP system. Additionally, the runtime system has access to all the stored thread-specific quantities. It should thus be in position to support the required transformations seamlessly. In this section we describe the actual implementation of this idea in the runtime system of the OMPi compiler.

3.1 The OMPi Compiler

OMPi is an experimental, lightweight OpenMP infrastructure for C. It consists of a source-to-source compiler and a runtime library. The compiler takes as input C code with OpenMP directives and outputs multithreaded C code augmented with calls to its runtime library, ready to be compiled by any standard C compiler. It conforms to V3.0 of the specifications while also supporting parts of the recently announced V3.1 [9].

Here we provide a brief description of portions of OMPi and its tasking implementation that are necessary for our discussion. A more detailed description was given by Agathos et al [1]. The compiler uses *outlining* to move the code residing within a `parallel` or a `task` region to a new function and then, depending on the construct, inserts calls to create a team of threads or a task to execute the code of the new function.

The runtime system of OMPi has a modular architecture in order to facilitate experimentation with different threading libraries. In particular, it is composed of two largely independent layers. The upper layer (ORT) carries all required OpenMP functionality by controlling a number of abstract *execution entities* (EEs). The lower layer (EELIB) is responsible for actually providing the EEs, along with some synchronization primitives. A significant number of EELIBs is available. The default one is built on top of POSIX threads, while there also exists a library which is based on high-performance user-level threads [6].

OMPi provides a tasking layer within ORT which can be used with any EELIB, although the runtime design allows for the latter to provide its own tasking functionality, if desired. Each execution entity (thread) is equipped with a queue (TASK_QUEUE) which is used to store all the pending tasks it has created. OMPi's task scheduler is based on work stealing [2], whereby a thread that has finished executing its own tasks tries to steal tasks from other threads' TASK_QUEUEs. After a new task is created, it is placed in the thread's queue until some thread decides to execute it. Task queues have fixed length, which means that they can store up to a certain number of pending tasks. This number is one of OMPi's runtime parameters, controlled through an environment variable (`OMPI_TASKQ_SIZE`). The manipulation of task queues is based on a highly efficient lock-free algorithm.

When a thread is about to execute its implicit task (parallel region), a new task descriptor is allocated and the task code is executed immediately. Whenever a thread reaches an explicit `task` construct, it can either allocate a new task node and submit the corresponding task for deferred execution, or it can suspend the execution of the current task and execute the new task immediately; OMPi's default behavior is to choose the former. That is, it implements a *breadth-first* task scheduling policy. It resorts to the second alternative (*depth-first* task execution) when the task queue is full. In that case the thread enters *throttling* mode, where every encountered task is executed immediately to completion. Notice that in this case the current task (although temporarily suspended in favor of the new task) does not enter the task queue, so it can never be resumed by another thread. In effect, all tasks are *tied*. Throttling mode is disabled when 30% of the task queue capacity becomes again available.

3.2   Automating the Process

In order to apply our technique we had to modify the code produced by the OMPi compiler as well as add new functionality to the runtime system. The actual changes in the compiler were rather minimal and limited to the case where a combined `parallel for` construct is encountered. An (identical) outlined function is still created which includes all the code needed for sharing the loop iterations among threads. However, the call to create the team of threads now includes a new parameter to let the runtime know that this is a combined loop construct. This covers nested and orphaned construct cases alike.

The changes in the runtime system (ORT) were more extensive. Whenever a team of threads needs to be created, if the team is going to operate in nesting level > 1 and the parallel region is actually coming from a combined `parallel for` construct[3], then, instead of threads, an equal number of explicit tasks are created. However, as noted previously this is not enough to cover the cases where the user code accesses thread-specific data.

OMPi associates a control block (EECB) with every execution entity it manages. The EECB contains everything ORT needs in order to schedule the thread, including the size of the team, the thread ID within the team, its parallel level etc. The only thread-specific data not actually stored in a threads EECB are `threadprivate` variables. These are allocated at the team's parent control block (in order to guarantee persistence across parallel regions, as required by the OpenMP rules). The EECB makes them available through a pointer to the parent EECB (thus a tree of EECBs is formed at runtime). In conclusion, everything a running thread requires is serviced through its control block. Whenever a thread starts the execution of a parallel region, ORT assigns a new EECB to it, which is later freed when the team is disbanded.

Based on the above, the main idea behind our implementation is that the produced tasks try to mimic threads. Every task produced (instead of a thread) when a nested combined parallel loop is encountered, carries a special flag along with the ID number the corresponding thread would have. The tasks are inserted as normal in the TASK_QUEUE of the outer-level thread that encountered the nested construct. When such a task is scheduled for execution (either by the same thread or a thief), the flag will cause the following actions:

– A new EECB is created, as would be done if a new nested thread was created in the first place, updating the tree of EECBs correspondingly.

---

[3] and if the user allows; a new environmental variable lets the user decide whether the new technique should be applied or not.

- The outer-level thread that is about to execute the task assumes temporarily the new EECB and sets its thread ID equal to the ID stored within the task.
- The task becomes tied to this thread.

In essence, an outer level thread while executing the task in question, obtains all the characteristics of the inner level thread that would be created normally. As such it is able to handle thread-specific data accesses, overcoming all the previously mentioned limitations. Notice for example that because the old control block of the thread remains intact in the tree, all information needed to service runtime calls such as `omp_get_level()`, `omp_get_active_level()`, etc, is readily available. When the task execution is finished, the temporary EECB is freed and the thread resumes its original control block, continuing with its normal operation.

3.3 Ordered

The above implementation is able to substitute a nested team of threads by an equivalent set of tasks, for any OpenMP schedule type. However, one of our initial concerns was the possible presence of the `ordered` directive. This particular directive forces ordering dependencies among the iteration executors; when the executors are threads there is no problem whatsoever but what about tasks? Is there a possibility that particular task scheduling sequences lead to deadlock? In all cases but one, the answer is no. This is because even if there is only one thread available to execute the generated tasks, there will always be at least one task active, advancing the iteration count and obtaining the next chunk of iterations. For example, consider the case of `dynamic` schedules; if there is a thread (task) blocked at an ordered directive then there must exist at least one other thread that obtained the (sequentially) previous chunk; eventually the latter will be executed and the turn of the former will come.

The single problematic case is the `static` schedule with specified chunk size. Although it is a matter of implementation, the straightforward way of executing it is by using a double loop; the outer loop iterates over the series of chunks while the inner loop goes over the actual iterations of a particular chunk. As the loops bounds are *pre-calculated* (since for this particular schedule they are not subject to competition among the executors), imposing an `ordered` directive may lead to a deadlocked situation, depending on how tasks are implemented / scheduled.

To see this consider the case of having M (level-1) threads to execute $N > M$ tasks generated by the level-2 parallel loop. When all threads have gone through their first chunk of iterations, they will be blocked at an `ordered` region waiting for their next chunk's turn. However, if tasks are executed on a run-to-completion basis, the remaining $N - M$ tasks will never be given a change to run and advance the iteration count, resulting in a deadlock.

OMPi by default executes tasks to completion and is thus susceptible to this problem. The engineering solution we currently follow is to avoid the problem altogether: if the loop schedule is `static` and an explicit chunk size is given and an `ordered` clause is present, nested parallelism is generated as usual, instead of

```
delay() {
  volatile i, a;
  for (i=0; i < TASK_LOAD; i++)
    a += i;
}
testpfor() {
  for(i=0; i <= REPS; i++)
    #pragma omp parallel for num_threads(N)
    for (j=0; j < N; j++)
      delay();
}
main() {
  #pragma omp parallel for num_threads(16)
  for (i=0; i < 16;t++)
    testpfor();
}
```

Fig. 4. Code for synthetic benchmark

tasks. We are currently working on the support for OpenMP V3.1 which includes a new `taskyield` directive. Yielding upon an imminent `ordered` block should allow the possibility of other tasks to be executed and thus make progress.

4   Evaluation

We have run several experiments in order to evaluate the performance gains of our implementation. We report here the results obtained on a server with two 8-core AMD Opteron 6128 CPUs operating at 2GHz and a total of 16GB of main memory. The operating system is Debian Squeeze based on the 2.6.32.5 Linux kernel. In our experiments, apart from OMPi, we had the following compilers available: GNU GCC (version 4.4.5-8), Intel ICC (version 12.1.0) Oracle SUNCC (version 12.2). We used "-O3 -fopenmp" flags for GCC, "-fast -openmp" flags for ICC and "-fast -xopenmp=parallel" flags for SUNCC. GCC with the "-O3" flag was used as a back-end compiler for OMPi. For all compilers, the default runtime settings were used. These settings also happened to produce the best results.

4.1   Synthetic Benchmark

Our first experiments aim at showing directly the performance gains possible with our methodology in the given system. A synthetic benchmark is used, measuring the time taken to execute the code shown in Fig. 4. This code is based on the EPCC microbenchmarks [3] which are used to estimate OpenMP construct overheads. We instead measure the total execution time. In the main function a team of 16 threads is created and each thread calls the `testpfor()` function once. In there a thread executes REPS times a combined `parallel for` directive, creating N second-level threads, each one performing work, the granularity

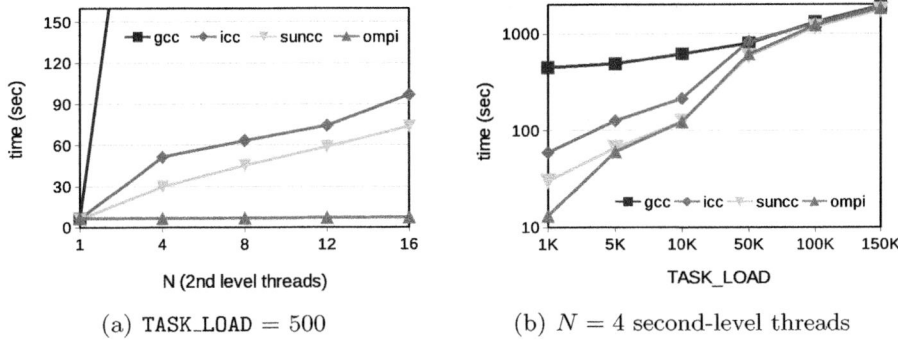

(a) TASK_LOAD = 500   (b) $N = 4$ second-level threads

Fig. 5. Synthetic benchmark execution times

of which is controlled by the TASK_LOAD parameter in the delay() function. We used REPS= 100000 and varied the TASK_LOAD value.

We present the results in Fig. 5. In Fig. 5(a) we consider fine grain work (TASK_LOAD = 500) and vary the number of second-level threads in order to stress the runtime system. The growing number of threads results in considerable overheads that are clearly depicted in the total execution time. Because OMPi avoids creating nested parallelism, it exhibits remarkable stability in its performance, which is only very slightly affected by an increasing number of generated tasks.

In figure 5(b) we fixed the number of second-level threads to $N = 4$ and varied the work granularity, with TASK_LOAD values in the range of 1K to 150K. We use a logarithmic scale due to the wide range of timing results. As expected, for finer grain work our methodology results in significantly faster execution as compared to other compilers. As the work gets coarser, all compilers tend to exhibit similar performance since the task or thread manipulation stops being the performance bottleneck and execution time is dominated by the actual computation. For the coarser load, all compilers execute the benchmark in about 2000 sec.

4.2 Face Detection

As already mentioned in Section 2, we also experimented with a full face detection application, which has been described in detail by Hadjidoukas et al [5]. It takes as input an image and discovers the number of faces depicted in it, along with their position in the image. The code has been parallelized with OpenMP, utilizing nested parallelism in order to obtain better performance than what is possible with only single-level loop parallelization.

In Fig. 6 we outline the structure of the main loop nest of the application. Initially the image is subsampled repeatedly to create a pyramid of different scales, the number of which is dependent on the images size and is usually less than 14. For each scale (this is the first-level loop) a series of convolutional filters and non-linear subsamplings are applied through the 3 nested for-loops.

```
for each scale {        /* level 1 */
    for i=1 to 4 {
        <body1>
    }
    for i=1 to 14 {
        <body2>
    }
    for i=1 to 14 {
        <body3>
    }
}
```

Fig. 6. Structure of the main computational loop

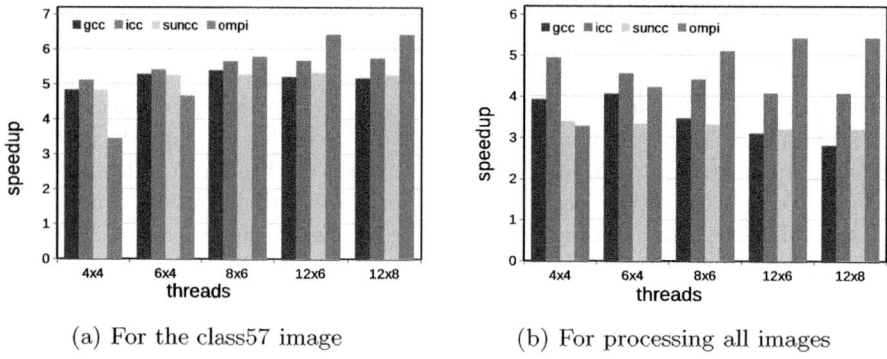

(a) For the class57 image   (b) For processing all images

Fig. 7. Face detection results (for each compiler the speedups are calculated in comparison to its own sequential execution time)

Because of the load imbalance between the different image scales, the level-1 loop is parallelized through a `parallel for` directive with dynamic schedule, while for the inner loops a `parallel for` directive with a static schedule is applied.

In our experiments we vary the number of participating threads per parallelism level; a configuration of $M \times N$ threads uses M (≤ 12) threads in the first level and N (≤ 8) threads for the second level. In Fig. 7 we show the performance obtained when each of the available compilers was used. We do not include results for single-level parallelization ($N = 1$) as they were inferior to what we obtained when $N > 1$. For these plots the speedups for each compiler are calculated in relation to the sequential execution time obtained by the same compiler so that we can show how it behaves under nested parallelism. In Fig. 7(a) the application used as input a particularly demanding image which contains 57 faces (the 'class57' image from the CMU test set [11]). For obtaining the results in Fig. 7(b) we processed a series of 161 images with varying sizes and faces, one after the other.

Table 1. Best execution times and comparison with OMPi when processing all images (speedup is calculated in comparison to the best sequential time overall)

Compiler	Sequential time (sec)	Best configuration	Parallel time (sec)	Speedup	OMPi improvement
GCC	37.329	6x4	9.210	3.219	25.5%
ICC	37.282	12x8	9.163	3.236	25.2%
SUNCC	29.656	4x4	8.778	3.378	21.9%
OMPi	37.329	16x8	6.853	4.327	–

All compilers, except OMPi are using nested parallelism, spawning $M \times N$ threads, while OMPi uses only M threads that execute $M \times N$ tasks in total. The results lead to similar conclusions in both plots. For the 4×4 configuration OMPi exhibits the lowest speedup due to the few (4) available threads while all other compilers employ 16 threads in total, potentially exploiting all the 16 cores of the system. On the other hand, when 8 or more threads are used in the first level, OMPi exhibits the highest speedups. ICC exhibits the second best performance and when processing image class57 it attains stable speedups for all thread configurations. For the set of all images ICC exhibits its best behavior when 4×4 threads are used, while for more threads synchronization overheads cause poorer speedups. GCC get its best speedup for image class57 for 8×6 threads, whereas for set of all images maximum speedup is shown for 6×4 threads. SUNCC exhibits similar execution times compared to ICC for both inputs in all thread configurations. The lower speedups shown for SUNCC are due to its shorter sequential execution times compared to all other compilers.

For completeness, in Table 1 we report the best performance attained by each compiler based on absolute execution times. For each compiler, we include the time required for a sequential run, the best observed configuration and the parallel execution time for that configuration. Speedups are then calculated in relation to the lowest sequential execution time, which is achieved using the SUNCC compiler. The last column demonstrates the performance improvement OMPi achieves in comparison to each compiler, based on the parallel execution times. Notice that for a fair comparison we also considered the $16 \times N$ configuration, which, although not advantageous for the rest of the compilers, it gives OMPi the chance to utilize all the available processors. It should be clear that our task-based technique outperforms the conventional implementations which utilize nested thread teams.

5   Conclusion

We have proposed a novel technique for executing nested `parallel for` loops using tasks instead of threads, thereby avoiding the overheads associated with nested parallelism in such cases. The technique we present is potentially applicable to any OpenMP runtime system that supports tasking and requires almost no changes in the compiler-produced code. It has been implemented in the framework of the OMPi compiler and has been shown to offer significant performance gains. While in this work we were mostly interested in showing the performance potential, as a future work we envisage an adaptive application of our technique. In particular, we believe that appropriate decisions can be made at runtime, depending on the number of active threads; if the active threads are much less than the available system processors it may be more appropriate to create nested threads instead of tasks.

Our technique can be applied to nested `parallel sections` regions without any alterations, as well, and this is currently under implementation in OMPi. It is not applicable, though, to general nested parallel regions. This is because parallel regions produce threads that may contain barrier synchronizations, which are not allowed within tasks. Nevertheless, it seems plausible to investigate this further and we are actually working on this possibility within our PSTHREAD library [6,1]; this library is based on user-level threads that are used to instantiate both OpenMP threads and OpenMP tasks.

References

1. Agathos, S.N., Hadjidoukas, P.E., Dimakopoulos, V.V.: Design and Implementation of OpenMP Tasks in the OMPi Compiler. In: Proc. of 15th Panhellenic Conference on Informatics, PCI 2011, pp. 265–269. IEEE, Kastoria (2011)
2. Blumofe, R.D., Joerg, C.F., Kuszmaul, B.C., Leiserson, C.E., Randall, K.H., Zhou, Y.: Cilk: An efficient multithreaded runtime system. J. Parallel Distrib. Comput. 37(1), 55–69 (1996)
3. Bull, J.M.: Measuring Synchronisation and Scheduling Overheads in OpenMP. In: Proc. of 1st European Workshop on OpenMP, EWOMP, pp. 99–105. Lund, Sweden (September 1999)
4. Dimakopoulos, V.V., Leontiadis, E., Tzoumas, G.: A portable C compiler for OpenMP V.2.0. In: Proc. of 5th European Workshop on OpenMP, EWOMP 2003, Aachen, Germany, pp. 5–11 (September 2003)
5. Hadjidoukas, P.E., Dimakopoulos, V.V., Delakis, M., Garcia, C.: A high-performance face detection system using OpenMP. Concurrency and Computation: Practice and Experience 21, 1819–1837 (2009)
6. Hadjidoukas, P.E., Dimakopoulos, V.V.: Nested Parallelism in the OMPi OpenMP/C Compiler. In: Kermarrec, A.-M., Bougé, L., Priol, T. (eds.) Euro-Par 2007. LNCS, vol. 4641, pp. 662–671. Springer, Heidelberg (2007)
7. Leiserson, C.E.: The Cilk++ concurrency platform. J. of Supercomputing 51, 244–257 (2012)
8. OpenMP ARB: OpenMP Application Program Interface V3.0 (May 2008)
9. OpenMP ARB: OpenMP Application Program Interface V3.1 (July 2011)
10. Reinders, J.: Intel threading building blocks, 1st edn. O'Reilly & Associates, Inc., Sebastopol (2007)
11. Rowley, H., Baluja, S., Kanade, T.: Neural network-based face detection. IEEE Trans. on Pattern Analysis and Machine Intelligence 20, 23–28 (1998)

SPEC OMP2012 — An Application Benchmark Suite for Parallel Systems Using OpenMP

Matthias S. Müller[1,2], John Baron[1,4], William C. Brantley[1,3], Huiyu Feng[1,4], Daniel Hackenberg[1,2], Robert Henschel[1,5], Gabriele Jost[1,3], Daniel Molka[1,2], Chris Parrott[1,6], Joe Robichaux[1,7], Pavel Shelepugin[1,8], Matthijs van Waveren[1,9], Brian Whitney[1,10], and Kalyan Kumaran[1,11]

[1] SPEC High Performance Group
info@spec.org
http://www.spec.org/hpg
[2] Center for Information Services and High Performance Computing (ZIH), Technische Universität Dresden, 01062 Dresden, Germany
[3] Advanced Micro Devices, Inc.
[4] Silicon Graphics International
[5] Indiana University
[6] Portland Group
[7] IBM
[8] Intel Corporation
[9] Fujitsu Systems Europe Ltd
[10] Oracle
[11] Argonne National Laboratory

Abstract. This paper describes SPEC OMP2012, a benchmark developed by the SPEC High Performance Group. It consists of 15 OpenMP parallel applications from a wide range of fields. In addition to a performance metric based on the run time of the applications the benchmark adds an optional energy metric. The accompanying run rules detail how the benchmarks are executed and the results reported. They also cover the energy measurements. The first set of results provide scalability on three different platforms.

Keywords: Benchmark, OpenMP, SPEC, Energy Efficiency.

1 Introduction

The Standard Performance Evaluation Corporation's (SPEC) High Performance Group (HPG) has a long history of producing industry standard benchmarks for comparing high performance computer systems and accompanying software. The group's members comprise leading HPC vendors, national laboratories and universities from across the globe. The group currently has two science application benchmark suites based on the OpenMP and MPI programming models. The

B.M. Chapman et al. (Eds.): IWOMP 2012, LNCS 7312, pp. 223–236, 2012.

targeted HPC systems include multi-CPU shared memory servers to distributed memory clusters.

The current effort is aimed to refresh the OpenMP benchmark suite that was released in 2001. This initial suite, SPEC OMP2001, comprising a collection of OpenMP based applications was released in June, 2001. An update containing a larger dataset was released in June, 2002. Until February 2012 more than 370 results were published for this benchmark clearly proving the popularity of the benchmark. SPEC OMP2001 was based on version 1.0 of the OpenMP specifications, that were released in 1998[1]. Most of the applications were based on codes from SPEC CPU2000 with added OpenMP directives. In the meantime OpenMP has evolved to version 3.0, containing new directives and clauses. The increased use of OpenMP, the evolution of the standard and the fact that typical applications will change over time in terms of algorithms, physics and language standards, provided the motivation to develop a new SPEC benchmark for OpenMP.

The development of the benchmark suite included identifying candidate applications from different science domains making use of a variety of OpenMP directives in different programming languages and, very importantly, stressing various hardware features on a node including the processor core and various memory hierarchies. Like any SPEC benchmark suite the new suite comes within a harness with scalable data sets for running and validating. The harness and the benchmark has been built and tested on a variety of platforms. The suite comes with run rules that result submitters must adhere to. The run rules are similar to other current SPEC benchmarks. Run times are compared to a reference architecture and the geometric mean of all run time ratios is computed to calculate the performance metric.

Another interesting facet of this benchmark suite is the addition of an experimental power metric. The HPG worked closely with the Power group within SPEC to make use of their work on power analyzers, power daemons, and run rules for making power measurements to include a power metric. Result submissions are encouraged to make power measurements along with performance, but it is not mandatory to do so.

Some aspects of the benchmark are still under development. This paper describes the almost final version. For definite performance numbers the official benchmark reports at the SPEC web page should be consulted once the benchmark is released. The next section discusses a few of the principles that guided the development of SPEC OMP2012. In Section 3, we provide a short description of the applications contained in the benchmarks. Following that we describe how we added energy measurements to the suite. In Section 5 we describe the initial results and discuss the scalability achieved on the benchmarks. Section 6 puts the benchmark in perspective compared to related work. Section 7 concludes the paper.

---

[1] Fortran Version 1.0 was released Oct. 1997, C/C++ Version 1.0 was released Oct. 1998.

2   Design and Principles of SPEC OMP2012

2.1   General Design

The SPEC OMP2012 benchmark and its accompanying run rules has been designed to fairly and objectively benchmark and compare high-performance computing systems runing OpenMP applications. The rules help ensure that published results are meaningful, comparable to other results, and reproducible. SPEC believes that the user community benefits from an objective series of tests which serve as a common reference.

A SPEC OMP2012 result is an empirical report of performance observed when carrying out certain computation- and communication-intensive tasks. It is also a declaration that the observed level of performance can be obtained by others. Finally it carries an implicit claim that the performance methods it employs are more than just "prototype" or "experimental" or "research" methods; it is a claim that there is a certain level of maturity and general applicability in its methods.

The SPEC HPG committee reviews SPEC OMP2012 results for consistency and strict adherence to the run rules, whether enough details have been supplied for reproduction of the results, and whether only allowable optimizations have been used. If the committee accepts the results, they get published on the SPEC website. On the website, HPC users can view the results and compare them to results of others.

2.2   Run Rules

The run rules cover the building and running of the benchmark and the disclosure of the benchmark results. The SPEC OMP2012 benchmark suite supports base, peak and power metrics. The overall performance metric is the geometric mean of the run time ratios of the system under test with the run time of a reference machine. The reference system chosen for this benchmark suite is a Sun Fire X4140 with two AMD Opteron 2384 processors (quad-core 'Shanghai' , 2.7 GHz) with 32 GB RAM.

A set of Perl tools is supplied to build and run the benchmarks and automatically validate the output. To produce publishable results, these SPEC tools must be used. This helps ensure reproducibility of results by requiring that all individual benchmarks in the suite be run in the same way and that a configuration file be available that defines the optimizations used.

The optimizations used are expected to be safe and it is expected that system and compiler vendors would endorse the general use of these optimizations by customers who seek to achieve good application performance.

For the base metric, the same compiler must be used for all modules of a given language within a benchmark suite. Except for portability flags, all flags or options that affect the transformation process from SPEC-supplied source to completed executable must be the same for all modules of a given language. For the peak metric, each module can be compiled with a different compiler and a different set of flags or options. In addition, for the peak metric, source code changes are allowed. Changes to the directives and source are permitted to facilitate generally useful and portable optimizations, with a focus on improving scalability. Changes in algorithms are not permitted.

As used in these run rules, the term "run-time dynamic optimization" (RDO) refers broadly to any method by which a system adapts to improve performance of an executing program based upon observation of its behavior as it runs. Run time dynamic optimization is allowed, subject to the provisions that the techniques must be generally available, documented, and supported.

Differences between Run Rules of OMP2001 and of OMP2012. The main differences between the OMP2001 and OMP2012 relate to power measurements, feedback driven optimization and run time dynamic optimization.

Power measurements make their entry in the HPG benchmarks with OMP2012. They were not supported in OMP2001. Thus the OMP2012 run rules devote quite a few rules to the measurement of power.

Feedback driven optimization relates to allowing the compiler to do two passes through the code: the first pass generates feedback information, and this information is used in the second pass for optimization purposes. This type of optimization was allowed for in OMP2001, but in OMP2012 it is not allowed.

Run time dynamic optimization is a concept that makes its entry in OMP2012. Run time dynamic optimization is allowed in OMP2012, subject to the provisions that the techniques must be generally available, documented, and supported.

3   Description of the Benchmark

The following section should provide a short description of the applications used in SPEC OMP2012. This includes the scientific area of each code and contains a brief explanation of the specific workload. Table 1 contains an overview of all applications providing the programming language, the code size, memory demand, the amount of OpenMP usage and the code area. For reporting the lines of code (LOC) we use the Unified CodeCount tool (UCC) [15] and report the logical SLOC.

350.md. The IU-MD code performs molecular dynamics simulations of dense nuclear matter such as occurs in Type II supernovas [4], the outer layers of neutron stars, and in white dwarf stars. The IU-MD code simulates fully ionized atoms via a classical screened Coulomb interaction. An exponential screening factor models the screening effect of the background electron gas. These simulations have been used to study a number of properties of dense matter in compact stellar objects, such as chemical and phase separation, thermal conductivity, phase diagrams, and mechanical properties. The benchmark performs a short run of a realistic 27648 ion system consisting of carbon and oxygen ions.

351.bwaves. 351.bwaves [11] numerically simulates blast waves in three dimensional transonic transient laminar viscous flow. The initial configuration of

Table 1. Application key facts

Code	Memory MB	LOC	Language	OMP call sites	OMP directives	Area
350.md	5	1,768	Fortran	14	3	Molecular Dynamics
351.bwaves	22,800	876	F77	29	1	Computational Fluid Dynamics
352.nab	618	11,485	C	60	5	Molecular Modeling
357.bt331	11,188	2,331	Fortran	44	5	Computational Fluid Dynamics
358.botsalgn	156	1,277	C	4	3	Sequence Alignment
359.botsspar	7,179	209	C	8	4	LU factorization
360.ilbdc	16,482	978	Fortran	7	1	Lattice Boltzmann
362.fma3d	5,205	19,681	F90	142	5	Finite Element Method
363.swim	6,490	212	Fortran	14	3	Finite Difference
367.imagick	1,733	96,810	C	312	6	Image Processing
370.mgrid331	13,972	806	Fortran	20	5	Multi-Grid Solver
371.applu331	14,884	1,782	Fortran	81	9	PDE/SSOR
372.smithwa	177	2,561	C	22	3	Optimal Pattern Matching
376.kdtree	119	287	C++	4	3	Sorting and Searching
377.DROPS2	5,340	8,350	C++	55	5	Finite Element Method

the blast waves problem consists of a high pressure and density region at the center of a cubic cell of a periodic lattice, with low pressure and density elsewhere. Periodic boundary conditions are applied to the array of cubic cells.The algorithm implemented is an unfactored solver for the implicit solution of the compressible Navier-Stokes equations using the biconjugate gradient stabilized (Bi-CGstab) algorithm, which solves systems of non-symmetric linear equations iteratively. The code is made OpenMP parallel with 29 *parallel do* directives.

352.nab. 352.nab is based on Nucleic Acid Builder (NAB), which is a molecular modeling application that performs the types of floating point intensive calculations that occur commonly in life science computation [13]. The calculations range from relatively unstructured "molecular dynamics" to relatively structured linear algebra.

357.bt331. BT is a simulated CFD application that uses an implicit algorithm to solve 3-dimensional (3-D) compressible Navier-Stokes equations. The finite differences solution to the problem is based on an Alternating Direction Implicit (ADI) approximate factorization that decouples the x, y and z dimensions. The resulting systems are Block-Tridiagonal of 5x5 blocks and are solved sequentially along each dimension. This version is derived from the NPB 3.3.1 benchmark suite [9].

358.botsalgn. This application is part of the Barcelona OpenMP tasks suite [6]. All protein sequences from an input file are aligned against every other sequence using the Myers and Miller algorithm. The outer loop is parallelized with an *omp for* worksharing directive with tasks created inside this parallel loop. This allows the implementation to break the iterations when the number of threads is large compared to the number of iterations and when there is imbalance. To be able to use untied tasks several global variables, used as temporal space, were moved to local variables.

359.botsspar. This application is part of the Barcelona OpenMP tasks suite [6]. An LU matrix factorization over sparse matrices is computed. A first level matrix is composed by pointers to small submatrices that may not be allocated. Due to the sparseness of the matrix, a lot of imbalance exists. Matrix size and submatrix size can be set at execution time. While a dynamic schedule can reduce the imbalance, a solution with task-based parallelism seems to obtain better results. In each of the sparseLU phases, a task is created for each block of the matrix that is not empty.

360.ilbdc. The benchmark kernel is geared to the collision-propagation routine of an advanced 3-D lattice Boltzmann flow solver using a two-relaxation-time (TRT-type) collision operator for the D3Q19 model [2]. The benchmark kernel is not a complete flow solver. Lattice Boltzmann flow solvers use a velocity-discrete Boltzmann equation and discretize space and time in such a way that an explicit (finite difference) numerical scheme with Euler forward time-stepping is obtained. The resulting fluid mechanical results satisfy the incompressible athermal Navier-Stokes equations with second order accuracy. The specific data structures of the benchmark kernel use a list-based "sparse" data representation resulting in indirect data access patterns. However, especially for flow in porous media or blood flow simulations, such data structures are highly beneficial to efficiently recover the complex geometries.

362.fma3d. FMA-3D [10] is a finite element method program designed to simulate the inelastic, transient dynamic response of three-dimensional solids and structures subjected to impulsively or suddenly applied loads. As an explicit code, the program is appropriate for problems where high rate dynamics or stress wave propagation effects are important. In contrast to programs using implicit time integration algorithms, the program uses a large number of relatively small time steps, with the solution for the next configuration of the body being explicit (and inexpensive) at each step. To further reduce the computational effort, the program has a complete implementation of Courant subcycling in which each element is integrated with the maximum time step permitted by local stability criteria. More than 100 *parallel do* directives are contained in the code and the *threadprivate* directive is used.

363.swim. Swim is a weather prediction benchmark program for comparing the performance of current supercomputers [16]. The swim code is a finite-difference approximation of the shallow-water equations and is known to be memory bandwidth limited. It computes on a 1335x1335 area array of data and iterates over 512 timesteps.

367.imagick. ImageMagick[1] is a software suite to create, edit, compose, or convert bitmap images. It can read and write images in a variety of formats (over 100) including DPX, EXR, GIF, JPEG, JPEG-2000, PDF, PhotoCD, PNG, Postscript, SVG, and TIFF. Use ImageMagick to resize, flip, mirror, rotate, distort, shear and transform images, adjust image colors, apply various special effects, or draw text, lines, polygons, ellipses and Bzier curves.

370.mgrid331. MG demonstrates the capabilities of a very simple multigrid solver in computing a three dimensional potential field. This version is derived from the NPB 3.3.1 benchmark suite [9]. The code makes use of the OpenMP directives for loop parallelism, including the *collapse* clause to parallelize a nested loop construct.

371.applu331. Solution of five coupled nonlinear PDE's, on a 3-dimensional logically structured grid, using an implicit psuedo-time marching scheme, based on two-factor approximate factorization of the sparse Jacobian matrix. This scheme is functionally equivalent to a nonlinear block SSOR iterative scheme with lexicographic ordering. Spatial discretization of the differential operators is based on second-order accurate finite volume scheme. Insists on the strict lexicographic ordering during the solution of the regular sparse lower and upper triangular matrices. As a result, the degree of exploitable parallelism during this phase is limited to $O(N^{**}2)$ as opposed to $O(N^{**}3)$ in other phases and it's spatial distribution is non-homogenous. This fact also creates challenges during the loop re-ordering to enhance the cache locality. This version is derived from the NPB 3.3.1 benchmark suite [9].

372.smithwa. The C program runSequenceAlignment is derived from the Matlab program RUN_sequenceAlignment that was written by Bill Mann (formerly of MIT Lincoln Labs) and distributed as version 0.6 of DARPA SSCA #1. Whereas the Matlab code is serial, the C code has been modified for parallel execution under OpenMP, following the suggestions given in the "parallelization.txt" file that is included in the version 0.6 distribution.
The program operates as follows. A similarity or "scoring" matrix is generated by genSimMatrix.c. Two random sequences of amino acid codons are generated by genScalData.c, and then six pre-determined verification sequences are embedded therein. Then in Kernel 1 each OpenMP thread compares sub-sequences of the two sequences via the local-affine Smith-Waterman algorithm, and builds a list of the best alignments and their endpoints. Next, in Kernel 2A each OpenMP thread or MPI process begins at each endpoint and follows each alignment back to its start point, and outputs a list of the best alignments and their start points, endpoints and codon sequences. Kernel 2B merges the results of Kernel 2A from all of the OpenMP threads or MPI processes, and outputs a final list of the best alignments.

376.kdtree. The program builds a k-d tree using random coordinate points, then searches the k-d tree for points that are proximate to each point in the tree. The build phase is single threaded, but the search phase is multithreaded using the OpenMP task directive. The points that are sorted into the tree are defined using a random number gener ator to generate either 3D (x,y,z) or 4D (x,y,z,w) points that are stored one large 2 D array, xyzw. In order to build the k-d tree, four index arrays xi, yi, zi and wi are created then heap-sorted using the x, y, z and w coordinate data from the xyzw array. The k-d tree is a balanced tree, and is built in O[n*log(n)] time. Once the k-d tree is built, the k-d tree is walked to visit each point, and that point is used as a query point to search the k-d tree for all other points that lie within a specific radius of that query point. The default value for that radius is one-tenth the range of the random numbers. The total number of points found by using each point successively as a query point, as well as the total execution time, are reported. Note that the walking and searching of the k-d tree imply two recursive traversals of the k-d tree.

377.DROPS. This research is partially supported by the Deutsche Forschungs-gemeinschaft (DFG) within SFB 540 (Model-based experimental analysis of kinetic phenomena in fluid multi-phase reactive systems). The software aims at simulating flows consisting of two phases, e.g., an oil drop in water [Bertakis:2010] or a liquid film flowing downward a wall [Gross:2005]. To this end, it employs advanced numerical techniques. The computational domain is discretized by a hierarchy of tetrahedral grids which is adaptively modified while evolving in simulation time. The level set method captures the interface between both phases. Additionally, the numerical techniques include iterative solvers based on multigrid methods, extended finite elements to represent the pressure jump at the interface, and a continuum surface force term for treating the surface tension. A detailed description of the numerical techniques is given in [Gross:2006] [Gross:2007]. The shared-memory parallelization of the submitted DROPS code is based on an OpenMP for reducing the runtime of the main computational expensive parts, i.e., setting up the non-linear equation systems and their solution.

4   Energy Efficiency

Our approach to add energy measurements is based on the SPEC Power and Performance Benchmark Methodology that describes in detail how testers can integrate a power metric into their benchmarks. Following this methodology allows OMP2012 to use the PTDaemon. The PTDaemon can control a large set of professional power analyzers and temperature sensors. Its feature set is rich and includes aspects such as range checking, uncertainty calculation, multichannel measurements and more.

Moreover, the methodology requires users to follow strictly defined run rules (e.g. regarding the power measurement setup) and to provide detailed documentation of their benchmark configuration (e.g. hardware/software setup). For example, it is required that the power analyzer be supported by the measurement framework and be calibrated once a year. The temperature needs also to be measured and a minimum temperature is required to prevent people from reducing the power consumption by using air that is colder than a typical environment.

The energy consumption has been added as a separate and optional metric. It compares the energy consumption of each benchmark with the energy

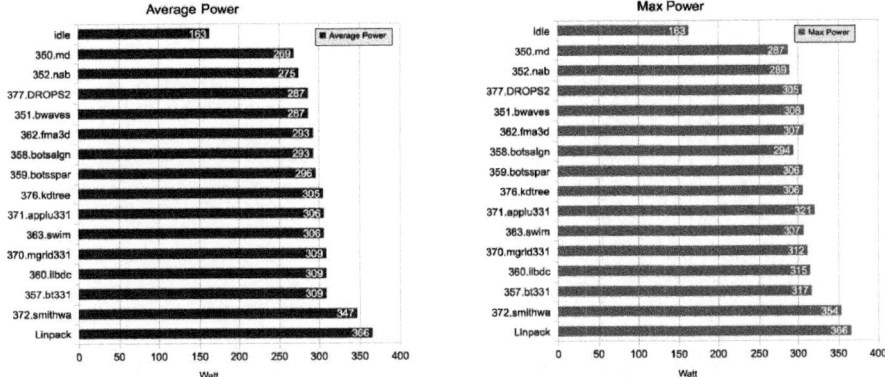

Fig. 1. Average and maximum power consumption of the different applications on the reference system compared to idle and linpack power

consumption of the reference machine. An energy metric of 2 means that a benchmark run on a given system consumes half of the energy (in Joules) of the benchmark run on the reference machine. This could for example be caused by

- the system under test having the same power consumption but twice the performance (half the benchmark runtime) of the reference machine, or
- the system under test delivering the same performance as the reference machine at half the power consumption.

We also report the average and maximum power consumption of each benchmark run. To measure idle power we include a 15-minute idle period, of which we report the last 5 minutes as the average idle power consumption of the system. Fig. 1 shows the power consumption on the reference system. The average power consumption varies between 82% and 97% of the reported max power consumption. This reported max power consumption is smaller than the value reported by the vendor. It is also smaller than the power consumed by a power intensive benchmark like Linpack. A large difference between the value for average and max power of the individual benchmarks indicates high variations of the power consumption in time. Fig. 2 shows the power consumption of 359.botspar as an example.

5   First Scalability Results

Figure 3 shows the scaling of the benchmarks on a four socket system with Opteron 6274 processors. The results were obtained with PGI compilers version 12.3 and the flags: `-mp -fast -Mvect=sse -Mipa=fast,inline -Msmartalloc`. The processors have 16 cores with 2.2 GHz base frequency and up to 2.5 GHz with turbo. Each 16-core processor is implemented as multi-chip-modules that consist of two

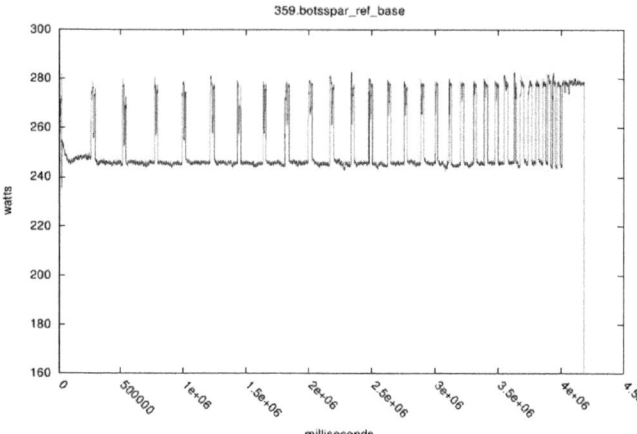

Fig. 2. Power consumption of 359.botspar over time on a two socket system with Intel Xeon X5670 processors

8-core dies. Each die has a shared last level cache and an integrated dual-channel DDR3 memory controller. Therefore, the 64 cores in the 4 socket system are partitioned into 8 NUMA domains with 8 cores each. The eight cores of each die are composed of four dual-core modules. The two cores in a module share the floating point unit as well as L2 and instruction caches.

The scaling with the number of utilized modules (FPUs) is depicted in Figure 3a. While execution resources scale linearly, the level 3 cache capacity and the memory bandwidth are shared by all modules. Despite this some benchmarks scale almost linear, i.e. are not constrained by the shared resources. On the other hand 363.swim mirrors the memory bandwidth scaling. In between there are some more or less memory bound benchmarks. 376.kdtree does not show any scaling as the used compiler version does not support the nested tasking in this benchmark.

Figure 3b shows how the performance increases if multiple sockets (dies) are used. In this case execution resources as well as last level cache capacity and memory bandwidth scale linearly. Therefore, most benchmarks achieve better scaling. This is most noticeable with 363.swim that scales linearly with the increasing memory bandwidth. 350.md, 358.botsalgn, 370.mgrid331, 371.applu331, and 372.smithwa scale almost linearly as well. The speedup of 351.bwaves, 352.nab, 357.bt331, and 360.ilbdc is slightly lower. However, with more than 85% parallel efficiency when going from 1 to 4 sockets, they still scale very well. 359.botsspar does not scale as well as it does within a single die. This behavior could be caused by frequent remote memory accesses that cause contention on the processor interconnects. To a lesser degree this applies to 362.fma3d as well. 377.DROPS2 does not scale well with the number of sockets. 376.kdtree again is limited by the nested task issue of the PGI 12.3 compilers.

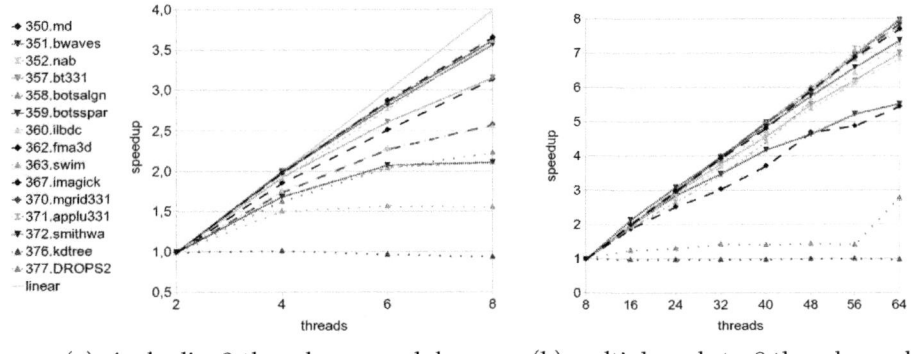

(a) single die, 2 threads per module   (b) multiple sockets, 8 threads per die

Fig. 3. Scaling of SPEC OMP2012 on an quad socket Opteron 6274 system (367.imagick is missing because of segmentation faults that occur with the used compiler version)

Fig. 4a shows up to which thread counts the benchmarks scale on an SGI Altix UV. Therefore, measurements are omited if the runtime increases when more threads are used. 350.md scales almost linearly up to 512 threads on that architecture. 372.smithwa shows good speedup up to 384 threads. 358.botsalgn scales almost linearly up to 128 threads. 363.swim, 370.mgrid, and 351.bwaves scale well up to 256 threads with approximately 75% parallel efficiency. They also achieve more than 50% parallel efficiency with 512 threads. While 363.swim and 370.mgrid did not show any sign of being affected by inter-socket communication on the four socket Opteron system, the more complex topology in the SGI Altix UV seems to affect their scalability. 359.botsspar and 376.kdtree also achieve a high parallel efficiency with up to 256 threads, but do not scale well beyond that. The scalability of the remaining benchmarks is seriously constricted on the Altix UV system. Their parallel efficiency is below 50% with 256 threads. 357.bt331, 360.ilbdc, and 362.fma3d show noticeable reductions in runtime when using more than 256 threads. The runtime of 352.nab and 367.imagick reduces marginally when going from 256 to 512 threads.

Fig. 4b shows the scalability up to 128 threads on a Sun Fire E25K system from Oracle. The parallel efficiency of 128 threads compared to 16 threads is in the 50% to 100% range with two exceptions: 372.smithwa shows slightly superlinear speedup while 371.applu331 does not scale well on that architecture.

6   Related Work

There are numerous efforts to create benchmarks for different purposes. The goal of SPEC OMP2012 is to create an application benchmark consisting of codes using OpenMP. There are only a few efforts that share this goal. One of the benchmark that is in wider use is the NAS Parallel Benchmark [9]. They consist of a

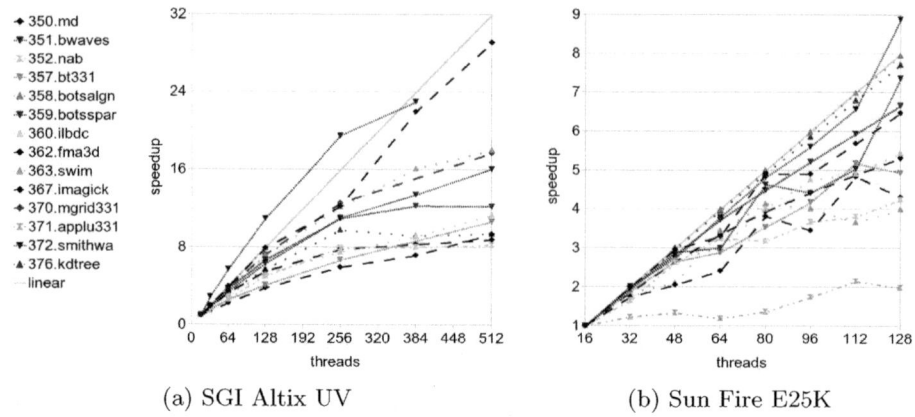

(a) SGI Altix UV   (b) Sun Fire E25K

Fig. 4. Scalability of SPEC OMP2012 on large SMP systems

small set of programs designed to help evaluate the performance of parallel super-computers. The benchmark, which is derived from computational fluid dynamics (CFD) applications, consists of five kernels and three pseudo-applications. The Rodinia Benchmark [5] is a collection of different algorithms with implementations for CUDA, OpenCL and OpenMP. The EPCC Microbenchmarks [3] focus on measuring the overhead of specific directives of OpenMP.

The need to add energy consumption measurements into benchmarks has been identified by various communities. The Green500[2] list uses Linpack as workload and combines the achieved performance with an extrapolated energy consumption to an energy efficiency metric [7]. Since June 2008 the Top500[3] list also contains the overall power consumption of the system.

The Open Systems Group within SPEC has created SPECpower_ssj2008 [12], a benchmark with a concise power measurement methodology and precise run-rules. Instead of an HPC workload it combines a Java server workload at different load levels from 0 to 100% and measures the power consumption of the server. An extensive list of benchmark results from all major server vendors is publicly available on the SPEC website, thus making it easy to compare the energy efficiency of e.g. CPUs or system designs. The power consumption of SPEC MPI2007 was also analyzed [8], but unlike the work presented here, power is not a standardized feature in the SPEC MPI2007 benchmark.

There are also a number of application benchmark suites developed and published by SPEC. Characteristics of the SPEC benchmark suites CPU2006, OMP2001 [17,14], and OMP2012 are shown in Table 2. The provided runtimes are for execution on the different reference machines.

The benchmark suites differ in the systems or applications they focus on. SPEC CPU2006 focuses on serial applications. SPEC OMPM2001 focuses on

---

[2] http://www.green500.org

[3] http://www.top500.org

Table 2. Comparison of CPU2006, OMPM2001, OMPL2001, and OMP2012

Characteristic	CPU2006	OMPM2001	OMPL2001	OMP2012
Max. working set	0.9/1.8 GB	1.6 GB	6.4 GB	23 GB
Memory needed	1 or 2 GB	2 GB	7 GB	32 GB
Single runtime	20 min	90 min	4 hrs	60 min
Language	C, C++, F95	C, F90	C, F90	C, C++, F95
Focus	Single CPU	< 16 cores	> 16 cores	> 8 cores
System type	Desktop	MP workstation	SMP	SMP
Total runtime	288 hours	34 hours	72 hours	> 72 hours
Run modes	speed and rate	parallel speed	parallel speed	parallel speed
Applications	29	11	9	15
Iterations	Median of 3	Worst of 2, median of ≥3	Worst of 2, median of ≥3	Median of 3
Source mods	Not allowed	Allowed	Allowed	Allowed
Reference system	1 CPU 300 MHz	4 CPU 350 MHz	16 CPU 300 MHz	8 cores 2.7 GHz

multiprocessing workstations with less than 16 CPUs, while SPEC OMPL2001 focuses on systems with more than 16 CPUs.

7 Summary and Conclusion

SPEC OMP2012 is a benchmark suite, which uses real parallel applications which use OpenMP. They stress the whole system under test, e.g. compiler, run time system, operating system, memory, and CPU. The selected applications come from a wide field of scientific areas, and also cover a significant range of OpenMP usage, including features added with OpenMP 3.0. The benchmark suite comes with an elaborate set of run rules, which help ensure that published results are meaningful, comparable to other results, and reproducible. The energy metric is another important feature. Its value increases with the growing cost of the energy. SPEC also has an extensive review procedure, which is followed before results are published on the public SPEC web site.

This unique combination of properties distinguishes SPEC OMP2012 from other OpenMP benchmark suites. SPEC believes that the user community benefits from an objective series of realistic tests, which serve as a common reference.

Acknowledgements. This work has been partially funded by the Bundesministerium für Bildung und Forschung via the Spitzencluster CoolSilicon (BMBF 13N10186) and the research project eeClust (BMBF 01IH08008C). This research used resources of the Argonne Leadership Computing Facility at Argonne National Laboratory, which is supported by the Office of Science of the U.S. Department of Energy under contract DE-AC02-06CH11357.

References

1. Image magick homepage (March 2012), http://www.imagemagick.org
2. Axner, L., Bernsdorf, J., Zeiser, T., Lammers, P., Linxweiler, J., Hoekstra, A.G.: Performance evaluation of a parallel sparse lattice Boltzmann solver. Journal of Computational Physics 227(10), 4895–4911 (2008)
3. Mark Bull, J., O'Neill, D.: A microbenchmark suite for OpenMP 2.0. In: Proceedings of the Third Workshop on OpenMP (EWOMP 2001), pp. 41–48 (2001)
4. Caballero, O.L., Horowitz, C.J., Berry, D.K.: Neutrino scattering in heterogeneous supernova plasmas. Phys. Rev. C 74, 065801 (2006)
5. Che, S., Boyer, M., Meng, J., Tarjan, D., Sheaffer, J.W., Lee, S.-H., Skadron, K.: Rodinia: A benchmark suite for heterogeneous computing. In: Proceedings of the 2009 IEEE International Symposium on Workload Characterization, IISWC 2009, pp. 44–54. IEEE Computer Society, Washington, DC (2009)
6. Duran, A., Teruel, X., Ferrer, R., Martorell, X., Ayguadé, E.: Barcelona OpenMP tasks suite: A set of benchmarks targeting the exploitation of task parallelism in OpenMP. In: ICPP, pp. 124–131. IEEE Computer Society (2009)
7. Feng, W.-C., Cameron, K.W.: The green500 list: Encouraging sustainable supercomputing. Computer 40(12), 50–55 (2007)
8. Hackenberg, D., Schöne, R., Molka, D., Müller, M.S., Knüpfer, A.: Quantifying power consumption variations of HPC systems using SPEC MPI benchmarks. Computer Science – Research and Development 25, 155–163 (2010), doi:10.1007/s00450-010-0118-0
9. Jin, H., Frumkin, M., Yan, J.: The OpenMP implementation of NAS parallel benchmarks and its performance. Technical report, NASA (1999)
10. Key, S.W., Hoff, C.C.: An improved constant membrane and bending stress shell element for explicit transient dynamics. Computer Methods in Applied Mechanics and Engineering 124(12), 33–47 (1995)
11. Kremenetsky, M., Raefsky, A., Reinhardt, S.: Poor Scalability of Parallel Shared Memory Model: Myth or Reality? In: Sloot, P.M.A., Abramson, D., Bogdanov, A.V., Gorbachev, Y.E., Dongarra, J., Zomaya, A.Y. (eds.) ICCS 2003. LNCS, vol. 2660, pp. 657–666. Springer, Heidelberg (2003), 10.1007/3-540-44864-0_68
12. Lange, K.-D.: Identifying shades of green: The SPECpower benchmarks. Computer 42, 95–97 (2009)
13. Macke, T.J., Case, D.A.: Modeling Unusual Nucleic Acid Structures, ch.25, pp. 379–393. American Chemical Society (1997)
14. Müller, M.S., Kalyanasundaram, K., Gaertner, G., Jones, W., Eigenmann, R., Lieberman, R., van Waveren, M., Whitney, B.: SPEC HPG benchmarks for high performance systems. International Journal of High Performance Computing and Networking 1(4), 162–170 (2004)
15. Nguyen, V., Deeds-Rubin, S., Tan, T., Boehm, B.: A sloc counting standard. Technical report, University of Southern California: Center for Systems and Software Engineering (2007)
16. Sadourny, R.: The Dynamics of Finite-Difference Models of the Shallow-Water Equations. Journal of Atmospheric Sciences 32, 680–689 (1975)
17. Saito, H., Gaertner, G., Jones, W., Eigenmann, R., Iwashita, H., Lieberman, R., van Waveren, M., Whitney, B.: Large System Performance of SPEC OMP2001 Benchmarks. In: Zima, H.P., Joe, K., Sato, M., Seo, Y., Shimasaki, M. (eds.) ISHPC 2002. LNCS, vol. 2327, pp. 370–379. Springer, Heidelberg (2002)

An OpenMP 3.1 Validation Testsuite

Cheng Wang, Sunita Chandrasekaran, and Barbara Chapman

University of Houston,
Computer Science Dept, Houston, Texas
{cwang35,sunita,chapman}@cs.uh.edu
http://www2.cs.uh.edu/~hpctools

Abstract. Parallel programming models are evolving so rapidly that it needs to be ensured that OpenMP can be used easily to program multicore devices. There is also effort involved in getting OpenMP to be accepted as a de facto standard in the embedded system community. However, in order to ensure correctness of OpenMP's implementation, there is a requirement of an up-to-date validation suite. In this paper, we present a portable and robust validation testsuite execution environment to validate the OpenMP implementation in several compilers. We cover all the directives and clauses of OpenMP until the latest release, OpenMP Version 3.1. Our primary focus is to determine and evaluate the correctness of the OpenMP implementation in our research compiler, OpenUH and few others such as Intel, Sun/Oracle and GNU.

We also aim to find the ambiguities in the OpenMP specification and help refine the same with the validation suite. Furthermore, we also include deeper tests such as cross tests and orphan tests in the testsuite.

Keywords: OpenMP, validation suite, task constructs, tests.

1 Introduction

OpenMP [5] has become the *de facto* standard in shared-memory parallel programming for C/C++ and Fortran. Defined by compiler directives, library routines and environment variables, the OpenMP API is currently supported by a variety of compilers from open source community to vendors (for e.g. GNU [18], Open64 [1], Intel [11], IBM [8]). OpenMP ARB ratified the version OpenMP 3.0 in 2008 and 3.1 in 2011. The main difference between versions 2.5 (released in 2005) and versions 3.0/3.1 is the introduction of the concept of tasks and the task construct. The task-based programming model enables the developers to create explicit asynchronous units of work to be scheduled dynamically by the runtime. This model and its capabilities address the previous difficulties in parallelizing applications employing recursive algorithms or pointers based data structures [2]. OpenMP version 3.1 was a minor release that offered corrections to the version 3.0. The main purpose of OpenMP version 3.1 is to improve efficiency for fine grain parallelism for tasks by adding `final` and `mergeable` clauses along with other extensions such as `taskyield`.

B.M. Chapman et al. (Eds.): IWOMP 2012, LNCS 7312, pp. 237–249, 2012.
© Springer-Verlag Berlin Heidelberg 2012

The goal of the work in this paper is to build an efficient framework, i.e. a testing environment, that will be used to validate the OpenMP implementations in OpenMP compilers. OpenMP is evolving with the increase in the number of users, as a result, there is an absolute need to check for completeness and correctness of the OpenMP implementations. We need to create an effective testing environment in order to achieve this goal. In prior work, we collaborated with colleagues at University of Stuttgart, to create validation methodologies for OpenMP versions 2.0 and 2.5 reported in [16,17] respectively. We have built our current framework on top of the older one. We have improved the testing environment and now the OpenMP validation testsuite covers all tests for the directives and clauses in OpenMP 3.1. This testing interface is portable, flexible and offers an user-friendly framework that can be tailored to accommodate specific testing requirements. Tests could be easily added/removed adhering to the changes in the OpenMP specification in future. In our current work we have ensured that the bugs in the previous validation testsuite have been fixed.

The organization of this paper is as follows: In Section 2 we describe the design and execution environment of the OpenMP validation suite. Section 3 shows the implementations and basic ideas for each of the tests. Here, we mainly focus on the concept of OpenMP tasks. In Section 4 we evaluate the validation suite using several open-source and vendor compilers. We discuss the related work in Section 5. Finally, we present the conclusion and the future work in Section 6.

2   The Design of an OpenMP Validation Suite

The basic idea in the design of the OpenMP validation suite is to provide short unit tests wherever possible and check if the directive being tested has been implemented correctly. For instance, the `parallel` construct and its corresponding clauses such as `shared` are tested for correctness. A test will fail if the corresponding feature has not been implemented correctly. We refer to such typical tests as *normal tests*.

Basically a number of values are calculated using the directive being tested and we compare the result with a known reference value. There is one type of failure called performance failure, in this case, even if the implementation of a directive is incorrect, it is not directly related to the correctness factor but it would just degrade the performance, for e.g. the `untied` clause in `task` construct. So it is at times not quite enough to only rely on the result calculated, but would require carefully written tests to check for the correctness of the implementation in a given compiler.

In a given code base, there might be more than a few directives being used at a given time. However, it is a challenge to check for correctness for a particular directive of interest, for instance `loop`, among several others. To solve this issue, we perform another test methodology called *cross test*, to validate only the directive under consideration. If this directive is removed from the code base, the output of the code will be incorrect.

Besides, we also need to ensure that the directive is serving its purpose. For instance lets consider a variable declared as `shared`. We also know that the

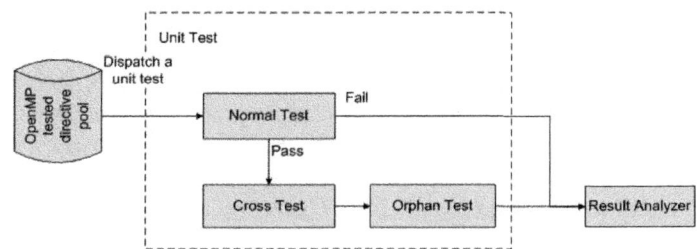

Fig. 1. The OpenMP Validation Suite Framework

variable is `shared` by default irrespective of explicitly declaring it as `shared`. Let us replace the `shared` with a `private` clause or any other clause which does not contain the functionality of the directive being tested, which in this case is `shared`. As a result, the *cross test* will check for the output result, which has to be incorrect because the variable is no longer being `shared`.

Moreover, in order to ensure that the directive being tested also gets executed correctly when "orphaned" from the main function, we creat a new test methodology named as *orphan test*. In the *orphan test*, the directive to be tested is placed into a children procedure which is called by the main function.

All test results will be statistically analyzed. Each test will be repeated multiple times. This is to ensure that the directive being tested functions correctly at all times. In order to estimate the probability that a test is passed accidentally we take the following approach: if n_f is the number of failed cross tests and M the total number of iterations, the probability of that test will fail is $p = \frac{n_f}{M}$. Thus the probability that an incorrect implementation passes the test is $p_a = (1 - p)^M$, and the certainty of test is $p_c = 1 - p_a$, i.e. the probability that a directive is validated.

Currently the validation suite contains more than 70 unit tests covering all of the clauses in the OpenMP version 3.1 release. Each of the unit tests has three types of tests: *normal, cross,* and *orphan test*. One of the challenges is that if we implement each of these tests separately, the entire suite would be ad-hoc and error-prone. It would also be challenging to manage and analyze the results generated out of so many tests. So we created an execution environment that will manage these several tests methodically.

Figure 1 shows the proposed framework i.e. the execution environment of the OpenMP validation suite. In this framework, we create a test directive pool that will consist of templates for the unit tests for each of the OpenMP directives being tested. This framework has been developed mainly using the Perl scripting language. We use this framework to parse through the several templates that have been written for each of the OpenMP directives. Executing this framework will deliver the source code for the three types of tests, namely *normal, cross* and *orphan* tests. The *normal* tests will be the first test to be performed in this process. If this particular test fails then there is no need to perform the *cross* and *orphan* tests. As a result, the corresponding source codes for *cross* and *orphan* tests will not be generated. This has been carefully crafted into our framework. If the *normal* tests pass successfully, the framework will automatically generate source codes for the other two tests. Note that we had to create only one template in order to generate source codes for all the three types of tests. As a result we emphasize that the framework adopts an automatic approach while creating the different kinds of tests necessary to check the correctness of the directives. There is very little manual labor involved in this process. Once these different tests have been created, our framework will compile and execute them as and when necessary. There is also a result analyzer component as part of the framework that will collect the results from each of the unit tests once all of them have completed execution. These results will be in the form of log files and the analyzer component will help in generating a complete report in a user-friendly manner.

The advantages that the execution environment offers are as follows:

- Creates one template for each test that is sufficient to automatically generate source codes for the three types of tests, i.e normal, cross and orphan tests.
- Creates bug reports that consist of adequate information about the compiler being used for testing purposes. The report will consist of version numbers of the compiler, build and configuration options, optimization flags used, and so on.
- Launches all the tests automatically, although individual tests will be performed only for those directives that are being tested.
- Generates reports that are easy to read and understand. These user-friendly reports will contain information about the bugs that have been identified. The details of the compilation and execution are also provided.

The framework is easy to use and maintain. It is quite flexible enough to accommodate changes as and when OpenMP specification gets updated with newer features.

3   Implementation

In this section, we discuss the unit tests for the OpenMP directives and clauses. We primarily discuss the unit tests for the directives and clauses in the latest versions of OpenMP (version 3.0 and 3.1). Previous publications [16,17] also discusses some of the ideas for the unit tests used to evaluate OpenMP Version 2.5 directives and clauses.

3.1   Directives and Clauses

Task is a new construct in OpenMP 3.0. It provides a mechanism to create explicit tasks. Tasks could be executed immediately or delayed by any assigned thread. Figure 2 shows the test for OpenMP `task` construct. The basic idea is to generate a set of tasks by a single thread and execute them in a parallel region. The tasks should be executed on more than one threads. In the cross test, the task *pragma* is removed. As a result, every task is executed only by one thread since the tasks are in the `single` region hence delivering incorrect outputs.

```
int test_omp_task(){
 int i, result=0;
 int tids[NUM_TASKS];

 /*Initialization*/
 for (i=0; i<NUM_TASKS; i++)
 {
  tids[i]=0;
 }

 #pragma omp parallel
 {
  #pragma omp single
  {
   for (i = 0; i < NUM_TASKS; i++){
    int myi = i;
    #pragma omp task
    {
     sleep (SLEEPTIME);
     tids[myi]=omp_get_thread_num();
    } /* end of omp task */
   } /* end of for */
  } /* end of single */
 } /*end of parallel */

 /*now check for results*/
 for (i = 1; i < NUM_TASKS; i++){
  if (tids[0] != tids[i])
   return (result = 1);
 }

 return result;
} /* end of test */
```

Fig. 2. Test for `task` construct

```
int test_omp_taskwait(){
 int i, result = 0;
 int array[NUM_TASKS];

 /*Initialization*/
 for(i=0;i<NUM_TASKS;i++)
 {
  array[i]=0;
 }

 #pragma omp parallel
 {
  #pragma omp single
  {
   for (i = 0; i < NUM_TASKS; i++){
    int myi = i;
    #pragma omp task
    array[myi] = 1;
   } /* end of for */

   #pragma omp taskwait

   /*check for all tasks finish*/
   for (i = 0; i < NUM_TASKS; i++){
    if (array[i] == 0)
     result++;
   } /*end of for*/
  } /* end of single */
 } /*end of parallel */

 return (result == 0);
}/*end of test*/
```

Fig. 3. Test for `taskwait` construct

The `taskwait` construct specifies a synchronization point where the current task is suspended until all children tasks have completed. Figure 3 shows the code listing for testing the `taskwait` construct. A flag is set to each element of an array when a set of tasks are generated. If `taskwait` executes successfully, all elements in the array should be 1; otherwise, the elements should be zero. In the cross test, we remove the `taskwait` construct and check the value of elements in the array. Obviously, part of the values will be 0 while others will be 1 if there is no "barrier" at the completion of tasks. Consequently, it is able to validate the `taskwait` construct.

The `shared` clause defines a set of variables that could be shared by threads in `parallel` construct or shared by tasks in `task` construct. The basic idea to test this would be to update a shared variable i.e. say i by a set of tasks and check whether it could be shared by all tasks. If this is the case, the value of the shared variable should be equal to number of tasks. In the cross test, we check if the result is wrong without the `shared` clause. As discussed in section 2, `shared` is replaced by the `firstprivate` clause, i.e., the attribute of i is changed to firstprivate. As a result, the value of i should be incorrect.

As opposed to `shared` clause, the `private` clause defines that variables are private to each task or thread. The idea of testing for the `private` clause is first to generate a set of tasks as before and each task to update a private variable, e.g., *local_sum*. We compare the value with the *known_sum* which is calculated in prior. In the cross test, we remove the `private` clause from `task` construct. Thus the private variable now becomes `shared` by default. As a result, we see that the value of `local_sum` should be incorrect.

The `firstprivate` clause is similar to `private` clause except that the new item list has been initialized prior to encountering the `task` construct. As a result, in contrast to `private` clause, we do not need to initialize variables declared as `firstprivate`. Consequently, test for the `firstprivate` is similar to the test for the `private` clause except that variable `local_sum` does not need to be initialized to zero in the `task` region. In the cross test, the `firstprivate` is removed and hence the variable `local_sum` becomes a `shared` variable once again.

The `default` clause determines the data-sharing attributes of variables implicitly. In C language, the variables declared as `default` is shared, while in Fortran from OpenMP 3.0, variables are declared as `private` or `firstprivate` by default. In addition, OpenMP 3.0 also allows variables to not have any predetermined data-sharing attribute declared as `none`. As a result, the idea of testing for `default` clause is actually the same as to testing for `shared` clause in C and `firstprivate, private` in Fortran.

The `if` clause controls the `task` implementation as shown in Figure 4. If the `if` is evaluated as false then the encountering task will be suspended and a new task is executed immediately. The suspended task will be resumed until the generated task is finished. The idea of testing the `if` clause is to generate a set tasks by a single thread and pause it immediately. The parent thread shall set a counter variable that the task which is paused, will consider when the thread wakes up. If the `if` clause is evaluated to false, the `task` region will be suspended and the counter variable *count* will be assigned to 1. When the `task` region resumes, we evaluate the value of the counter variable *count*. In the cross test, we removed `if` clause from the `task` construct, since `if` is evaluated to true by default, the `task` region will be executed immediately and the counter variable `count` will still be 0.

In OpenMP 3.0, task is executed by a thread of the team that generated it and is tied by default, i.e., tied tasks are executed by the same thread after the suspension. If it is the `untied` clause, any thread could resume the task after the suspension. The implementation of untied clause introduces newer kinds of compiler bugs and performance failures. But degradation in performance is unrelated to the implementation of the clause and its correctness. Testing such

```
int test_omp_task_if(){
 int count, result=0;
 int cond_false=0;

#pragma omp parallel
{
 #pragma omp single
 {
  #pragma omp task if (cond_false)
  {
   sleep (SLEEPTIME_LONG);
   result = (0 == count);
  } /* end of omp task */

  count = 1;
 } /* end of single */
} /*end of parallel */

 return result;
} /*end of test */
```

Fig. 4. Test for `if` clause

```
int omp_for_collapse(){
 int is_larger = 1;
#pragma omp parallel
{
 int i,j,my_islarger = 1;
 #pragma omp for schedule(static
       ,1) collapse(2) ordered
 for (i = 1; i < 100; i++)
  for (j =1; j <100; j++)
  {
   #pragma omp ordered
    my_islarger = my_islarger &&
       check_i_islarger(i);
  } /* end of for */
 #pragma omp critical
  is_larger=is_larger &&
       my_islarger;
} /*end of parallel*/
 return (is_larger);
} /*end of test*/
```

Fig. 5. Test for `collapse` clause

features require the test codes to be very carefully created, since if the clause is not implemented correctly, it will not yield incorrect results but just degrade the performance and moreover the purpose of validating the feature will not be achieved.

We discuss the idea of testing the `untied` as shown in figure 6. First we create a set of tasks in parallel region and save the thread id executed by each task. Then we suspend all the tasks using `taskwait`. We send half of the threads into a busy loop so that at least half of the other idle threads could be rescheduled to the suspended tasks. We compare the thread number before and after the suspension. Since task is untied, tasks could be rescheduled by different threads after the suspension. In the cross test, the `untied` clause is removed so that the tasks are tied with the execution thread by default. As a result, the thread number before and after the task suspension should be the same delivering incorrect result.

Besides the `tasking` model, OpenMP 3.0 defines a new `collapse` clause for the `loop` construct that handles perfectly nested multi-dimensional loops. This clause collapses the loops, it is associated with, into one single loop,and controls the number of loops associated with one larger loop. The order of iterations in the collapsed loop is determined by the order of iterations in all loops before the collapse. If no `collapse` clause specified, the only loop that is associated with the `loop` construct is the one that immediately follows the construct.

Figure 5 shows the basic idea of testing the `collapse` clause that binds the two loops together. With the `ordered` clause, both i and j loops should be executed in order, thus the variable *my_islarger* should be TRUE. In the cross test, since the `collapse` clause is removed, the only loop that is associated with the `loop` construct is the i loop, the one that immediately follows the construct which should be executed in parallel and the only j loop will be executed in order. Consequently, the result will be incorrect.

```
int omp_task_untied(){
 int init_tid[NUM_TASKS];
 int curr_tid[NUM_TASKS];
 int i, count=0;

 /*Initialization*/
 for(i=0; i<NUM_TASKS; i++){
   init_tid[i]=0;
   curr_tid[i]=0;
 }

#pragma omp parallel
{
 #pragma omp single
 {
  for (i = 0; i < NUM_TASKS; i++){
   int myi = i;
   #pragma omp task untied
   {
    init_tid[myi]=
       omp_get_thread_num();
    #pragma omp taskwait
    if ((init_tid[myi]%2) == 0){
     sleep (SLEEPTIME);
     curr_tid[myi]=
        omp_get_thread_num();
    } /*end of if*/
   } /* end of omp task */
  } /* end of for */
 } /* end of single */
} /* end of parallel */

 for(i=0;i<NUM_TASKS;i++){
  if(curr_tid[i]!=init_tid[i])
   count++;
 } /*end of for*/
 return count;
} /*end of test*/
```

```
int test_omp_task(){
 int tids[NUM_TASKS];
 int i, error=0;

 /*Initilization*/
 for(i=0; i<NUM_TASKS; i++)
 {
   tids[i]=0;
 }

#pragma omp parallel
{
 #pragma omp single
 {
  for (i = 0; i < NUM_TASKS; i++){
   int myi = i;
   #pragma omp task
          final(myi>=THRESH)
   {
    sleep (SLEEPTIME);
    tids[myi]=
       omp_get_thread_num();
   } /* end of omp task */
  } /* end of for */
 } /* end of single */
} /*end of parallel */


 /*check tid beyond thresh*/
 for (i =THRESH;i < NUM_TASKS;i++)
 {
  if (tids[THRESH] != tids[i])
   error++;
 }

 /*check for if result is correct*/
 return (error==0);
} /* end of test */
```

Fig. 6. Test for `untied` clause   **Fig. 7.** Test for `final` clause

3.2   Support for OpenMP 3.1

OpenMP version 3.1 was released in July 2011, a refined and extended version of OpenMP 3.0. The `taskyield` construct defines an explicit scheduling point, i.e. the current task is suspended and switched to a different task in the team. The test for the `taskyield` construct is similar to the test for `untied` clause, except for the `taskwait` begin replaced by `taskyield`.

The OpenMP 3.1 also provides a new features to reduce the task generation overhead by using `final` and `mergeable` clause. If the expression in `final` clause is evaluated to true, the task that is generated will be the final task and no further tasks will be generated. Consequently, it reduces the overheads of generating new tasks, especially in recursive computations such as in *Fibonacci* series when the *Fibonacci* numbers are too small. The test for the `final` clause is shown in Figure 7. The idea is to set a threshold and if the task number is larger to the threshold, that particular task will be the final task. We save the *task id* to check if the task larger to the threshold is executed by the same task.

In OpenMP 3.1, the `atomic` is refined to include the `read, write, update,` and `capture` clauses. The `read` along with the construct `atomic` guarantee an atomic read operation in the region. For instance x is read atomically if `v=x`. Similarly, the `write` forces an atomic write operation. It is much more lightweight using `read` or `write` separately than just using `critical`. The `update` clause forces an atomic update of an variable, such as $i++$, $i-$. If no clause is presented at the `atomic` construct, the semantics are equivalent to atomic update. The `capture` clause ensures an atomic update of an variable that also captures the intermediate or final value of the variable. For example, if `capture` clause is present then in `v = x++`, x is atomically updated while the value is captured by v.

OpenMP 3.1 also extends the `reduction` clause to add two more operators: `max` and `min`, that is to find the largest and smallest values in the reduction list respectively.

For our tests, we use a common search/sort algorithm to discuss the reduction clause and compare the results with a known reference value.

4   Evaluation

In this section, we use the OpenMP validation suite to evaluate the correctness of some of the open source an vendor compilers including OpenUH, GNU C, Intel and Oracle Studio compiler (suncc). The experiments were performed on a Quad dual-core Opteron-880 machine and we used eight threads to perform the evaluation.

To begin with, we use our in-house OpenUH compiler [14,13], to test the correctness of OpenMP implementation in the compiler. Currently, OpenUH supports OpenMP Version 3.0. OpenUH compiler is a branch of the open-source Open64 compiler suite for C, C++, Fortran 95/2003, with support for a variety of targets including x86 64, IA-64, and IA-32. It is able to translate OpenMP 3.0, Co-array Fortran, UPC, and also translates CUDA into PTX format. An OpenMP implementation translates OpenMP directives into corresponding POSIX thread code with the support of runtime libraries.

The versions of the other compilers that we have used for the experimental purposes are:

- GNU compiler is 4.6.2 (gcc)
- Intel C/C++ compiler 12.0 (icc)
- Oracle Studio 12.3 (suncc)

For the first round of experiments, we disable the optimization flags to avoid any potential uncertainties, e.g. code reconstruction while compiling the unit tests. And then we turn on the -O3 optimization as most of the time compiler optimizations are highly used by programmers.We did not find any differences with the turning off/on of the optimizations flags. Almost all the tests passed with 100% certainity.

Table 1 shows the experimental results of evaluating the directives on several compilers. For each sub-column, N is normal test, C is cross test, O is orphan

Table 1. Experimental results on several compilers

	OpenUH				Gnu				Intel				Oracle			
Directive	N	C	O	OC	N	C	O	OC	N	C	O	OC	N	C	O	OC
has_openmp	100	100	100	100	100	100	100	100	100	100	100	100	100	100	100	100
para_shared	100	100	100	100	100	100	100	100	100	100	100	100	100	100	100	100
para_private	100	100	100	100	100	100	100	100	100	100	100	100	100	100	100	100
para_firstpriv	100	100	100	100	100	100	100	100	100	100	100	100	100	100	100	100
para_if	100	100	100	100	100	100	100	100	100	100	100	100	100	100	100	100
para_reduction	100	100	100	100	100	100	100	100	100	100	100	100	100	100	100	100
para_copyin	100	100	100	100	100	100	100	100	100	100	100	100	100	100	100	100
para_num_thres	100	100	100	100	100	100	100	100	100	100	100	100	100	100	100	100
para_default	100	100	100	100	100	100	100	100	100	100	100	100	100	100	100	100
for_private	100	100	100	100	100	100	100	100	100	100	100	100	100	100	100	100
for_firstpriv	100	100	100	100	100	100	100	100	100	100	100	100	100	100	100	100
for_lastpriv	100	100	100	100	100	100	100	100	100	100	100	100	100	100	100	100
for_reduction	100	100	100	100	100	100	100	100	100	100	100	100	100	100	100	100
for_sche_dynam	100	100	100	100	100	100	100	100	100	100	100	100	100	100	100	100
for_sche_static	100	100	100	100	100	100	100	100	100	100	100	100	100	100	100	100
for_sche_guided	100	100	100	100	100	100	100	100	100	100	100	100	100	100	100	100
for_collapse	100	100	100	100	0	-	0	-	100	100	100	100	100	100	100	100
for_ordered	100	100	100	100	100	100	100	100	100	100	100	100	100	100	100	100
for_nowait	100	100	100	100	100	100	100	100	100	100	100	100	100	100	100	100
sec_private	100	100	100	100	100	100	100	100	100	100	100	100	100	100	100	100
sec_firstpriv	100	100	100	100	100	100	100	100	100	100	100	100	100	100	100	100
sec_lastpriv	100	100	100	100	100	100	100	100	100	100	100	100	100	100	100	100
sec_reduction	100	100	100	100	100	100	100	100	100	100	100	100	100	100	100	100
sec_nowait	100	100	100	100	100	100	100	100	100	100	100	100	100	100	100	100
sing_priv	100	100	100	100	100	100	100	100	100	100	100	100	100	100	100	100
sing_firstpriv	100	100	100	100	100	100	100	100	100	100	100	100	100	100	100	100
sing_copypriv	100	100	100	100	100	100	100	100	100	100	100	100	100	100	100	100
sing_nowait	100	100	100	100	100	100	100	100	100	100	100	100	100	100	100	100
para_for_priv	100	100	100	100	100	100	100	100	100	100	100	100	100	100	100	100
para_for_fpriv	100	100	100	100	100	100	100	100	100	100	100	100	100	100	100	100
para_for_lpriv	100	100	100	100	100	100	100	100	100	100	100	100	100	100	100	100
para_for_ordered	100	100	100	100	100	100	100	100	100	100	100	100	100	100	100	100
para_for_reduc	100	100	100	100	100	100	100	100	100	100	100	100	100	100	100	100
para_for_if	100	100	100	100	100	100	100	100	100	100	100	100	100	100	100	100
para_sec_fpriv	100	100	100	100	100	100	100	100	100	100	100	100	100	100	100	100
para_sec_lpriv	100	100	100	100	100	100	100	100	100	100	100	100	100	100	100	100
para_sec_priv	100	100	100	100	100	100	100	100	100	100	100	100	100	100	100	100
para_sec_reduc	100	100	100	100	100	100	100	100	100	100	100	100	100	100	100	100
task	100	100	100	100	100	100	100	100	100	100	100	100	100	100	100	100
task_private	100	100	100	100	100	100	100	100	100	100	100	100	100	100	100	100
task_firstpriv	100	100	100	100	100	100	100	100	100	100	100	100	100	100	100	100
task_if	100	100	100	100	100	100	100	100	100	100	100	100	100	100	100	100
task_untied	100	100	100	100	100	100	100	100	100	100	100	100	100	100	100	100
task_default	100	100	100	100	100	100	100	100	100	100	100	100	100	100	100	100
master	100	100	100	100	100	100	100	100	100	100	100	100	100	100	100	100
critical	100	100	100	100	100	100	100	100	100	100	100	100	100	100	100	100
barrier	100	100	100	100	100	100	100	100	100	100	100	100	100	100	100	100
taskwait	100	100	100	100	100	100	100	100	100	100	100	100	100	100	100	100
atomic	100	100	100	100	100	100	100	100	100	100	100	100	100	100	100	100
flush	100	100	100	100	100	100	100	100	100	100	100	100	100	100	100	100
threadprivate	100	100	100	100	100	100	100	100	100	100	100	100	100	100	ce	-
get_wtick	100	100	100	100	100	100	100	100	100	100	100	100	100	100	100	100
get_wtime	100	100	100	100	100	100	100	100	100	100	100	100	100	100	100	100

test while OC is orphan cross test (the cross test within orphan test). Each row contains the directive to be tested. For instance, the `para_shared` is to test the `shared` clause in the `parallel` construct. Other terms such as `ce` means compile error and textttto means time out (reach the maximum execution time threshold we set in case of deep dead).

Using statistical analysis approach, the tests are repeated several times (the number of times to be repeated is configured at the beginning) and the number of times the tests pass/fail is calculated. Through this strategy, we can capture uncommon circumstances, where a compiler would still fail but pass under normal circumstances. From the experimental results, we see that most of the tests pass with 100% certainty. However, we could still see that the `collapse` implementation fails for the GNU C compiler, and the `threadprivate` implementation fails for the Oracle Studio compiler.

It is quite challenging to analyze the reason behind why a compiler would fail certain tests. But our validation suite still tries to provde as much detail as necessary to the compiler developers in order to assist them in improving the implemenation of the features in the compiler. Also we believe that the validation suite will help resolve ambiguities in the OpenMP specification and help refine the same if necessary.

5   Related Work

To the best of our knowledge, there is no similar public efforts reporting on the validation of OpenMP implemenations on compilers. Vendors have their own internal testsuites but this does not allow for open validation of implemented features which may be of great importance to application developers. As mentioned in Section 1, [16,17] report on the validation methodologies and testsuite for older OpenMP versions (2.0 and 2.5). Since there is no means with OpenMP specification by which an user can obtain dynamic feedback on the success or otherwise of a specific feature, open means for testing features' availability is a matter of concern. A path to extend OpenMP with error-handling capabilities was proposed in [19]. This effort was to address OpenMP's lack of any concept of errors (both OpenMP runtime and user code errors) or support to handle them. A number of works report on evaluation of peformance measurement using OpenMP, for e.g. EPCC [6],PARSEC [4],NAS [12],SPEC [3],BOTS [10] and SHOC [9].

A methodology called *randomized differential testing* [20] was developed that employs random code generator technique to detect compiler bugs. This is an hand-tailored program generator methodology that took about three years to complete, this work identifies compiler bugs that are not uncommon. Although this effort has helped find more than 325 bugs so far in common compilers, the execution environment is quite complex, this tool generates programs that are too large, consequently bug reports are hard to understand. In order to clean this up, manual intervention will be required, since automated approach would introduce unidentifiable undefined behavior. Also it requires voting heuristics to determine which compiler implementation is wrong, this can be hard to determine at times. In our approach we use fine-grained unit tests for each of the OpenMP directives, this will help us determined the faults due to erroneous implementations very easily. Other approaches to detect bugs in compilers include [7,15]. Our approach is slightly different in a way that we designed an efficient, portable and flexible validation framework that will detect bugs in OpenMP implementations in various compilers.

6   Conclusion

The work in this paper presents a validation testsuite evaluating OpenMP implementations on several different compilers, both academic and commercial compilers. The validation suite basically validates OpenMP Version 3.1 specification. We developed a framework, that employs an automatic approach to run different types of tests such as *normal, cross* and *orphan* tests. The framework provides a flexible, portable and user-friendly testing environment.

Acknowledgements. Development at the University of Houston was supported in part by the National Science Foundation"s Computer Systems Research program under Award No. CRI-0958464. Any opinions, findings, and conclusions or recommendations expressed in this material are those of the authors and do not necessarily reflect the views of the National Science Foundation.

References

1. The Open64 Compiler, http://www.open64.net/
2. Addison, C., LaGrone, J., Huang, L., Chapman, B.: OpenMP 3.0 Tasking Implementation in OpenUH. In: Open64 Workshop at CGO, vol. 2009 (2009)
3. Aslot, V., Domeika, M., Eigenmann, R., Gaertner, G., Jones, W.B., Parady, B.: SPEComp: A New Benchmark Suite for Measuring Parallel Computer Performance. In: Eigenmann, R., Voss, M.J. (eds.) WOMPAT 2001. LNCS, vol. 2104, pp. 1–10. Springer, Heidelberg (2001)
4. Bienia, C., Kumar, S., Singh, J.P., Li, K.: The PARSEC Benchmark Suite: Characterization and Architectural Implications. In: Proceedings of the 17th International Conference on Parallel Architectures and Compilation Techniques, PACT 2008, pp. 72–81. ACM, New York (2008)
5. Board, O.A.R.: OpenMP Application Program Interface, Version 3.1 (July 2011)
6. Bull, J.M.: Measuring Synchronisation and Scheduling Overheads in OpenMP. In: Proceedings of First European Workshop on OpenMP, pp. 99–105 (1999)
7. Burgess, C., Saidi, M.: The Automatic Generation of Test Cases for Optimizing Fortran Compilers. Information and Software Technology 38(2), 111–119 (1996)
8. Cappello, F., Etiemble, D.: MPI versus MPI+ OpenMP on the IBM SP for the NAS Benchmarks. In: ACM/IEEE 2000 Conference on Supercomputing, p. 12. IEEE (2000)
9. Danalis, A., Marin, G., McCurdy, C., Meredith, J.S., Roth, P.C., Spafford, K., Tipparaju, V., Vetter, J.S.: The Scalable Heterogeneous Computing (SHOC) Benchmark Suite. In: Proceedings of the 3rd Workshop on General-Purpose Computation on Graphics Processing Units, GPGPU 2010, pp. 63–74. ACM, New York (2010)

10. Duran, A., Teruel, X., Ferrer, R., Martorell, X., Ayguade, E.: Barcelona OpenMP Tasks Suite: A Set of Benchmarks Targeting the Exploitation of Task Parallelism in Openmp. In: Proceedings of the 2009 International Conference on Parallel Processing, ICPP 2009, pp. 124–131. IEEE Computer Society, Washington, DC (2009)
11. C. Intel and C. User. Reference guides. Available on the Intel Compiler Homepage (2008), http://software.intel.com/en-us/intel-compilers
12. Jin, H., Frumkin, M., Yan, J.: The OpenMP Implementation of NAS Parallel Benchmarks and its Performance. Technical report (1999)
13. Liao, C., Hernandez, O., Chapman, B., Chen, W., Zheng, W.: OpenUH: An Optimizing, Portable OpenMP Compiler. Concurrency and Computation: Practice and Experience 19(18), 2317–2332 (2007)
14. Liao, C., Hernandez, O., Chapman, B., Chen, W., Zheng, W.: OpenUH: An Optimizing, Portable OpenMP Compiler. In: 12th Workshop on Compilers for Parallel Computers, p. 2006 (2006)
15. McKeeman, W.: Differential Testing For Software. Digital Technical Journal 10(1), 100–107 (1998)
16. Müller, M., Neytchev, P.: An OpenMP Validation Suite. In: Fifth European Workshop on OpenMP, Aachen University, Germany (2003)
17. Müller, M., Niethammer, C., Chapman, B., Wen, Y., Liu, Z.: Validating OpenMP 2.5 for Fortran and C/C
18. Stallman, R.M., GCC DeveloperCommunity: Using The Gnu Compiler Collection: A Gnu Manual For Gcc Version 4.3.3. CreateSpace, Paramount, CA (2009)
19. Wong, M., Klemm, M., Duran, A., Mattson, T., Haab, G., de Supinski, B.R., Churbanov, A.: Towards an Error Model for OpenMP. In: Sato, M., Hanawa, T., Müller, M.S., Chapman, B.M., de Supinski, B.R. (eds.) IWOMP 2010. LNCS, vol. 6132, pp. 70–82. Springer, Heidelberg (2010)
20. Yang, X., Chen, Y., Eide, E., Regehr, J.: Finding and Understanding Bugs in C Compilers. In: Proceedings of the 32nd ACM SIGPLAN Conference on Programming Language Design and Implementation, PLDI 2011, pp. 283–294. ACM, New York (2011)

Performance Analysis of an Hybrid MPI/OpenMP ALM Software for Life Insurance Policies on Multi-core Architectures

Francesca Perla and Paolo Zanetti

Dipartimento di Statistica e Matematica per la Ricerca Economica
Università degli Studi di Napoli "Parthenope"
Via Medina 40, I-80133 Napoli, Italy
{perla,zanetti}@uniparthenope.it

1   Introduction

The application of new insurance and reinsurance regulation introduced by the European Directive 2009/138 (Solvency II) [4] leads to a complex valuation process to assess risks and determine the overall solvency needs. The development of an "internal model" – "a risk management system developed by an insurer to analyse its overall risk position, to quantify risks and to determine the economic capital required to meet those risks" [5] – generates hard computational problems. The perfect timing of measurements and consequent management actions must be further safeguard. It stands to reason that the computational performance of the valuation process plays a relevant role; this motivates the need to develop both accurate and efficient numerical algorithms and to use High Performance Computing (HPC) methodologies and resources. The literature on the application of HPC in the development of "internal model" is very poor; a relevant contribution is given in [1] where is introduced DISAR (Dynamic Investment Strategy with Accounting Rules), a Solvency II compliant system designed to work on a grid of conventional computers. In [2] numerical experiments carried out applying to DISAR a parallelisation strategy based on the distribution of Monte Carlo simulations among processors are reported. The developed parallel software is tested on an IBM Bladecenter using pure MPI implementation and treating every core as a separate entity with its own address space.

Now, we show some of experiences in adding a layer of shared memory threading trying to optimize the application built using MPI and OpenMP. At this aim, we use some tools and techniques for tuning the hybrid MPI/OpenMP DISAR implementation.

2   The ALM Software for Life Insurance Policies

We investigate the performance of Asset-Liability Management (ALM) software for monitoring portfolios of life insurance policies on multi-core architectures. We refer to the methodological ALM valuation framework used in DISAR that

B.M. Chapman et al. (Eds.): IWOMP 2012, LNCS 7312, pp. 250–253, 2012.

is detailed in [3]. The analysis is carried out on "Italian style" *profit-sharing life insurance policies* (PS policies) with minimum guarantees. In these contracts – widely diffused in Italy – the benefits which are credited to the policyholder are indexed to the annual return of a specified investment portfolio, called the *segregated fund* (in Italian *gestione separata*). In Italian insurance market, the crediting mechanism typically guarantees a minimum to the policyholder. A profit sharing policy is a "complex" structured contract, with underlying the segregated fund return; the models for the market-consistent valuation of the policy require the solution of partial stochastic differential equations and the use of Monte Carlo (MC) simulation techniques. Then, to speed-up the valuation process of portfolio of PS policies, we applied to DISAR a parallelisation strategy based on the distribution of Monte Carlo simulations - the most time consuming tasks involved in the valuation process - among processors.

3   Performance Results

We test the parallel MC-based version of the ALM software on an IBM Bladecenter LS21, installed at the University of Naples "Parthenope", with six blades equipped with two Dual-Core AMD Opteron 2210HE, a L2 cache memory of 1 MByte and a L1 cache of 64 Kbyte per core. The system is supplied with OpenMP release 3.1, MPICH2 1.3.1 with hydra process manager and hwloc 1.2.1. We use the Mersenne Twister generator included in the *Intel Math Kernel Library* for generating distributed pseudo-random sequences.

We simulate a real portfolio containing about 78000 policies aggregated in 5600 fluxes. The time horizon of simulation we consider is 40 years. The segregated fund includes about 100 assets, both bonds and equities. The values of MC trajectories used are N=5000, 20000, 50000.

We develop the hybrid MPI/OpenMP and the MPI pure versions from the same code base; that is, both the versions maintain the same numerical accuracy. It is the Monte Carlo loop that is parallelised using OpenMP to create the hybrid code. Communication among nodes is limited to the final phase, since communication consists only in the collective operation MPI_REDUCE to compute global averages from the partial ones, which give the MC method results. Each MC simulation size and processor core count is tested with three combinations of MPI processes and OpenMP threads (Fig. 1(a)): one MPI process for each core, no OpenMP thread (pure MPI); one MPI process on each host, all other cores filled with OpenMP threads (hybrid 1); one MPI process on each node, all other cores filled with OpenMP threads (hybrid 2). We use TAU profiler to track the performance of the application and PAPI framework for measuring hardware related events. To improve performance of the hybrid versions, we properly set thread affinity to specify which core each thread should run on; the thread affinity has a large performance impact on a NUMA-system based. For binding of processes we use hwloc - a sub-project of the overall OPEN MPI project - which further aims at gathering a detailed knowledge of the hardware topology (Fig 1(b)). To get a time comparison, in Fig. 2(a) the ratio of timings of the

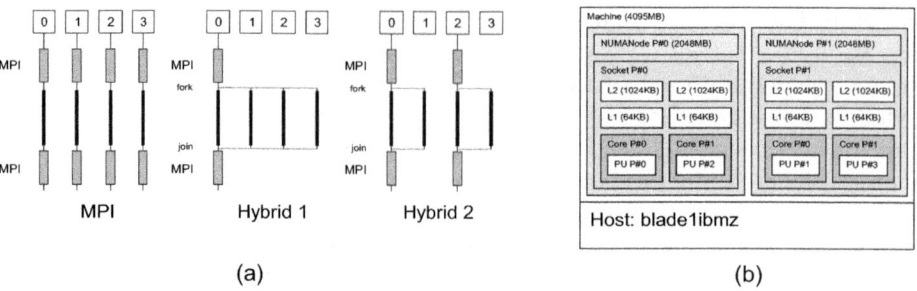

Fig. 1. (a) Pure MPI and hybrid versions. - (b) Graphical output of the lstopo tool describing the topology of the host.

hybrid 2 version with and without thread affinity is shown, for the total number of cores increasing from 4 to 24. In any case the ratio is smaller than 1, confirming the advantage in setting thread affinity. At the same aim, in Fig. 2(b) we report the ratio of timings of the hybrid versions, both of them with thread affinity, with pure MPI code. We observe that the hybrid 2 version performs better than the other two codes; the pure MPI implementation instead outperforms the hybrid 1 version. Those results point out that, in terms of execution time, 1) the hybrid 2 version exhibits the optimal combination of #MPI processes and #OpenMP threads - that is consistent with the hardware topology of the machine; 2) an hybrid version can perform worse than pure MPI when the impact of NUMA memory is not considered. In Fig. 3(a) we plot the parallel efficiency of pure

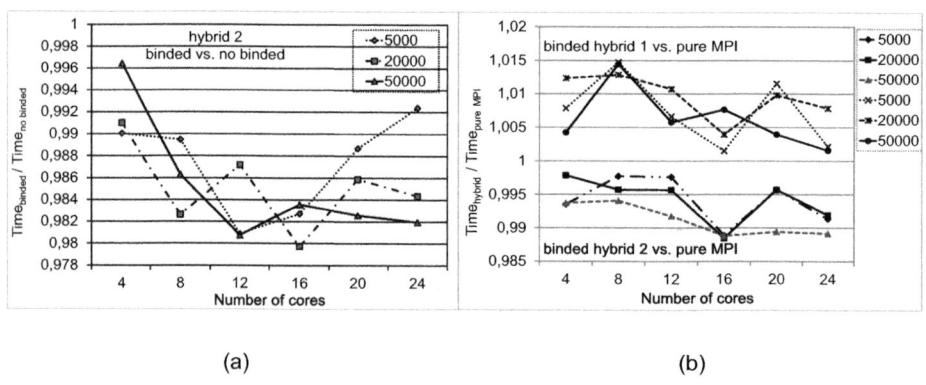

Fig. 2. Time comparison of (a) hybrid 2 version binded vs. no binded. (b) hybrid versions vs. pure MPI.

MPI and hybrid 2 versions. Both of codes scale very well - the efficiency values always very close to the ideal value 1 -, due to the perfect load balancing as displayed by TAU profile; further hybrid 2 version scales better than pure MPI since the time spent carrying out collective communication is much lower, as the TAU communication time profiles show (Fig. 3(b)). Note that for N=50000 the execution time on 1 core is about 16 hours while it takes about 41 minutes on 24 cores with the hybrid 2 version. Another advantage of the hybrid version over pure MPI is in the data memory consumed. For a fixed MC simulation size, the ALM software requires for each generated MPI process a replication of almost all of data arrays; this implies that halving the number of MPI processes, the data memory usage reduces by almost a factor two.

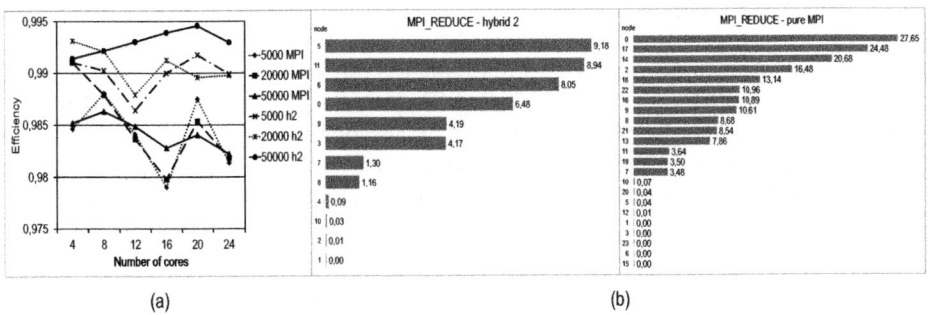

(a)   (b)

Fig. 3. (a) Efficiency of pure MPI and hybrid 2 - (b) Time profile of MPI_REDUCE for N=20000 on 24 cores, on the left hybrid 2 version, on the right pure MPI

All our experiments show that an hybrid combination of MPI processes and OpenMP threads, consistent with the hardware architecture, improves the overall performance of ALM software thus allowing to efficiently face the complex valuation process in "internal models".

References

1. Castellani, G., Passalacqua, L.: Applications of Distributed and Parallel Computing in the Solvency II Framework: The DISAR System. In: Guarracino, M.R., Vivien, F., Träff, J.L., Cannataro, M., Danelutto, M., Hast, A., Perla, F., Knüpfer, A., Di Martino, B., Alexander, M. (eds.) Euro-Par-Workshop 2010. LNCS, vol. 6586, pp. 413–421. Springer, Heidelberg (2011)
2. Corsaro, S., De Angelis, P.L., Marino, Z., Perla, F., Zanetti, P.: On parallel asset-liability management in life insurance: a forward risk-neutral approach. Parallel Comput. 36(7), 390–402 (2010)
3. De Felice, M., Moriconi, F.: Market Based Tools for Managing the Life Insurance Company. Astin Bull. 35(1), 79–111 (2005)
4. Directive 2009/138/EC of the European Parliament and of the Council of 25 November 2009 on the taking-up and pursuit of the business of Insurance and Reinsurance. Official Journal of the European Union (2009)
5. International Association of Insurance Supervisors: Guidance Paper on the Use of Internal Models for Regulatory Capital Purpose (2008)

Adaptive OpenMP for Large NUMA Nodes

Aurèle Mahéo[1], Souad Koliaï[1], Patrick Carribault[2,1], Marc Pérache[2,1],
and William Jalby[1]

[1] Exascale Computing Research Center, Versailles, France
[2] CEA, DAM, DIF, F-91297, Arpajon, France

1 Introduction

The advent of multicore processors advocates for a hybrid programming model like MPI+OpenMP. Therefore, OpenMP runtimes require solid performance from a small number of threads (one MPI task per socket, OpenMP inside each socket) to a large number of threads (one MPI task per node, OpenMP inside each node). To tackle this issue, we propose a mechanism to improve performance of thread synchronization with a large spectrum of threads. It relies on a hierarchical tree traversed in a different manner according to the number of threads inside the parallel region. Our approach exposes high performance for thread activation (parallel construct) and thread synchronization (barrier construct). Several papers study hierarchical structures to launch and synchronize OpenMP threads [1,2]. They tested tree-based approaches to distribute and synchronize threads, but they do not explore mixed hierarchical solutions.

2 Adaptive OpenMP Runtime

Multiple tree shapes exist to perform thread synchronization. The most straightforward solution is a *flat tree* with one root and one thread per leaf. It allows fast synchronization for a few number of threads: the master thread iterates through leaves to flip one memory cell. But with an increasing number of threads, performance drops. A tree mapping the topology of the underlying architecture is more suitable. Such tree exposes more parallelism for synchronizing a large number of threads, but invoking few threads requires a high overhead for tree traversal.

Our approach is to bypass some parts of the tree when the number of threads is small enough to impact only a sub-tree of the topology tree. Figure 1 depicts this mechanism on a 32-core node (4 processors with 8 cores). Thus, when the number of threads is lower than 8, the master thread starts at the second level (leftmost child of the root). For a larger number of threads, the topology tree is still fully used.

3 Experimental Results

We implemented our mechanism in MPC [3] inside the existing OpenMP runtime. We conducted experiments on a Bull bullx 6010 server embedding a

B.M. Chapman et al. (Eds.): IWOMP 2012, LNCS 7312, pp. 254–257, 2012.
© Springer-Verlag Berlin Heidelberg 2012

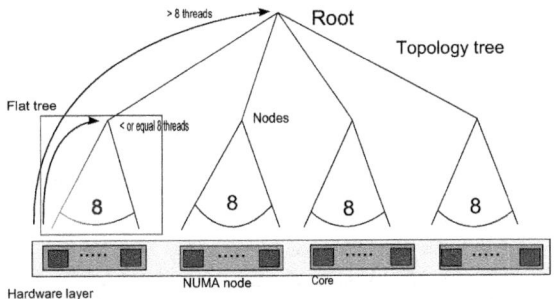

Fig. 1. Tree Structures for 32-Core Node

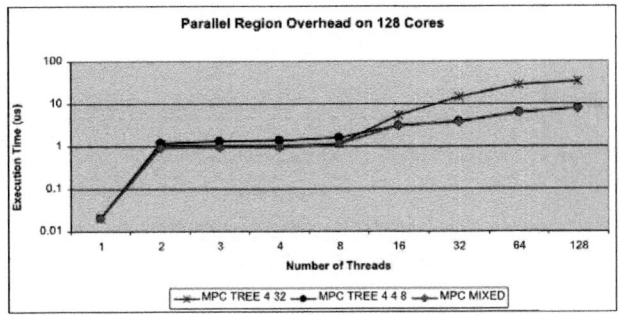

-a- Tree Evaluation

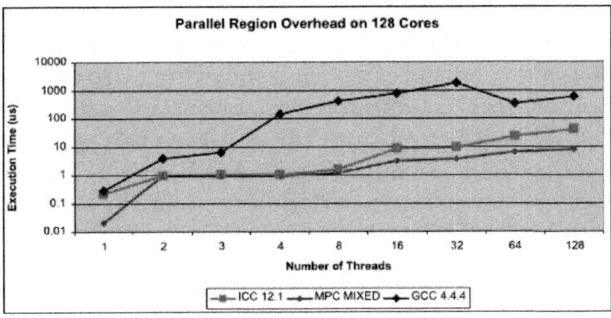

-b- Runtime Evaluation

Fig. 2. Parallel Overhead Evaluation on 128 Cores

memory controller for cache coherency called Bull Coherency Switch (BCS). This ccNUMA system allows configuration with up to 16 processors sockets (4 modules containing 4 processor sockets and a BCS) sharing a single coherent memory space. Thus these 16 processor sockets provide 128 CPU cores.

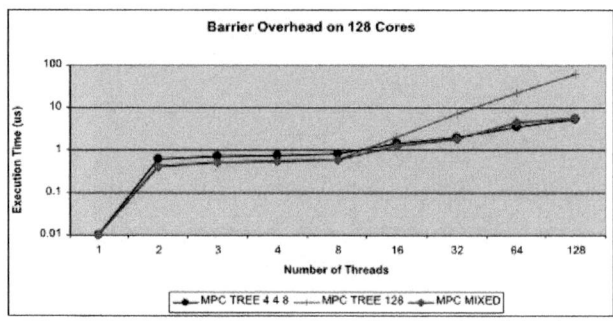

-a- Tree Evaluation

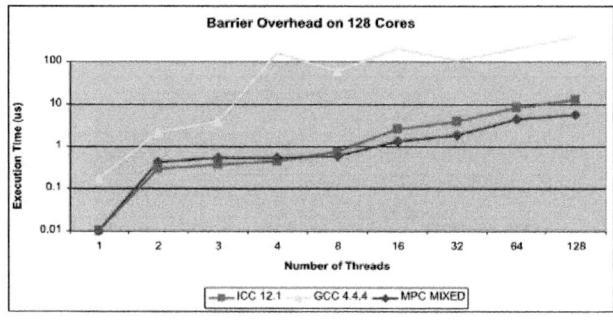

-b- Runtime Evaluation

Fig. 3. Barrier Overhead Evaluation on 128 Cores

Figures 2 and 3 present the results of EPCC benchmarks [4] up to 128 threads. Figure 2-a depicts the overhead of entering and exiting a parallel region for different trees: 2-level tree (MPC 4-32), topology tree (MPC 4-4-8) and our approach (MPC MIXED). We benefit from both trees by using this bypass mechanism: the overhead is equal to the minimum of trees. Furthermore, Figure 2-b illustrates that our approach achieves better performance than state-of-the art implementations. Figure 3-a and 3-b illustrate the same experiments for the OpenMP barrier construct.

4   Conclusion and Future Work

We introduced a new mechanism to increase the performance of OpenMP thread activation and synchronization for a wide spectrum of threads. It shows significant performance improvement on a 128-core node on EPCC microbenchmarks. For future work, we have to investigate more this strategy by extracting a generic algorithm to bypass trees in a flexible way. Finally, it would be interesting to integrate OpenMP tasks and check the influence of task scheduling.

References

1. Nanjegowda, R., Hernandez, O., Chapman, B., Jin, H.H.: Scalability Evaluation of Barrier Algorithms for OpenMP. In: Müller, M.S., de Supinski, B.R., Chapman, B.M. (eds.) IWOMP 2009. LNCS, vol. 5568, pp. 42–52. Springer, Heidelberg (2009)
2. Broquedis, F., Furmento, N., Goglin, B., Wacrenier, P.A., Namyst, R.: ForestGOMP: an efficient OpenMP environment for NUMA architectures. International Journal on Parallel Programming 38(5), 418–439 (2010)
3. Carribault, P., Pérache, M., Jourdren, H.: Enabling Low-Overhead Hybrid MPI/OpenMP Parallelism with MPC. In: Sato, M., Hanawa, T., Müller, M.S., Chapman, B.M., de Supinski, B.R. (eds.) IWOMP 2010. LNCS, vol. 6132, pp. 1–14. Springer, Heidelberg (2010)
4. Bull, J.M., O'Neill, D.: A Microbenchmark Suite for OpenMP 2.0. SIGARCH Comput. Archit. News 29(5), 41–48 (2001)

A Generalized Directive-Based Approach for Accelerating PDE Solvers

Francesco Salvadore

CASPUR - via dei Tizii 6/b 00185 Rome, Italy
salvador@caspur.it

1 Cube-Flu

Cube-Flu is a Python software application that produces Fortran code for solving Partial Differential Equations (PDEs), according to the input provided by the user. The code produced by Cube-Flu is designed for exploiting distribuited memory architectures as well as Graphics Processing Units, as shown in the next section. The software solves equations of the form $\frac{\partial \mathbf{u}}{\partial t} = f(\mathbf{u})$ on cartesian grids, using Runge-Kutta time integration, and finite difference schemes. The idea behind the application is to provide a simple framework for solving a wide class of systems of equations, using a natural and intuitive syntax. For instance, considering the 2D Poisson equation

$$\frac{\partial \theta}{\partial t} = \nu \left(\frac{\partial^2 \theta}{\partial x^2} + \frac{\partial^2 \theta}{\partial y^2}, \right)$$

we have to specify the forcing term as

```
nuu*(#[dsx]{tem}+#[dsy]{tem}),
```

together with all parameters and information describing our system and domain.

Discrete differential operators are directly translated by the software into the corresponding linear combinations of array elements. Hence, given the operator

```
"ds":{"coeff":{"-1":"1.","+0":"-2.","+1":"-1."}}
```

the software will perform a transformation that looks like:

```
#[dsx]{tem}  ⟶  tem(i-1,j)*1.+tem(i,j)*(-2.)+tem(i+1,j)*(1.)
```

where the x suffix stands for the first component of the array. Although the code is still under development, a few significant tests have been performed providing an interesting insight into implementation and performance issues.

B.M. Chapman et al. (Eds.): IWOMP 2012, LNCS 7312, pp. 258–261, 2012.
© Springer-Verlag Berlin Heidelberg 2012

2   Parallelization and Directive-Based GPU Porting

We briefly describe how the OpenMP parallelization and the PGI-Accelerator GPU porting of our code is achieved in Cube-Flu. The `mirror` and `update` clauses provided by PGI have been used to minimize the performance impact of time-consuming data transfers from/to the GPU and to allow for a simple code design. Most of the variables reside in Fortran modules embedding, when needed, the `mirror` for GPU counterparts.

The major part of the Fortran code is made up of nested loops spanning the cartesian grid points. The OpenMP parallelization of such loops is straightforward provided that no data dependencies between subsequent iterations of the parallelized loop are present. This condition is often fulfilled by the computation of field derivatives in finite difference schemes. To achieve reasonable occupancy values on the GPU, a suitable choice is to parallelize loop nests along two directions. Loops that do not require particular attention to be parallelized are referred to as standard, and are marked with a preprocessing parallel directive called `!PARALLEL_STANDARD` in the generated Fortran code. This directive gets then translated into either OpenMP (left) or PGI-Accelerator (right) directives.

```
                              !$acc region
   !$omp do                   !$acc do independent
   do i_z=istart_z,iend_z     do i_z=istart_z,iend_z
      do i_y=istart_y,iend_y  !$acc do independent
         do i_x=istart_x,iend_x   do i_y=istart_y,iend_y
            <loop body>             do i_x=istart_x,iend_x
         enddo                        <loop body>
      enddo                        enddo
   enddo                        enddo
   !$omp end do              enddo
                              !$acc end region
```

where the `independent` clause has been added as a further hint to the compiler.

Other loop nests have to be partially adapted to be parallelized: this is the case, for instance, for in-place translations of a vector, required to impose boundary conditions. Since the translation direction cannot be easily parallelized, we resort to reordering the loop nest to bring this direction in the innermost loop, making the first two loops parallelizable. When producing Fortran code, we use the token `!PARALLEL_REORDER` to mark this kind of loops. Once the required reordering is performed, OpenMP and PGI-Acc translations are straightforward.

We then have to consider simple scalar operations performed on arrays or scalars, that we mark by inserting `!PARALLEL_ONLYONE`. For OpenMP, a `!$omp single` directive does the job. For PGI-Accelerator a trick is required to prevent the compiler from performing scalar operations on CPU, thereby adding unnecessary data transfers. Writing the scalar operation as the body of a one-iteration loop allows for the `!$acc do seq` directive to be applied, so that the computation gets executed (by a single thread) on GPU.

Another critical point is detecting scalar variables – e.g., used as temporary storage for array values – which have to be privatized trough the `private` clause (for both paradigms). In OpenMP this is needed to avoid wrong results due to race conditions, while PGI-accelerator's default behavior is to disable parallelization.

Finally, another case of special attention is given by loops involving random values. Since the Fortran intrinsic `random_number` subroutine is not supported in PGI-Accelerator we decided to manually parallelize a random number function: the parallelization for the general case is not trivial and requires a certain amount of additional memory to store variables for random evolution.

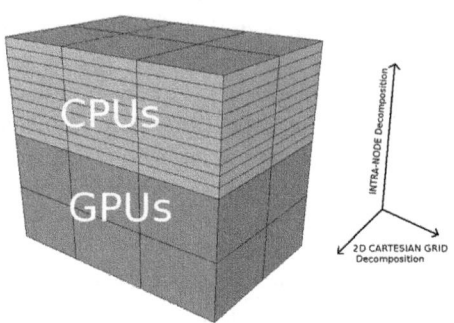

The Fortran code produced by Cube-Flu also features a 3D MPI decomposition. allowing for MPI+OpenMP or MPI+GPU hybrid parallelizations. We conceived a 3D MPI decomposition where a 2D MPI cartesian grid maps computing nodes, and the third direction is used for intra-node parallelization. Within a node, it is possible to assign a larger amount of work to cores that control GPUs, with respect to cores that directly perform computations. Furthermore, this can be done at run-time, by setting the ratio between the domain portions assigned to the two different purposed kinds of core.

3   Performance Results

The solution of compressible Navier-Stokes equations for a triperiodic system with random forcing has been carried out with Cube-flu in different configurations to assess performance results. A 192^3 point grid, and single precision real variables have been used. Tests have been performed on a cluster composed by Dual-Socket, six cores Intel Xeon X5650 (Westmere) CPU nodes, featuring two Tesla S2050 GPUs each.

MPI parallelization yields similar results with respect to the MPI+OpenMP case. The limited scaling is probably due to the large amount of memory accesses saturating the memory bandwidth. The MPI+OpenMP-socket parallelization employs OpenMP within each socket, and MPI for inter-socket and inter-node communications. The MPI+OpenMP-node parallelization uses one MPI process for each node, employing OpenMP for all the cores of the same node. The MPI+OpenMP-socket version seems to be slightly faster compared to both pure MPI or MPI+OpenMP-node ones. In the MPI-GPU flavour, each MPI process controls a GPU (the figure shows results for 1, 2 and 4 GPUs). The comparison

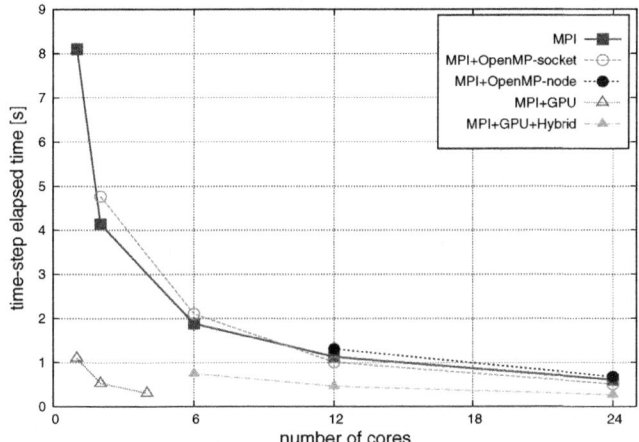

between 1 core and 1 GPU gives a speed-up close to 8, and using more GPUs, a reasonable (even though not linear) scaling is observed. The hybrid version (MPI+GPU+Hybrid in the figure) uses 6 MPI processes for each socket with one process controlling a GPU and the other 5 processes exploiting the CPU cores. The domain decomposition among cores and GPUs has been manually tuned and is crucial to get the best performance results.

In conclusion, our impression is that PGI Accelerator directives end up to be a viable choice to perform a fairly simple heterogeneous porting of a realistic code. Many issues arising in OpenMP parallelization can be transferred to GPU-acceleration directives, supporting the inclusion of GPU-acceleration directives into the OpenMP standard as a suitable choice. However, the OpenACC standard, a potential candidate for this integration, does not include the `mirror` directive, that played a significant role in porting our code. The code generated by Cube-Flu can be also viewed as a starting point for writing a more complex and tuned GPU-hybrid code, possibly based on more low-level programming models (CUDA, OpenCL,...).

References

2010. The Portland-Group, PGI Accelerator Programming Model for Fortran and C, v1.3 (November 2010), `http://www.pggroup.com/resources/accel.htm`
2011. The OpenACC Standard, `http://www.openacc-standard.org`
2012. NVIDIA CUDA Architecture, `http://www.nvidia.com/object/cuda_home.html`
2010. Jespersen, D.C.: CFD Code Acceleration on Hybrid Many-Core Architectures. Journal Scientific Programming 18(3-4) (2010)
1998. Orszag, S.A., Patterson, G.S.: Numerical Simulation of Three-Dimensional Homogeneous Isotropic Turbulence. Phys. Rev. Lett. 28 (1972)
2009. Thibault, J.C., Senocak, I.: CUDA implementation of a Navier-Stokes solver on multi-GPU platforms for incompressible flows. In: Proc. 47th AIAA Aerospace Sciences Meeting, AIAA 2009-758 (2009)

Design of a Shared-Memory Model for CAPE

Viet Hai Ha and Éric Renault

Institut Télécom – Télécom SudParis
Samovar UMR INT-CNRS 5157
Évry, France
{viet_hai.ha,eric.renault}@it-sudparis.eu

1 Introduction

Checkpointing Aided Parallel Execution (CAPE) is the paradigm we developed to use checkpointing techniques to automatically run parallel programs on distributed-memory architectures. Two versions of CAPE have been developed and tested. The first one was based on complete checkpoints and has proved the feasibility of the paradigm but did not have good performance [1]. The second one based on incremental checkpoints improved performance a lot and made it comparable with MPI similar programs [2]. However, both versions are applicable only to problems containing parallel regions that verify the Bernstein's conditions. In this case data in parallel regions are processed independently in each parallel thread and result are combined at the end of each region. To overcome this restriction, two main tracks have been investigated: the first one consists in implementing a shared-memory model and the second one in processing all requirements of OpenMP data-sharing clauses and directives. In this paper, we present the design of a shared-memory model based on the Home-based Lazy Release Consistency model and the algorithm to implement it.

2 Shared-Memory Models on Distributed Systems

The straightforward idea to implement OpenMP on distributed systems is to use the virtually global address space of a software SSI to replace the memory in case of SMP systems. The most important advantage of this approach is the feasibility of a fully compliant implementation. At the opposite, the global address space is located across machines and causes a strong overhead to the global performance. To reduce this overhead, shared data could be copied into many nodes but this leads to consistency issues. Many consistency model haves been built with different performance such as Sequential Consistency (SC), Relaxed Consistency (RC), Lazy Release Consistency (LRC). An implementation of LRC is Home-based Lazy Release Consistency (HLRC). In this last model, each shared page is associated with a home page. This home page always hosts the most updated content of the page, which can then be fetched by any non-home node that needs an updated version. The hight efficiency of this model for implementing an OpenMP compliant was shown in [3].

B.M. Chapman et al. (Eds.): IWOMP 2012, LNCS 7312, pp. 262–266, 2012.
© Springer-Verlag Berlin Heidelberg 2012

3   OpenMP `flush` Directive and Memory-Consistency Mechanism

In OpenMP, the consistency between local and common memory is done via `flush` directives. A `flush` enforces consistency between a thread's temporary view and memory, and does not effect the other threads. There are two types of `flush` in OpenMP: one specifying a set of variables called the *flush-set* and another without any parameter. In [4], they are called *selective-flush* and *global-flush* respectively and the same names are used in this paper. For the selective flush, consistency is applied on the given flush set, and for the global flush the consistency is applied on the whole memory space. Within the advantage has been proved in [3], we use the HLRC model with some modifications to implement the memory model of CAPE.

4   Updated Home-Based Lazy Release Consistency Model

As presented in Section III of [2], the basic implementation of CAPE in homogeneous systems ensured the consistency between the memory of the master thread and the slave threads in the sequential regions and at the begin and end points of parallel regions. For the beginning and in sequential regions, all threads run the same set of instructions, so they have the same memory spaces in these regions. It is also the case for the beginning of parallel regions (before the devision into jobs of parallel constructs). At the end of parallel constructs, all threads injects the same set of updated memory items that makes their memory spaces become consistent. Thus, the only problem remaining to ensure the consistency between threads is implementing a mechanism for `flush` directives.

For most approaches using HLRC model, a `flush` on a copy of a page on a distant node involves three main phases:

- On the distant node: computing the differences between pages, sending those differences to the home node.
- On the home node: applying the received differences to the home page, computing the differences between pages and send those differences to the distant node.
- On the distant node: applying the received differences to the page.

For the global flush, the above phases are applied for each process' shared page.

In the case of CAPE, the above algorithm can be directly used while considering the master node is the home node and its memory pages are home pages. However, as a result of checkpointing, there are two advantages that can reduce the cost of the `flush` execution. First, on slave nodes, `create` function of incremental checkpointers can replace the `diff` function as they do exactly the same job. Second, on the master node, the number of comparisons can usually be significantly reduced if a list of memory updated items of all shared pages is maintained and the `diff` function is applied on this list instead of home pages. As a replacement of the updated list for the set of home pages, this model is called the Updated Home-based Lazy Release Consistency (UHLRC) model. Two other main operations are necessary to implement the mechanism:

- The initialization of the updated list on the home node: in parallel sections, after having divided jobs to slave nodes, the master thread creates a null list as the updated list. As an example, for the prototype in Fig. 2 of [2], an instruction is inserted after line 7.
- The organization of a mechanism to capture `flush` requests and for the synchronization between slave nodes and the master node. In this design, an auxiliary thread called the monitor is used on each node and executed in event-driven mode. Each time a `flush` request occurs on slave node, a signal is sent to the local monitor. This monitor then coordinates with the one on the master node to execute all `flush` operations.

5   The Global Flush Using the UHLRC Model

In this case, the above mechanism can be used as is.

On the slave nodes:

- The slave thread creates a *diffs* list using the `create` function (refer to sec. III of [2]) then calls the `stop` function to temporary stop the checking process. Then a signal is sent to the local monitor.
- The local monitor sends a request to the master's monitor and waits the acknowledgement.
- The local monitor sends the *diffs* list to the master's monitor and waits the returned data.
- The local monitor receives the returned *diffs* list, merges it into the process memory space, calls the `start` function to restart the checking process and notifies the slave thread to resume the execution.

On the master node:

- After the master's monitor receives the *flush* request, it sends an acknowledgement to the slave's monitor and waits the *diffs* list.
- After the master's monitor receives the *diffs* list, it computes the differences between the current updated list and the received list and sends the result back to the slave's monitor.
- The master's monitor applies the received *diffs* list to the current updated list.

6   The Selective Flush Directive Using the UHLRC Model

This case is slightly different from the global flush case and the associated algorithm is far simpler. Below algorithm is designed for the specific case where the flush set contains a single variable. For more than one variable the solution can be easily derived from the case of single variable. Also note that OpenMP does not distinguish between reading or writing from/to the memory to/from the temporary view of the thread. This leads to an ambiguous problem that is out of the scope of this paper.

On the slave nodes:

- The slave's monitor compares the current value of the variable given in the flush set with the initial value. If they are different then this means it is a write flush. Otherwise, this is a read operation. Then a signal is sent to the local monitor.
- The local monitor sends a request to the master's monitor and waits the acknowledgement.
- In case of read flush:
  - The local monitor sends the address of the variable to the master's monitor and waits the returned value.
  - The local monitor receives the returned value, if it is not null merges it into the process memory space. Then notifies the slave thread to resume its execution.
- In case of write flush:
  - The local monitor sends the value of the variable to the master's monitor and notifies the slave thread to resume its execution.

On the master node:

- The master's monitor receives the `flush` request.
- The master's monitor sends the acknowledgement to the slave's monitor and waits for data.
- In case of read flush:
  - Master's monitor searches for the given variable in the updated list. When found it reads and sends back the updated value to the slave's monitor. Otherwise it sends back a null value to the slave's monitor.
- In case of a write flush:
  - The master's monitor receives the returned value, updates it into the updated list and keeps on executing.

7   Conclusion and Future Works

This paper presented the UHLRC model, an improved version of the HLRC model to make it more appropriate to CAPE. In the near future work will consist in implementing this model and evaluating its performance. Finding solutions for OpenMP data-sharing directives and clauses is also planed to make CAPE become an fully OpenMP compliant for distributed memory systems.

References

[1] Renault, É.: Distributed Implementation of OpenMP Based on Checkpointing Aided Parallel Execution. In: Chapman, B., Zheng, W., Gao, G.R., Sato, M., Ayguadé, E., Wang, D. (eds.) IWOMP 2007. LNCS, vol. 4935, pp. 195–206. Springer, Heidelberg (2008)

[2] Ha, V.H., Renault, É.: Design and Performance Analysis of CAPE based on Discontinuous Incremental Checkpoints. In: Proceedings of the Conference on Communications, Computers and Signal Processing (PacRim 2011), Victoria, Canada (August 2011)
[3] Tao, J., Karl, W., Trinitis, C.: Implementing an OpenMP Execution Environment on InfiniBand Clusters. In: Mueller, M.S., Chapman, B.M., de Supinski, B.R., Malony, A.D., Voss, M. (eds.) IWOMP 2005 and IWOMP 2006. LNCS, vol. 4315, pp. 65–77. Springer, Heidelberg (2008)
[4] Karlsson, S., Lee, S.-W., Brorsson, M.: A Fully Compliant OpenMP Implementationon Software Distributed Shared Memory. In: Sahni, S.K., Prasanna, V.K., Shukla, U. (eds.) HiPC 2002. LNCS, vol. 2552, pp. 195–206. Springer, Heidelberg (2002)

Overlapping Computations with Communications and I/O Explicitly Using OpenMP Based Heterogeneous Threading Models

Sadaf R. Alam[1], Gilles Fourestey[1], Brice Videau[2], Luigi Genovese[2],
Stefan Goedecker[3], and Nazim Dugan[3]

[1] Swiss National Supercomputing Centre, Switzerland
[2] CEA—Grenoble, France
[3] University of Basel, Switzerland
{alam,fourestey}@cscs.ch,
brice.videau@imag.fr, luigi.genovese@cea.fr,
{stefan.goedecker,nazim.dugan}@unibas.ch

1   Introduction and Background

Holistic tuning and optimization of hybrid MPI and OpenMP applications is becoming focus for parallel code developers as the number of cores and hardware threads in processing nodes of high-end systems continue to increase. For example, there is support for 32 hardware threads on a Cray XE6 node with Interlagos processors while the IBM Blue Gene/Q system could support up to 64 threads per node. *Note that, by default, OpenMP threads and MPI tasks are pinned to processor cores on these high-end systems and throughout the paper we assume fix bindings of threads to physical cores for the discussion.* A number of OpenMP runtimes also support user specified bindings of threads to physical cores. Parallel and node efficiencies on these high-end systems for hybrid MPI and OpenMP applications largely depend on balancing and overlapping computation and communication workloads. This issue is further intensified when the nodes have a non-uniform access memory (NUMA) model and I/O accelerator devices. In these environments, where access to I/O devices such as GPU for code acceleration and network interface for MPI communication and parallel file I/O are managed and scheduled by a host CPU, application developers could introduce innovative solutions to overlap CPUs and I/O operations to improve node and parallel efficiencies. For example, in a production level application called BigDFT, the developers have introduced a master-slave model to explicitly overlap blocking, collective communication operations and local multi-threaded computation. Similarly some applications parallelized with MPI, OpenMP and GPU acceleration could assign a management thread for the GPU data and control orchestration, an MPI control thread for communication management while the CPU threads perform overlapping calculations, and potentially a background thread can be set aside for file I/O based fault-tolerance. Considering these emerging applications design needs, we would like to motivate the OpenMP standards committee, through examples and empirical results, to introduce thread and task heterogeneity in the language specification. This will allow code developers, especially those programming for large-scale distributed-memory HPC systems and

B.M. Chapman et al. (Eds.): IWOMP 2012, LNCS 7312, pp. 267–270, 2012.
© Springer-Verlag Berlin Heidelberg 2012

accelerator devices, to design and develop portable solutions with overlapping control and data flow for their applications without resorting to custom solutions.

2 Heterogeneous OpenMP Model: BigDFT Implementation

BigDFT is a density functional electronic structure code and it uses a Daubechies wavelet basis [1][7] and has been implemented using MPI, OpenMP, CUDA and OpenCL. In the build up phase for the total electronic charge density, there are MPI collective operations (MPI_Allreduce, MPI_Allgatherv and MPI_Reduce_Scatter) within an OpenMP region, which could be overlapped with the OpenMP computation. The code developers devise a solution where the master thread is responsible for the MPI communication explicitly in communication and computation intensive phases while the other threads perform local computation only. There is no memory contention for the two sets of operations. Figure 1 provides the code listing with a simple example highlighting how the code is structured in a complex simulation code.

```
! Overlap of communication and computation is devised using nested OpenMP
! parallelization. Thread 0 makes the MPI communication. Computation
! is distributed to remaining threads with the internal OpenMP parallel region.
 nthread_max=omp_get_max_threads()
 if (nthread_max > 1) then
    call OMP_SET_NESTED(.true.)
    call OMP_SET_MAX_ACTIVE_LEVELS(2)
    call OMP_SET_NUM_THREADS(2)
 end if
!$OMP PARALLEL DEFAULT(shared), PRIVATE(ithread,nthread,ith_int,nth_int,s)
 ithread = OMP_get_thread_num()
 nthread = omp_get_num_threads()
. . . .
 ! thread 0 does mpi communication
 if (ithread == 0) then
    call MPI_Bcast( dat, ndat, MPI_DOUBLE_PRECISION ,0, MPI_COMM_WORLD,ierr)
 end if
 if (ithread > 0 .or. nthread==1) then
    ! only the remaining threads do computations,
    if (nthread_max > 1) call OMP_SET_NUM_THREADS(nthread_max-1)
    !$OMP PARALLEL DEFAULT(shared), PRIVATE(ith_int,nth_int,s) !internal parallel
    ith_int = omp_get_thread_num()
    nth_int=omp_get_num_threads()
    ! dynamic scheduling avoided
    s = 0.d0
    !$OMP DO
    do j=1,100000000
       s = s+1.d0
    enddo
    ss(ith_int+1)=s
    !$OMP CRITICAL
    sumtot=sumtot+s
    !$OMP END CRITICAL
    !$OMP END PARALLEL !internal end
 end if
!$OMP END PARALLEL
```

Fig. 1. Sample code demonstrating the collective communication and local computation overlap during different calculation phases in the BigDFT application

There are two routines where the explicit computation and collective communication overlap is being implemented in the application of Hamiltonian on a wave function. The call to the `communicate_density` subroutine in turn invokes either `MPI_Reduce_Scatter` or `MPI_Allreduce`. The threading model is initiated with `MPI_THREAD_FUNNELED` and therefore in the above implementation thread 0 initiates MPI collective calls. As illustrated in the above example, the master thread does not participate in the computation parts, however, the results in the next section show that this improves efficiency up to 15% for different numbers of the cores.

3   Experiments and Results

Figure 2 shows results of the BigDFT runs with and without overlap on the two Cray systems with identical interconnect but different core counts and NUMA resgions: 32 cores and 4 regions on Cray XE6 vs. 16 cores and 2 regions on Cray XK6 [2][3]. Consequently, twice as many nodes are used for the Cray XK6 experiments than for the Cray XE6 experiments resulting in different runtimes. For example, for runs on 552 cores, 35 Cray XK6 nodes are used while on the Cray XE6 system, 18 nodes are used. The runtime per simulation step on the Cray XK6 system without overlap is 9.6 seconds and with overlap is 1.75 seconds while on the Cray XE6 system time per step on without explicit overlap is 2.16 seconds and with overlap is 1.86 seconds.

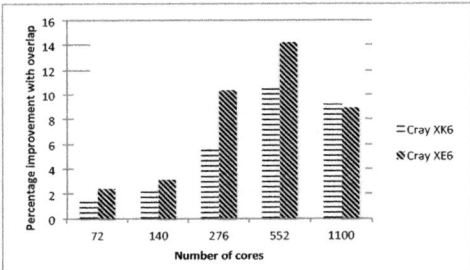 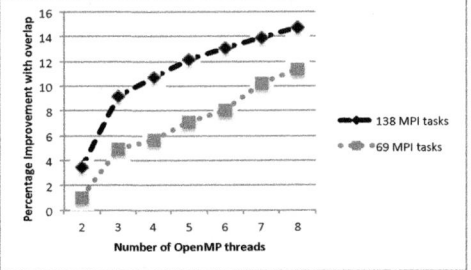

Fig. 2. Relative improvements on two target platforms are shown in the figure (left). On each platform, experiments are performed with 4 OpenMP threads per MPI task. Noticeable differences are observed when the latencies for the MPI collective communication operations increase. Graph on the right shows OpenMP tuning opportunities on the Cray XK6 platform as the number of threads increase for the local computation.

A second motivating scenario is the work-sharing concept that has been introduced for the programming models for accelerators, where diverse sets of threads (CPU and GPU) work together in separate memory address spaces. For example, we obtained over a Teraflops for split DGEMM on a single server device with multiple GPU devices [6]. The third scenario in which a subset of threads can deliver additional functionality, for example in memory or file I/O based fault-tolerance, while the others perform computation [8][9]. As there is an abundance of hardware threads per node, a subset of threads can be dedicated to perform peripheral operations thereby reducing overhead of these necessary operations.

4   Discussion and Proposal for OpenMP Extensions

In all three scenarios and potentially others, where explicit overlapping is desired between MPI communication, OpenMP computation and code acceleration using I/O attached devices, an extension to the OpenMP standard that allows for characterization of threads in a manner that a code developer can express their bindings and affinities at runtime could be the only portable solution. For example, in case of the BigDFT implementation with master and slave threads, users can specify placement of the master thread according to the node memory and its network interface layout. As the numbers of threads continue to increase, users can have flexibility of including additional threads to the master thread pool. Likewise, in the heterogeneous environment where there could be a large number of accelerator threads with respect to fewer CPU threads (for computation) plus a CPU management thread for the accelerators, users can specify at runtime the composition of threads and their affinities. The split DGEMM example for instance takes a CPU thread away from DGEMM computation for each GPU device on the node and assigns it to the GPU DGEMM management. Thus, as the OpenMP committee reviews proposals for extension to the standards for heterogeneous nodes [4][5], we would like to stress that the proposal should also take into account heterogeneity of CPU threads thereby allowing code developers to design applications with a greater degree of flexibility for overlapping on-node computation with other operations. In future, we plan on extending the explicit thread control in additional phases of the BigDFT application and introducing OpenMP task heterogeneity in a quantum systems simulation code.

References

1. BigDFT code, http://inac.cea.fr/L_Sim/BigDFT/
2. Cray XE6 system, http://www.cray.com/Products/XE/CrayXE6System.aspx
3. Cray XK6 system, http://www.cray.com/Products/XK6/XK6.aspx
4. Ayguade, E., Badia, R.M., Cabrera, D., Duran, A., Gonzalez, M., Igual, F., Jimenez, D., Labarta, J., Martorell, X., Mayo, R., Perez, J.M., Quintana-Ortí, E.S.: A Proposal to Extend the OpenMP Tasking Model for Heterogeneous Architectures. In: Müller, M.S., de Supinski, B.R., Chapman, B.M. (eds.) IWOMP 2009. LNCS, vol. 5568, pp. 154–167. Springer, Heidelberg (2009)
5. Beyer, J.C., Stotzer, E.J., Hart, A., de Supinski, B.R.: OpenMP for Accelerators. In: Chapman, B.M., Gropp, W.D., Kumaran, K., Müller, M.S. (eds.) IWOMP 2011. LNCS, vol. 6665, pp. 108–121. Springer, Heidelberg (2011)
6. Fatica, M.: Accelerating Linpack with CUDA on heterogeneous clusters. In: GPGPU-2 Proceedings of 2nd Workshop on General Purpose Processing on Graphics Processing Units. ACM, New York (2009)
7. Genovese, L., Neelov, A., Goedecker, S., Deutsch, T., Ghasemi, A., Zilberberg, O., Bergman, Rayson, M., Schneider, R.: Daubechies wavelets as a basis set for density functional pseudopotential calculations. J. Chem. Phys. 129, 14109 (2008)
8. Jones, W.M., Daly, J.T., DeBardeleben, N.A.: Application Resilience: Making Progress in Spite of Failure. In: Eighth IEEE International Symposium on Cluster Computing and the Grid (CCGRID), pp. 789–794 (2008)
9. Park, B.H., Naughton, T.J., Agarwal, P.K., Bernholdt, D.E., Geist, A., Tippens, J.L.: Realization of User Level Fault Tolerant Policy Management through a Holistic Approach for Fault Correlation. In: IEEE Symp. on Policies for Distributed Systems and Networks (2011)

A Microbenchmark Suite for OpenMP Tasks

J. Mark Bull[1], Fiona Reid[1], and Nicola McDonnell[2]

[1] EPCC, The King's Buildings, The University of Edinburgh,
Mayfield Road, Edinburgh EH9 3JZ, Scotland, U.K.
{m.bull,f.reid}@epcc.ed.ac.uk
[2] ICHEC, Trinity Technology and Enterprise Campus,
Grand Canal Quay, Dublin 2, Ireland
nix@ichec.ie

Abstract. We present a set of extensions to an existing microbenchmark suite for OpenMP. The new benchmarks measure the overhead of
the `task` construct introduced in the OpenMP 3.0 standard, and associated task synchronisation constructs. We present the results from a
variety of compilers and hardware platforms, which demonstrate some
significant differences in performance between different OpenMP implementations.

1   Introduction

The EPCC OpenMP microbenchmark suite [1], [2] contains a set of tests which
measure the overhead of various OpenMP constructs, including synchronisation,
loop scheduling and and handling of thread-private data. The most significant
new features added to OpenMP in Version 3.0 of the language specification [6]
were the `task` and `taskwait` constructs which permit the creation, execution
and synchronisation of independent units of execution.

We extend the microbenchmark suite to measure the overheads associated
with the new constructs. The basic technique remains the same as in previous
versions of the suite: we compare the time taken for a section of code executed
sequentially to the time taken for the same code executed in parallel, which
in the absence of overheads, should complete in the same time. Some similar
benchmarks are described in [3], though our set covers more patterns and we
report results on more platforms. Our benchmarks are intended to complement
those described in [4] and [5], which consist of computational kernels and focus
more on evaluating task scheduling mechanisms than on the overheads associated
with task creation and dispatch.

2   Benchmark Design and Implementation

The first test we consider is **ParallelTasks** where every thread generates (and
possibly executes) tasks. We also implement **MasterTasks**, where all the tasks
are generated by the master thread, and the remaining threads are free execute

B.M. Chapman et al. (Eds.): IWOMP 2012, LNCS 7312, pp. 271–274, 2012.
© Springer-Verlag Berlin Heidelberg 2012

them, and **MasterTasksBusySlaves** where the master thread generates tasks, while the remaining threads perform the same computation, but not enclosed in a task construct. **ConditionalTasks** is the same as **ParallelTasks**, except that all the tasks constructs have an if clause which always evaluates to 0 (false).

There are four tests where tasks are created nested inside other tasks. In **NestedTasks**, each thread creates innerreps/nthreads tasks (where nthreads in the number of threads in the parallel region), and each of these tasks creates a further nthreads tasks and waits for their completion before proceeding to the next outer task. **NestedMasterTasks** is similar, except that the master thread creates all the outer tasks. In **TreeBranchTasks**, every thread creates tasks recursively in a binary tree structure, executing the delay function in every task. **TreeLeafTasks** is similar, except that the delay function is only executed in leaf tasks (i.e. when tree_level is zero), rather than in every task. These two tests are desgined to reflect task generation patterns typical of recursuve divide-and-conquer algorithms. Finally there are two tests which measure the overhead of task synchronisation. **Taskwait** and **TaskBarrier** are the same as **ParallelTasks**, with the addition of a taskwait or **barrier** directive respectively, inside the innermost loop.

3   Benchmark Results

3.1   Hardware

We have run the benchmark suite on the following platforms:

- **Cray XE6 (Magny-Cours node)** with GCC 4.5.2, Cray CCE C compiler 7.3.4 and PGI C 11.3.0.
- **Cray XE6 (Istanbul node)** with GCC 4.6.2, Cray C compiler 8.0.0 and PGI C 11.10.0.
- **IBM Power7 server** with IBM XL C/C++ for AIX 11.1.
- **AMD Magny-Cours server** with GCC 4.6.1 and Oracle Solaris Studio 12.2 for Linux suncc.
- **SGI Altix ICE 8200EX Westmere node**, using GCC 4.5.1 and Intel icc 12.0.0.
- **SGI Altix 4700** using Intel icc 11.1.

3.2   Results

We do not have space here to show the results of all the benchmarks on all the platforms, so we have selected some of the more interesting results for presentation.

Figure 1 shows the overheads for the **ParallelTasks** benchmark. We observe a wide range of values, depending on the compiler and hardware used. The Intel compiler on the Westmere system has the lowest overheads (much less than 1 microsecond on 12 threads), while GCC generally has the highest overheads: over 1 millisecond on the Magny-Cours system for larger thread counts. Also of

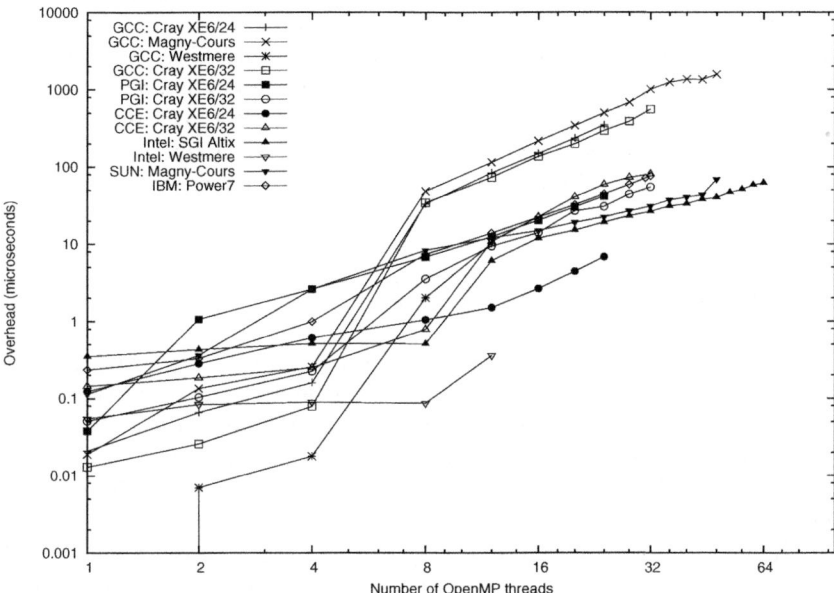

Fig. 1. Overheads for **ParallelTasks** benchmark

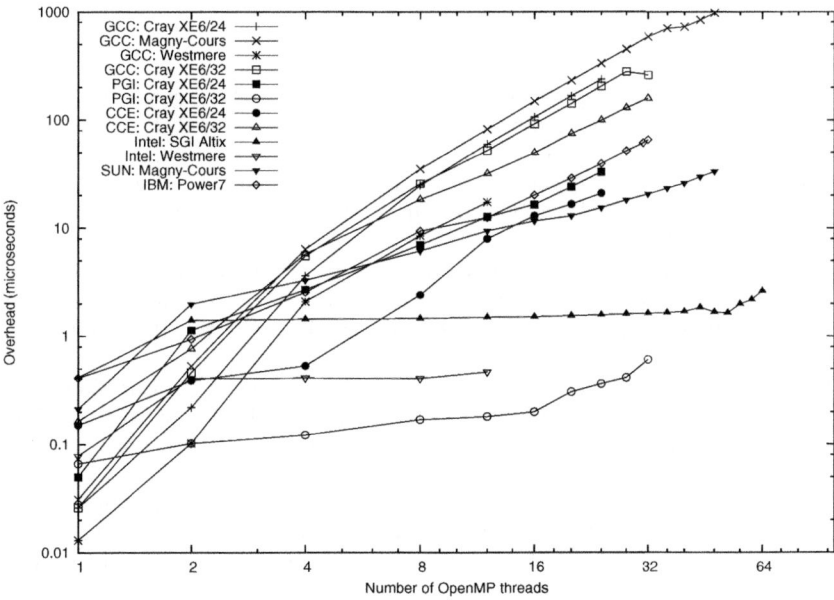

Fig. 2. Overheads for **TreeBranchTasks** benchmark

note is an increase of a factor of around 10 in the overheads of the Cray compiler on the 32-core nodes compared to the 24-core nodes.

Figures 2 shows the overheads for the **TreeBranchTasks** benchmark. Two of the implementations show much reduced overheads compared to the **ParallelTasks** benchmark: the most recent version of PGI (running on the Cray XE6/32 system) and the Intel compiler on the SGI Altix. For larger thread counts, there are some three order of magnitude between the best and worst implementations.

4   Conclusions

We have presented an extension to our existing suite of OpenMP microbenchmarks to cover the `task` construct and associated synchronisation. We have executed these benchmarks on a variety of OpenMP implementation, and on a number of different hardware platforms. The results show that there are some very significant differences in the overheads measured between different OpenMP implementations: up to three orders of magnitude in some cases: this is much larger than is typically observed for other OpenMP constructs, and indicates that there is significant scope for optimisation of some implementations. The results of these benchmarks should also serve to assist OpenMP programmers in indicating the granularity of task which will be required to avoid excessive overhead due to task generation and execution.

References

1. Bull, J.M.: Measuring Synchronisation and Scheduling Overheads in OpenMP. In: Proceedings of First European Workshop on OpenMP, Lund, Sweden, pp. 99–105 (September 1999)
2. Bull, J.M., O'Neill, D.: A Microbenchmark Suite for OpenMP 2.0. In: Proceedings of the Third European Workshop on OpenMP (EWOMP 2001), Barcelona, Spain (September 2001)
3. LaGrone, J., Aribuki, A., Chapman, B.: A set of microbenchmarks for measuring OpenMP task overheads. In: Proceedingis of International Conference on Parallel and Distributed Processing Techniques and Applications, vol. II, pp. 594–600 (July 2011)
4. Duran, A., Teruel, X., Ferrer, R., Martorell, X., Ayguade, E.: Barcelona OpenMP Tasks Suite: A Set of Benchmarks Targeting the Exploitation of Task Parallelism in OpenMP. In: Proceedings of 38th International Conference on Parallel Processing (ICPP 2009), Vienna, Austria (2009)
5. Teruel, X., Barton, C., Duran, A., Martorell, X., Ayguade, E., Unnikrishnan, P., Zhang, G., Silvera, R.: OpenMP tasking analysis for programmers. In: Proceedings of the 2009 Conference of the Center for Advanced Studies on Collaborative Research (CASCON 2009), pp. 32–42 (2009)
6. OpenMP ARB, OpenMP Application Programming Interface Version 3.0 (2008)

Support for Thread-Level Speculation into OpenMP

Sergio Aldea, Diego R. Llanos, and Arturo González-Escribano

Departamento de Informática, Universidad de Valladolid,
Campus Miguel Delibes, 47011 Valladolid, Spain
{sergio,diego,arturo}@infor.uva.es

Abstract. Software-based, thread-level speculation (TLS) systems allow the parallel execution of loops that can not be analyzed at compile time. TLS systems optimistically assume that the loop is parallelizable, and augment the original code with functions that check the consistency of the parallel execution. If a dependence violation is detected, offending threads are restarted to consume correct values. Although many TLS implementations have been developed so far, robustness issues and changes required to existent compiler technology prevent them to reach the mainstream. In this paper we propose a different approach: To add TLS support to OpenMP. A new OpenMP *speculative* clause would allow to execute in parallel loops whose dependence analysis can not be done at compile time.

Keywords: TLS systems, speculative parallelization, OpenMP.

1 Introduction

Manual development of parallel versions of existent, sequential applications requires an in-depth knowledge of the problem, the architecture, and the parallel programming model. On the other hand, using automatic parallelization mechanisms we can only extract parallelism from a small fraction of loops, decided at compile time.

The most promising runtime technique to extract parallelism from fragments of code that can not be analyzed at compile time is called software-based Speculative Parallelization (SP). This technique, also called Thread-Level Speculation (TLS) [2,4,5] or even Optimistic Parallelization [6,7] aims to automatically extract loop- and task-level parallelism when a compile-time dependence analysis can not guarantee that a given sequential code is safely parallelizable. SP optimistically assumes that the code can be executed in parallel, relying on a runtime monitor to ensure correctness. The original code is augmented with function calls that distribute iterations among processors, monitor the use of all variables that may lead to a dependence violation, and perform in-order commits to store the results obtained by successful iterations. If a dependence violation appears at runtime, these library functions stop the offending threads and re-starts them in order to use the updated values, thus preserving sequential semantics.

B.M. Chapman et al. (Eds.): IWOMP 2012, LNCS 7312, pp. 275–278, 2012.

The purpose of this paper is to discuss how to add SP support into OpenMP. Parallel applications written with OpenMP should explicitly declare parallel regions of code. In the case of parallel loops, the programmer should classifies all variable used inside the loop, according to their use, in "private", or "shared". This task is extremely difficult when the parallel loop consists of more than a few dozen lines.

To help the programmer in the development of a parallel version of a sequential loop, our proposal is to offer a new "speculative" clause. This clause would allow the programmer to handle variables whose use can potentially lead to a dependence violation, and therefore should be monitored at runtime in order to obtain correct results. Note that the use of such a category effectively frees the programmer from the task of deciding whether a particular variable is private or shared. To the best of our knowledge, no production-state parallel programming model incorporates support for thread-level speculation.

Our research group has worked for a decade in the field of software-based speculative parallelization. The research carried out so far have led to both a production-level SP runtime library [3] and a prototype of a SP compiler framework [1]. We believe that adding support for speculative parallelization in OpenMP will help to reduce the intrinsic difficulties of manual parallelization of existent code. If successful, parallel code will be much easier to write and maintain.

2   Our Proposal

We have developed a software-only TLS system [2] that has proven its usefulness in the parallel execution of loops that can not be analyzed at compile time, both with and without dependence violations [3].

Our TLS system is implemented using OpenMP for thread management. The loop to be parallelized is transformed in a loop with as many iterations as available threads. At the beginning of the loop body, a scheduling method assigns to the current thread the block of iterations to be executed. Read and write operations to the speculative structure are replaced at compile time with `specload()` and `specstore()` function calls. `specload()` obtains the most up-to-date value of the element being accessed. `specstore()` writes the datum in the version copy of the current processor, and ensures that no thread executing a subsequent iteration has already consumed an outdated value for this structure element, a situation called "dependence violation". If such a violation is detected, the offending thread and its successors are stopped and restarted. Finally, a `commit_or_discard()` function is called once the thread has finished the execution of the chunk assigned. If the execution was successful, the version copy of the data is committed to the main copy; otherwise, version data is discarded.

From the programmer point of view, the structure of a loop being speculatively parallelized is not so different from a loop parallelized with OpenMP directives. Current OpenMP parallel constructs force the programmer to explicitly declare the variables used into the parallel region according to their use, which can be an extremely hard and error-prone task if the loop has more than a few dozen lines.

The problem of adding speculative parallelization support to OpenMP can be handled from two points of view. One requires the addition of a new directive, for example `pragma omp speculative for`. However, this option demands more effort, because there are many OpenMP related components that should be modified. We believe that it is preferable to use a different approach to add a new clause to current parallel constructs that allows the programmer to enumerate which variables should be updated speculatively. The syntax of this clause would be

$$speculative(variable[, var\_list])$$

In this way, if the programmer is unsure about the use of a certain structure, he could simply label it as speculative. In this case, the OpenMP library would replace all definitions and uses of this structure with the corresponding `specload()` and `specstore()` function calls. An additional `commit_or_discard()` function should be automatically invoked once each thread has finished its chunk of iterations, to either commit the results, or restart the execution if the thread has been squashed.

In order to integrate our TLS system, already written using OpenMP, into an experimental OpenMP implementation that also supports speculative parallelization, the particularities of our TLS system should be taken into account. For example, our TLS system needs to set its own control variables as *private* and *shared*. This implies that, if a *speculative* clause is found by the compiler, declaring that there are variables that should be handled speculatively, the use of our TLS system to guide the speculative execution needs to add several *private* and *shared* variables to the current lists. Fortunately, OpenMP allows the repetition of clauses, so the implementation of this new *speculative* clause may add additional *private* and *shared* clauses that will later be expanded by the compiler.

There are two additional issues to be considered. First, the current scheduling methods implemented by OpenMP are not enough to handle speculative parallelization. These methods assume that the task will never fail, and therefore they do not take into account the possibility of restarting an iteration that has failed due to a dependence violation. Therefore, it is necessary to use an speculative scheduling method. This method assigns to each free thread the following chunk of iterations to be executed. If a thread has successfully finished a chunk, it will receive a brand new chunk not been executed yet. Otherwise, the scheduling method may assign to that thread the same chunk whose execution had failed, in order to improve locality and cache reutilization.

We have already developed both Fortran and C versions of our TLS system. Since implementation of OpenMP for C, C++ and Fortran only differs in their respective front ends, adding TLS support for a different language should not require to modify the middle or the back end.

3   Conclusions

Adding speculative support to OpenMP would greatly increase the number of loops that could be parallelized with this programming model. The programmer may label some of the variables involved as *private* or *shared*, using *speculative* for the rest. With this approach, in the first parallel version of a given sequential loop, the programmer might simply label all variables as *speculative*. Of course, the execution of such a loop would lead to an enormous performance penalty, since all definitions and uses of all variables would have been transformed into `specload()` and `specstore()` function calls, that will not perform any useful task if the variables are indeed private or read-only shared. Note that our proposal would let to transform *any* loop into a parallel loop, although the parallel performance will depend of the number of dependence violations being triggered at runtime. The approach described here is being currently implemented.

Acknowledgments. This work has been partially supported by MICINN (Spain) and the European Union FEDER (CENIT OCEANLIDER, CAPAP-H3 network, TIN2010-12011-E, TIN2011-25639), and the HPC-EUROPA2 project (project number: 228398) with the support of the European Commission - Capacities Area - Research Infrastructures Initiative. Sergio Aldea is supported by a research grant of Junta de Castilla y León, Spain.

References

1. Aldea, S., Llanos, D.R., Gonzalez-Escribano, A.: Towards a compiler framework for thread-level speculation. In: PDP 2011, pp. 267–271. IEEE (February 2011)
2. Cintra, M., Llanos, D.R.: Toward efficient and robust software speculative parallelization on multiprocessors. In: ACM PPoPP 2003 (June 2003)
3. Cintra, M., Llanos, D.R.: Design space exploration of a software speculative parallelization scheme. IEEE TPDS 2005 16(6), 562–576 (2005)
4. Dang, F., Yu, H., Rauchwerger, L.: The R-LRPD Test: Speculative Parallelization of Partially Parallel Loops. In: IEEE IPDPS 2002 (April 2002)
5. Gupta, M., Nim, R.: Techniques for speculative run-time parallelization of loops. In: Proc. of the 1998 ACM/IEEE Conference on Supercomputing, pp. 1–12 (1998)
6. Kulkarni, M., Pingali, K., Ramanarayanan, G., Walter, B., Bala, K., Paul Chew, L.: Optimistic parallelism benefits from data partitioning. In: ACM ASPLOS 2008, pp. 233–243. ACM, Seattle (2008)
7. Kulkarni, M., Pingali, K., Walter, B., Ramanarayanan, G., Bala, K., Paul Chew, L.: Optimistic parallelism requires abstractions. In: ACM PLDI 2007, pp. 211–222. ACM, San Diego (2007)

Author Index

GPSR Compliance

*The European Union's (EU) General Product Safety Regulation (GPSR)
is a set of rules that requires consumer products to be safe and our
obligations to ensure this.*

*If you have any concerns about our products, you can contact us on
ProductSafety@springernature.com*

In case Publisher is established outside the EU, the EU authorized
representative is:

Springer Nature Customer Service Center GmbH
Europaplatz 3
69115 Heidelberg, Germany

Batch number: 09478804

Printed by Printforce, the Netherlands